BERLIN GAMES

ALSO BY GUY WALTERS

The Traitor

The Leader

The Occupation

The Voice of War
(co-editor)

The Colditz Legacy

BERLIN GAMES

HOW THE NAZIS STOLE
THE OLYMPIC DREAM

Guy Walters

wm

WILLIAM MORROW
An Imprint of HarperCollins*Publishers*

This book was published in Great Britain in 2006 by John Murray (Publishers), a division of Hodder Headline.

BERLIN GAMES. Copyright © 2006 by Guy Walters. All rights reserved. Printed in the United States of America. No part of this book may be used or reproduced in any manner whatsoever without written permission except in the case of brief quotations embodied in critical articles and reviews. For information, address HarperCollins Publishers, 10 East 53rd Street, New York, NY 10022.

HarperCollins books may be purchased for educational, business, or sales promotional use. For information, please write: Special Markets Department, HarperCollins Publishers, 10 East 53rd Street, New York, NY 10022.

FIRST U.S. EDITION

Library of Congress Cataloging-in-Publication Data has been applied for.

ISBN-13: 978-0-06-087412-4
ISBN-10: 0-06-087412-0

06 07 08 09 10 RRD 10 9 8 7 6 5 4 3 2 1

This book is for my parents,
Martin and Angela Walters

Contents

Illustrations

Preface

THE SMALL TOWN of Dallgow-Doeberitz lies some 20 miles west of Berlin. It is a down-at-heel place, and its unmanned and heavily graffitied railway station greets the visitor with an air of tired menace. A few all-day drinkers sitting in a scratchy beer garden add a sense of decay, and it quickly becomes clear that the name of Dallgow-Doeberitz will never trouble the pages of any guidebook. Unsurprisingly, there is no taxi rank at the station, and the only way to summon a taxi is to ask one of the drinkers whether he knows of a firm. In return for a Pilsener, a telephone number will be issued, and after an uneasy wait, a creaky Mercedes might well turn up. The driver's surprise at seeing that he has a tourist for a fare will be magnified when he is told of his destination: *die Olympische dorf.*

After a five-minute drive along a main road, the driver turns right on to a track that runs over some rolling scrubland. The noise of crickets fills the air, which is still warmed by a setting September sun. The cabbie then turns right again, and heads towards a stand of unkempt fir and silver birch. The occasional dilapidated rooftop can be seen through gaps in the trees. After confirming that this is really where his fare wants to go, the driver heads down the ever worsening track into what remains of a village that housed over four thousand of the world's finest athletes in the summer of 1936.

Seven decades and the Soviet army have taken their toll on what should be a preserved national monument. The 150 single-storey stone huts are being consumed by undergrowth, and those windows that are not boarded up are smashed. The large crescent-shaped Housing Building, which boasted forty kitchens, each of which specialised in a different national cuisine, resembles a derelict block of flats on the most deprived of estates. On the practice running track, its cinders tufted with weeds, a flock of sheep grazes. A row of foot-high concrete blocks gives the suggestion of a viewing platform, from where athletes could monitor their rivals' abilities and techniques.

The dereliction and the eeriness of the village make it hard to envisage it as a centre of bustling joy. Could this really be what one American athlete described as 'a sight to behold', with its 'wild animals running over the grounds . . . and green grass mowed like a golf course'? It is more reminiscent of a concentration camp, the buildings giving the impression that something bad happened here. Like so many other decaying structures from the Nazi period, there is the normal sense of Ozymandias, the ruins symbolic of collapsed majesty. It is not a place to be after dusk, and with the taxi's meter running, it is soon time to leave.

Unlike the village, the other relic from the Eleventh Olympiad of the Modern Era is a far more impressive and intact affair. Situated halfway between Dallgow-Doeberitz and the centre of Berlin, the mighty Olympiastadion is as awe-inspiring as Adolf Hitler intended it. Clad in pale Franconian limestone, the stadium almost glows in the sunlight, its magnificent pillared curves elegant and powerful.

It is only upon entering the building that its sheer scale can be appreciated. As the stadium sinks 40 feet below ground level, the outside of the building gives the lie to its capacity. In 1936, it accommodated some 100,000 spectators, although today, because of the use of seats, that number has shrunk to 76,000. Nevertheless, it is vast, and unlike so many of today's steel-and-glass structures, the limestone gives the building a more natural air.

In contrast to the Olympic village, it is easy to imagine the dramatic events that took place here seventy years ago. The VIP platform where Hitler and his acolytes watched the infuriatingly fast progress of Jesse Owens eighty feet below still stands. The brazier that contained the Olympic flame is here too, along with the names of the gold medal winners carved in stone near by. Through the gap in the stadium's west end can be seen the 247-foot bell tower on the other side of the immense May Field. The tower once contained a bell that weighed over 30,000 pounds, its toll 'summoning the youth of the world' to the Games. Its chimes would have filled the stadium, but not as effectively as the sound of 100,000 singing 'Deutschland über Alles' whenever a German took gold.

Whereas other Nazi edifices such as the rally grounds at Nuremberg are rightly abandoned, this is a building still very much in use – even playing host to the 2006 World Cup final. Although some argue that a structure so closely associated with the Nazi period should not be used, it would seem churlish (and uneconomical) to abandon so handsome and vast a building. In 1936 it may well have been regarded as an architectural embodiment of the waxing power of the new German Reich, but in 2006, the seventieth anniversary of the Nazis' Olympics, it stands as a symbol that Germany has the ability to come to terms with its past. Why should it not be used? What harm does it do? The shape of the Olympic Stadium does not register as a symbol of evil in the same way as the infamous entrance to Auschwitz, with its railway lines converging to pass under its all-seeing watchtower. The stadium may well not be free from guilt, but like many associated with the Nazi regime, it does not necessarily deserve the death penalty.

What follows is the story of what happened inside that village and stadium. But the story is set elsewhere too, from the plains of the American Midwest to the hilltop villages of the Korean peninsula. And if its locations are global, then its themes are of a similar stature, because this is not just a story about sport. It is also about politics, about the titanic fight between fascism and democracy. It is about racism and those who struggled to overcome it. It is about the glory of winning medals, and the despair that sees men putting bullets through their own heads. It is about Olympism itself, and how the Games of 1936 saw an ideal marriage between it and Nazism. Above all, the story shows how it is impossible to keep sport out of politics, for the simple reason that there are those who will always use athletes as their unwitting tools. Those two weeks in Berlin show how easily the naive worthiness of the Olympics could be corrupted to suit the ambitions of repellent men. It is a lesson that still needs to be learned.

Guy Walters
Heytesbury
February 2006

Author's Note

This book has a large cast of characters, and for simplicity's sake I have used the names under which athletes competed. Obviously, many of the female athletes have since changed their names. As a rule, I have kept to the names used in the official Olympic Report, except in the case of Kitei Son, whom I call Son Ki-Jung for reasons the book makes apparent.

Beware: there are numerous abbreviations that use the letter 'A'. Although I have endeavoured to spell out repeatedly what each stands for – and indeed to minimise their use – it might be helpful for readers to have an easily accessible list.

AAA   Amateur Athletics Association (UK)
AAU   Amateur Athletic Union (US)
AOA   American Olympic Association
AOC   American Olympic Committee
BOA   British Olympic Association
BOC   British Olympic Committee
BWSA   British Workers' Sports Association
IAAF   International Association of Athletics Federations
IOC   International Olympic Committee
GOC   German Olympic Committee
NWSA   National Workers' Sports Association (UK)

HONOURABLE CHARLES ZARAKA: A most illuminating spectacle, Mr Chan. The nations of the world about to struggle for supremacy on the field of sports. Yet behind all this there is another struggle going on constantly – for world supremacy in a more sinister field. It is not a game for amateurs, Mr Chan. I hope you get my meaning.

CHARLIE CHAN: Could not be more clear if magnified by 200-inch telescope.

From *Charlie Chan at the Olympics* (1937)
Script by Paul Burger, Robert Ellis and Helen Logan

Prologue

~

'I LOOKED DOWN that field to the finish 109 yards and 2 feet away and then began to think in terms of what it had taken for me to get there . . . And as I looked down at the uniform of the country that I represented and realised that after all I was just a man like any other man, I felt suddenly as if my legs could not carry even the weight of my body.'

It was coming up to 4.55 p.m. on Monday, 3 August 1936. A light rain fell on Jesse Owens as he waited for the start of the 100 metres final. The temperature was mild – some 19 to 20 degrees – and a light 6 mph wind was blowing diagonally from behind him. Owens had easily got through the heats, and now just a ten-second run stood between him and an Olympic gold medal. He looked around the stadium, spotting Adolf Hitler, the patron of the Games, waiting to see whether an Aryan would triumph over this '*Neger*', in the same way as Germany's Max Schmeling had defeated America's Joe Louis earlier in the year at the Yankee Stadium in New York City.

Owens had been drawn on the inside lane. Next to him stood Strandberg of Sweden, and in lane three stood Hitler's hope, the mighty Erich Borchmeyer. The German was the Nordic archetype, every inch of his six foot pure Aryan. In lane four stood Osendarp of Holland, with the Americans Frank Wykoff and Ralph Metcalfe – Owens' fellow African-American – in lanes five and six. Owens knew that he could beat them all, but he also knew that the same was true of Metcalfe and Borchmeyer. He recalled his coach's words: 'Imagine you're sprinting over a ground of burning fire.'

At 4.58 the men dug their feet into the cinders. Hitler strained forward in his seat in the box of honour, beating his right fist on the rail in front of him. Borchmeyer *had* to win. For a mere Negro to walk away with gold would be unthinkable.

The starter's words rang out.

'*Auf die platz . . .*'

Owens looked down the lane. He could just about make out the finishing tape.

'*Fertig!*'

Simultaneously, the six men raised their haunches. Owens swallowed, trying to control his breathing. The pistol went off, the recoil jolting the starter's right arm. A large cloud of white smoke filled the air around his head. Owens launched himself forward, his arms starting to pump furiously. Within 20 metres, Owens was already ahead, sprinting at his top speed of 22½ mph. 'There never was a runner who showed so little sign of effort,' wrote one observer. 'He seemed to float along the track like water.' One second and 10 metres later, he had widened the gap to a whole metre, making his lead seemingly unassailable. Ralph Metcalfe had had an appalling start and was in last place, while Borchmeyer was struggling in fourth between Strandberg and Osendarp.

After 80 metres, Owens noticed that someone was closing on him. The figure was too far away to be Borchmeyer – in fact this challenger was on the other side of the track. It was Metcalfe, who was clipping away at Owens' lead with every stride. As the two men approached the tape, it looked as if Metcalfe might overtake him. More muscular than Owens, Metcalfe displayed a running style that appeared far more powerful than Owens' graceful light-footedness. He had beaten Owens before, and it looked as though he was going to beat him again.

'Ralph and I ran neck and neck,' Owens recalled. 'And then, for some unknown reason I cannot yet fathom, I beat Ralph, who was such a magnificent runner.' The 'unknown reason' was Metcalfe's appalling start. Had Metcalfe started as quickly as Owens, then the race would have been his.

Much to the Fuehrer's chagrin, the crowd went ecstatic. They shouted 'Yess-say Oh-Vens! Yess-ay Oh-Vens!', not seeming to mind that Borchmeyer had come second from last. If Nazi Germany was racist, then its prejudice was seemingly put aside for a few minutes of fanatical cheering. Owens grinned, although his natural modesty made him refrain from anything more demonstrative. He had won in a time of 10.3 seconds, although the world record was denied him because of that 6 mph tail wind. Owens didn't care: 'The greatest moment of all, of course, was when we knelt and received the Wreath of Victory and standing there facing the stands we could hear the strains of the "Star Spangled Banner" rise into the air and the Stars and Stripes was hoisted to the skies.' The flag would be hoisted three more times in Owens' honour. He was doing his best to make the Games his own, but there were others for whom they represented more than the chance of winning a few races.

I

Sporting Spirit

~

WITH ITS GRAND classical façade, the town hall in Barcelona makes a suitable setting for momentous decisions. Gathered there on the morning of Sunday, 26 April 1931, were twenty men, all of whom had breakfasted well and were ready to discuss the most important matter on the agenda of their two-day meeting – the venue for the 1936 Olympic Games. The men were members of the International Olympic Committee, and this, their twenty-eighth annual meeting, was chaired by the committee's president, the fifty-five-year-old Count Henri de Baillet-Latour. The Belgian had been a member of the IOC since 1903, just nine years after it had been created to establish the first of the modern Olympic Games in Greece in 1896. A former diplomat and a keen horseman, Baillet-Latour had successfully organised the 1920 Olympics in Antwerp, a feat that had been regarded as extraordinary as he had only a year to accomplish it in a country that had been ravaged by war. Tall, with balding white hair and a large but trim moustache bristling under a long nose, Baillet-Latour commanded much respect from his fellow members of the IOC.

Also present were three men who hoped to gain much from the meeting. Their names were State Excellency Dr Theodor Lewald, Dr Karl Ritter von Halt and the Count de Vallellano. Lewald and von Halt were both German members of the IOC, and they felt confident that Berlin, after years of lobbying, would be awarded the prize. Nevertheless, Vallellano, a representative of the Spanish Olympic Committee and a powerful financier with his own palace in Madrid, was hopeful that the IOC members would award the 1936 Games to Barcelona.

Although Berlin and Barcelona were the two front-runners for the prize, there were two other potential candidates for host city – Budapest and Rome. After an introduction by Baillet-Latour, the first members to speak were two Italian members of the IOC, General Carlo Montu and Count Bonacossa. To the relief of the Germans and the Spaniard, they told the meeting that 1936 was not the right time for Rome to host the Games, but they begged the committee to consider the city at some future date. The next to speak was the Hungarian, Senator Jules de Muzsa, who instead of lobbying for his capital spoke in favour of Berlin, much to the delight of Lewald and von Halt.

Lewald then addressed the meeting. For him, that Sunday morning was the potential culmination of nearly two decades of intense effort to get the Games staged in Germany. A member of the IOC since 1924, Lewald had also been head of the German Organising Committee that had been planning the 1916 Olympics, which were awarded to Berlin at Stockholm in 1912. The Germans had set to work immediately, and had constructed a magnificent stadium outside Berlin that had been dedicated by the Kaiser in 1913. Surprisingly, the outbreak of war in 1914 did little to damage the chances of the Games being held in Germany. 'In olden times it happened that it was not possible to celebrate the Games, but they did not for this reason cease to exist,' Baron Pierre de Coubertin, the founder of the modern Olympics and the then president of the IOC, declared in the spring of 1915. In April, the Germans announced that the Games would simply be delayed until the end of the war, a decision agreed by the IOC.

On the 22nd of that month, however, a grey-green cloud was observed by 8,000 French colonial soldiers entrenched north of Ypres in northern France. The cloud was in fact a truly terrifying weapon. It was chlorine gas, and its sinister, billowing appearance caused the soldiers to flee. The Germans, wary of their own gas, failed to capitalise on the French retreat and the gap in the line was quickly reinforced by Allied troops. The deployment of those first few tons of chlorine changed the nature of the war, however, and soon poison gas was used on both sides. As a result of the war losing its 'gentlemanliness', Coubertin finally felt obliged to cancel the Games.

After the war ended, Lewald was to encounter more disappointments, as Germany was forbidden from taking part in the Games of 1920 and 1924. Nevertheless, along with Dr Carl Diem, his sidekick on the German Olympic Committee, he persisted in lobbying the

IOC, whose new head, Baillet-Latour, was more amenable to their approaches. Lewald's efforts paid off. In 1928, Germany once more competed in the Olympics. Her performance at Amsterdam was stunning; the country came second only to the United States in the tally of medals. With eight gold medals, seven silver and fourteen bronze, Germany had firmly re-established herself as an Olympic power. Naturally, Lewald was determined to capitalise on the German success. In May 1930, the IOC held its congress in Berlin. Setting the tone for the gathering, President Hindenburg declared that 'physical culture must be a life habit'. But the meeting was more of a showcase for Lewald than the ageing president. If Lewald could sufficiently impress the visiting Olympic dignitaries, then there was a good chance that Berlin might soon host the Games. Lewald was mercenary, even reminding the delegates that it was thanks to the work of German scholars that so much was known about classical Olympism. Rooted in antiquity, Germany was the natural home for the Games, he claimed.

Lewald drew on the same themes at the meeting that Sunday morning in April 1931. As a former under-secretary of state, the seventy-year-old Lewald was used to the sophisticated parley of the committee room. He made the case for Berlin impressively, with no need to draw on the smooth charm of his colleague, the handsome financier and war hero von Halt. Lewald said that Berlin deserved the Games, not least because it had been denied them in 1916, and also because Berlin, being in the heart of Europe, would attract far more visitors than Barcelona. The Count de Vallellano then made the case for Barcelona, and Baillet-Latour called for the votes to be cast.

There was a problem, however, a problem that should have been dealt with sooner. The attendees present did not even constitute half the membership of the IOC, which was nearly sixty strong. In the days before jet aircraft, such a poor showing was by no means uncommon, but with such an important decision at stake, it was decided to wait for the votes of absent members to be mailed or sent by telegram to the IOC headquarters in Lausanne. The votes that had already been cast were sealed. Now there was nothing the IOC could do but wait.

Lewald and his team had to kick their heels for nearly three agonising weeks. At last, on Wednesday, 13 May, the final count was held in the Swiss lakeside town. In the presence of the vice-president of the IOC, Baron Godfroy de Blonay, and the magistrate of Lausanne, Mr Paul Perret, the envelopes were opened. Eight IOC members, dissatisfied by both cities, abstained. Sixteen votes were cast for Barcelona. Berlin received a commanding forty-three votes, which represented three-quarters of those available. It was a triumphant victory not only for Lewald but also for Germany. The vote signified that thirteen years after the war, she was ready to be readmitted to the pantheon of 'respectable' nations.

It is easy to underestimate how desperately Germany wanted to be regarded as a civilised country. Since the legal establishment of the Weimar Republic in August 1919, the grip of democracy in Germany was anything but strong. For the twelve years leading up to her being awarded the Olympics, the country suffered a succession of left-wing and right-wing putsches and economic crises. In March 1920, when the new national government was less than year old, a group of far-right paramilitaries — members of the infamous Freikorps — seized Berlin and installed Wolfgang Kapp, a right-wing journalist, as Chancellor. The legitimate government called for a general strike, and within four days the Kapp putsch had failed. It was the left's turn next, and the Ruhr soon fell under the command of a 50,000-strong 'Red Army'. This was quashed by an amalgam of the regular army and Freikorps units.

On the evening of Thursday, 8 November 1923, yet another putsch was mounted, this time by the fledgling Nazi Party. Under the command of their firebrand thirty-four-year-old leader, Adolf Hitler, and General Erich Ludendorff, the Nazis attempted to seize power in Munich by storming the Buergerbräukeller, where Gustav von Kahr, the Bavarian commissar, was addressing a crowd of 3,000. The Beer Hall Putsch was a failure. Far from being the 'national revolution' that Hitler announced when he mounted the stage, the attempted coup disintegrated into violent farce. After a night of confusion, Ludendorff decided the following morning that the Nazis should do something proactive and march – although quite where, no one knew. When the column of around two thousand neared the Defence Ministry, shots were fired, resulting in the deaths of four policemen and fourteen insurgents. Hitler was captured and subsequently sentenced to five

years in Lansdberg Prison, where, assisted by Rudolf Hess, he wrote
Mein Kampf.

It was not just political turbulence which threatened the integrity of
the Weimar Republic. In 1923, the government defaulted on its repa-
rations payments, demanded by the Treaty of Versailles, and as a result
the French and Belgians occupied the Ruhr in January. A series of
strikes further damaged the economy, and in order to pay the striking
workers their benefits the government decided to print currency. The
now infamous hyper-inflation took hold, and by November of that year
it required 4,200,000,000,000 marks to buy one dollar. At the beginning of the year the exchange rate had been 4.2 marks to the dollar.
Nevertheless, after a revaluation, the situation was brought under
control, and until 1929 Germany enjoyed a relatively stable six years.

In 1930, however, Germany was hit by the Great Depression. The
political result was a resurgence of extremist parties, and in the election
of September 1930 the Nazis became the second-largest party in the
Reichstag, holding 107 seats, or 18.3 per cent of the vote. Hitler, who
had been released from prison just over a year after the Beer Hall
Putsch, ruled his party by means of the *Fuehrerprinzip*, which demanded
absolute loyalty to him as leader. His style of leadership appealed not
just to established Nazis, but also to the masses of farmers, veterans and
members of the middle class who had voted for him. Furthermore, the
party's emphasis on ritual, the wearing of uniforms and elaborate ceremony, elevated the image of the party above that of merely another
manifestation of the lunatic fringe. To many Germans, the appeal of
Nazism lay in its look, which suggested in an almost cultist fashion the
virtues of discipline, order and strength.

By the time Theodor Lewald had learned that Berlin had secured the
Olympics, 4 million Germans were unemployed. Nevertheless, despite
the country reeling punch-drunk from crisis to crisis, Lewald and
Diem were not discouraged. Lewald was fortunate to have the vigorous forty-eight-year-old Diem as his colleague. Initially a sporting
journalist, Diem had captained the German team that had competed
at the Stockholm Olympics of 1912. In 1920, with the backing of
Lewald, he founded a university – the Deutsche Hochschule fuer
Leibesuebungen – dedicated to the study of sport. What was remarkable was that Diem had no formal education, and yet he was soon to

8

be regarded as a formidable scholar. With his intellectual and organisational abilities, he was a natural choice to become the secretary of the German Olympic Committee.

Like Lewald, Diem was an enthusiastic supporter of Baron Pierre de Coubertin, the founder of the modern Olympics. 'It will be my most ardent desire to arrange the Olympic Games of 1936 in the spirit as desired by their originator,' he wrote to Coubertin in October 1931. At the age of sixty-eight, Coubertin was living in Lausanne, where he could reflect on his achievement of founding what had become the most successful international sporting event the world had seen. A French educationist and historian, Coubertin believed that sport not only promoted a healthy body but also provided much moral enrichment, a view he had arrived at after observing the British. 'Since ancient Greece has passed away,' he wrote, 'the Anglo-Saxon race is the only one that fully appreciates the moral influence of physical culture and gives to this branch of educational science the attention that it deserves.'

Two Anglo-Saxons in particular had influenced Coubertin's thinking. One was Thomas Arnold, the famous headmaster of the British boys' school, Rugby. Although Arnold had died over twenty years before Coubertin's birth, his legacy of combining sport with religion to create boys of 'character' greatly appealed to Coubertin, who saw the success of schools like Rugby as being vital to the formation of the British Empire. The other Anglo-Saxon was William Brookes, the driving force behind the annual 'Olympian Games' held in Much Wenlock in Shropshire since 1850. A forerunner to the modern Olympics, Brookes's 'Olympics' was a village fête that had transmogrified into a significant athletic pageant that attracted much international attention. One of the characteristics of the Shropshire games was their use of ritual and ceremony – laurels were awarded by women to the victors, specially composed music was played, flags with ancient Greek mottoes were hoisted; the Greek king had even donated a silver cup to be awarded at the Games. Although Coubertin never saw the Games, he visited Much Wenlock in October 1890, and he and Brookes struck up a friendship of sorts. Whether Brookes's games alone gave Coubertin the idea for a modern Olympics is unclear, but there is no doubt that he owed a debt to the Englishman.

After his visit, Coubertin wrote, 'If the Olympic Games, that Modern Greece has not yet been able to revive, still survived today, it is due, not to a Greek, but to Dr W. P. Brookes.'

Four years after his visit to Much Wenlock, in June 1894, Coubertin convened an international congress at the Sorbonne in Paris. It was there that he proposed the revival of the Games, which would draw upon the ancient Greek Olympic ideals of amateurism and fair play. Using a mixture of charm and lavish entertainment, Coubertin convinced a collection of sportsmen and sports education- ists of the merits of his idea. The congress decided that the Games should be held every four years, with the first scheduled to take place in Greece in 1896.

On 6 April of that year, the first Olympic Games of the Modern Era were opened in the newly restored Panathenaic Stadium in Athens. Eighty thousand crowded into the stadium, including King George I of Greece, who started the Games with the unashamedly patriotic words: 'I declare the opening of the first international Olympic Games in Athens. Long live the Nation. Long live the Greek people.' The king had neglected to mention that the representatives of twelve other nations were waiting to compete, having come from as far afield as Australia and the United States to help make the Games a success.

Even though the standard of competition was almost abysmal – no world records were set, and the only two nations whose athletes had trained for the events were Great Britain and the United States – the Games were considered a success. The Greeks found a new national hero in the form of Spiridon Louis, a water-carrier who won the marathon in a time of 2:58:50, his efforts fuelled by wine, milk, beer, orange juice and even an Easter egg. When Louis won, the Greeks in the stadium went wild. 'Here the Olympic Victor was received with full honour; the King rose from his seat and congratulated him most warmly on his success,' reads the official report of the Games. 'Some of the King's aides-de-camp, and several members of the Committee went so far as to kiss and embrace the victor, who finally was carried in triumph to the retiring room under the vaulted entrance. The scene witnessed then inside the Stadion cannot be easily described, and even foreigners were carried away by the general enthusiasm.'

The closing ceremony was held on 12 April. Over 100,000 packed into the stadium and massed on the surrounding hills to watch as the athletes received their medals and laurel wreaths. Pigeons with blue-and-white streamers were released, and flower petals were tossed into the air. Spiridon Louis then led the athletes in a lap round the track, his presence once more causing a massive outburst of nationalist fervour. After the lap, King George closed the ceremony with the portentous words: 'I proclaim the ending of the first Olympiad.' Later, King George declared that the Games should be held in Greece for all time. This went against the wishes of Coubertin, who had found himself almost as a bystander during the past week. Coubertin wished to see the Games held in a different city every four years, thus encouraging internationalism. Many of the athletes were not in agreement, however; even most of the American athletes signed a petition to the Crown Prince of Greece asking for the Games to be held in Athens in perpetuity.

Nevertheless, Coubertin got his way. Over the next few decades the Olympics were held in Paris in 1900, St Louis in 1904, London in 1908 and, Stockholm in 1912; there was also an 'Intercalated Games' in Athens in 1906. The Paris and St Louis Olympics had been considered failures, overshadowed by massive international exhibitions held concurrently in their host cities. The Athens Games of 1906 were a successful attempt to reinvigorate the Games, but it was not until the 1912 Games that the Olympics became recognisable in the form they maintain today. For the first time athletes came from all five continents, thus ensuring that the symbolism of the five Olympic rings was truly representative. The ceremonies and rituals also became more elaborate, and the establishment of national Olympic committees ensured a high level of competition.

By the early 1930s, however, the ageing baron in Lausanne was not as happy as he should have been. After standing down from the presidency of the IOC after the 1924 Paris Games, Coubertin watched as the Olympic movement swelled and outgrew its founder. He grew increasingly bitter, partly because he felt he had not received the international recognition that he deserved, and also because he was worried about his dwindling financial resources. In the late summer of 1934 he was to be found in a positively suicidal mood. 'He seemed in excellent health, though he still pronounced that he wished soon to die,' wrote Sigfrid Edström, the vice-president of the IOC, to Baillet-Latour. 'He said that he had nothing to live for. His wife is very ill.' Coubertin also told Edström in confidence that 'he had lost all his money', and that he would have to sell the furniture and paintings that his wife had left in the Olympic museum, items that the couple had wished to leave to the city of Lausanne. It was unsurprising, therefore, that Edström found Coubertin 'difficult to handle'.

One of Lewald's and Diem's first actions upon securing the Olympics for Berlin was to head to the United States for the Los Angeles Olympics of 1932. The two men, along with the million other visitors to California, were impressed. Despite the depression, the Californian Treasury Department had managed to donate $1 million (nearly $11 million in 2005), and a special bond raised $1.5 million (over $16 million in 2005), all of which ensured that Los Angeles was able to hold a glittering Games. A massive stadium meant that 104,000 could watch the athletes competing under – for the first time – the Olympic flame. This new piece of ritual was invented by Hollywood, and it had no roots in ancient Greek culture. One element that did have its roots in Olympism, albeit of the modern variety, was the releasing of pigeons, which had been a feature of the 1896 Games. The most important addition to the Olympic pageant, however, at least from the point of view of anybody who organises Olympic Games, was the Los Angelenos' building of an Olympic village. Previously, athletes had been housed in cheap hotels or had had to stay with friends, but the provision of purpose-built cottages and halls meant that the athletes had their first chance to mingle 'after hours'.

Lewald and Diem spent their time furiously making notes. Diem went so far as to take photographs of workshops, and even noted the culinary preferences of each participating country. With their country in an even worse financial state than the United States, the two men knew they would be pushed to duplicate, let alone better, the tenth Olympiad. Their mood was not improved by the poor showing Germany made in the medals table, lagging in ninth place with a mere three gold medals, twelve silver and five bronze. The Americans were the victors by a long chalk, with a total of 103 medals, forty-one of which were gold. The Italians and the French were second and third respectively, and the British came eighth, with a total of sixteen medals, four of which, being gold, secured them a place above Germany.

Germany's showing caused much upset back home. The most virulent reaction came in the pages of *Der Angriff* (The Attack), the Nazi newspaper. A fortnight after the German team returned from Los Angeles, the newspaper commented that members of the German Olympic Committee were 'traitors' for allowing German athletes to compete against Jews and 'niggers'. For the time being, Lewald and Diem were able to dismiss such rantings as the outpourings of extremists, but they would soon find themselves having to curry favour from those who shared such execrable views.

In the meantime, they had work to do. On 11 November 1932, the German Olympic Committee met to found the Organising Committee, and it was swiftly agreed that Lewald should become its chairman. The Olympic Committee also pondered the adoption of a symbol for the Games, and after some discussion Lewald's idea of a bell was chosen. On 24 January the following year, the Organising Committee held its first meeting at the Berlin Town Hall. There, Lewald estimated that some four thousand athletes and one thousand team leaders and trainers would attend the Games – an unprecedented number. He also advocated that the existing stadium should have its capacity increased to around 80,000–85,000. The money for all this, he said, would come from the sale of tickets, which would raise some 3 million Reichsmarks ($712,589 – $10,000,000 in 2005). A million Reichsmarks would be raised by the addition of a small levy on postage stamps, and an unspecified amount would be earned from the payment by spectators at sporting events of an 'Olympic penny'. The economics minister, Dr Hjalmar Schacht, had also given his blessing to a lottery that would run for three years.

Six days after Lewald's meeting, however, the entire face of Germany changed: the Nazis came to power. Since the election of September 1930, Hitler's path to power had been steady but not quite sure. In 1932 he stood against Hindenburg in the presidential election, and although he came second, he won nearly 37 per cent of the vote. In the Reichstag election of July that same year, the Nazis won 230 seats, thus becoming the largest party in parliament. Franz von Papen, the beleaguered

Chancellor, soon lost a no-confidence vote, and a further election was called for November. Frantic efforts by Papen to secure Nazi support for his Centre Party failed, and although the Nazis lost seats in the November election, they remained the largest party. Papen was fired by Hindenburg and was replaced by General Kurt von Schleicher, who had promised he could form a majority government without the Nazis. Unsurprisingly, his attempt failed, and Hindenburg reluctantly called upon Hitler to assume the chancellorship. On the morning of 30 January 1933, Hitler was sworn in.

Hitler's elevation represented a severe threat to the efforts of the Organising Committee. The previous year, Hitler had declared that the Olympics was 'an invention of Jews and Freemasons' and 'could not possibly be put on in a Reich ruled by National Socialists'. Lewald and Diem now feared that the Olympics in Germany might be cancelled for a second time, not through external pressure, but through inimical forces within. The Organising Committee had another problem, however, which no amount of smooth talking to the Nazis by Lewald would be able to banish: Lewald's paternal grandmother had been a Jew. Although his father had converted to Christianity at the age of seventeen – some 110 years earlier – Lewald knew that as far as the Nazis were concerned he was still a de facto Jew. What made matters worse was that Diem's wife, Liselott, also had Jewish forebears, an association that made some Nazis describe Diem as a 'white Jew'.

Lewald was canny enough to have anticipated the difficulty of his and Diem's position in the event of the Nazis coming to power. The Organising Committee was founded as a not-for-profit private society, which meant that if the Nazis respected the German legal system, they would not be able to oust Lewald for being a Jew. Lewald's influence and range of contacts meant that he was able to register the company in far less than the normal six weeks. In fact, the Organising Committee of the 1936 Olympics was registered in just one hour.

In March, Lewald met the Chancellor and his new Minister for Popular Enlightenment and Propaganda, Josef Goebbels. Although Goebbels, who showed little interest in sport, saw the advantages of the Olympics as a showcase for the regime, Hitler remained unconvinced. According to the official Olympic Report, however, Lewald appeared to have impressed Hitler to the extent that his opinion of the previous year was turned round: 'The Games, he [Hitler] asserted, would contribute substantially towards furthering understanding among the nations of the world and would promote the development of sport among the German youth, this being in his opinion of vast importance to the welfare of the nation.' Naturally, the report is anodyne, but with Lewald securing an official public statement from Hitler pledging his support for the Games, there is little doubt that Hitler was at least paying lip-service to them. What the report does not mention is the question of Lewald's Jewishness. The Nazis wanted Lewald to relinquish his post, but Baillet-Latour would not have it. The Nazis relented, and allowed him to stay, with the proviso that he step down from the German Olympic Committee as soon as the Games were finished. In effect, Lewald would be nothing more than a titular head of the Organising Committee, while the bulk of the work would be carried out by Diem, who would in turn report to the government through the figure of Hans von Tschammer und Osten, the Reich's sports minister, one of Hitler's oldest allies. Furthermore, both Diem and Lewald had to relinquish their posts at the Deutsche Hochschule fuer Leibesuebungen, the sports university they had established.

Nevertheless, on 1 April Lewald felt sufficiently confident to write a letter soothing the disquiet any of his fellow IOC members may have felt about the new regime:

> During the last few weeks the foreign press reported in many instances that the National Government of the Reich opposed the Olympic Games being held in Berlin 1936. This is one of the numerous wrong news [sic] about Germany which recently have been set afloat; it is as unfounded as all the widely circulating rumours about atrocities occurring in this country. The fact of the matter is that the Chancellor Herr Hitler, the Minister of Foreign Affairs, the Minister of the Interior, the Propaganda Minister and the Minister of Defence have expressed their willingness to further the cause of the Olympic Games by all means in their power.

Unsurprisingly, Lewald did not mention his Faustian pact with his new rulers. It would be the first of many times that Lewald would mislead the Olympic movement, mendacities all the more shocking coming from a man whose career had been threatened by the regime for reasons of race.

Lewald's letter did not work. The IOC remained troubled by what it heard coming from Germany. With each week, its members, along with the rest of the world, heard more and more stories concerning prejudice against Jewish sportsmen and women. One of them was Brigadier General E. Charles Sherrill, one of three American members of the IOC. Like many, Sherrill was appalled by the situation in Germany, and wrote to the American Jewish Congress, promising them that he would 'stoutly maintain the American principle that all citizens are equal under all laws'. The IOC was also concerned about the stranglehold the Nazis were already starting to exert on the Games. On 5 May Baillet-Latour wrote to Lewald, von Halt and the Duke of Mecklenburg-Schwerin, the third German member of the IOC, warning them that measures 'taken against certain athletes have created a hostile movement of opinion in the sporting world overseas and in international federations, against the celebration in Berlin of the XIth Olympiad'. Baillet-Latour laid down the Olympic law firmly, insisting that Hitler should be made to realise that the Games were the IOC's and not his. If Hitler did not offer a written guarantee saying that he would leave the Games alone, then Berlin would have to withdraw as the host city. He then invited the three men to attend the next IOC congress in Vienna in June to explain their position.

An incensed von Halt replied on 16 May, claiming that he understood Baillet-Latour's worries, but that he did not understand the content of his letters, fearing that the IOC president had been influenced by biased newspapers. He did not deny, however, that discrimination had taken place.

> Events in Germany are solely to do with domestic politics. In individual cases sportsmen have been affected. If a certain anti-German press feels called upon to deliver these domestic German matters on to the Olympic stage, then this is extraordinarily regrettable and shows their unfriendly attitude towards Germany in the worst possible light. [. . .] Germany is in the middle of a national revolution that must be described as an example of the greatest, never-before-seen discipline. If, in Germany, individual voices rise up against the Olympic Games, then

they emanate from circles that do not understand the Olympic spirit. These voices must on no account be taken seriously.

Von Halt then scoffed at the idea of seeking Hitler's written guarantee, saying that Hitler's spoken confirmation would have to do. 'I request your understanding, Mr President, that the head of a government of a nation of 65 million people cannot be made to confirm in writing an affirmation given orally.' Von Halt had clearly never heard of treaties, but then written guarantees from Hitler were to become infamously worthless.

Baillet-Latour was clearly affronted by von Halt's attitude. Ten days later, he wrote back to von Halt from Lausanne. He dismissed the charge that he had been influenced by a hostile press, and claimed that he had gathered his knowledge from official declarations. Was it not true, he said, that Lewald had in fact been replaced by the Reich Sports Minister, and that his participation was only a sham? Were German Jews able to take part in the Olympics representing Germany? If not, this would be 'contrary to the Olympic charter'. Once more, he demanded that the three German members of the IOC present themselves at Vienna.

So what evidence did Baillet-Latour have that the Jews – and in particular Jewish sportsmen and women – were being discriminated against? The list of measures taken against Jews is extensive, but one law that did affect Germany's right to stage the Games was a decree issued on 26 April, which banned Jews from membership of sports organisations. This directly contravened the clause in the Olympic Charter that read: 'The Olympic Games assemble together the amateurs of all nations on an equal footing and under conditions as perfect as possible'.

By the time the IOC gathered in Vienna on 7 June, the matriculation of Jews from schools, colleges and universities was limited to just 1.5 per cent of the student body. Any Jews beyond this percentage found it impossible to attend classes, let alone play sports at school. Specific sports were targeted as well. On 8 May, for example, Jews were excluded from tennis competitions. Later that month, any rowing club affiliated to the German Rowing Association was allowed to accept only 'Aryan' members. The German boxing federation banned Jews on 1 April. On 2 June, just five days before the Vienna meeting, Jews were barred from gymnastic clubs. That same month the German Skiing Union forbade any subordinate clubs from accepting Jews.

One Jew who was affected by these measures was the eighteen-year-old Margaret 'Gretel' Bergmann. An exceedingly talented all-round athlete, Bergmann was a member of the Ulmer Fussball Verein (the Ulm Football Club), which despite its name trained its members in all manner of track and field disciplines. Bergmann discovered her niche as a high-jumper, and she soon found her technique improving under expert tutelage. 'The fact that I had developed a gigantic crush on the coach was also helpful,' she later wrote; 'trying to impress him I worked twice as hard.' Bergmann recalls her days with the UFV spent at Ettlingen training camp in the Black Forest as idyllic and free from prejudice: 'When the day's labours were done we all got together for our meal and an evening of socialising. I do not know if any other Jews, besides me and a friend from the UFV, were among these atheletes; nobody cared anyway. Many a close and lasting friendship was formed.' By the end of 1931, Bergmann found herself ranked fourth in Germany.

Her talent did not stop a letter arriving in April 1933, a few days before her nineteenth birthday. 'It was not a very nice birthday present,' she wrote. 'The letter informed me that my membership in the UFV had been terminated and that I was no longer welcome. Forgotten were the good times we had together, forgotten were the many medals I had won for them, forgotten was the camaraderie.' By the autumn, Bergmann's parents had decided to send her to England, where she dreamed of joining the British Olympic team. She would soon be sucked back to Germany, however.

At 2.45 on the afternoon of 7 June, the IOC met in yet another fine building at the heart of a European city. The room on this occasion was the Festive Hall of the Academy of Sciences in Vienna, a gaudy affair with marble stucco and a baroque ceiling fresco. The turnout was only marginally better than in Barcelona two years before, with some thirty members in attendance. After welcoming new members, and bemoaning the death of Prince Leon Ouroussoff of Russia, the committee elected four new members to the IOC, two of whom were British – the champion hurdler Lord Burghley, and the author Sir Noel Curtis-Bennett.

Baillet-Latour then turned to the vexatious question of Germany. He briefed his colleagues on the exchanges that had taken place between himself and the Germans, reminding them of the necessity of ensuring that the Olympic code was adhered to. Diplomatically, Baillet-Latour paid tribute to the Olympic spirit and loyalty of the German delegates – Lewald, von Halt and Mecklenburg-Schwerin. He then read out a statement:

> The President of the International Olympic Committee asked the German delegates if they would guarantee the observance of the articles in the Charter dealing with the Organising Committee and the Rules of Qualification. On behalf of the three Delegates, His Excellency Doctor Lewald replied that, with the consent of his Government [. . .] All the laws regulating the Olympic Games shall be observed [and] as a principle German Jews shall not be excluded from German Teams at the Games of the XIth Olympiad.

There were two weasel clauses here. The first, 'with the consent of his Government', indicated that the German Organising Committee was not in charge of the Berlin Games; rather the government was. In Germany the government meant only one man: Hitler. The second weasel clause was 'as a principle'. Although this convinced many of the delegates, it still allowed the Nazis to mete out punitive measures against their Jewish sportsmen and women. Jews may have had the right to compete, but they had little or no opportunities to do so. The provision did not, for example, restore to Gretel Bergmann her membership of her beloved UFV. It did not stop Jews being banned from swimming in public baths, for fear that they would 'infect' the water. It did not stop the Jews being banned from equestrian clubs, lest the German horses were 'sullied' by Jewish riders. Like so many other Nazi so-called guarantees, it was valueless. Nevertheless, the IOC members took it at face value. General Sherrill, who had openly questioned Lewald about the rights of Jews to compete, wrote to Rabbi Stephen Wise back in New York, telling him that the negotiations with the Germans had been 'a trying fight' but that Lewald and his colleagues had 'finally yielded because they found that I had lined up the necessary votes'. There was an air of finality about the proceedings, as if this distasteful business regarding the Jews was finally over, a teething trouble, nothing more. Nevertheless, the trouble would not go away.

The IOC was clearly turning two blind eyes to what was going on in Germany. Fine words echoing in fine buildings were not representative of the true situation. In fact, the farcical nature of the Vienna congress was revealed just a few days after it was held. Towards the end of June, von Tschammer und Osten, the Reich's sports minister, made a speech in Berlin which contradicted the empty words spoken by Lewald to Baillet-Latour. 'We shall see to it that both in our national life, and in our relations and competitions with foreign nations, only such Germans shall be allowed to represent the nation as those against whom no objection can be raised.' That meant only one thing – no Jews were to be allowed to compete. If any IOC member wanted further confirmation of this attitude, then he could have found it more vulgarly expressed in *The Spirit of Sport in the Third Reich*, written by Bruno Malitz, the sports leader of the Berlin SA. After expressing the most un-Olympian sentiment that he could 'see no positive value for our people in permitting dirty Jews and Negroes to travel in our country and compete in athletics with our best', the author then stated:

> There is no room in the German land for Jewish leadership in sport, nor for pacifists and those betrayers of the people, the pan-Europeans, or others infected by the Jews. They are worse than cholera, tuberculosis, syphilis, worse than the pillaging hordes of Kalmucks [Mongols], worse than fire, starvation, flood, drought, poison gas. The most fearful battle of all still confronts the world – the battle against Jewry.

The irony of these words, when one considers the eventual fate of Europe's Jews, is sadly clear. So enamoured was Goebbels of Malitz's words that he insisted that every sports club in Germany should have a copy.

Despite the continued persecutions, preparations for the Games continued over the summer without any significant controversies. Then, on 5 October, Hitler decided to pay a visit to the Olympic Stadium, a visit that would have far-reaching consequences. Wearing a beige overcoat and without a hat, Hitler intended his presence to be low-key, which suggested that he was not on state business. It was clear that the self-styled Fuehrer, who had been in power only for eight months, was still not manifestly convinced of the merits of staging a festival he regarded as Semitic, Masonic and Negroid.

Besides an elite detachment of SS bodyguards, four other men were accompanying Hitler. Dr Wilhelm Frick was one of the Fuehrer's most devoted disciples. He had taken part in the Beer Hall Putsch of 1923, and his loyalty had seen him earn high office as the minister of the interior, in charge not only of the police, but also of the nascent concentration camps. Similarly, Hans von Tschammer und Osten had also been with Hitler since the early days. Well groomed, Tschammer und Osten wore the uniform of an army captain – brown riding breeches, leather boots and a peaked cap. Although he was subordinate to Frick in the ministry, there was no doubt that the newly appointed Reich Sports Minister cut the more impressive figure, more impressive even than Hitler.

The third man was Werner March. Unlike Frick and Tschammer und Osten, March had only recently joined the Nazi Party, taking up his membership at the beginning of April. Like many, he had done so because he would otherwise have found it impossible to have maintained his career. For March, becoming a Nazi was simply a matter of expediency and not of ideology. He was not going to see such an important commission undone simply because he had refused to sign a piece of paper. The fourth man was Lewald.

The five men walked slowly away from the two armour-plated Mercedes that had driven them the ten miles from the centre of Berlin. Hitler looked up at the vast concrete stadium. This was March's project, a project that had been started by his celebrated father Otto in 1913. Now that Otto had died, Lewald had entrusted his son with the task of enlarging it in time for the Games. As Hitler and his retinue approached, they could see workmen busying themselves all over the building, their industry stepped up by the presence of the German leader. Much of the activity was centred on the floor of the stadium, which Hitler noticed was being excavated.

'Why are they digging?' the Fuehrer asked.

'It's the only way we can increase the capacity,' Lewald answered. 'We cannot go up, because the Berlin Horseracing Association has insisted that we cannot spoil the view of their track.'

Hitler's reply was to the point.

'Is the racecourse necessary?'

He was right to pose the question. Berlin had two other tracks, and the one here at the Grunewald was making a loss. The representatives told Hitler that the racecourse was indeed unnecessary.

'This stadium must be demolished!' Hitler ordered. 'A new one must be built in its place, capable of seating 100,000 people. It will be the task of the nation! If Germany is to stand host to the entire world, her preparations must be complete and magnificent.'

None of the men was willing to point out that this was a remarkable volte-face on the part of Hitler. For reasons of personal prestige, each of them needed the Games as much as Germany did – who were they to complain that the dictator had changed his mind? Besides, now that the Fuehrer himself was behind the Games, they were bound to be a triumph, a tremendous celebration of sportsmanship. But sportsmanship was the last thing that concerned Hitler. For him, the Games would have little to do with athletics. Instead, they would prove that his fascist regime was an example other nations would have to follow. The XIth Olympiad would prove that Germany, after nearly two decades of subjugation since 1918, was once more on top of the world. Far from being a festival of internationalism, the Games would be one of over-arching nationalism.

2

'A party in such a house may not be a pleasant experience'

~

'I AM NOT personally fond of Jews and of the Jewish influence,' wrote Count Baillet-Latour on 3 November 1933, 'but I will not have them molested in no way whatsoever, I know that they shout before there is no reason to do so and I have always been struck by the fact that all the horrors which took place in Russia for instance, much more barbarous than anything which took place in Germany has never excited public opinion in the same way. Why? Because the propaganda was not made as cleaerverly.'

The recipient of this letter would no doubt have forgiven the count's somewhat tortuous use of English, and more especially his views on the Jews. The letter, unsurprisingly marked 'CONFIDENTIAL', was addressed to Avery Brundage, the forty-six-year-old head of the American Olympic Committee (AOC) and Amateur Athletic Union (AAU). As well as being the United States' leading sports administrator, Brundage had made a fortune from his Chicago-based construction business. In fact, he had made two fortunes, the first being lost during the Great Crash of 1929. When he faced bankruptcy, Brundage was determined to maintain appearances, and went around Chicago with his 'chest out and not a nickel in my pocket, but no one knew that except my accountant and my secretary'. His chutzpah was rewarded, and unlike so many other businessmen of that period, he did not succumb to the swift fall from a skyscraper or the placing of a revolver in his mouth. Brundage was later to comment that not one of these suicides 'had the character-building discipline of competitive sport'.

Brundage's obsession with competitive sport was not simply a product of his administrative roles. He had been a highly successful pentathlete and had competed in the 1912 Stockholm Olympics, where he came a creditable sixth. Brundage was disappointed with his performance, however, especially since he dropped out of the 1,500 metres when he realised that he would never make enough points to win a medal. The victor was Jim Thorpe, the American Indian who was subsequently stripped of his gold when it was discovered he had breached the strict amateur code laid down in the Olympic charter. Despite this, Brundage viewed the Stockholm Games later in life as if they were the highest expression of the noble ideals of Olympism. 'What social, racial, religious or political prejudices of any kind might have existed', he wrote, 'were soon forgotten and sportsmen from all over the world, with different ideas, assorted viewpoints, and various manners of living, mingled on the field and off with the utmost friendliness, transported by an overflowing Olympic spirit.' In fact, the whole experience touched Brundage so deeply that the spirit seemed to flow into him. 'My conversion, along with many others, to Coubertin's religion, the Olympic Movement, was complete.'

Brundage's comparison of Olympism to a religion was not merely a figure of speech. For many, the Olympic Games were indeed like religious experiences, complete with their increasingly sophisticated rites and rituals. Coubertin was almost regarded as Christ, and Baillet-Latour as his disciple. These men were infallible, because they embodied an idealism that far transcended the grubby quotidian strivings of humanity. It was a pagan idealism, its pageantry godless, but its chauvinist adherents were nothing less than fanatics, men for whom no other point of view was acceptable. If anyone obstructed their ideals, then they would be subjected to the most vicious *ad hominem* attacks.

Brundage also saw in Olympism an enshrinement of his own racist ideals, ideals he shared with the Chicago Association of Commerce in November 1929:

> Perhaps we are about to witness the development of a new race, a race of men actuated by the principles of sportsmanship learned on the playing field, refusing to tolerate different conditions in the other enterprises of life; a race physically strong, mentally alert and morally sound; a *race* not to be imposed upon, because it is ready to fight for right and physically prepared to do so; a race quick to help an adversary beaten in fair combat yet fearlessly resenting injustice or unfair advantage . . .

There was little to distinguish this from the 'teachings' of Hitler. Brundage clearly shared the Nazis' admiration of the body, and its use as a military machine. For both Brundage and Hitler, sport was a way of honing the body militaristic.

Baillet-Latour's letter to Brundage reflected not just his anti-Semitism, but also a desire to do well for the Jews despite it. As news of Germany's punitive measures against 600,000 of her own people continued to spread, Baillet-Latour was keen to ensure that the Germans kept to the promises they had made at Vienna. In order to achieve this, he turned to Brundage.

> What I believe should be a useful move would be from the Amateur Athletic Union of the United States, at the annual meeting to decide that a request should be addressed to the Athletic Union of Germany in view to make sure that as a consequence of the promise made at Vienna, certain definite measures have been repealed. The German AAU ought to be told as well that if it was not so, the participation of American Athletes is very doubtful and that very likely the consequence would be the refusal by the American Olympic Committee of the invitation of the American [sic – German] Committee.

Baillet-Latour added that support in the United States would considerably strengthen his position, as he still felt vulnerable to the accusations that he was personally prejudiced against Nazi Germany. Attacks on the Germans from other quarters would, he maintained, make them 'think the thing over with care'. For the present, Baillet-Latour was unsuccessfully able to rebut Lewald's claim that the moves being made against Germany were solely inspired by 'the hate felt by American Jews against the new Germany'. Lewald's implication that this was simply a problem for Jews suggests that he was aware of Baillet-Latour's anti-Semitism. After all, was not the hate felt by American Jews entirely justified? Did they not have a point? Only someone who did not care for Jews would disagree with them.

Baillet-Latour timed his approach to Brundage well. On Saturday, 18 November 1933, the grand William Penn Hotel in downtown Pittsburgh was invaded by the delegates attending the forty-fifth annual convention of the AAU. On the agenda for their meeting was not just the matter of whether to scrap the recently imposed metric system, but also the question of going to Berlin. The delegates were divided between those who saw the internal workings of another country as being none of the business of a sports association, and those who saw it as morally repugnant that the United States should play sports with a country that was not allowing its Jews to compete. Brundage was firmly placed in the latter camp. He agreed with Baillet-Latour, and thought ill of the Germans not so much because their stance was anti-Semitic, but more because it was anti-Olympic.

The meeting was protracted, and lasted from Sunday until three o'clock on Monday morning. Put to the floor was a resolution that called for members of the AAU to boycott the Games, as well as calling on the American Olympic Association to take a similar stand at its meeting in Washington the following day. The resolution was presented by Gustavus Town Kirby, the former president of the AOC, and was supported by Brundage. The resolution was put to a vote by viva voce, and the room filled with a baritone rumble of 'ayes'. The 'nays' could barely be heard – only three voted against the resolution.

One of them was a German-American called Dietrich Wortmann, of the German-American Athletic Club of New York. Wortmann had represented the United States at the St Louis Games of 1904, and had won bronze as a welterweight wrestler. An active member of the AAU, Wortmann was a keen crusader for an improvement in the standard of the national team. At the Pittsburgh convention, Wortmann spoke against the resolution, saying that the AAU had 'no right to discuss the matter because it was entirely within the sphere of the IOC'. He also accused both the AAU and the AOC of hypocrisy, suggesting that both organisations were culpable of prejudice against African-Americans, citing the recent transferral of two major athletic competitions away from the South to Lincoln, Nebraska, and Boston, two cities in which black competitors would not be allowed to compete. The charge that the United States' sporting organisations treated the blacks little better than the Germans treated their Jews would be made many times over the next few years, and with much justification. Many members of the AAU suspected, however, that Wortmann was a Nazi sympathiser, and his appeal was fruitless. He would, however, soon find support from the most unlikely of people – Avery Brundage.

The Germans were quick to react to the news, although it was news that was not to find itself printed in German newspapers. On the evening of 21 November Lewald issued a cable that stipulated that the 'obligations incurred' by the Germans regarding Jews would be 'strictly fulfilled'. (That Lewald saw giving the Jews the right to compete as being an 'obligation' is surely indicative.) He had the backing of Tschammer und Osten, who that day issued Lewald with a letter that crisply denied that the Nazis were in any way restricting the abilities of Jews to compete:

1) Neither Reich government nor I have issued any order excluding Jewish members from athletic clubs,
2) Neither Reich government nor I have issued any order barring Jewish clubs from public training facilities,
3) Neither Reich government nor I have issued any order prohibiting Jews from competitions.
4) If I should learn of any local authorities having issued any order contrary to the above statements I should investigate them and make them conform.

The four points were blatant lies, as the decree of 26 April 1933 specifically banned Jews from sporting associations. Lewald, as a target of anti-Semitism, must have known that Tschammer und Osten's points were false, but he chose to telegraph them round the world. In doing so, he showed that his desire to stage the Olympics was even greater than his loyalty to the tenets of Olympism. His malleability ensured that he was a perfect cover for the Nazi hijacking of the Games.

Lewald's cable and Tschammer und Osten's lies appear to have had an effect, however. At the American Olympic Association meeting in Washington on Wednesday 22nd, the tone was far more temperate. Once again, Gustavus Kirby presented a resolution similar to that agreed by the AAU, but on this occasion it met with a more lukewarm response. General Sherrill, supported by Dietrich Wortmann, suggested that the threat of non-participation should be withdrawn, or else it would defeat the very purpose it sought to achieve, namely the improvement of the conditions of Jewish sportsmen and women. 'I oppose the resolution in its present threatening form,' added

Sherrill, 'chiefly because it promises to start a wave of anti-Semitism in our country among a class which hitherto never even knew the word – the youth disgruntled by being deprived of participation in the 1936 games because of the Jews. It would be unreasoning, but it would sweep the country.' This statement could have been viewed in two ways. It could either have been taken at face value, or it could have been seen as a warning from Sherrill for the Jews to stop meddling. Subsequent events would soon suggest that the second interpretation was the correct one.

The opposing argument came from Charles Ornstein, a representative of the Jewish Welfare Board, who claimed that a resolution that made no threat was like passing a law without a penalty. Brundage's solution was to convene a five-strong committee that drew up a new resolution. This committee included both Ornstein and Sherrill, and after some frank negotiations a new resolution was presented, which stated that the AOA 'expresses its ardent hope . . . that all disabilities affecting the rights and privileges of Jews training, competing and being upon German sports teams will have been removed'. The resolution was passed, but many, including Kirby, felt that the sting had been removed from its tail. Brundage, however, still had a tough message to deliver to the Germans. This resolution was 'an inference rather than a direct threat and carries the same implication,' he said. 'If Germany does not live up to the Olympic pledge, then we will not certify our athletes. We say that specifically.'

There were some who doubted Brundage's apparent open-mindedness. One was George S. Messersmith, the consul-general in the US embassy in Berlin. Messersmith was troubled by both the German and the American Olympic committees. On 28 November 1933, he wrote to the State Department, advising it that the AOC

> . . . knew that the Jewish athletes in Germany were being discriminated against in a wholesale and absolutely definite manner and were not given an opportunity to train nor participate and that this extended not only to preparations for the Olympic Games in Berlin, but also for sport competitions within the country with no reference to the Games. To this Dr. von Lewald [sic] could make no answer because he knew that he could not deny to me that this was the situation.

Messersmith's warning went unheeded. The State Department did not regard it as its business to interfere in a private sporting event, and would show little or no interest in the question of participation.

It was not just the Americans who were taking issue with the Germans. In Britain, the British Olympic Association (BOA) seriously discussed withdrawing its team from Berlin. At Vienna, the British IOC member, Lord Aberdare, had strongly supported the American members' stance against the Germans, and his backing was no less strong a few months later. Having had a good war, the forty-six-year-old Aberdare was renowned as a notable tennis player, having won more than fifteen championships in the United States, Canada and Britain. His stance was supported by Evan Hunter, the secretary of the BOA, who said that 'to keep an athlete from training on account of his race or religion is clearly just as much a violation of the Olympic rules as to prevent him from competing'. After meeting on Friday, 24 November, however, the BOA committee decided not to copy the Americans, but chose instead to wait for further information from Germany.

The British stance may have seemed like fence-sitting, but it was anything but. On New Year's Day, 1934, Lord Aberdare wrote to Lewald, demanding to know whether the German government was 'keeping the spirit of its promise' and whether the Jews were being 'reinstated to their previous positions in the world of sport in Germany'. Furthermore, he enquired as to the fate of four specific Jewish sportsmen, all of whom had lost their positions – the championship tennis player Daniel Prenn; Dr Nussbaum of Munich, a water-polo referee; J. Stern of Berlin, the secretary of the International Diving Committee; and Walther Binner, the honorary secretary of the Deutscher Schwimm Verband. Aberdare demanded a reply by 2 February, the date of the next BOA meeting.

Lewald had to take notice of Aberdare's letter. The British were important for the Olympics, as at that time Britain was seen as the cradle of world sports. It was in Britain that the notion of 'fair play' was established, and it was from Britain that so many sports originated. If Britain did not go to the Games, then many other nations would follow suit. If both the United States and Britain boycotted the Games, then the event would surely have been scuppered. Lewald's reply was strident. After claiming that the three German members of the IOC and Tschammer und Osten were 'desirous' to conform with the Vienna meeting, he went on the attack, saying that the fate of the sportsmen Aberdare wrote about was of no consequence in respect of the Germans' promise. 'I do not feel obliged to reply in detail to these questions,' he wrote. 'As they are, however, typical for quite wrong informations of the British Olympic Council, I shall do so.' Lewald then dealt with each of the Jewish sportsmen in turn, claiming that Nussbaum had resigned voluntarily and that Stern had been corrupt. Binner was not Jewish, so that should not concern them, and as tennis was not an Olympic sport, the fate of Prenn was irrelevant. Lewald's claims were groundless, and in order to mask their weakness he waved the problem away as an irrelevance.

> I asked you kindly to let me know whether there was only one Jewish participant between the British athletes in Los Angeles, and I want to inform you that there were only three among the 414 German participants at Amsterdam, Los Angeles and Lake Placid [. . .] This will prove the British Council that the whole question misses of any real importance.

This last sentence was extraordinarily callous. Lewald's argument appeared to be that because Jews played only a minority role in sporting life, then their feelings could be ignored. In fact, it was hardly surprising that German Jews had not excelled in sports, because, by Lewald's own admission *in that same letter*, 'quite a great number of German Athletic Clubs [. . .] followed since their foundation – 40 or 50 years ago – the principle not to accept Jewish members'.

Lewald's tactic paid off, however. On 5 February Aberdare adopted a far more conciliatory tone, and thanked Lewald for taking the trouble to deal with each of the sportsmen in turn. Aberdare said that, as a result he felt sure 'that my confidential utterance to the B.O. Council has improved the situation enormously'. As the BOA's minutes no longer exist, the precise nature of Aberdare's utterance can only be guessed at, but it would be fair to assume that it would have been based on the information in Lewald's letter, and would therefore have attempted to placate any doubters on the council. For the time being, the Nazis could rest easy. There would be no more talk of boycott, at least not for a while.

One name that Lord Aberdare should have included in his New Year's Day letter to Lewald was that of a fencer called Helene Mayer, who was regarded as one of the most impressive athletes in the world. At the age of seventeen, she won gold at the 1928 Olympics in Amsterdam. At the Los Angeles Games, she came fifth, but that was seen as an uncharacteristically poor performance. What few knew at the time was that two hours before the finals she was informed that her boyfriend had been one of the sixty-nine men who had drowned when the German navy schooner the *Niobe* was accidentally sunk. At 5 foot 10 inches, weighing 150 pounds and with long golden hair, the imposing Mayer was nicknamed the Golden 'He' (pronounced 'Hay') by the German public. 'The whole world loves her!' gushed one commentator. 'The most stark contrasts come together in a strangely unopposed way in this blonde girl – sinews and grace, energy and naiveté, gruffness and elegance.' She was, to many, the embodiment of all the 'Aryan' virtues, a potential poster girl for any Nazi propagandist wishing to find the ideal Germanic woman. There was a problem with the Golden He, however, a problem very much like that suffered by Lewald: her father, a prominent doctor, was a Jew.

Before the Nazis came to power, neither Mayer nor her ranks of fans regarded her Jewish heritage as an issue. Although her birth certificate identified her as *Israelitischen*, neither Mayer nor her family were practising Jews. She grew up in Offenbach am Main, a genteel suburb of Frankfurt, and her childhood was dominated by sport rather than by faith. Hours were spent fencing with her older brother, Eugen, and with Offenbach being the home of fencing in Germany, Mayer's talents were noticed when she was as young as ten. In 1923, at the age of thirteen, she won the German National Youth Championship. The following year she came second in the senior championship, and in 1925 she won it, as she would do for the next six years.

Mayer went to the Schiller School in Frankfurt, where her classmates remembered her with some affection. Despite being a figure of international renown, Mayer seemed to have adopted few airs and graces. 'What was striking was that her success in sports did not make her snooty or arrogant,' one classmate remembered. 'When she occasionally did tell us something about her other life that distinguished her from us, she talked about it in a very matter-of-fact way.' Mayer's other distinguishing feature was of course her Jewishness. Her father was determined not to allow it to become an issue, however, so when Mayer started school he wrote to the headmaster requesting that his daughter be excused participation in Jewish religious instruction.

Mayer's winning of the gold at Amsterdam in 1928 naturally made her a star, not just at school, but throughout Germany. Although the praises poured on her were justifiably fulsome, some were tinged with references to her Jewishness. In September, Mayer's headmaster received a letter from a professor enquiring as to her faith. The headmaster replied that although his student was indeed of the Jewish faith, that 'says nothing about her race affiliation, because one look at a picture of Helene Mayer shows every knowledgeable person where things stand. As is sometimes the case, she mendels completely to the aryan side'. ('Mendels' was a reference to Gregor Mendel, the plant geneticist, who suggested that offspring adopted the characteristics of the dominant genes within their parents, rather than inheriting a simple fifty-fifty split.) It is easy to detect a sense of satisfaction in the headmaster's words that Mayer's 'mendelling' went 'Aryan'. It is unlikely that he would have had commissioned a portrait of his star pupil to hang in the school's entrance had she looked closer to the anti-Semitic stereotype.

After the Los Angeles Games, Mayer did not return to Germany with her teammates. Instead, she took up a position at Scripps College in California to study foreign languages for two years. With a mere 200 students, Scripps was an exclusive place, an impression reinforced by its bucolic campus nestling beneath the San Gabriel Mountains. Mayer fitted in well there, setting up a fencing club, which was a great success. 'She has persuaded the whole college to follow her own love of this sport, which is indeed as much art as sport,' commented a school magazine.

Hitler's coming to power had little impact on Mayer's life in California. Although she was once heard to have described the new Chancellor as 'mad, completely mad', Mayer continued her studies and her fencing without any outward shows of concern. According to her fellow students, she made little mention of the persecutions in Germany, although she did acknowledge that her half-Jewishness was problematic. In April 1933, however, Mayer's idyllic bubble was burst. She was expelled by the Offenbach Fencing Club. The club hid behind an insulting piece of legalese to sugar the pill: 'Hereupon they [the Mayers] are not suspended, but they are no longer registered as members.' Mayer kept the news to herself, hoping the trouble would blow over. Worse was to come, however. In June her sponsorship from the German government was withdrawn on 'racial grounds'. Fortunately, Scripps had both the will and the funds to allow her to stay on. All Mayer could do was to keep her head down and hope that the situation in Germany would improve.

By the late spring of 1934 Count Baillet-Latour seemed happy with the way the Germans were behaving. At the IOC convention in Athens in May, Lewald and von Halt convinced their fellow members that the promises made at Vienna were being kept. On 26 May Baillet-Latour cabled Brundage to inform him that 'Lewald [and] Halt have in my opinion settled Jewish question quite satisfactorily [. . .] Hope German invitation shall be accepted now'. His opinion was shared by the IOC's vice-president, Sigfrid Edstrøm, who wrote to Brundage from Italy on 29 May. He began by telling Brundage that the Jewish issue was irrelevant for many of the competing nations: 'It is only the USA and Great Britain that are concerned [with the Jews]. In these countries, the Jews are very strong and utilise the might that the Ol. Games carry for their own political purposes.' This was a refrain from a letter that Edstrøm had written to Brundage the previous December, in which he had said that 'the day may come when you will have to stop the activities of the Jews. They are intelligent and unscrupulous. Many of my friends are Jews, so you must not think I am against them, but they must be kept within certain limits.' The suggestion that the move to boycott the Games was a Zionist plot was being sown in Brundage's mind. Edstrøm went on to claim that 'German Jews of both sexes are invited to prepare themselves for the Games and take part if they can qualify'. It was a big 'if'. No longer allowed to be members of clubs, Jews were denied the facilities and coaches that were available to non-Jewish athletes.

Edstrøm then went on to address a subject very dear to Brundage – membership of the IOC. As head of the American Olympic Committee, Brundage was not automatically a member of the powerful international committee, a position he desperately sought. Apart from

General Sherrill, the other two American members of the IOC were Colonel William May Garland and Commodore Ernest Lee Jahncke, a former assistant secretary of the navy. An outsider in terms of the sporting establishment, Jahncke was not much liked by many of his fellow IOC members. They were desperate to oust him and replace him with someone far more fitting – Brundage. 'As regards the third member of Int. Ol. Com. for the USA,' Edstrøm wrote, 'your election is clear as soon as Jahncke resigns. He has paid his dues and took part in the meeting at Los Angeles. Being thus a member in good standing nothing can be done at present. We shall have to wait.'

The Swede was not clear as to why Jahncke might wish to resign, or what could be done to him. Nevertheless, Brundage knew that if he wanted to succeed him, then he would have to do exactly as the president and the vice-president wished. With the two men looking benevolently on Germany, Brundage decided that he would change his opinion to coincide with theirs. It was nothing more than toadying. From this moment on, Brundage would do everything in his power to ensure that his masters were satisfied, and the best way he could do that was to ensure American participation at Berlin. Had Brundage not been so personally ambitious, then a boycott would have been, if not inevitable, certainly more likely. Nevertheless, the road to Berlin was long, and it was to be heavy going.

Brundage's first task was to go to Germany at the behest of the American Olympic Association, a decision that had been taken in February. His mission was to examine the conditions of Jewish sportsmen and women, and to report back with a recommendation as to what course of action the Association should take. Even before he left in July, Brundage left people in little doubt what decision he would reach. 'The German committee is making every effort to provide the finest facilities and plans to reproduce the Los Angeles Olympic village,' he wrote in an issue of the *Olympic News*. 'We should see in the youth at Berlin the forebears of a race of free, independent thinkers accustomed to the democracy of sport; a race disdainful of sharp practice, tolerant of the rights of others and practicing the Golden Rule because it believes in it.'

Before Brundage arrived in Germany, he attended the International Association of Athletics Federations' meeting in Stockholm in August. There, at Edstrøm's villa outside Stockholm, Vestoraäs, he saw Carl Diem, whom he had met before in 1929 when Diem and Lewald were on a five-week tour of the United States. There then followed a lunch in Stockholm with Lewald, Diem, von Halt and Justus W. Meyerhof, a Jewish member of the Berlin Sports Club and the IAAF. Meyerhof appeared to have behaved himself, as Diem was delighted by the way the lunch had gone. 'We showed Brundage documents indicating that the Jews are able to participate freely in sports and to train for the Olympic team,' he wrote. 'Meyerhof told us that he had offered to resign from the Berlin Sports Club but that the resignation had not been accepted. I was seldom as proud of my club as at that moment. Brundage was visibly impressed.' That night, Brundage and his wife had dinner in one of the small cosy dining rooms in the Gyldene Freden restaurant in Stockholm with Diem, von Halt and Edstrøm and his wife. After the women withdrew, Diem was toasted handsomely by Brundage and Edstrøm.

Brundage arrived in Germany at Konigsberg in East Prussia on 12 September. His tour lasted little less than a week, and predictably he was presented with a sanitised version of Nazi Germany. He met Jewish sports leaders, who, under the watchful eyes of Nazi handlers, assured Brundage that conditions were not as the foreign newspapers were suggesting. Brundage was further handicapped by his inability to speak German, so any inferences that the Jewish sportsmen may have made would have been blocked out by the Nazis' interpreters. Brundage also met his old friend von Halt, who assured him that there were no obstacles to Jews making the Olympic team, a pledge echoed by von Tschammer und Osten, with whom the American got on well. By the end of the week, Brundage not only felt content that the Jews were getting a fair deal, but he was also dazzled by the seeming prosperity and order of the new Germany. 'America could learn much from Germany,' he was to say in a speech eighteen months later. 'She is efficient and hard working and has spirit.' The notes for the same speech also reveal how deeply Brundage was impressed by the Nazis leadership:

    Hitler   a god
                given back self respect
                a man of people.

Brundage, a man of moderate tastes, also noted that Germany in the 1930s had suffered from 'despair', 'debt', 'youth undernourished', 'feverish gayety' and, worst of all, 'night life'. It was hardly surprising that he should speak approvingly of the SS and the SA, who consisted of the 'hardest young men', who were 'apparently doing useful work and no leaf raking'. The Germans were 'hospitable – courteous – good hearted – friendly people', and although they had their 'political problems, so do we'. The Jews, he noted, were 'leaders in communism', and it was only right that Germany should have 'Germany for the Germans'. For Brundage, the new Germany must have seemed not just a Nazi Germany, but also an Olympic Germany, a place in which there were no rewards for those who could not go faster, higher or stronger.

It came as no shock that Brundage returned to the United States with the news that there was nothing in Nazi Germany that gave cause for a boycott. On 26 September the AOC met to discuss Brundage's report. It soon became clear that the meeting would go Brundage's way, as Gustavus Kirby, the drafter of two previous resolutions against participation, spoke in favour of the president. 'I honestly believe that Germany will live up to her pledges,' he said. 'Mr President, we have every right to believe from your report that Germany will not dare recede from the position she has taken.' General Sherrill went further, and stated that the pressure put on the Germans by the AAU and the AOC had in fact improved conditions for Jews in Germany. This was breathtakingly myopic, and proved that Sherrill had been completely hoodwinked. Unsurprisingly, the eighteen members of the AOC voted unanimously that the United States should not only go to Germany for the Summer Olympics, but also for the Winter Olympics, which were to be held in the Bavarian villages of Garmisch-Partenkirchen in February 1936. Lewald, naturally, was delighted. 'Considering the importance of American sports,' he said, 'the Olympics would not be complete without the Americans.' He then added that the 'Jewish question' was 'definitely settled, so far as sports were concerned'.

The opposition was not going to cave in quite so easily, however. That same day, Brundage had received a letter from Samuel Untermeyer, the president of the wordily named Non Sectarian

Anti-Nazi League to Champion Human Rights, which protested against the holding of the Games. 'These games in Germany would violate the economic boycott and cultural isolation which the civilised world has been forced to employ against the brutalities of the current regime,' he wrote. 'It will be impossible for any self-respecting Jew from any part of the world to enter Germany or to subject himself to the degradation that would be involved in his participating in the Olympiad [. . .] either as a contestant or an observer.' Brundage himself was also openly criticised. Democrat Senator Edmund Celler stated that he had 'prejudged the situation before he sailed [. . .] The Reich Sports Commissars have snared and deluded him'.

Although Untermeyer's words were fine, they did not take into account the situation of a young German-Jewish woman living in Britain. Ever since she had arrived in October the previous year, Gretel Bergmann had found her new home to be somewhat less than ideal. The food was bland and terrible, the climate was miserable, and her small room in London was so cold that it was impossible to read in bed at night, because her hands froze. Nevertheless, it was not Germany, and Bergmann found it a delight 'to be able to walk freely into a Lyons to sit over a cup of their sinfully delicious tea'. Such a simple pleasure would of course be denied to Bergmann back home in Ulm.

Bergmann desperately wanted to continue jumping, and as soon as the athletics season started, she found that the British winter had deprived her of none of her talents. At her school, the London Polytechnic, she was so superior to her competitors that she had to race and jump with a handicap. It made no difference – Bergmann kept winning. Her successes made her feel that her dream of joining the British Olympic team might yet be realised. Even though she knew that her nationality – although certainly not her talent – would be one bar over which she would probably never be able to jump, Bergmann was keen to send out a personal message to the Nazis: 'Look, you bastards, this is what a Jew can do.' Bergmann's attitude was therefore diametrically opposed to that of Untermeyer – despite the risk of degradation, she actually wanted to use her body to show the Nazis that their racial policies were shams.

On 30 June 1934 Bergmann had her first chance to show the world just how good she was. The event was the British Championships, which were being held at Herne Hill in south-east London. At 32 degrees, it was almost unbearably hot, but Bergmann still made sure that she warmed up properly, aware that her father, who had come over from Germany on a business trip, was watching her. She had entered for two events, the shot put and the high jump, although poor organisation by the officials meant that she had to pull out of the shot put halfway through the event. By the time she arrived at the high jump the bar was already at 4 feet 5 inches (just under 1.35 metres). After a brief measuring out of her run-up, Bergmann ran up to the bar and soared over it, flabbergasting her fellow competitors.

After several rounds, the only two competitors remaining were Bergmann and Mary Milne, the winner of the event for the previous two years. Both easily jumped over 4 feet 10 inches, 4 feet 11 inches and 5 feet. At 5 feet 1 inch (a fraction under 1.55 metres), however, Milne muffed her first jump, and Bergmann did the same. At the second attempt, Milne once again knocked the bar down. Despite her best effort, Bergmann also knocked it down. Both women were clearly nervous, as they knew that the event would possibly be decided at the next jump. Once more, Milne ran up, leaped and grazed the bar, striking it just enough to send it to the ground.

If she got over the bar, then Bergmann would be the British champion. Trying to calm herself, she shook out her hands and feet. She then accelerated and launched herself into the air, her right leg first. It cleared the bar, but there was still the matter of her left leg to get over. She strained to lift up her heel, and that too left the bar untouched. She was over. She had won. 'I could hear my father and my friends whoop and holler from the sidelines,' she recalled. 'And, had there still been a doubt, Milne came over to congratulate me. Her handshake would not have melted an ice-cube!'

The euphoria of winning was to last only a few hours. Back at her father's hotel room, she was to learn that she was being ordered back to Germany to try for the Olympic team. She found the order almost impossible to comprehend. Hadn't she been thrown out of her athletic club only a year before? Her first reaction was to refuse the Nazi 'offer', but her father soon explained the entirety of the situation. The

Nazis needed some token Jews in training to show the world that they were being given a fair chance to compete. If Bergmann did not return, then it would put her family in great danger. Veiled threats had been made, and although her father said that the choice was his daughter's, and hers alone, Bergmann knew that there was no choice. It was blackmail. She recalled how, on the trip back to Germany, she was violently sick while crossing the English Channel. 'I felt that I was cleansing myself of some evil forces,' she wrote, 'by dedicating each spurt of vomit to that symbol of hate, the swastika.'

Throughout the rest of 1934, the calls for a boycott were sporadic. By the time the AAU gathered in Miami in December for its convention, the mood was positively mellow, although a few delegates maintained that the matter was not closed. Avery Brundage even felt sufficiently relaxed to step down from presidency of an organisation he had headed for a record six years, handing over the office to a former justice of the New York Supreme Court, the fifty-six-year-old Jeremiah T. Mahoney. (Brundage still retained presidency of the American Olympic Association, however.) Allowing the appointment of Mahoney would prove to be a stupendous tactical error for Brundage, for the two men would clash violently over the course of the next eighteen months.

In Britain, the mood was a little more hostile. On 16 December Lord Aberdare wrote to Lewald, expressing his unhappiness 'about the possibilities of there not being the Olympic atmosphere in Berlin by 1936 because of the action taken in Germany against the Jews'. Referring to the German behaviour as 'uncivilised', Aberdare went on to lambast the Americans for passing resolutions in support of the Games too quickly and without consulting the British. He then went for the jugular. 'I am sure you quite appreciate that even Great Britain could not have sent an Olympic team to Berlin if the Games had been 1934, because it could not be expected that Jews of the rest of the world [. . .] would all accept to enter Germany of if they did that they would be able to give of their best because of their mental attitude in the midst of a German crowd.'

Despite Aberdare's stylistically poor prose (his English was perhaps worse than Lewald's), there was no doubt that this was fighting talk.

To Lewald, the letter would have been problematic, as there was nothing he could do to change the nature of the 'German crowd'. The only way to do this would be to unseat the Nazis and to reverse centuries of ingrained anti-Semitism, both of which would be impossible, even for the wily Lewald. Aberdare offered Lewald a pathetically simple solution, however.

> There is a very strong body of opinion that soon signs of what they call a 'Change of Spirit' should be shown. It would be a splendid thing, if you could give me proof of the re-Appointment of some eminent Jew who has been displaced (in sport) or of some young Jews who are joining with others in 'preparation' for the Olympic Games of 1936.

This was tokenism at its worst. Not only was Aberdare's demand utterly cynical, its compete insincerity was revealed by his use of inverted commas. Aberdare was merely looking for examples he could show to critics of the Games, examples that even he knew would be misleading. Although Lewald's reply has not been preserved, he doubtless would have pointed to the examples of Gretel Bergmann and others as athletes who were in 'preparation'.

One Briton whose objection to the persecutions was sincere was William Temple, the Archbishop of York. On 14 May 1935 he wrote to the British Olympic Association, asking – somewhat naively – whether it could forward a letter to Hitler. The letter was written by the archbishop, but it was to purport to come from the BOA.

> The British Olympic Committee have resolved to appeal to your Excellency to follow the precedent of the ancient Olympic Games which were, as Your Excellency is aware, inaugurated by a general truce.
>
> We appeal to Your Excellency to show yourself no less generous than the Greeks, and to issue a general act of amnesty for the benefit of all those who are suffering imprisonment for religious or racial reasons.

Temple's letter then suggested to Hitler that sport could either encourage friendly relations between countries or damage them.

The idea for the letter and much of its text was not Temple's, however, but that of Arnold Lunn, who had invented ski slalom racing in 1922 and had organised the first world championship in Combined Downhill and Slalom in 1931. His father, Sir Henry Lunn, was a Methodist reverend and the founder of Lunn's Travel Agency, which would eventually become better known as Lunn Poly. In April, Arnold Lunn had written to Temple, telling him that he would be officiating at the Winter Olympics. 'I feel curiously disinclined to accept hospitality at a banquet in Germany,' he wrote, 'so long as men are imprisoned in concentration camps merely because they refuse to render unto Caesar the things which are God's.' Lunn suggested that the archbishop should write to the British Olympic Association, although he stopped short of recommending a call for a boycott. 'There is nothing that the Germans at this moment would dislike more than a protest from British athletic bodies against the treatment of Christians in Germany.' In a later letter, Lunn told Temple that the Germans were 'artlessly snobbish, and extremely anxious to be thought sporting'. He added, however, that it was 'rather pathetic that none of them seem to mind being thought cruel, brutal, oppressive or unjust'.

One BOA member who supported Temple's letter was Harold Abrahams, the British 100 metres champion at the 1924 Paris Olympics, whose exploits were later to be depicted in the 1981 film *Chariots of Fire*. By now a renowned sports writer, the Jewish Abrahams presented a cogent argument in favour of writing to Hitler. After claiming that the letter might indeed cause Hitler to make some small concession, Abrahams addressed the broader, and more philosophical, point of the purpose of Olympism.

. . . if I rightly understand the fundamental principles which underlie our enthusiasm for international sport, it is that we have here a means of emphasising the similarities between nations, and we are, I think, shutting our eyes to reality, if we believe that the mere organisation and support of such institutions as the Olympic Games, constitutes the end of our duty in this matter. Quite legitimately the common bond of sport can be used to ameliorate international relationships, and unless all our professing that the Olympic Games are a good thing is so much eyewash, a body such as the British Olympic Association can legitimately regard it as within its provinces to point out that racial and religious prejudices such as exist in Germany to-day tends [*sic*] to undermine the good which sport hopes to achieve.

This encapsulated precisely what the Olympic Games were meant to be for. Abrahams was shrewd enough not to remind the BOA of his own faith; its members might well have seized upon it to dismiss the affair as purely a Jewish matter. Abrahams's argument showed that sport could indeed meddle in politics, and was in fact desirable if it could be used to promote good.

The BOA was in no rush to reply. On 8 July, exactly eight weeks after the archbishop had written his letter, Evan Hunter informed Temple that writing to Hitler was 'outside the province' of the BOA. Abrahams' words had not been heeded, further confirmation of Aberdare's tokenism. Had he and the BOA been genuinely concerned about the plight of the Jews in Germany – and indeed the Olympic charter – then they would have backed any move that applied pressure to the Nazi regime.

Meanwhile, Gretel Bergmann was doing her best to train under the eyes of the Nazis. Having won an Olympic trial at Ulm in June, in July 1935 she found herself back at Ettlingen training camp in the Black Forest. The camp was used for training a select group of Jews, a fact advertised by Tschammer und Osten. In August, a brief interview in the *New York Times* with the Reich's sports leader captured the phoniness of the training. When the correspondent asked what opportunities Jews who lived far from Ettlingen had of training there, Tschammer und Osten replied, 'They can become members of athletic clubs that have not excluded non-Aryans.' The correspondent responded by asking how such clubs could exist in Germany. Tschammer und Osten initially refused to answer, but the correspondent pressed him. Eventually, the flummoxed Nazi spectacularly passed the buck: 'If you do not believe me you can ask Count Baillet-Latour [. . .] who will tell you that everything is all right with the Olympiad and that the Germans are fulfilling all their promises that were made concerning facilities for Jewish athletes.'

Bergmann considered herself warily fortunate to be able to train at what was an idyllic island, with its views across the Rhine to Vogesen. 'We felt that we had suddenly been lifted from our everyday spheres of life and carried to a sportsman's paradise,' gushed one anonymous attendee in a propaganda article about the camp. Bergmann recognised that the Jews' attendance was simply a gesture, but the athletes tried to have as good a time as possible. The same anonymous writer tells of how, in the evening after a hard day's training, 'songs were sung accompanied by stamping, some of them drawn out and others short and lively; the tones of an accordion were heard, and below in the Rhine valley the first lights appeared'. The writer describes how, on another evening, during a pause between the songs, the athletes gazed out across the twilit hilltops, a view that caused one of them to remark, 'And they say we are not at home here.' Apparently, 'no one answered either affirmatively or negatively, since there was nothing to deny and affirmation was not necessary'. Germany was indeed their home, just as much their home as that of those who were persecuting them.

Bergmann found herself at Ettlingen again in the autumn, but on this occasion she was the only Jew. Her room-mate was a seventeen-year-old high jumper called Dora, who Bergmann found a little strange. Dora never joined the other girls in the shower, instead always shutting herself into a room with a bath. Bergmann wondered about Dora's modesty, but she kept her musings to herself, because 'a Jewish girl could not afford to say anything derogatory about an Aryan'. Bergmann was right not to ask too many questions about Dora, as she had been secretly appointed by the Nazis to rival her. That was not Dora's only secret, however. There was something else about her that Bergmann would not discover for another thirty years.

In California, Helene Mayer also found herself wrestling with the Nazi regime. After learning of her expulsion from the Offenbach Fencing Club in April 1933, and the cessation of her government sponsorship in June, Helene did her best to continue her studies blithely. She graduated from Scripps in May 1934, knowing that her dream of joining the German Foreign Office would remain just that. Fortunately, she was offered a teaching post at the exclusive all-female Mills College in the foothills of Oakland on the eastern shore of San Francisco Bay. When she arrived in the autumn, Mayer made an immediate impact. Her fencing skills impressed everybody, and her tall, chic presence around the campus was hard to miss. One of her friends remembered Mayer being 'more fun than a barrel of monkeys', a young woman who loved to go to parties and to dance with men – so long as the men were taller than she. In the spring of the following year, Mayer appears to have had a week-long affair with a German naval officer serving on the light cruiser *Karlsruhe III*, which was docked in San Francisco. The officer would have been taking a terrible risk consorting with a Jew, but no doubt the distance from home made him jettison caution. Mayer not only danced and slept with men, but she also fenced against them. In competition after competition she beat countless fencers of the opposite sex. At one event, an observer noted: 'Any mental hazard the men may have felt at lunging towards a woman soon disappeared when they met her skillful foil.'

The spectre of the forthcoming Games still taunted her, however. Would she be allowed to compete? Or would she indeed want to? In an interview with a Mills College magazine in May 1935, she admitted that it would be an 'honour' if Germany invited her to participate. As a former Olympic champion, she should not have regarded it as an 'honour' – it was merely her due. It soon became clear that her loyalty to her sport and her personal ambition were greater than her loyalty to her Jewish ancestry. In August, the *American Hebrew* asked her a series of questions: 'Did you receive and accept reported invitations to participate in the Olympics for Germany? Do you think in light of continued discrimination, America and other countries should withdraw? Do you regard yourself as a refugee from Germany? Did you know Nazi papers repeatedly and tendentiously reported your suicide?' Mayer told the paper that she had not received an invitation from Germany. She then said that she was 'unable to answer your second question' and that she did not consider herself a refugee. She added that she was 'amused' by the suicide rumours.

Mayer's unwillingness to comment directly on the boycott movement may well have been because her family still lived in Germany, and could be punished if she made anti-Nazi remarks from the safety of California. Like Bergmann, she seemingly had little room to manoeuvre, although so far she had yet to be coerced back to Germany. There were those who maintained, however, that Mayer had been invited back to Germany, and that she was secretly stalling in order to try to improve conditions for her family. In September, Gustavus Kirby wrote to Avery Brundage, stating that he had heard that Mayer 'has been not only invited but urged to return to Germany but that she has refused or is reticent to do so by reason of the fact that her brother, who is a physician, has been treated so badly by the Hitler government that he is now reduced to cleaning out hallways in an apartment house'. If Mayer was stalling in order to help her family, then she was playing a dangerous game. The Nazis were not just another male fencer who thought he could make easy work of this 'blonde girl'.

Someone who certainly thought he could get the better of the Nazis was General Charles Sherrill of the IOC. In the late summer of 1935, he visited Germany, where he met Hitler himself in Munich at midday on 24 August. Although Sherrill was visiting the Chancellor to talk about the issue of Jewish participation, it is evident from the letter he wrote to Franklin Roosevelt some two weeks later that he was both charmed and bamboozled by Hitler. Sherrill recalled the meeting in oozing detail, his description as breathy as that of an enraptured teenager:

> This German's face and figure showed he is in perfect health – good color, but not too much, well-built, but not too heavily, good height, but not really tall.
>
> His eye is clear, his glance is frank, his replies prompt, but limited. About what he said and how he said it, there was no July 4th nonsense (as we call it at home) – no speechifying, such as politicians are prone to use even with an audience of one.
>
> Especially did I notice the clarity and neatness of his German – if all Germans spoke so, we poor foreigners would better understand them! His precision of phrase reveals the practised orator. He evidently knows exactly what he wants to say. No great political leader in any country had ever had his text-book so widely read as has been Hitler's 'Mein Kampf.' But very few foreigners notice the accent he therein casts upon two things – the importance of the spoken (as contrasted with the written) word, and his constant demand for physical fitness throughout Germany. Well, he himself is a perfect example both of the finished orator, and of the physically fit [. . .] His photographers do him great injustice in two regards – they do not show enough the strengths of his upper head (above the expressive eyes) and give no hint of the engaging human being he can be when he wants to be. Never until this talk did I understand how he gathered the personal following that started his Nazi movement, but now I do.

It comes as no surprise to discover that Sherrill was thrilled to be invited to the Nuremberg Rally the following month.

Sherrill did not relate the precise nature of his conversation with Hitler to Roosevelt, but did so later in a letter to Marguerite Lehand, Roosevelt's secretary. At the end of the meeting, Sherrill had tentatively brought up the question of Jewish participation in the Games. 'Explosion! Was shocked to find he knew nothing of June 1933 pro-Jew letter from his own Ministerium des Inneren [Ministry of the Interior] which I secured for Int. Olympic Com. and is flatly opposite to dreadful <u>new</u> anti-Jew move he had just said he projected.' This exchange reveals the hollowness of the promises made by Lewald and Tschammer und Osten. Men like Brundage – and indeed Sherrill – had been hoodwinked, taking the Nazis at face value. Sherrill then tried appealing to Hitler's better nature – which was surely a very small part of his character. The General had presented Hitler with a book on Bismarck and Mussolini, and Sherrill gauchely asked the Chancellor, 'What would Bismarck, master of foreigners' psychology, do today?' Hitler didn't reply.

A few days later, however, Sherrill experienced what he felt to be a significant breakthrough. At a lunch in Berlin with Tschammer und Osten, an official said that he had shown a copy of the June 1933 letter to Hitler, and that the Fuehrer had said that he would 'fulfill its terms for German Jews, and that the <u>new</u> move against them was dropped – <u>thank</u> God!' Sherrill's delight clearly reveals that he trusted Hitler's words.

That misplaced trust would be shattered at the Nuremberg Rally in mid-September. It was here that punitive new racial laws were announced – the infamous Nuremberg Laws – which prevented marriage between Jews and Gentiles. That alone must have flabbergasted Sherrill, but the passing of the 'Reich Citizenship Law' must have made him realise that his efforts were in vain. Under these new laws, Jews, half-Jews and even quarter-Jews were stripped of their German citizenship, which meant they had no rights whatsoever. In sporting terms, this meant that they would no longer be able to represent their country, as they no longer were part of any country. Sherrill described his four days in Nuremberg as 'very difficult'. He spent his time constantly negotiating with Tschammer und Osten, who eventually agreed that a Jewish athlete could join the German team. Sherrill declared himself to be satisfied: 'I went to Germany for the purpose of getting at least one Jew on the German Olympic team, and I feel that my job is finished.' This was untruthful. Sherrill had wanted to do more than secure one Jew his or her place, but because he knew his mission had failed, fobbed off by another show of tokenism, he felt he had to present his efforts as successful.

But Sherrill was to go further with his lies. 'I would have no more business discussing that [anti-Jewish obstacles in sport] in Germany than if the Germans attempted to discuss the Negro situation in the American South or the treatment of the Japanese in California.' Sherrill's meetings with Hitler and Tschammer und Osten had been precisely an attempt to discuss the 'Jewish question' in sport. What was he doing in Germany if not that? Swapping pleasantries with Hitler about Bismarck? Sherrill had been astutely played by the Nazis, and the general, rather than losing face, had decided to modify his stance. It would have been more honourable of him to have admitted failure and to have supported the boycott movement, but instead he found himself on the same side as anti-Semites such as Brundage, Edström and Baillet-Latour.

The special Jewish athlete singled out by the Nazis would be Helene Mayer. After Sherrill's meeting there followed an almost bewildering succession of exchanges between the fencer and the Nazi sporting authorities. On 25 September, Lewald stated that he was posting a 'personal invitation' to Mayer to attend the Olympic trials in February. 'We hope she will come over,' he exhorted. 'Believe me, we wish more than anybody in America that we had some Jewish athletes of Olympic calibre. But we have none, and I believe no one in America would want us to put a second-rate athlete on our team just because he is Jewish. That certainly isn't the Olympic spirit.' Lewald was lying. Gretel Bergmann, for one, was of Olympic calibre. His bandying of the 'Olympic spirit' was ironic, to say the least.

The following day, von Tschammer und Osten released a statement he had made to Sherrill, in which he invited both Mayer and Bergmann. The statement contained letters he said were being sent to the two women, which he claimed were 'evidence that Germany is acting entirely within the spirit of the Olympic statutes'. The letter to Mayer read, in part:

> [. . .] I am asking you whether you would take part in the Olympic Games in 1936 in Berlin.
>
> If you agree, I beg you to consider yourself as a member of the pre-selected German team, which will definitely be composed in the Spring of 1936 after test matches. If you are prevented from taking part in these test matches I am prepared to accept American sport tests as sufficient qualifications.

Tschammer und Osten offered no reasons as to why Mayer would be prevented from taking part. Clearly the Reich Sports Minister was not in a strong enough position to be able to guarantee Mayer freedom from his fellow Nazis' attempts to eradicate Jews from public life. Mayer denied receiving any communication from Tschammer und Osten or Lewald. By the end of the month, it was claimed that Mayer had been publicly invited by the Germans on four occasions, but each time she had not actually received an invitation.

On 26 October, it looked as though the situation had been resolved – Mayer had indeed received and accepted a formal invitation from the Germans. Her reply to Lewald was bizarrely affectionate: 'Sickness delayed answering you and Tschammer. Acceptance left yesterday. Love. H.' To papers like the *American Hebrew*, Mayer was the victim of Nazi arm-twisting, the threats to her family implicit. 'There are those who will condemn Miss Helene Mayer accepting the [. . .] invitation to compete for the Reich under the swastika. [. . . She] will offer the probability that she will win honours of the Fatherland and shame Hitler himself, with the admission that he is wronging the Jews of Germany.'

Like any good fencer, Mayer now sought to strike while she had her opponent on the back foot. Aware that it would be impossible for the Nazis to withdraw their invitation, Mayer told the Germans on 4 November that she demanded full citizenship rights. This sent Lewald into a flurry; he maintained that Mayer had accepted the invitation without any such stipulations. Mayer held her position, and once more insisted that she be granted full citizenship. This was daring, to say the least. In order to formalise the process, she even approached the German consul-general in San Francisco, who reported his discussion with Mayer to the embassy in Washington on 18 November. 'She declares she is free of any religion,' Consul Hinrich wrote, 'and that she has never been in touch with the synagogue community [. . .] She further explained to me that she feels all the more bitter about her present situation because she does not want to have anything to do with Jewish circles and that she regards herself in no way as Jewish nor does she want to be regarded as Jewish by others.'

This had the ring of truth. Mayer had not been brought up as a Jew, and her identification with the Jewish faith had been non-existent. Culturally, as well as anatomically, she had 'mendelled' into an Aryan. There was, however, something distasteful about her brusque disavowal of her heritage. Unlike Bergmann, who was keen to compete to show Hitler that his racial policies were bunkum, Mayer's ambition was purely personal. Her plea to the consul was clearly convincing, because he recommended that Mayer's citizenship be granted immediately. Hinrich cautioned his superiors that in the event of Mayer being denied it, then her 'impulsive temperament' might see her make remarks 'which will do us unnecessary harm considering the typical, prominent big spread of the American press'.

Mayer's appeal paid off. On 26 November, the *New York Times* reported that the Germans 'had assured the famous fencer she would be considered a full German citizen despite her Jewish blood'. In what was becoming a familiar scenario, however, Mayer declared that no one had contacted her directly, and once more she rescinded her acceptance. A few days later matters were finally resolved when a telegram arrived from Mayer's mother, which informed her that her brothers had been made citizens of the Reich, the implication being that their sister had as well. Although she had no way of confirming this, or whether her mother had been coerced into issuing a false statement, Mayer decided this was good enough. She was on her way home.

'The Jewish proposal to boycott the Games of the Eleventh Olympiad which I thought was safely buried last year, has come to life again and the situation is very serious indeed.' So wrote Avery Brundage to Count Baillet-Latour on 24 September 1935. The AOC president's *bête noire* was the recently appointed president of the AAU, Jeremiah Mahoney. According to Brundage, Mahoney had been elected on a Jewish, pro-boycott ticket, and he was now using his position to stop the United States team from sailing to Berlin the following summer. By now Brundage was adamant that the boycott movement was purely a sinister Jewish plot. Like all anti-Semites, he saw Shylockian conspiracy everywhere he looked. 'Articles appearing in the metropolitan press are almost entirely anti-Nazi. The picture of conditions in Germany obtained from reading our newspapers is entirely different from that gained by an inspection of that country. The great Jewish merchant advertisers may have something to do with this.'

Brundage claimed that, to compound his woes, because of his insistence that amateur sport and the Olympics were 'above political, racial and religious considerations', he was 'being denounced and threatened with great violence'. Brundage would repeat ad nauseam the view that sport was above all, not just for the next year, but also for the rest of his life. This may well have been sincere, but it exposed his dreadful political naivety. Brundage certainly had the strength of character and the determination to be a politician, but his pig-headedness and the lack of sophistication of his views made him a political neophyte. He was too ready to see the world in bipolar terms, a world in which Jews and communists were out to get him.

Brundage's chief worry was the forthcoming AAU convention in December in New York. He informed Baillet-Latour that the delegates were being 'deluged' with propaganda from the boycott movement. According to Brundage, they were being threatened with all manner of tactics – 'the same tactics which they profess to deplore in Germany, are being adopted to gain their end'. The difference between aggressive lobbying and locking someone up in Dachau is a great one, but as Brundage never saw a concentration camp on his tour of Germany, perhaps it is understandable that he alone could discern some equivalence.

Brundage feared that the AAU would vote against participation. 'If such a resolution were adopted solely with the idea of striking a blow at Hitler and the Nazis, it would, in my opinion, wreck the AAU.' He was not willing to admit what sort of damage would be wrought on Nazi Germany – he was more concerned with the fate of a sporting body than that of a murderous regime. Brundage cannot be excused his respect for the Nazis on the grounds that to damn him would be to fall prey to the historian's fallacy of 'presentism', in which the antecedent is judged by the consequent. Although the gas chambers were yet to start up, the maimings, the murders and the measures were already taking place, reported by newspapers worldwide.

If the AAU voted against participation, then Brundage was prepared. He asked Baillet-Latour whether it would be possible for the AOC to certify the athletes to go to the Games and not the AAU. Although this appears arcane, Brundage was effectively prepared to write off the wishes of the United States' largest and most powerful sporting body – a body he himself had headed for six years – in order to get a team to Berlin. Baillet-Latour was to agree with Brundage, and declared that it was the job of the national Olympic committee of each country to certify its sportsmen, and not the relevant national sporting federations of which athletes were members.

Despite his 'Plan B', Brundage was not going to give in to the boycott movement. On 27 September he wrote to the key members on the AOC, telling them it was their 'duty' to 'expose those who would use the Olympic Games as a weapon to take a swipe at Hitler'. Almost ominously, Brundage said that it was time 'we took an aggressive stand, and you will hear more from me anon on this subject'. Baillet-Latour also rallied the American members of the IOC for the forthcoming clash. In October he wrote to Garland, Sherrill and Jahncke, stressing, like Brundage, that it was their 'duty' to support the Berlin Games. He also reassured them that all was well in Germany.

Since March I have been in close touch with Mr. Tschammer und Osten, who gave me the assurance that Jews had been asked to join German teams and that non Aryan athletes, holders of sufficient records, would be admitted in the trials. We have also at hand many articles from Jewish German sporting newspapers, where it is admitted that unfortunately very few Jews hold Olympic form.

Baillet-Latour had forgotten that there was no such thing as a free press in Nazi Germany. As well as taking Tschammer und Osten at his word, he then compared the situation of the Jews in Germany with that of African-Americans. Although African-Americans – and indeed Jews – suffered from all manner of vile prejudice in the United States of the 1930s, that prejudice was not enacted into federal law.

With one exception, Baillet-Latour was preaching to the converted. On 16 October William Garland declared to Baillet-Latour that he agreed with the IOC president 'absolutely in all you have said'. The California-based Garland claimed that he was 'well informed' regarding the position of Tschammer und Osten and the German Olympic Committee, and had no doubt that the whole boycott movement was simply a result of Jewish and Catholic propaganda. Garland reiterated his position a few days later in another letter to Baillet-Latour, when he stated that the American press was 'full of innuendoes, lies, vituperations, insinuations and malice [. . .] reports would make it appear that Hitler has nothing else to do but persecute the Jews and the Catholics'.

The one IOC member who would not fall in with Baillet-Latour's demands was Ernest Lee Jahncke, who with Jeremiah Mahoney of the AAU would form a redoubtable opposition against the likes of Brundage and those who wanted to go to Berlin. It was Mahoney who fired the first major salvo, which was aimed at Lewald. In a letter written on 20 October Mahoney reminded Lewald that the German, because of his Jewish ancestry, was a 'hostage' of his government, and that he was being used as a screen to conceal the Nazis' violations of the Olympic ideals. He then called on Lewald to resign, because

> [. . .] your country [. . .] cannot observe the principles of democracy and of equality upon which the Olympic Games are based. The Olympic Code which recognises in the realm of sports the absolute equality of all races and of all faiths is the direct antithesis of Nazi ideology which has as its cornerstones the dogma of racial inequality.

The letter continued for some twenty pages. As might have been expected from a former judge, it was coherent and well argued. Mahoney could not see how Lewald could deny his four principal charges: that Jews were being excluded from participation on grounds of race; that the conditions for Jews made it impossible for them to participate; that the German government had injected race, religion and politics into the Olympics; and that the reason for Jewish underperformance was a lack of training facilities. Mahoney also asked why, if the Games were organised by the IOC, the German Olympic Committee had to continually seek consent for its actions from the Nazi government. More questions followed, all of which were pertinent and hard hitting. Why did Hitler's face appear on the German Olympic calendar? Why was all athletic training under the aegis of the Reich's sports minister? Why had Jewish athletes been barred from any club associated with the Reich Association for Physical Culture? Why were Catholic and Protestant sports clubs made to ally with the Hitler Youth? Why did winners of any sports contest in Germany have to master Nazi ideology before being declared victors? Why would no visitors to the Olympics be allowed to stay in the homes of Jews? Why were there anti-Semitic placards up all over Germany, and why could Lewald not get them removed? Would Lewald agree that the provision of six weeks' worth of training for the few Jews allowed was not sufficient to bring athletes up to an Olympic standard? How could Lewald reconcile the recently passed Nuremberg Laws with his agreement to stick to the Olympic code? Mahoney finally ended the letter with an encapsulation of his views:

> You state that participation in the Olympic Games does not involve recognition of the Hitler government's claim to moral equality with other regimes. I believe that participation in the Games under the swastika implies the tacit approval of all that the swastika symbolises. Surely it does not imply the disapproval and abhorrence which so many Americans feel. I believe that for America to participate in the Olympics in Germany means giving American moral and financial support to the Nazi regime which is opposed to all that Americans hold dearest. Therefore I hope that all Americans will join with me in opposing the American participation in the Olympic Games and aid me in having the Games transferred to another country.

Lewald's response was considerably shorter than Mahoney's accusatory letter – a mere page and a half. He answered not one of Mahoney's questions, and instead sought refuge in the fact that he, Tschammer und Osten, Avery Brundage and the three American IOC members were 'entirely satisfied with our attitude and preparation'. This arrogance hardly constituted a defence. Not only was it absurdly unlikely that either Tschammer und Osten or Lewald himself would admit to being dissatisfied, but Lewald was also incorrectly assuming Jahncke's complicity. He dismissed Mahoney in a letter to Coubertin, saying that the former judge was a 'fanatical Catholic of Irish origin, who wished to become the governor of the state of New York and who lives in a quarter of New York in which a majority of the inhabitants are Jews and Communists'. Like Brundage, Lewald could not see the 'agitation' as anything more than a Jewish-Catholic plot, assisted by the 'Jewish newspapers' in the United States, which spread 'lies' that were 'too stupid to be believed, even by the most credulous'.

An enraged Brundage took his case directly to the American people. The American Olympic Committee released a hefty booklet entitled *Fair Play for American Athletes*, which set out the case for sending a team to Germany. In the introduction, Brundage posed the question 'Shall the American athlete be made to be a martyr to a cause not his own?' This was a barely covert implication that the boycott movement was to do with Jews and not 'real' Americans. To his credit, Brundage reminded the public that this issue was not just in the political ether, but it has something that affected what he called 'the Forgotten Man – America's Olympic Athlete'. Brundage said it was his 'duty' to the 'vigorous youth' to ensure they were his – and other officials' – primary considerations. A boycott of the Olympics would thwart many youthful ambitions, and it was not Brundage's job to do that.

Brundage's views on the boycott were shared by many athletes in the United States and the rest of the world. Adolph Kiefer, who as the holder of the world record for the 100 metres backstroke was guaranteed a place on the team, recalled how 'although all us athletes were in favour of going, the only discussion took place by those not in the know. It was an opposition largely built by the press'. It would be convenient to dismiss Kiefer's views as those of a seventeen-year-old, but seven decades later he maintained that not to have gone would have been 'a terrible mistake'. Kiefer, like many athletes, saw the Olympics as above everything else. 'The Olympics represent the world,' he said. Another American athlete, pentathlete Charles Leonard, claimed he had 'no concept' of a boycott. 'All of us were just going over to compete,' he said. 'We paid no attention to political aspects.' Swimmer Velma Dunn admitted that she didn't 'pay much attention to it'. In

Britain, a similar feeling of political apathy reigned among the potential Olympians. Pole vaulter Dick Webster recalled the boycott debate
in Britain 'very slightly'. 'There were one or two people who had *con-
sciences*,' he said. 'There were always a few of these. But there weren't
that many.' Rower Martin Bristow maintained that the issue of a
boycott 'never came up'. 'As young people, we weren't politically
interested. If you were, you were probably someone radical like
[Anthony] Blunt.' In Australia, swimmer Percy Oliver said that he
could not 'recall any boycott movement'. In Greece, hurdler Domnitsa
Lanitis said that the Greeks, although they didn't like Nazism, could
'not even think of not going – after all, the Games came from Greece'.
In Turkey, female fencer Halet Çambel, whose mother was an active
communist, said, 'we all knew what was going on in Germany. There
were many Jewish and Socialist refugees in Turkey, and we heard what
they said.' Nevertheless, this was not enough to stop her going to
Berlin. 'I didn't think of not going,' she said. 'There was not a political problem in going to the Olympics.'

The reason for this apathy probably lies in the words of Martin
Bristow. It is easy to assume that political apathy among those in their
early twenties is a modern malaise, yet apathy appears to have been just
as widespread – if not more so – among the young of the 1930s. One
was either apathetic or a radical, and there were very few radicals. The
athletes above did not come from backgrounds in which people took
an interest in world affairs. Except for the radicals, political engage-
ment, if it comes at all, arrives a little later in life. For many of these
young athletes, the priority was not worrying about the fate of a few
Jews in a foreign land, but to get on the Olympic team. A twenty-year-
old in 1935 worrying about the rights of minorities in Nazi Germany
would have been a rare thing. He would have been accused of being
sanctimonious, or he may well have been Jewish.

Nevertheless, the pressure to boycott continued, not just from the
AAU, but from non-sporting institutions such as colleges and labour
unions. Many would have agreed with the words expressed by sports
writer John Kieran in the *New York Times*:

[. . .] What goes on in there [Germany] may be the affair of Herr
Hitler and his fellow residents.

But we have been invited to a party in the house. In this corner, it seems that the invitation makes a big difference in the matter of minding our own affairs. If we go in there, what goes on in the house is a matter of much concern to us. Standing on the outside and hearing the crash of crockery, the smashing of furniture, and the screams of the wounded, it seems to more than a few in this country that going to a party in such a house may not be a pleasant or profitable experience.

In October, Baillet-Latour decided to regain the initiative and visited Germany, where he had a meeting with Hitler. The German leader soothed the ruffled Olympic chief, by assuring him that Jews were being given a fair chance. In order to prove quite how highly the Nazis regarded the Olympics, however, Hitler agreed to Baillet-Latour's request that anti-Semitic signs should be removed during the Games. This was quite a concession for Hitler, as he had been adamant that they should stay. Back in April, Fritz Wiedemann, one of Hitler's adjutants, reported to Martin Bormann: 'I've told the Fuehrer about the reservations over these signs on account of the Olympics. Nothing has changed in the Fuehrer's decision that there is no objection to these signs.' Baillet-Latour regarded this climb-down as a significant triumph, and was cockahoop when he told Brundage of it. 'It is a success,' he reported on 17 November, 'because this has nothing to do with sport itself and the IOC had no right to require it.' Baillet-Latour was seemingly aware of his own double standards. On the one hand, the Olympics were not supposed to be a political matter, and yet he had made a request that was overtly political. When the request was agreed to, Baillet-Latour was happy to take the credit, albeit with a kind of faux sheepishness.

In the same letter, Baillet-Latour told Brundage that the boycott campaign was 'weakening'. The count felt himself to be a world leader, on a par with Hitler and Roosevelt. He had just pulled off a great coup, and had shown the world that the Olympics were truly a force for good. He could point to the fact that Jews were on the German Olympic team, and that the Germans had reversed some of their anti-Semitic measures – all at the bidding of the mighty IOC. Never mind that this was tokenism, and that the signs would be hidden only for the duration of the Games. Never mind that the half-handful of Jewish athletes who were notionally on the Olympic team were there for appearance's sake. As far as Baillet-Latour was concerned, what he saw was indeed good, despite the passing of the Nuremberg Laws, despite the numerous pieces of evidence that showed that Jews were being denied participation not just in sports, but in society at large.

Baillet-Latour's confidence was shattered just a few days later. On the evening of Thursday, 21 November Madison Square Park in New York City was filled with 10,000 anti-Nazi demonstrators. The peaceful protesters listened to some twenty speakers in the cold, and broke up at around nine o'clock. On the same day, 138 leading Protestant clergymen and educationists issued a statement demanding a boycott of the Olympics. Any claims that the boycott movement was merely a 'Jewish-Communist plot' could no longer be taken seriously.

Now it was the turn of Ernest Lee Jahncke to strike. On 25 November he wrote from his home in New Orleans to Count Baillet-Latour. The letter was just as damaging as that written by Mahoney to Lewald. Jahncke reminded Baillet-Latour that he was the only American member of the IOC who was of German descent, and that he was 'proud of that origin'. He then informed the count that he would not do as he had been asked the month before; in fact, he would 'do just the opposite of what you so confidently ask of me'.

> I shall urge upon my countrymen that they should not participate in the Games in Nazi Germany because it is my opinion that under the domination of the Nazi government the German sports authorities have violated and are continuing to violate every requirement of fair play in the conduct of sports in Germany and in the selection of the German team, and are exploiting the Games for the political and financial profit of the Nazi regime.
>
> [. . .] I am convinced, moreover, that to hold the Games in Nazi Germany will be to deal a severe blow to the Olympic idea. And, tragically enough, it will have been damaged by the International Olympic Committee [. . .] If our Committee permits the Games to be held in Nazi Germany, the Olympic idea will cease to be the conception of physical strength and fair play in unison, and there will be nothing left to distinguish it from the Nazi ideal of physical power.

One can only imagine the near-apoplexy Baillet-Latour must have suffered reading this at his desk in the Olympic headquarters in

Lausanne. But there was worse to come. Less specifically than Mahoney, Jahncke outlined the evidence that the Nazis were breaking the Olympic code by denying the Jews a fair chance to compete. Baillet-Latour would have been used to such charges, however. It was not until the final paragraph that Jahncke delivered his body blow. 'Let me beseech you to seize your opportunity to take your rightful place in the history of the Olympics alongside of de Coubertin instead of Hitler. De Coubertin rescued the Olympic idea from the remote past. You have the opportunity to rescue it from the immediate present and safeguard it for posterity.' This was too much for Baillet-Latour to bear. The cheek, to mention the name of the Christ-like de Coubertin in this way! What made matters worse was that Jahncke had released his letter to the press simultaneously. This enabled Brundage to immediately dispatch a telegram to Brussels which counselled: 'Jahncke statement most unfortunate. He has no official connection American sport. Suggest strong answer from you.'

Baillet-Latour was not to reply, however, until after the crucial AAU vote over participation was taken in early December. Instead of responding to Jahncke's specific allegations, he instead wrote that he had been reassured about the Germans' behaviour by an impressive list of IOC members and officials, presidents and officials of international sporting federations, high authorities in many countries, as well as the German Jewish sporting associations. Naturally, Baillet-Latour was unable to name any of these officials and authorities, and neither would he tell Jahncke which German Jewish sporting associations he had spoken to (even if he had, they were hardly likely to be able to give a true picture). Baillet-Latour was most splenetic over Jahncke's mention of Coubertin: 'The light manner in which you have taken for granted all those various reports is enlightened [sic] by the liberty you have taken in quoting even Baron de Coubertin [. . .]. In doing so, you have gone over the limit, because the Baron that you rightly praise has on this important question the same opinion as all the Members of the IOC.' In fact, Coubertin's enthusiasm for the Games was certainly not a given. In October, Lewald had written to Coubertin asking whether he could make a public statement against the boycotters, a request to which Coubertin did not appear to accede. If anybody was taking Coubertin's name in vain it was

Baillet-Latour, who ended his letter to Jahncke by demanding the American's resignation.

As December and the AAU convention approached, the British were carefully watching events on the other side of the Atlantic. At the British Olympic Association committee meeting on 3 December, Harold Abrahams spoke in favour of participation, arguing that it was up to the IOC to withdraw from the Games and not the British. Abrahams believed that participation would help to tie Germany into the community of nations. If the Games were boycotted, Abrahams suggested, then Germany might well turn more belligerent. This was a classic piece of appeasement. Abrahams also thought that it was in the best interests of British sport for Britain to attend the Games. In this respect, he was similar to Brundage, who appeared more worried about the impact of a boycott on sport rather than the potential bolstering of the Nazi regime that might be engendered by attending the Games.

Not all former British Olympians were in concord with Abrahams, however. Philip Noel-Baker, who captained the British Olympic team at Antwerp in 1920 and Paris in 1924, wrote to the *Manchester Guardian*, stating that the BOA should make its own mind up:

> [. . .] will not the British Olympic Association decide for itself that sending teams to Berlin will involve risks to the Olympic principle which it would be unwise and, indeed, disastrous for us to run?
>
> It would be a grave matter to abandon the Berlin Games at this late stage. But [. . .] it would be a far graver matter to condone by our participation the flagrant violation of the vital principle upon which alone a world organisation for friendly rivalry in international sport can be built up.

Noel-Baker's opinion was supported by the publication of a photograph in the *Manchester Guardian* of a sign in Germany which read 'Jews Forbidden'. Of course, such signs were commonplace around Germany, but what made this sign significant was that it could be found in the Bavarian villages of Garmisch-Partenkirchen, which were hosting the forthcoming Winter Olympics.

The sign naturally enraged Jewish communities all over the world, nowhere more so than in Britain. Neville Laski, president of the Board of Deputies of British Jews, wrote to Harold Abrahams, protesting at the BOA's continued support of the Games. 'It passes the bounds of the knowledge which I possess to understand how any national or international Olympic committee, in view of the existence of this notice, could think for one moment of holding the Games in Berlin. [. . .] I should like to understand how the Committees [. . .] reconcile their continued association with the Games in Berlin with the statutes upon which the Games are founded.'

Laski's appeal fell on stony ground. On the evening of 6 December, the same day on which the AAU delegates were meeting at the Hotel Commodore in New York City, the BOA formally accepted the German invitation to attend the Games. As Evan Hunter, the secretary of the BOA, told Brundage in a short letter written the day before Hunter sailed to Australia, the association 'accepted the invitation absolutely unconditionally'. The confidence of the members was no doubt boosted by the recent playing of a football match between England and Germany in Tottenham in North London. Ten thousand Germans attended the match, in what was – and still is – an area of the city inhabited by many Jews. Despite fears of sieg-heiling German fans inflaming the locals, the game passed peacefully, and even Germany's losing by three goals to nil did nothing to bring about the anticipated rioting. Among the 10,000 Germans were none other than Tschammer und Osten, Lewald and Diem, for whom a dinner was held at the Victoria Hotel the following evening by the Anglo-German Fellowship, a group composed largely of British society figures who admired Nazi Germany.

Despite the success of the match and the BOA's resolution, Hunter was jittery. In a subsequent letter, he enclosed a copy of the Association's latest minutes concerning participation, but insisted that Brundage keep them secret. Hunter was not explicit as to why they had to be kept 'strictly confidential', although he cautioned that 'we are not out of danger yet'. Unfortunately, the contents of the minutes can only be speculated at, as they were either deliberately destroyed or lost in a later flood at the BOA headquarters. Brundage's copy is not to be found in his collection in the United States. In Britain, portions of the Harold Abrahams collection from around this period are closed to researchers. Hunter was chiefly worried about attacks coming from three camps – 'Church bodies', 'the labour people' and 'some Press'. His tactic was to 'keep quiet and to work away without publicity'. No doubt there was something in the minutes that would have enraged one or more of those camps. It is quite possible that the BOA may have made some form of clandestine deal with Tschammer und Osten, Lewald and Diem while they were in Britain. Whatever the truth, it is clear that Hunter wanted to hide something. Unfortunately for him, the following months would be anything but quiet.

On Friday, 6 December, while he was in London, Carl Diem wrote in his diary: 'Today, the American Olympic Committee is meeting in New York to decide the question of its participation in the Olympic Games.' Perhaps it was nervousness which compelled Diem to make this uncharacteristic error – he of course meant the AAU. Although the British were being compliant, Diem knew that the Americans were divided. Despite Brundage's assurances that he could deliver the correct result, the vote was anything but predictable. Brundage was nervous as well, arriving in New York from Chicago a day earlier than expected. There was much lobbying to do in the wide corridors of the Hotel Commodore. Brundage was nevertheless outwardly bullish, saying that even if the vote went against him, neither the AOC nor the IOC would be moved.

Jeremiah Mahoney convened the executive committee of fifteen delegates that Friday afternoon. Their task was to vote on the resolution that called for the AAU to refuse to send its members to Berlin. Their vote would not be final – but its result would be a useful indicator for the two hundred or so delegates who would have the final say. The meeting was short, but bitter. Brundage said that the AAU had no business deliberating on a matter that was the business only of the AOC. Mahoney abruptly overruled him. Some of Brundage's placemen, in the form of the AAU's foreign relations committee, joined the meeting and stated that it was not for the executive committee to decide on participation, but for them to do so. Mahoney overruled them as well. A vote was then taken. Seven delegates voted against the resolution to boycott the Games. There was one abstention, leaving six votes cast in favour. Brundage was delighted, and declared that the resolution had been defeated, squashed before it had even been put to the rest of the AAU. Mahoney was too wily for that, and said that he as chair would now vote. This made the vote seven against seven. The seven anti-boycotters shouted, 'Tammany methods! Tammany methods!' but Mahoney had his way. It was agreed that the resolution should be put to the remaining delegates 'without recommendation'. The next day's meeting was bound to be a stormy one.

The two hundred delegates assembled at nine o'clock the following morning. Prior to the meeting, a gentleman's agreement had been reached, in which each side allowed the other two hours to state its case. The meeting descended into chaos, however, with insults and accusations of 'parliamentary trickery' being hurled to and fro across the floor. Amendments and counter-amendments were tabled, and by the end of the session no clear decision had been reached. It was remarkable that a tone of relative civility reigned during that evening's dinner, at which the delegates deliberately chose not to discuss the Olympic issue.

At 9.30 on the morning of Sunday 8th, the delegates reconvened. Five hours of speeches ensued, before it was eventually agreed to vote on an amended resolution that incorporated a provision for a three-man investigative team to be sent to Germany. This was the key vote. If the AAU voted against participation, the boycotters would have won a crucial battle. Brundage's 'Plan B' would have to come into effect, and with the majority of the AAU against him, it would have been hard for the AOC to ignore their wishes without looking arrogant and out of touch.

The count came in. The quirkiness of AAU voting methodology meant that there were quarter-votes to cast. Out of 114 votes, 55.75 were cast for the resolution, 58.25 voted against it. With a mere 2.5 votes between the factions, it could scarcely have been closer. Nevertheless, despite the margin, it was a clear result, a result that saw Mahoney resign. 'I bow to the will of the majority,' he said, 'but I could not in good conscience carry it out. When conditions change in Germany, the evidence will change my views.' He was replaced by none other than a beaming Avery Brundage. He had delivered what Baillet-Latour and Edstrøm had wanted. With Jahncke's position on the IOC now looking fragile, Brundage must have thought that his ascension was imminent.

A few days later, he received a letter from the Olympic president. 'I congratulate you very sincerely on the issue of your struggle with the Mahoney group,' Baillet-Latour wrote. 'You have fighted [*sic*] like a lion and deserve great praise for your achievement. I realise that you have not reached yet the end of your troubles. The money is still to be found. But you have saved the principle and succeeded in having the sporting spirit defeating the politic aims of our enemies.' A satisfied Brundage wrote back to Baillet-Latour in the new year. It was evident that he saw his victory not just in sporting terms. 'It became far more than a matter of sport,' he wrote, 'it was really a test case on a national issue.'

Brundage was right. The American sports world had not only believed the Nazis, but it had appeased them, a stance that was being adopted by the worlds of politics and diplomacy. For Hitler, the Olympics were another game of bluff, another game that he had won. The next stage of the game would be played out at a couple of small villages in the Bavarian mountains.

3

A Winter Warm-up

~

THE OLYMPIC YEAR was greeted by the *Reich Sports Journal* in typical Nazi militaristic fashion. 'How much goodwill, how much time, hard work and personal sacrifice on the part of thousands of Germans and friends of the German people have been necessary in the past year to – yes, to fight the battle that we now have behind us and to prepare for the coming decisive warfare of the new year.' The journal was referring not only to preparation for the Summer Olympics, but also for the imminent Winter Olympics, which were due to open at Garmisch-Partenkirchen on 6 February. The citizens of 'Ga-Pa' were preparing themselves for an almighty invasion of athletes and visitors, and by early January the villages were already festooned with countless swastikas and Olympic flags.

The preparation involved more than just hanging up bunting, however. A new ski-jump had been built, which boasted a 142-foot tower that overlooked a new 15,000-capacity stadium. The two entrances to the stadium were flanked by two huge pillars, on the faces of which were mounted 25-feet high Greek figures, one of which was holding the German eagle in her left hand – a sculptural blend of Olympism and Nazism. A new 10,000-seater ice stadium had also been constructed, its surface artificially frozen so it could be used all year round. Everything had been tested in 1935 for the national championships, and all the facilities had performed admirably. There was only one thing that was lacking, one thing that no amount of organisation could produce – snow.

If the German Olympic Committee feared one thing more than a boycott, then it was the foehn, a warm wind that habitually visited Garmisch, erasing its slopes of snow. At the beginning of January, the foehn had been doing its unwelcome work, and the resort was beset by a warm drizzle. The slopes, far from being covered with several feet of beautifully compacted snow, were adorned with brown-grey runs of slush. The GOC feared a repeat of the 1932 Winter Olympics held at Lake Placid, New York, in which the weather had been so warm that it looked as if the Games would have to be abandoned. Some thought the Winter Games were in fact cursed – those held at Chamonix in 1924 were often described as a 'swimming contest'.

While the Germans were worrying about the weather, the Americans were worrying about money. With the cost of sending the US team to the Summer Games estimated at around $350,000, there was little money left to finance a vast winter team. As it was, the team was some seventy strong, and all of them had to be put up in the Husar Hotel and the Post House Hotel for around $35 ($464 in 2005) for dinner, bed and breakfast. Perhaps aware of the steepness of the price, the German Organising Committee hand-wringingly attempted to mollify the Americans by claiming that it was 'a special pleasure for us to choose the hotels for your Olympic team and that no other nation will be better lodged'.

Economies were required, and the AOC decided that the less able athletes on the team would have to pay their own way. One of them was Albert Lincoln 'Link' Washburn, who was entered for the Combined Downhill and Slalom. The twenty-four-year-old Washburn had been brought up in New Hampshire, and had spent much of his boyhood skiing in the White Mountains around Hanover. In September, Washburn received a letter from the AOC, informing him that it was 'unable to advance any money towards your expenses', but that he would be allowed to join the team if he could pay his way to and from Germany. The cost would be $400, some $5,350 in 2005. Fortunately, Washburn's family had the money – his father had been a distinguished diplomat – and he was able to tell the AOC that he could go. Economies had also been made with the uniforms. When Robert Livermore, one of Washburn's fellow skiers, received his uniform, he remarked in his diary that it was 'quite useless for skiing'. It consisted of 'light blue knickerbockers of a cheap gabardine, blue sweat shirts with USA on the front, turtle-neck jerseys, a cap that looks like a New Hampshire farmer's, and a skater's headpiece!' Livermore did, however, approve of the 'very fine' greatcoats, which were from the US Naval

Academy and emblazoned with an Olympic shield on the breast pocket. Avery Brundage did not care for them, and thought they made the athletes resemble 'street–car conductors'.

The AOC had other worries as well. With the fallout from the bad-tempered AAU convention still in the air, the AOC was concerned that some of its athletes might not show the Germans the right amount of respect when they were in Garmisch. On 6 January, Gustavus Kirby, the AOC's treasurer, wrote to Carl Diem telling him that he had heard from an anonymous source that 'there will be some who will be out both to make trouble and bring themselves notoriety – some one, let us say, who would jump up in a public place and cry out "Down with the Nazis" or "To Hell With Hitler" '. Kirby antici-pated that if such an event did happen, and if the offending athlete were thrown into prison, then he would be made a martyr by the pro-boycott movement. He also warned Diem against any German 'over-radical elements' at Garmisch insulting the Jewish members of the American team, because that too would help the boycotters. Kirby ended the letter by asking Diem to convey his best wishes to his 'good friends' Lewald and 'von Holst'.

If the budget for the American team was tight, for the British it was even tighter. In fact, the Winter Games were costing the BOA almost nothing, as it was not paying any expenses to athletes whatsoever. It was felt that Britons who were capable of competing were clearly already rich enough to travel, as they wouldn't have been able to learn their sports in Britain. The secretary of the BOA, Evan Hunter, held a pretty low opinion of the event, a view he shared with Brundage in December, when he told him: 'I wish there were no winter sports on the Olympics.' For the British, they were almost an inconvenience, and Hunter hoped that he didn't have to go. Nevertheless, he did have to, a decision that was clearly taken at the last moment, as he had no hotel booked. 'The hotels are absolutely packed,' he wrote to Brundage on 16 January, 'but of course they must find me a bed somewhere.' He also proudly told the American that he had purchased a new plus-four suit, 'which I am sure if friend Hitler sees he will immediately produce an iron cross from his hip pocket and present it to me!!'

The Olympians started to arrive in Garmisch a good two to three weeks before the Games. Many were struck by the picture-postcard prettiness of the place. 'There is a touch of comic opera in all things Upper Bavarian,' wrote one correspondent. 'The chromatic towns in the valleys, the Werdenfelser Alps that are almost majestic but somehow not quite large enough to provide a sense of Alpine solemnity, are all part of a slightly fantastic picture.' Garmisch itself was a maze of pretty timbered buildings, its cosy coffee houses luring tourists with a calorific selection of torte and strudel. The one element that everybody noticed was the abundance of swastika flags, which hung from every pole, lamp-post and balcony. The athletes had little time to take in the sights, however. Despite the lack of snow, they managed to practise on some of the higher slopes. The Americans and the British soon found themselves to be hopelessly outclassed by the Scandinavians. While the likes of Robert Livermore were working out just how to ski over bumps, the Norwegian Ruud brothers, Sigmund and Birger, were dazzling them with their skills. 'Those two are amazing in their ability, to stand up on impossible bumps at high speed,' Livermore wrote on 20 January. 'Hunter [Edgar H. Hunter, an American skier] made a really good "boner" when Birger came hurtling down from the gully, across the little bridge, and jumped through the air off a bump, landing on his side. Instead of crumpling like an ordinary runner, he bounced back into position and ended up in a jump-turn on his feet.'

Birger Ruud was one of the most impressive alpine sportsmen of the last century, and at Garmisch he would compete in both the Combined Downhill and Slalom and the jumping, for which he had won the gold medal at Lake Placid. Livermore found himself in a practice race alongside the Norwegian and described the experience as somewhat depressing.

> January 25. – Race at 10.45. Up at the Hahnenkamm I found that I was to start No 1 and Birger Ruud No 2! He passed me about halfway down the course, when I fell for the nth time!
>
> I was in a blue funk all the way – and skied perfectly miserably. I picked up courage, however, after he passed me and trailed after him, but in the last field I misjudged the wood path and fell down below it into the trees, losing a minute in climbing back out again. At the finish, I found that Birger had fallen up above, hurting himself, and that I had passed him only to have him pass me again when I fell below the path! Anyway, the whole race was a nightmare of rotten skiing on my part.

Out of the 32 runners, Livermore came 24th. He was by no means the worst of the Americans – four of his teammates came 26th, 28th, 29th and 30th. It was no surprise to find that Livermore regarded it as 'a bad day for the American team, but I think very good medicine'.

While the athletes trained, there were others who were also warming up. Despite a warning from Gustavus Kirby that the Germans were not to use the Winter Olympics to promote the Nazi regime, Walther Funk, the state secretary under Goebbels at the Propaganda Ministry, ignored him. At a reception for several hundred members of the press in Garmisch on 4 February, Funk laid into the foreign journalists for not presenting the 'true' side of Nazi Germany. 'Use this opportunity', he demanded, 'to learn the truth about Germany. The Reich Government's press bureau will place at your disposal trained aides and guides.' The regime insisted that it had nothing to hide. Visitors were even welcome at Dachau concentration camp, 'where they will be convinced that we are detaining nothing but gangsters', said Adolf Wagner, the Bavarian minister of the interior. In case there was any doubt that the Nazis regarded the Games as a vehicle for self-promotion, Funk declared that 'when the new Olympic era is to dawn in the world, Germany must be its centre'.

This was brazen stuff. No doubt one of the offending journalists Funk had in mind was the distinguished William Shirer, the Berlin bureau chief of the American Universal News Service. A few days before, Shirer had been telephoned by Wilfred Bade, a zealous young Nazi in charge of the foreign press at the Propaganda Ministry who was also a member of the organising committee for the Winter Olympics. Bade upbraided Shirer for writing a story concerning the removal of anti-Jewish signs during the Games, which Shirer described as simply a method of hiding what was really happening to the Jews. Bade accused Shirer of lying, which Shirer naturally denied. By noon, the Nazi airwaves were beasting the American, denouncing him as a 'dirty Jew' (he was neither), and claiming that he wanted to scupper the Winter Games. Shirer repeatedly tried to call Bade, who was constantly 'out'. By nine o'clock that evening, an apoplectic Shirer stormed over to the ministry to find Bade sitting at his desk. The journalist insisted on an apology, a request that went down badly. 'He started to roar at me,' Shirer recalled. 'I roared back, though in moments of excitement I lose what German I speak and probably was most incoherent.' The slanging match grew so loud that a pair of concerned underlings interrupted them. Bade shooed them out, and the shouting recommenced. The meeting ended in the same tone in which it started, and by the time Shirer got down to Garmisch, he was to find himself a marked man.

Shirer was right about the signs, of course. The Nazis had not, however, managed to remove all of them. Some were noticed by none other than Count Baillet-Latour as he drove to Garmisch to open the Games. The IOC president was furious, and as soon as he arrived he asked to see Hitler. The German leader was adamant that he would not change German policy just to suit Olympic protocol, but Baillet-Latour was equally stubborn and threatened to cancel both the Winter and Summer Olympics. 'Hitler began to talk glibly,' observed one bystander, 'exciting himself more and more while staring at a corner of the ceiling. Soon he seemed oblivious to the presence of his companion and it was almost as though he was in a trance.' The two men both went silent for a few minutes. It was Hitler who broke it, by shouting out, 'You will be satisfied! The orders will be given.' He then stormed out of the room. Although Baillet-Latour was content, the conversation should have made him wary of Hitler's promises. Nevertheless, Baillet-Latour had executed a deft piece of brinkmanship. There was no way Hitler could have suffered a cancellation of the Games at such a late stage – the loss of Nazi face would have been incalculable.

On 5 February, the day before the Games opened, snow began to fall. The Nazis' luck was in – the dreaded foehn had gone. The opening ceremony was held in a near-blizzard, although this did not stop some fifty to sixty thousand assembling for the ceremony, either crowding into the stadium or thronging outside it. Although many were excited by the ten days' sport that lay ahead of them, most of the crowd were more thrilled by the imminent arrival of the star of the show – Adolf Hitler. The spectators could hear the cheers greeting Hitler, quiet at first, and then increasing in volume, as his train from Munich approached. 'You could hear the "*Sieg Heil! Sieg Heil!*" coming up the valley when he arrived,' Albert Washburn recalled. For the few American visitors, it was hard not to get caught up in the excitement – Washburn even stuck his arm out. His wife, Tahoe Washburn, did the same. 'Just hearing the sound gave you gooseflesh,' she said. 'A million people all yelling "Heil Hitler!" I had my own hand up going "*Sieg Heil!*" and I had to force it back down!' The Fuehrer, hatless and wearing a somewhat battered old trench coat, had overshadowed the event before it had started.

Hitler did not come alone. He brought with him Nazi heavy-weights such as Goering, Goebbels, that most vicious of anti-Semites Julius Streicher, Minister of the Interior Frick, and Minister of War Field Marshal Werner von Blomberg. Not one of these men would be alive a decade later. Goering would poison himself in his cell in Nuremberg during the war crimes trial, in which Streicher and Frick were tried and subsequently executed. Blomberg, who was exiled during the war, was detained at Nuremberg to serve as a witness, yet he died of natural causes while there. Hitler and Goebbels would famously take their own lives in the *Fuehrerbunker* during the battle for Berlin. With the possible exception of Blomberg, the men who now joined Baillet-Latour at 10.50 that morning were criminals, men who needed the Games to give their new regime legitimacy.

In case there was any doubt that this was going to be a Nazi spectacle, the band struck up not only 'Deutschland über Alles' but also the Horst Wessel Song. With its lyrics including the verse

The flag high, ranks closed,
The SA marches with silent solid steps.
Comrades shot by the Red Front and reaction
March in spirit with us in our ranks.

it was hardly the most Olympic of songs. At exactly eleven o'clock, the music stopped and the ceremony proper began. As is custom, the Greeks were the first team to enter the stadium, quickly followed by the Australians, whose participants were outnumbered two to one by their officials. In all, twenty-eight nations filed past Hitler and his cronies, and all dipped their flags to him except for the United States and Italy, whose flags are dipped only for their own heads of state. Most nations gave the Olympic salute, which sent the crowd wild, as many supposed the salute to have been the fascist salute. The difference between the two is slight. Whereas the Nazi version of the fascist salute calls for the right arm to be raised upward and thrust forward, with the Olympic salute the same arm is raised upward and extended nearly all the way to the side. In practice, however, with different people adopting differing angles for both types of salute, the difference can become negligible. Therefore, when the British marched past Hitler and gave him the Olympic salute, they were disturbed to hear the loudspeakers announce, 'The British greet the German Fuehrer with the German salute!' (Not all the British team attended the ceremony, however. Arnold Lunn and his son Peter, who was competing in the Combined Downhill and Slalom, stayed away from it. Arnold Lunn was to claim that only the British officials saluted Hitler, but the 'teams cut him dead'.) The Americans and the Dutch, fearful of similar misinterpretation, merely gave an eyes-right. 'As it turned out,' wrote Robert Livermore, 'we were not given enough practice in this gesture, and I believe we were all pretty sloppy in our untutored military bearing. The result was that the stands thought we were doing nothing.' The one person in the stadium who certainly gave the fascist salute was Hitler himself, who raised his arm to every flag that went past.

The procession took half an hour, after which Karl von Halt gave a brief speech and invited his leader to open the Games. 'I hereby declare', said Hitler over the loudspeakers, 'these Fourth Winter Olympic Games of the year 1936, held in Garmisch-Partenkirchen, open.' The band struck up, and on the side of the mountain the Olympic flame was lit, accompanied by the boom of a field gun. Then the flag-bearers formed a semicircle and the German skier Willi Bogner swore the Olympic oath, but only after he had saluted the swastika flag that he held in his left hand. During the proceedings the weather began to deteriorate, and Clarita Heath, an American skier, started to curse the poor kit the US ladies had been given. Luckily, chivalrous help was at hand. 'As we stood there getting colder and colder in our light windjackets,' she recalled, 'one member of the men's squad removed his handsome blue overcoat with the enameled buttons and placed it over my shoulders.'

Once more the nations marched around the stadium, and Hitler beamed when the team from Austria – Hitler's homeland – saluted him not with an Olympic salute, but with an emphatically Nazi one. 'The faces turned upward toward him seemed to say it was no formal courtesy,' wrote one observer. 'Those faces – or most of them – said as plainly as faces could say anything, "Our Fuehrer".' Hitler was seen to lean forward and look wistfully towards the mountains, no doubt in the direction of Austria. The significance of the gesture was noted not only by the German Chancellor, and for the next few days the future of Austria would be the talk of many.

The other talk of Garmisch was the twenty-three-year-old Norwegian figure skater Sonja Henie. A petite 5 foot 3 inches, Henie was more than the bubbly childish blonde that many men took her for. She had entered her first Olympics in 1924 when she was just eleven. Although she had no success that year, at St Moritz in 1928 she took gold, a feat that she repeated four years later at Lake Placid. She had also won nine consecutive ice skating championships, a record that remains unbroken. By 1936, then, Henie's star dominated the world of winter sports. A friend of royalty, Henie was like a monarch herself at Garmisch, skating in sheer white satin, her infectious charm and astonishing athleticism wooing the crowds. She seemed certain to take gold for a third time.

What Henie had not reckoned on was the presence of a fifteen-year-old girl from England. Cecilia Colledge may have lacked Henie's sophistication, but she was no less attractive or skilful. She had taken up the sport after watching Henie win her second world title in London in 1928. Colledge competed at Lake Placid in 1932, a few months younger than Henie had been at Chamonix in 1924. Technically, Colledge could do more advanced moves than Henie, and the more informed observers of the skating scene felt that Queen Sonja's crown might soon be snatched by this English upstart. Out of the twenty-three competitors, Colledge was unfortunately drawn to skate second. In subsequent Olympics, the favourites would be always held to the end, thereby giving the spectacle a great finale. Colledge's position meant that she was skating while spectators were still arriving, and the bustling in the stands no doubt distracted her. Wearing a black armband to commemorate the recent death of King George V, Colledge skated brilliantly, however, thrilling the 11,000-strong crowd with her performance. She also attracted the attention of many of the leading Nazis, particularly Goering, who, it was said, 'could not keep his eyes off her'. And then she fell. It was not a bad fall, but it was still an error. Until that moment, her performance had been faultless, breathtaking. Nevertheless, she had impressed the crowd, and at the end of her routine she was given a massive ovation. The judges were impressed too, and awarded her enough points to bring her total to a commanding 418.1. It seemed that the fall had hardly counted against her. Would it be enough to beat Henie?

The crowd had to wait until the end, as Henie was drawn last. As the light faded, the spotlights were switched on, making Henie appear even more like a jewel on the ice. (For subsequent Olympics, it was determined that the lighting had to be the same for all competitors.) Hitler sat captivated, admiring this specimen of Aryan womanhood. Henie, despite looking uncharacteristically nervous, disappointed neither the Fuehrer nor the rest of the stadium. In fact, she gave the performance of her life, her routine ending with a spectacular jump which was arrested by a split. The cheering did not start immediately, but when it did it was as loud as it had been for Colledge. The Ice Queen had lost none of her sparkle. There was a collective holding of breath while the judges deliberated. A few minutes later, the points appeared. Henie's score leaped to 424.5 – a mere 6.4 ahead of Colledge. Henie had won the gold, but only just. The gap between Colledge's silver medal and the bronze was nearly four times greater. Henie's success was cheered loudly, no more so than by Hitler, who was keen to be photographed with the winner. Henie was only too happy to oblige. In fact, she was very willing to be photographed with the Fuehrer, and had been on numerous occasions.

The other stars in the ice skating stadium were Maxie Herber and Ernst Baier, who were tipped to win gold in the pairs figure skating. Their natural talents were abetted by the Reich Sport Commission, which provided them with enough resources to train them and yet not to sour their amateur status. Music was specially composed for their routine, so that for the first time the skaters' movements and the music combined to produce a display of perfect synchronicity. Yet, just as Henie had her potential nemesis in the form of Colledge, Baier and Herber had the Pausins from Austria, a fifteen-year-old girl and her sixteen-year-old brother, whose routine was the antithesis of that of the German pair. The Pausin siblings swept around the rink to Strauss's

'Tales from the Vienna Woods', their movements seemingly spontan-
eous and off the cuff. It was a routine of much gusto and jollity, and it
saw the spectators baying at the judges to give them as many points as
possible. The judges sat firm, however, and awarded the Pausins 11.4
points to Herber and Baier's 11.5. The crowd, even though it was
largely German, hissed and booed the result. The reaction did nothing
to dampen Herber's feelings of joy. 'It was fantastic,' she remembered,
'I was so happy.' Herber recalled attending a medal-winners' lunch
with Hitler and shaking his hand. After the Games, she set up home
with Baier in Garmisch, and the couple dominated the World and
European Championships up to the war.

Up on the slopes, the competition was no less exciting. In the
Combined Downhill and Slalom, the Americans and the British found
themselves trying to keep up with the Germans and the Scandinavians.
Robert Livermore recalled his somewhat shaky progress down the
fearsome Neuner downhill course. He had been rendered especially
nervous by the fact that one of his teammates had crashed into the very
first tree, and had spent minutes extricating himself. Livermore's own
progress was hardly any less chaotic.

> I started out cautiously and was a little too cautious to Fade-Away
> Corner until I found the snow was perfect. At Damen Start I took the
> corner too slowly, but bucked up when I saw the Turk who had started
> a minute ahead of me. I passed him wildly yelling 'Bahnfrei!' [Make
> way!] and just made it, schussing down to Krembs. Before the Labyrinth
> I ran into a cloud and couldn't see the contours, so I took that slower
> than usual – but through the Labyrinth and down to the trough I went
> faster than I had dared before. The snow was perfect. I scraped my hand
> two corners above the Steilhang, but didn't lose any time. On the
> Steilhang I was scared of ice from reports I had had [. . .] It was icy, but
> much easier than I had expected, and I was exulting when I caught an
> edge on the soft snow and toppled into a bushy spruce.

Livermore had literally suffered pride before a fall. After taking a good
thirty seconds to extricate himself from his bushy spruce, he skied the
rest of the course well and clocked up a time of 6:04, which was certainly quicker than Washburn's 6:30. Times like these, however, would
not see the Americans troubling the podium. Birger Ruud's time
was 4:47, well over a minute faster than any American. At least the

Americans did a whole lot better than the four Turks. The Turk who had started before Livermore was Nazim Aslanbigo, who made it down in a sedate 13:56. Hot on his bindings were fellow countrymen Ülker Pamir with 14:18 and Mahmut Sevket with 14:29. The slowest Turk was Resat Erces, who took a staggering 22 minutes and 44 seconds to get down. One can only assume that he either got lost or walked.

The British fared marginally better than the Americans. Peter Lunn found the pressure of his distinguished parentage hard to bear. To make matters worse, his father Arnold was even the manager of the British team at Garmisch. In his practice runs, Lunn had taken a very fast line down the Neuner, but during the race itself he decided to adopt a more cautious approach. 'I did not take the same line in the race,' he recalled, 'because, overawed by the Olympic name, I felt I must not risk a heavy crash and a discreditable performance. I skied so carefully that this became the only major downhill in which I did not fall.'

Lunn got down in 5:35, and after his two slalom runs he ended up in 12th place, two places ahead of his fellow Briton, James Palmer-Tomkinson. The highest-placed American was Dick Durrance, who came 10th, while Robert Livermore came 23rd. Albert Washburn was disqualified for his second slalom run, and was unplaced, but is listed in the official report in 38th place. The Turks were all unplaced. Only two attempted the slalom, and both were disqualified in the first round. Birger Ruud, although he had the quickest downhill time, incurred a six-second penalty for missing a gate on his first slalom run, which meant that he came fourth. The Germans Franz Pfnuer and Gustav Lantschner took gold and silver respectively, while Emile Allais of France took bronze.

The German women did just as well in the Combined Downhill and Slalom as their male counterparts. The gold was won by the finest female skier of the 1930s, Christel Cranz. Before the Olympics, she already held numerous World Championship titles, and it looked as if the Olympic gold would be an easy picking for her. 'I was on top form at that time,' Cranz recalled, 'and almost believed myself unbeatable.' On the downhill part of the event, however, disaster struck: 'A small bump, just like ones I had skied over thousands of times on every downhill course in the world, a lump of ice on it, a wobble for one hundredth of a second – and I couldn't recover, a back flip – and I had fallen, was lying in a deep pit, in the soft new snow, scrabbling around like a beetle on its back.' It took Cranz fifty seconds to dig herself out and get back on course. She hurtled down, desperately trying to make up lost time, knowing that her attempt was surely futile. Her time of 5:23.4 meant that she came in nineteen seconds after the winner, Laila Schau-Nilsen of Norway, and found herself in sixth position. 'It seemed all over,' she recalled. 'No hope of a gold medal for Germany.' Everybody knew that it was impossible for Cranz to make up those crucial nineteen seconds in the two slalom runs, but she pushed herself as she had never done before, skiing beyond the limits of her ability. It was, she wrote, 'do or die'. She completed the first run in an astonishing seventy-two seconds, four seconds ahead of her fellow German, Käthe Grasegger, and fourteen seconds faster than Schau-Nilsen, who had incurred a six-second penalty for missing a gate. In her second run, Cranz made it in seventy seconds, astonishing herself as well as Grasegger and Schau-Nilsen, who were both over seven seconds slower. Cranz had pulled off what had seemed impossible and had won the gold, victorious in what she described as her 'greatest battle'. Grasegger and Schau-Nilsen won silver and bronze respectively.

Birger Ruud would find glory in the ski-jumping, where he took his second gold medal in the event. His fellow countryman, Ivar Ballangrud, however, won three gold medals and one silver in the speed skating, which made his achievement comparable with that of Jesse Owens in the Summer Games. Ballangrud is one of the forgotten great Olympians. As well as his four medals won at Garmisch, he won a silver medal at Lake Placid, and a gold and a bronze at St Moritz in 1928.

The Americans and the British fared better on the bobsleigh run than on the pistes. In the four-man event, the Americans entered into bobsleigh legend, when during their second run their brake man, James Bickford, was thrown out of the sleigh as it careered down the run at 80 mph. Nevertheless, he managed to hang on with one hand, his body being battered against the ice. One of his teammates, Richard Lawrence, managed to pull Bickford back into the sleigh – surely the stuff of Hollywood – and the team made it down in 1:23, two seconds faster than their first run. Despite such heroics, the team finished sixth, three places behind Britain. The Swiss took gold and silver. America's greatest achievement was in the two-man event, in which she took both gold and bronze, with the Swiss in second place.

The greatest sporting controversy of the Games was reserved for the ice hockey tournament. Evan Hunter, the BOA secretary, had predicted that there would be an 'almighty howl' over it, and he was proved right. Ten of the twelve members of the British team lived in Canada but had dual citizenship, and the Canadian team maintained that two of them – goalkeeper Jimmy Foster and Alec Archer – were not even amateurs because they had previously played on professional Canadian teams. Hunter's 'almighty howl' did indeed break out. The players were suspended, and were reinstated in the British team only after an emergency meeting of the International Ice Hockey Committee. Nevertheless, bad feeling reigned, with A. E. Gilroy, the president of the Canadian Amateur Hockey Association, even referring to British hockey as 'a racket', an insult that earned him censure on the floor of the Canadian House of Commons. The Canadians had won every Olympic hockey title since 1920, and for the first time they could sense defeat.

The two teams met at 9.45 in the evening of 11 February. By now there were four teams left in the final round: Britain, Canada, the United States and Czechoslovakia. An estimated 15,000 squeezed themselves into the stadium, most of them rooting for the British. The reason for this was more to do with anti-Canadian feeling than a particularly pro-British one. A few days before, Canada had faced Germany in a spectacularly violent and bad-tempered match that had almost caused a riot in the stadium. Both Goering and Goebbels had called for calm over the loudspeakers, an order that was scarcely heeded – one of the few such instances in Nazi Germany. To the Germans' chagrin, the Canadians beat them 6–2. That night the German crowd hoped the British would wreak revenge on behalf of the host nation.

With mounting excitement, the spectators watched the ice being prepared by hand, the sweepers smoothing the surface with huge two-handled spades. Even this mundane act was performed with balletic precision, as the sweepers undertook their tasks in formation. Ice hockey is played over three twenty-minute periods, and after the first period the teams were level at 1–1, with John Davey scoring for Britain, and Ralph St Germain for Canada. The second period was goalless. The final twenty minutes were even more aggressive than the sport's norm, and the crowd was baying for the British. The Canadians were very strong, and Jimmy Foster had to use every pound of strength and skill to stop the ferocious assaults on his goal. Just as it looked as if the game was going to end in a draw, the British player Edgar Brenchley slotted the puck into the Canadian goal ninety seconds before the whistle. The British won 2–1, a result that was met with 'a roar of cheers and *Heils*'. Many members of the crowd rushed on to the ice to embrace their new heroes, bursting through the military cordon.

There were plenty more games to play, however, before the band would know which national anthem to practise. Buoyed by their success against the Canadians, the British trounced the Czechs with a 5–0 victory two days later. The Czechs were to suffer an even worse defeat the following day, this time at the sticks of the Canadians, who annihilated them 7–0. Later that day the British drew 0–0 with the United States, who had beaten the Czechs 2–0. With one game to play, between Canada and the United States, the situation was tight. The British had won two and drawn one. The United States had won one and drawn one. The Canadians had won one and lost one. The Czechs, with three defeats, would of course remain in fourth place. The medals depended on the outcome of the final game. If the United States won, then she and Britain would have the same points, but would win gold because of goal advantage. If Canada won, then the British would win gold.

The crucial game started at 2.30 on the afternoon of 16 February. The Canadians were now doubly furious, because two days earlier they had once again fruitlessly taken their grievance with the British to the authorities, this time to the Olympic Ice Hockey Association. The Canadians complained that the points system gave the British an un-fair advantage, but their complaint was rejected. Unsurprisingly, the stadium was packed, and the British team sat nervously in the stands, hoping that their enemy would now be their saviour. It was a terrible situation for the Canadians, for if they decided to deprive Britain of gold by deliberately losing the match, then they would also be depriv-ing themselves of the silver medal. To win a mere bronze would be unthinkable. In the first period, David Neville of Canada managed to score. The British onlookers cheered reservedly – there was a long way to go yet. After the second period, the score remained at 1–0. For the British, the excitement was unbearable. They cheered the Canadians on, willing them to seal the victory with a second goal. The United States counter-attacked strongly, but they never managed to score. Thanks to Neville's goal, the British had won gold.

The Germans fêted the British team, even mobbing them outside their hotel. They were particularly drawn to Jimmy Foster, who had stopped 219 shots on his goal, and had let in a mere three. Meanwhile, the Canadians had to fester. On the floor of the Canadian House of Commons, Thomas Langdon Church, the Conservative member for Toronto-Broadview, himself a veteran sportsman, queried whether the Games were doing Canada any good at all. 'This government', he said, 'has appropriated $10,000 for these games and if they are to cause bad relations internationally, if they are to be bad advertising for Canada, I think something should be done. I ask the head of the government to make an investigation of this matter. There were rows before the Canadian sportsmen left, there were rows when they got over and there probably will be rows when they come back.'

As well as the ten Anglo-Canadian hockey players, the ice hockey tournament featured another controversial figure, the twenty-five-year-old German captain Rudi Ball. Like Helene Mayer and Gretel Bergmann, Ball was one of Tschammer und Osten's token Jews, invited back from a foreign land – in this instance, from exile in Italy – in order to show the world that the Jews were not being discriminated against. The Nazis had to invite Ball, because, like Mayer, he was undoubtedly the leading sportsman in his discipline. Ball had used this to his advantage, although he had played the Nazis better than the impetuous Mayer. He had cut a deal with them, insisting that he would return only if the regime allowed him and his parents to leave the country after the Games. The Germans accepted, not least because Ball's old linemate and best friend, Gustav Jaenecke, refused to play without him. The Germans knew that without Ball and Jaenecke, the team would not stand a chance of victory.

When Ball arrived at Garmisch, he was bemused to find a brass band to welcome him when he stepped off the train. He played well throughout the tournament, ignoring the great fuss made of him.

Unfortunately for the Germans, he was injured in the match against Hungary, and he missed the crucial and ferocious game against Canada. With the Germans taking only fifth place in the tournament, in sporting terms they got a bad deal, but in propaganda terms Ball had served a vital purpose. The following month, Avery Brundage issued a press release in which he used Ball and the five Jews who had represented Austria to hammer the boycotters. 'If conditions in Germany were truly as represented by the boycotters,' he wrote, 'why did these Jews participate? The fact is, the Jewish drive in this country [the United States] is incomprehensible to sports leaders in foreign lands. It does not exist beyond our borders.' After the Games, Ball's parents were permitted to emigrate, although Ball stayed in Germany, playing hockey both for Germany and Berliner SC throughout the war. In 1948, he emigrated to South Africa where he became a successful businessman, before dying in 1975.

The closing ceremony took place after the hockey match between the United States and Canada. In front of a reported 130,000 people, Karl von Halt presented the medals, field guns booming as he did so. The militaristic tone was augmented by the presence of an army regiment standing to attention, and the use of navy midshipmen to run the victorious countries' flags up and down the poles. Hitler, Goering and Goebbels watched proudly as the Germans were presented with a total of six medals, which put them in second place behind Norway. The British finished seventh, one place above the United States, which had also picked up a bronze in the 500 metres speed skating. The Canadians had to make do with their single silver, which placed them ninth. After the Olympic flame was extinguished, searchlights lit up the sky in a manner reminiscent of the Nuremberg rallies. Unlike at Nuremberg, however, the crowd control at Garmisch was not effective, and there were many reported injuries as the spectators tried to stampede out of the stadium in order to catch a glimpse of Hitler. They were manhandled by soldiers and SS men, and many had their clothes torn or were pushed down into ankle-deep mud and slush.

In fact, the closing ceremony was not the only part of the Winter Games which did not run smoothly. Because of the overcrowding during the ten days, hostelries had been unable to cope. There were often waits of an hour or more before food arrived, and usually the diners never received the food they had ordered, and had to make do with whatever the waiters had found. The Germans were also unable to cope with a slightly enlarged American team, and Charlie Gevecker from St Louis, a speed skating official, had to sleep in a bath. There was also excessive bureaucracy – dossiers on all the competitors and officials had to be completed in quadruplicate and sometimes more. Joan Dean, a British ice skater who was the non-playing captain of the British ladies' team, found it impossible to secure passes for the parents and guardians of the child athletes. The officials said that all the passes had already been issued. Dean was soon joined at Garmisch by her ice skating partner and husband, Fred, who tried to help his wife secure the passes. 'It was only after days of argument,' Fred Dean was to write, 'and by both of us banging the table harder and shouting louder than Ritter von Halt, the organiser and a typically arrogant Nazi, and by threatening to take the whole team back to London, which in point of fact we could not have done, for wild horses could not have stopped the competitors skating, that at last my wife got six cards with "Please admit to all parts of the stadium at all times".' American journalists hostile to the Nazis, such as William Shirer, also encountered bureaucracy, and were often prevented from entering the stadium whenever Hitler was present, although Shirer admitted that the Games had been 'a far more pleasant interlude' than he had anticipated. There were, in his opinion, far too many SS and army troops about, but 'on the whole', he wrote in his diary, 'the Nazis have done a wonderful propaganda job'.

Peter Lunn's father, Arnold, agreed with Shirer. In an article he wrote after the war, Lunn recalled that 'the young Nazis were encouraged to believe that a ski race was a competition in which Germans raced to prove, not that they were better skiers than other people, but that Nazism was better than democracy'. In the same article, Lunn accused the Germans of cheating, by closing the downhill course the day before the race, in order that they could practise on it themselves. It is hard to substantiate Lunn's claim. The downhill event took place on 7 February, the day after the opening ceremony. Robert Livermore's diary on the 6th makes no mention of practising or even being denied the opportunity – instead he writes about the opening ceremony. Perhaps the whole day was occupied by preparations for that, and there was simply no time for training. Certainly, Germany did brilliantly in the Combined Downhill and Slalom – she won gold and silver in both the men's and the women's competitions – but this may have had more to do with her skiers having months of training than sneaking in an extra day on the Neuner. Lunn's bitterness is easy to understand, but the truth is that the Germans had a much more professional approach to training, albeit a full-time approach that saw them skirt dangerously close to violating their athletes' amateur status. The British and American winter sportsmen were amateurs in the truest sense – they were competing for fun, and certainly not for any particular political prestige. As Arnold Lunn had counselled his son, 'compete seriously, but take the result light-heartedly'. James Palmer-Tomkinson felt that his compatriots would enjoy more success if they took a more gung-ho approach to the pistes. 'I still believe', he wrote to a friend during the war, 'that an Englishman is capable of getting somewhere near the top of a big ski race using the good old method of taking a five-to-one chance of holding a really fast line, or falling and finishing down the list. I used to get great amusement baiting the buggers on that subject, as they were always content to go for a mediocre place and get it, but I can't believe they got a quarter as much fun out of it.'

The greatest victor of the Games was Adolf Hitler. He had presided over them genially and diplomatically. He had gone so far as to send his personal congratulations to the victorious British hockey team and had autographed each of the British players' cards. Visitors to Germany were able to see that this man was not the monster that their newspapers had described, and that he seemingly had a heart. The regime could not be that bad, and besides, getting tough on a few unruly elements was something that many felt should be imitated back home in the democracies. There were therefore no grounds for athletes to fulfil the prediction of Kirby's anonymous source by shouting 'to hell with Hitler!' In fact, there were no reported demonstrations of any kind. As Arnold Lunn wrote to the Archbishop of York later in the year, the Germans 'were extremely affable, as it is their policy at the moment to keep Great Britain friendly while they deal with their enemies elsewhere'. Lunn, however, saw 'nothing reassuring at Garmisch so far as the peace of Europe is concerned'.

Neither was there much reassurance to be found elsewhere in Germany. One thing the Olympic visitors did not see was the arrest in Düsseldorf, on 10 February, of sixteen Catholics for activities 'inimical to the security of the German State'. Their 'crime' was their refusal to disband their youth club in favour of joining the Hitler Youth. Their previous leader had been shot dead 'while trying to escape' from prison in July 1934. Düsseldorf was also the subject of a letter written to Avery Brundage while he was staying in Garmisch. Purporting to come from one 'Lester Jack Brown', the clumsily handwritten letter was clearly written by a fearful German, as the inverted commas lay on the baseline.

> I am informing you of a flagrant violation of Germany regarding her promise to allow their Jewish citizens to practise Olympic sport.
>
> In Dusseldorf [. . .] the Jews since a few days must no more enter the public swimming pools.
>
> The reason given, 'in order to prevent difficulties', is a shabby pretext, for there is no danger, unless a dozen brownshirts is ordered to beat up the Jews, thereby creating the 'difficulties'.
>
> I am confident that you will take care that this state of affairs will be remedied.

It was a confidence that was misplaced. The letter showed just how desperate some Germans were to tell their visitors the true situation. Unfortunately, this particular German had written to the wrong visitor.

As well as not seeing anything untoward, something the visitors did not hear was a speech made by Hitler on 12 February in Schwerin at the funeral of Wilhelm Gustloff, the German leader of the Swiss Nazi Party, who had been shot by David Frankfurter, a Jewish medical student.

> Behind every murder stood the same power which is responsible for this murder; behind these harmless insignificant fellow-countrymen who were instigated and incited to crime stands the hate-filled power of our Jewish foe, a foe to whom we had done no harm, but who none the less sought to subjugate our German people and make of it its slave – the foe who is responsible for all the misfortune that fell upon us in 1918, for all the misfortune which plagued Germany in the years that followed [. . .] So our comrade has fallen a victim to that power

which wages a fanatical warfare not only against our German people but against every free, autonomous, and independent people. We understand the challenge to battle and we take up the gauntlet!

But Hitler had another challenge facing him, a challenge that would see him take the biggest gamble of his life. The Winter Olympics had provided him not only with an opportunity to reflect, but also a distraction that turned the eyes of the world away from a part of Germany that he so desperately coveted – the Rhineland.

4

On Their Marks

~

ON THE SAME day as Gustloff's funeral, Hitler convened a meeting with his minister for foreign affairs, Baron von Neurath, and Joachim von Ribbentrop, the eponymous head of the Büro Ribbentrop, a separate Nazi foreign office. Neurath and Ribbentrop despised each other, the latter regarding the sixty-three-year-old Neurath as a dinosaur who stood in his way. Neurath, however, saw Ribbentrop as a parvenu, a sycophantic upstart whose activities were encroaching on those of the official Foreign Office. According to Neurath, Ribbentrop was a man 'who did not have even the most primitive notions about foreign and political affairs'. As well as being professionally inferior, Neurath was disgusted by the forty-two-year-old Ribbentrop's social pretensions. Neurath would have agreed with Goebbels when he wrote that Ribbentrop had 'bought his name, married his money, and swindled his way into office'. Indeed, Ribbentrop's aristocratic 'von' was the product of his persuading his aunt – who had married a knight, and was thus able to use 'von' – to adopt him in return for providing her with an allowance. His wife Annelies did indeed have money, as she was the daughter of Otto Henkell, the largest manufacturer of Sekt, German sparkling wine. Nevertheless, Hitler was impressed by Ribbentrop, partly because he spoke French and English, and partly because as a former champagne salesman he exuded an air of faux sophistication. Despite his shortcomings, Ribbentrop had managed to pull off the 'impossible' Anglo-German Naval Treaty of June 1935, which enabled Germany to strengthen her navy while Britain agreed to withdraw her ships from the Baltic. As far as Hitler was concerned, Ribbentrop was a diplomatic genius, a man who delivered far more than the crustily timid Neurath.

The atmosphere was therefore less than warm at the meeting between the three men. The topic of conversation was the Rhineland. Under the terms of the Treaty of Versailles in 1919, the Germans were forbidden from engaging in any military activity whatsoever on the left bank of the Rhine, be it building fortifications or carrying out exercises. This exclusion also applied to a 50-kilometre strip along the right bank, thus providing a vast and reassuring buffer zone between France, the Low Countries and Germany. The Locarno Treaties of 1925 reinforced the demilitarisation, as well as providing a diplomatic Mexican stand-off, in which Germany, France and Belgium promised not to attack each other, with Britain and Italy acting as guarantors. If any of the first three countries attacked another, then the remaining three were obliged to help the country being attacked. The peace of Europe rested on 'the spirit of Locarno', and any violation would undoubtedly cause that spirit to dissipate. For Hitler, however, the fact that German troops were not allowed to occupy the Rhineland was a repellent affront to German pride. The Rhineland was, after all, Germany's, so why could Germany not station her troops there? In Hitler's eyes, the Rhine provided a line of defence against France, which Hitler regarded as a threat, one he distastefully described in *Mein Kampf*:

> The French people, who are becoming more and more obsessed by Negroid ideas, represent a threatening menace to the existence of the white race in Europe, because they are bound up with the Jewish campaign for world-domination. For the contamination caused by the influx of Negroid blood on the Rhine, in the very heart of Europe, is in accord with the sadistic and perverse lust for vengeance on the part of the hereditary enemy of our people, just as it suits the purpose of the cool calculating Jew who would use this means of introducing a process of bastardisation in the very centre of the European Continent and, by infecting the white race with the blood of an inferior stock, would destroy the foundations of its independent existence.

At the meeting on 12 February, Hitler presented Neurath and Ribbentrop with three options concerning the Rhineland, the third of which was the boldest – remilitarisation. Whereas Neurath was hesitant when asked which of the options he favoured, Ribbentrop instantly exclaimed: 'The third, *mein Fuehrer*, the third!' Neurath could only inwardly fume, knowing that this was just what Hitler wanted to hear. The object of Ribbentrop's adoration returned to the Winter Olympics with a more resolute outlook on the matter, although his mind was not yet fully made up.

Hitler knew that the repercussions of occupying the Rhineland would be immense. If it were seen by the fellow Locarno signatories as an act of straightforward aggression, then there was a strong possibility that the move could lead to war, a war for which Germany was ill prepared. A defeated Hitler would be a severely weakened Hitler, as all his nationalistic talk of a strong Germany would be seen to be nothing more than guff. If the gamble paid off, however, then Hitler's position would be immeasurably stronger. The occupation would be seen as a brilliant and daring *coup de main*, ensuring his esteem not only in the eyes of the German people, but also in those of the senior army officers, many of whom sceptically viewed the Chancellor as little more than a pipsqueak of a corporal. Furthermore, a military defeat would enlarge cracks that were beginning to appear in the regime. In his report to the Foreign Office at the beginning of the year, Sir Eric Phipps, the British ambassador to Berlin, opined that had Hitler really allowed free elections, then he would probably have lost. Many, he said, felt affronted by the Nazis' attitude to the Jews and the Catholics, and the food queues were far too long, especially when housewives found butter costing 1.6 Reichsmarks per pound (£5 or $8.50 in 2005) at the end of them.

The diplomatic community had been watching Hitler warily. They knew that 1936 would see her making some sort of bold move, but then there was a long list of potential bold moves. At the end of January, Phipps wrote to Sir Robert Vansittart, the permanent under-secretary at the British Foreign Office, outlining what he understood to be Hitler's demands. The first was cultural autonomy for the Germans in Czechoslovakia. The second was a referendum in Austria under British supervision. The third was a desire for greater economic opportunities in south-eastern Europe. The fourth was the return to Germany of her colonies. Phipps also noted that Hitler wanted to cultivate 'cordial relations' with Britain, and if this failed, to reconcile

France and Germany. But 'no mention was made [by Hitler or those close to him] of Locarno or the demilitarised zone'. The fact that it had not been mentioned did not mean that it was not an option that Hitler was considering.

Phipps ended his letter with a short paragraph about the Americans:

> [America's] recent declaration of neutrality was welcomed here and the general feeling is that there is much less likelihood that America will ever again intervene in European affairs. The experience of the last war – or rather the last peace – has so alienated public opinion that neutrality will be observed more strictly than in the last war.

Phipps's analysis was correct. The United States had indeed seemingly adopted an isolationist stance, by passing the Neutrality Act of 1935, which was strengthened by the Neutrality Act passed in February 1936. The acts prohibited American citizens from selling arms and war materials to belligerents at war, as well as outlawing the extending of credit to belligerents. The acts were indeed neutral, as they made no distinction between aggressor and victim. Nevertheless, they were supported by many in the United States, among them Avery Brundage, who was concerned that the Roosevelt administration was 'definitely committed to the British and French empires'. Roosevelt would later work around the acts, much to Brundage's disgust, but in the meantime, as far as Hitler was concerned, the United States posed no conceivable threat.

Phipps and Vansittart had much in common. As well as being brothers-in-law – Vansittart's wife Sarita was the sister of Frances Phipps – they shared a near-identical opinion of Germany and her leading figures. Their greatest odium, after Hitler, was reserved for Ribbentrop, who Phipps regarded as 'a lightweight (I place him near the bottom of the handicap), irritating, ignorant and boundlessly conceited'. Vansittart found him 'shallow, self-seeking and not really friendly'. 'No one who studies his mouth will be reassured,' Vansittart was to write. Whereas Ribbentrop was a *nouveau*, both Phipps and Vansittart were typically British old school. 'Van' was an Old Etonian, his intelligence matched by the tall and somewhat dandyish *bella figura* he cut. With his taste for whisky and his 'deft hand at intrigue', Vansittart was sometimes known as 'Machiavelli-and-soda', an appellation that was perhaps more common in the newspapers than within the corridors of the Foreign Office. Phipps was shorter than Vansittart, but just as well groomed. He was described by William Shirer as resembling a 'Hungarian dandy, with a perfect poker face'. Martha Dodd, the daughter of the US ambassador to Berlin, found Phipps's mandarin inscrutability almost inhuman. 'You felt that if suddenly you said, "Your grandmother has just been murdered," his facial muscles would not twitch, would show no sign of having heard your declaration, that he would go on quietly in the clipped, caught-in-throat, potato-laden English-well-bred voice, "Yes, yes, you don't say, yes, really, how extraordinarily interesting."' The difficulty in reading him was not helped by his sporting of a monocle – he had damaged an eye in a childhood accident.

Both Vansittart and Phipps held those who wished to appease Hitler in low regard. 'I realise that in our free country the Government cannot always prevent Mayfair from rushing Hitlerwards,' wrote Phipps, 'but if some of the visitors could be choked off I think it would be a good thing.' Many of the pro-Germans were indeed of the aristocratic 'Mayfair set'. Among them were Lord Redesdale – the father of the celebrated Mitford sisters; Sir Oswald Mosley – the leader of the British Union of Fascists and soon to be married to the Mitford sister Diana Guinness; Lord Londonderry – the former air minister whose rabid affection for Germany saw him nicknamed the 'Londonderry Herr'; the Duke of Wellington; and Lord Sempill – a noted aviator. There were countless other lords and MPs who flocked to Nazi Germany, many of whom were members of somewhat shadowy pro-German clubs such as the Link and the Anglo-German Fellowship. It would be wrong, however, to claim that those keen on improving relations with Germany were an upper-class collection of anti-Semitic quasi-Nazis. Appeasement was born not out of a love for Germany, but more out of hatred of war. There was much about Nazi Germany not to like, but then there was much about war that was even more repugnant. The public mood was certainly one of 'peace with Germany', and those such as Vansittart, Phipps and, of course, Winston Churchill were seen as Cassandras.

'Berlin trembles with tension,' wrote Goebbels on the morning of Saturday, 7 March. There was much to be tense about. That morning,

30,000 German troops had marched, ridden or driven into the Rhineland. Hitler had taken his gamble – his Rubicon was in fact the Rhine. It was to be the beginning of a tumultuous day, a day after which Europe would never be the same again. At the same time as his troops moved west, Hitler made a speech to the assembled members of the Reichstag. Nobody knew exactly what to expect, but there were many rumours. After a typically long rant against the injustices of the Treaty of Versailles, Hitler then announced: 'Germany no longer feels bound by the Locarno Treaty. In the interest of the primitive rights of its people to the security of their frontier and the safeguarding of their defence, the German government has re-established, as from today, the absolute and unrestricted sovereignty of the Reich in the demilitarised zone!'

One of those watching was Richard Helms, a twenty-two-year-old American reporter for the United Press. 'Suddenly [. . .] I noticed that Hitler had become pale,' he wrote, 'and that he was passing a handkerchief back and forth between his hands beneath the lectern. A few seconds later, he slowed his speech. Leaning forward over the lectern to command special attention, he said slowly, "At this moment German troops are crossing the Rhine bridges and occupying the Rhineland."'

The reaction was predictable. Six hundred deputies, all appointed by Hitler, showed an instant display of Nazi congratulation. William Shirer looked down from the gallery to see the 'little men with big bodies and bulging necks and cropped hair and pouched bellies and brown uniforms and heavy boots, little men of clay in his fine hands, leap to their feet like automatons, their arms outstretched in the Nazi salute, and scream '*Heils*,' the first two or three wildly, the next twenty-five in unison, like a college yell'. A further volley of cheers rang out when Hitler announced a general election to be held on 29 March, which would 'pass judgement' on his leadership.

Now all Hitler could do was to wait for the reaction of the Locarno powers. Would France mobilise her army? As Hitler had said in his speech, he had removed from the German press all hatred directed against the French. 'When, a few weeks ago, our French guests marched into the Olympic Stadium at Garmisch-Partenkirchen, they probably had occasion to determine whether, and how far, I have succeeded in bringing about such a remoulding of the German people.' There was no doubt that the Winter Games had been vitally important to Hitler. Through the reaction of the French team, he was able to gauge French public opinion. Had the French not attended the Games, then Hitler would have been far less likely to call their bluff. But they did come, and therefore he did gamble.

What would Britain do? In London, the British Foreign Secretary, Anthony Eden, was personally briefed by the German ambassador, Leopold von Hoesch. In a triumph of British understatement, the dapper Eden told the German that he 'deeply regretted the inform-ation' that Hoesch had given him. Nevertheless, Eden thought Hitler had made a cunning move. 'Most members of the British public would certainly see very little harm in Hitler's action,' he wrote. 'It would merely appear that he was taking full possession of a territory which was his by right.' Eden then summoned the French ambassador, and after telling him that he 'deeply regretted' Germany's action, he urged the French not to do anything to inflame the situation. Eden then rushed to Chequers, the British prime minister's country house some forty miles north-west of London. There, Stanley Baldwin told Eden that the British would not support any military action by the French, to which Eden agreed. When he arrived back in London, Eden found a cable from Phipps. 'I judged from [the cable] that Baron von Neurath had had the grace to seem embarrassed when announc-ing to him Hitler's decision,' Eden later wrote.

The eyes of the world were on France. She had the strength to expel the Germans, but did she have the will? No one was more anxious than Hitler. Albert Speer, the Nazi Party's chief architect, travelled down to Munich with Hitler later that day. 'The special train [. . .] was charged, compartment after compartment, with the tense atmosphere that emanated from the Fuehrer's section,' Speer wrote. Hitler knew that just one French division would be enough to turf the Germans out of the Rhineland. France did nothing, however, and neither did Britain. 'The reaction in the world was predicted,' wrote Goebbels that evening with a touch of retrospective certainty. 'The Fuehrer is immensely happy [. . .] The entry has gone according to plan [. . .] The Fuehrer beams. England remains passive. France won't act alone. Italy is disap-pointed and America uninterested.' Goebbels' comments, although terse, were correct. Hitler was later to claim that the forty-eight hours after the occupation were the most tense of his life. 'We had no army worth mentioning,' he told Speer. 'At that time it would not even have had the fighting strength to maintain itself against the Poles.'

The press reaction in Britain was just as Hitler would have hoped it to be. The *Observer* advised that the British should consider Hitler's move 'in a spirit of sympathy and goodwill'. This was classic appeasement, but far short of the *Daily Mail*'s zealous embracing of the German leader:

> Germany's latest stroke may be said, indeed, to have cleared the air. Like a fresh breeze from the mountaintops it has swept away the fog and shown exactly where she stands [. . .] This is a moment when it is most important to be beware of the Bolshevik trouble-makers. Their aim [. . .] is to involve the great Powers of Europe in a suicidal war.

Even the left-leaning *Morning Post* agreed with the *Daily Mail*: 'Herr Hitler may have performed a real service to the future peace of Europe by creating a situation which shows the futility of the whole sanctions policy.' The poet Robert Graves and Alan Hodge, a private secretary at the Ministry of Information, summed up the mood iron-ically in their 1940 book *The Long Week-end*: 'The Germans weren't such bad people really, though they did have a mania about the Jews – those Olympic Winter Sports at Garmisch had been marvellously organised, and everyone had been so polite and hospitable.'

Meanwhile, all the anti-appeasers could do was to fume. Ralph Wigram, an official at the Foreign Office, came home to his small house in Lord North Street in Westminster one night in a mood of utter dejection. '[He] sat down in a corner of the room where he had never sat before,' his wife recalled in a letter to Churchill, 'and said to me, "War is now *inevitable*, and it will be the most terrible war there has even been. I don't think I shall see it, but you will. Wait now for the bombs on this little house."' Both of Wigram's predic-tions were correct – war of course did come, and his house was indeed bombed.

In Germany, Phipps met Hitler, and found the dictator in an upbeat mood. As well as being cockahoop about the Rhineland, Hitler was also particularly impressed by Mussolini's recent conquest of Abyssinia. 'With dictators nothing succeeds like success,' Phipps wrote to Eden, 'and Herr Hitler is clearly lost in admiration of Mussolini. Before long he may have visions of the Holy Roman Empire (plus a big colonial empire) of his own.' Later in the month, Vansittart wrote to his brother-in-law, telling him that he had foreseen Hitler's move, 'but I admit I hardly expected to be justified so soon, for I had thought that Hitler would stay quiet until after the Olympic Games'.

So far, the Olympics had suited Hitler's purposes admirably. They had bought him time, and the Winter Games had given the opportunity not only to reflect, but to show the world that his regime was not how it was painted in the foreign press. The positive impression many gained of Germany at Garmisch made it easier for Europe to accept Hitler's occupation of the Rhineland. Had the Games been boycotted, then Hitler would not have had the nerve to enter the demilitarised zone, because countries that boycotted sports were not countries that would have tolerated a breach of Locarno. If Hitler had sat at Garmisch watching an Olympics that did not feature any American, British, French and Canadian athletes, would he have had the confidence to call their bluff? It is unlikely. The world of sport had the opportunity to show the world of diplomacy the way, and it had let it slip. The Games were now just six months away. War, some thought, might be even closer.

'We don't want nigger money!' the fat man shouted.

Inside the car, the three black athletes from Ohio State University waited in fear. The owner of the Indianapolis diner from which they had just bought some coffee and eggs reached through the car window and grabbed the plate from the driver's hands. The breakfast spilled into his lap, staining his only suit. The athlete jumped out the car, spoiling for a fight. One of his teammates followed him, restraining his companion from getting into a punch-up a few hours before a race meeting.

'No, Dave, no,' he implored him, 'we'll get something from the next place.'

The driver, who was called David Albritton, relented, although he was furious not to have had the chance of getting even with the owner, who was walking away with the plate. The two men got back into the 1914 Model-T Ford they had bought for $32.50. 'I'm going to run my balls off today,' said the teammate who had restrained him. He did just that. At the Butler Indoor Relays, a meet open to all, even African-Americans, he won the 60-yard dash in 6.2 seconds, the 60-yard hurdles in 6.9 seconds, and jumped over 25 feet to win the long jump. The athlete's name was Jesse Owens. Albritton won the high jump by clearing just over 2 metres.

It was 23 March 1936, and the twenty-three-year-old Owens was accustomed to both winning and suffering racist abuse. He and his fellow black athletes had often found themselves in towns where the only place to eat was in the car, and the only place to sleep was at a dosshouse. Owens constantly had to wrench the pugnacious Albritton away from a brawl. Just a few days earlier, in Richmond, Indiana, he had had to stop his friend punching a restaurant owner who had refused them admission. 'Now Pappa,' Owens had said, 'just take it easy.' This had happened countless times over the past three years, although the two men were never as scared as they had been in Kokomo, Indiana, in 1933, when they pulled into town the day after a young black boy had been lynched. Apparently, some of the town's populace had picknicked underneath the tree bearing its 'strange fruit'. What Owens and his friends was experiencing was somewhat similar to what the Jews were experiencing in Germany, a point that was made in *Der Angriff*, of all papers: 'In the last analysis, we do not hang any Jews who misuse a German woman, but we try them according to law and justice. In Germany we do not lynch persons of another race.' The paper neglected to mention that Nazi 'law and justice' hardly deserved to be described as such, and neither did it mention, for example, a pogrom held in July 1934 in Hirschberg, in which four Jews were shot while 'trying to escape' from SS men. '[Their bodies] remained in the ditch until Monday noon,' said one eyewitness, 'guarded by a few Storm Troopers. All four of them had been shot in exactly the same way: a revolver bullet through the jugular vein.' *Der Angriff* was quite right: persons of another race were indeed not lynched in Germany. They were shot.

The other difference was one of scale. Between 1933 and 1936 hundreds of Jews died at the hands of the Nazis in Germany, a significantly higher figure than the sixty-five African-Americans lynched in the same period. In 1936 there were just eight lynchings. This is not to minimise the repugnance of lynching, but to illustrate that while extra-legal racial murder was on the decrease in the United States, it was on the rise in Germany. To suggest that there was an equivalence, as General Sherrill had done the previous October with his talk of having 'no more business' discussing Jews in Germany than a German would have discussing the 'Negro situation' in the United States, was spuri-ous. His view was little different to that of *Der Angriff*. Indeed, the number of blacks lynched after 1936 was never to rise higher than eight per year. Throughout the six years of war, twenty-three blacks were lynched in the USA. The figure for the number of Jews killed in German-occupied territories during that same period is well known.

Nevertheless, race relations in the United States were desperately bad, something Jesse Owens, born James Cleveland Owens on 12 September 1913 in Oakville, Alabama, knew all too well. Owens' grandparents had been slaves, and his father Henry was a sharecropper who tilled several acres of his white landlord's estate. Henry Owens was a simple man, who believed that if he looked at any book other than the Bible, then a family member would fall sick. Owens worked hard – like a slave, in fact – although he knew his labour would not, and indeed should not, elevate him. 'It don't do a coloured man no good to get himself too high,' he once told Owens, ' 'Cause it's a helluva drop back to the bottom.' Owens' mother, Emma, gave birth to nine children, of whom Owens was the youngest. Growing up in a shack overcrowded with his siblings, Owens was not a healthy child, suffering from bronchial congestion and pneumonia. His mother, it was said, also removed several strange growths from his chest and legs with a knife.

Unsurprisingly, the family was extremely poor. Some of Owens' earliest memories concerned a lack of clothing. 'I didn't have enough clothing at that time to cover my entire body,' he recalled. 'The only time I remember being embarrassed was when I saw the neighbour girls and I didn't have enough clothing to cover my body [. . .] I would run and hide.' It was not only Oakville's black families, however, which suffered from poverty. Around 950 of the town's 1,138 inhab-itants were white, and many of them eked out a meagre existence on the land. Despite their mutual poverty, tensions between blacks and whites existed, largely because the whites regarded their colour as the only means of elevating themselves above their equally poor black neighbours. Owens often found himself getting into scraps with white boys, the worst being when he was pinned to the ground and threatened with having their initials carved into his face. Luckily, Owens' older brothers came to his rescue. As a result, Owens found that the best form of defence was simply to be as pleasant as possible to everybody. It was this attitude which was to make him so popular in later years. 'I try awfully hard for people to like me,' he once admitted.

Despite the poverty and the racism, life in Oakville had its pleasant side. The family was never short of food, and every autumn they killed a pig and smoked its meat. Owens and his brothers would go swimming in the village pond, and at night they would hunt possum and sit around campfires. Like any other child, Owens would play games like catch and hide-and-seek. If any game called for running away, however, then Owens could never be caught. 'I always loved running,' Owens later recalled. 'I wasn't very good at it, but I loved it because it was something you could do all by yourself, and under your own power.'

At some point after the First World War – the exact date is uncertain – the Owens family moved to Cleveland, Ohio. The reason for the family's move north is also unclear, but they were just eleven of 500,000 African-Americans who moved to northern cities between 1910 and 1920. Many who worked on the land found themselves being replaced by machinery, and the northern cities, with their promises of employment and better social conditions for blacks, were attractive prospects. Nevertheless, Cleveland was no paradise. Although there was no official racial segregation, it was nonetheless still there. The Ku Klux Klan was active as well, its membership some several thousand strong. One third of all those arrested were black, yet blacks accounted for just over 4 per cent of the population. Compared to Oakville, however, Cleveland was a cornucopia, and Owens senior and his three eldest sons found steady jobs at a steel mill. Even the young Owens found himself a job, working in a cobbler's.

Owens attended Bolton Elementary School, which is where he earned the name 'Jesse'. Legend has it that when his teacher asked for his name, Owens replied 'J. C. Owens' in his Southern drawl. When his teacher asked whether he had said 'Jesse Owens', the young boy, not wishing to contradict her, said that he had. The name stuck. After Bolton, Owens went to Fairmount Junior High School, where he met Ruth Solomon, with whom he fell in love. He also befriended David Albritton, who dated Ruth's sister, and the two boys formed a strong bond, based partly on their love of sports.

It was at Fairmount that Jesse met Charles Riley, to whom Owens would later credit much of his success. Riley was the school's PE teacher, a short, grey-haired Irishman. 'I grew to admire and respect his words and his actions and everything else,' Owens recalled. Riley identified Owens' natural talent, and started coaching him an hour before school started. Soon, Owens was running the 100 yards in eleven seconds, an astonishingly quick time for a teenage boy. Riley, it was said, had to check that his stopwatch was not broken. In 1928, at the age of fifteen, Owens started breaking records on both the track and in the long jump pit, a habit that would endure. It was Riley who taught Owens his running style, instructing him to sprint as if 'the ground was a burning fire'. Owens also learnt from Riley that not all whites were out to get him. 'He was the first white man I really knew [. . .] he proved to me beyond all proof that a white man can understand – and love – a Negro.'

By the late 1920s, the Owens family was suffering from the effects of the Great Depression. Their experience was not of course unique, but their plight was not helped by the fact that Henry Owens was laid off from his job because he had been knocked down by a car. Owens' siblings left school to find work, and by 1930 Owens was the only child who remained in education. In that year, he enrolled at East Technical High School, a place that was more used to teaching vocational skills than reading and writing. In fact, Owens was never to learn to read well, despite his spoken fluency. He continued to impress on the track, however, his technique still being improved by Riley's coaching. By 1932, Owens was already being labelled in the local press as 'a marvel'.

That year, Owens tried making it on to the Olympic team. His nerves meant that he 'tightened up', however, and he did not even get past the Midwestern preliminaries. But Owens was to show his off his talents after the Los Angeles Games, when he beat a selection of American and European Olympians in the 100 and 200 metres. He finished second in the long jump, only narrowly defeated by the Olympic gold medallist Edward Gordon.

In the meantime, Owens' relationship with Ruth Solomon had blossomed, and they supposedly married in July 1932. The principal reason for marrying so soon became apparent on 8 August when their daughter Gloria was born. Whether her parents were actually married remains open to doubt, however, as there is no record of their marriage, and there are inconsistencies in the accounts of their 'wedding'. The couple undoubtedly did get married – supposedly for a second time – three years later. It would be fair to assume that Owens and Ruth had fabricated the earlier wedding in order to allay family sensitivities.

Owens' new role as a family man did not impinge upon his athletic achievements – he won seventy-five out of the seventy-nine races in which he competed at East Tech. In May 1933 he won all his events in the Ohio Interscholastic State Finals, smashing the long jump record in the process. In June he was to do even better. At the National Interscholastic Championships in Chicago, he set a new world record for the 220 yards of 20.7 seconds, and in the 100 yards he equalled the world record of 9.4. Cleveland embraced him, and upon his return he was given a victory parade.

Unsurprisingly, many universities clamoured for Owens to join them. Although his grades were not up to the mark, Ohio State allowed him to take 'special tests' so that he could gain admission in the autumn of 1933. Owens found that the racial conditions in Columbus were almost as bad as they were in Alabama. He was barred from the men's dormitory because of his colour, and no restaurants near the university would allow him or his fellow black students to dine. Owens did manage to find a part-time job manning a lift in the State Office Building, although he was kept out of sight in the service lift at the rear of the building. He supplemented his income by giving talks to local schools, as well as by cleaning the cafeteria. He later claimed that he was earning some $350 per month ($5,000 in 2005). This seems to be a gross exaggeration, but there was no doubt that Owens was not a starving student. Academically, he fared less well, but then he was not expected to shine.

Over the next three years, Owens' star continued to rise. His two biggest rivals were his fellow Alabamans Ralph Metcalfe and Eulace

Peacock. Metcalfe was two years older than Owens, and far more experienced. He had won silver in the Los Angeles Olympics 100 metres, and bronze in the 200 metres. Peacock was a year younger than Owens, and they would run against each other several times. They were evenly matched, and in 1935 they even won alternate races.

Owens was soon to show his superiority over his two rivals at the Big Ten Championship meeting in Ann Arbor, Michigan, in May 1935. Owens arrived at the competition complaining of a bad back, which was sustained either through a fall or from a game of touch foot-ball. As with so many other stories associated with Owens, the precise details are lost in legend. Whatever the cause, the back was reputedly so painful that Owens doubted he could compete, yet willpower and a hot bath strengthened his resolve. He struggled through the prelim-inaries, and spent the night in agony. Fortunately, the weather was warm the next day, and Owens found that his back responded well to the heat. That day, 25 May, was soon to become one of the most remarkable in the history of sport, let alone athletics. At the long jump pit, Owens asked for a handkerchief to be placed at the 26 feet mark. He sprinted down the track and leaped past it, landing 8¼ inches beyond. The distance was a new world record, but as Owens did not wish to strain his back, he did not try to better it. In the 220 yards he won with a time of 20.3 seconds – smashing a world record that had been on the books for eleven years. In his weakest event, the 220-yard low hurdles, Owens' time of 22.6 seconds constituted yet another world record. In the 100 yards, Owens equalled the world record of 9.4 seconds, although the starter's stipulation that the watches should be stopped only when the runners' back feet crossed the line surely counted against him. What made Owens' accomplishments all the more remarkable was that they had taken place in just one hour. After the meet, Charles Riley drove Owens back to Cleveland, where he found his face all over the Sunday papers the following morning. With typical modesty, Owens told one reporter that he found all the praise 'a little too high'.

The next several months were not to be the easiest of Owens' life. Mobbed wherever he went, he soon found that he had attracted the attention of many adoring female fans, who were charmed not only by his physique but also by his radiant grin and utterly charming manner. One fan, Quincella Nickerson, would prove to be a femme especially fatale. The daughter of a rich Californian businessman, Nickerson fell for Owens, and from all appearances he did for her. Soon, the glamorous couple were being photographed wherever they went – most heartbreakingly for Ruth, even in a jeweller's shop. The affair made the front pages of the national papers, which speculated about when the couple might get engaged. Ruth did not let her man get away with it. She harangued him over the telephone in July before the AAU championships in Lincoln, Nebraska, and even more distressingly, Owens was confronted by a journalist who threatened to expose Owens' daughter on the front page unless Owens married Ruth. As a result, Owens' performance at Lincoln was poor – he finished third behind Peacock and Metcalfe in the 100 metres, and second to Peacock in the long jump. Owens left the championships as soon as he could, and when he arrived back in Cleveland he married Ruth in her parents' living room on the evening of 5 July.

For the next few races, Owens found that he had lost his form, and Peacock beat him five times in a row. Some thought Owens was 'burned out' and championed Peacock as the star of the forthcoming Olympics. Worse was to come, however. In August, Owens found that his job as a page at the Ohio House of Representatives was being investigated by the AAU, which felt that his acceptance of the job – essentially an honorary position – was a breach of his amateur status. On 12 August Owens was summoned to attend a meeting of the Northeastern Ohio AAU in Cleveland. The committee members heard that Owens had never done 'anything that really discredits him', although one committee member disgracefully thought it pertinent to bring up the matter of Owens' marriage. This was dismissed as an irrelevance. The committee found that Owens had not breached their rules, but Owens announced that he would return $159 that he had earned in order to soothe any doubters. Nevertheless, the affair rumbled on, and it was not until December that the AAU issued its final verdict. 'We have considered Owens to be a victim of circumstances,' it reported.

Owens continued to attract controversy. In November, when he was asked his opinion of the boycott movement, Owens replied, '[. . .] if there is discrimination against minorities in Germany then we must withdraw from the Olympics'. This statement earned him an immediate censure from his new coach, Larry Snyder, who warned Owens that if he continued to preach against the Games, he would be 'a forgotten man'. If his athletic and personal lives were problems enough, a few days after Christmas Owens found that his academic life was similarly troublesome. His report showed that he had performed so poorly that he would not be eligible for the winter indoor track season. If his grades were as bad the following term, the report warned, he would not even be allowed to compete during the summer outdoor season.

Winning the Butler Indoor Relays in March 1936 was therefore an important part of Owens' rehabilitation. What gained him even more applause was his behaviour at an indoor meet in Cleveland's public hall. Once again, Owens found himself lined up against Eulace Peacock in a final – this time the 50-yard dash. As soon as the gun went off, Owens shot out of his blocks, but Peacock's block slipped, and he fell to the floor. All he could do was to get up and watch helplessly as his rival glided effortlessly to breach the tape. As soon as Owens heard what had happened, he insisted that the result did not count. The defective starting block was repaired, and the race was held again. This time, Peacock won, but the star of the day was undoubtedly Owens, who had showed a remarkable degree of sportsmanship.

Magnanimity does not win places on the Olympic team, however, something of which Owens was all too aware. Although his 'scholastic troubles' had abated, his athletic performance was still not as good as it might be. In the six major races in which he had competed against Peacock since the previous July, Peacock had beaten him five times. There was no doubt that Owens was a tremendous athlete, but it looked as if he had peaked at Ann Arbor. Once again, cynics started to write him off, and his enforced 'idleness' during the winter season appeared to have taken its toll. If any American was going to win gold in Berlin that August, it was almost certainly going to be Peacock. Indeed, very few would have bet against him. Owens may have had the charm, the fascinating and somewhat controversial private life, but Peacock had the raw ability and the results to prove it. It looked as if combining athletics, academic work and family life was just too much for the twenty-two-year-old from Oakville. 'It's going to take a special man to defeat Eulace Peacock,' said Owens. 'You see, I've already reached my peak. Peacock is just now reaching his. He's a real athlete. I don't know whether I can defeat him again.'

1,400 miles west of Cleveland, another young man from a small town was dreaming of Olympic glory. His name was Glenn Morris, and he came from Simla, Colorado, the smallest of the little towns on the prairie. If Jesse Owens was not a poster boy for the archetype of All-American Athlete, then the handsome Morris, at 6 foot 2 inches and weighing 182 pounds, most certainly was. In fact, the twenty-three-year-old's life was the epitome of the small-town-boy-makes-good story. The second of seven children, Morris moved from St Louis, Missouri, to Simla when he was just three. His parents grew kidney beans on a 160-acre farm some three miles out of town, and life was predictably hard. Like Owens, he may have worn raggedy clothes, but he was well fed.

The 5-kilometre track to town was the key to Morris's athleticism. 'We walked to school,' his brother Jack recalled, 'hiked it in summer and winter.' Sometimes, Morris would run to school, but his brother said that he never ran back as it was uphill and 'would have been real tough'. Nevertheless, back at the farm Morris had made himself a mini-sports ground, complete with a high jump pit, a long jump pit and even a selection of hurdles made out of old sticks. Morris's father found his son's obsession with athletics somewhat trying, and Jack recalled how Glenn and his father had 'some real set-tos' as Morris would much rather be practising his athletics than hoeing the kidney beans. Apart from that difficult uphill stretch on the way back from school, Morris would run everywhere, jumping over fences and creeks. However, he struggled against an affliction that could have ended his athletic career early – he had asthma. Sometimes he would fall to the ground, struggling to catch his breath while his helpless mother looked on, terrified. But Morris's single-mindedness meant that he did not treat the disease as a handicap, merely as something that needed to be overcome.

Unsurprisingly, Morris excelled in sports at school. Unlike Owens, he also performed well in the classroom, and even edited the school newspaper. It was not until 1930, however, that Morris began to show some real promise. At the Eastern Colorado League high-school track meet, he won first place in six different events, and broke the records for the high jump and the discus. At the Colorado State meet, he came third in the hurdles, a result with which the driven young man was disappointed. His hunger for victory was noticed by many, and some saw him as a little moody and introspective. 'Glenn was more of an observer,' one school friend recalled. 'He liked to watch other people, quietly, and think about things.' Despite, or perhaps because of, this moodiness, Morris was, according to his brother Jack, 'always good with the girls'.

That year, Morris was admitted to Colorado State College in Fort Collins, some 160 miles from Simla. Like Owens, Morris found himself a good coach. Morris's was Harry Hughes, his football coach, who later recalled that Morris was 'as green as the stadium grass, but I knew I had a natural born athlete in the rough [. . .] He was as quick on his feet as a cat, and he had a hair-trigger mind.' Morris played right end at football, and he was renowned for catching even the longest of passes. For a while, it looked as if he would take up the sport professionally, but it was while competing in the hurdles at the Kansas Relays of 1935 that Morris's head was turned by another sport – the decathlon. When Morris returned to Simla, he told Harry Hughes that he could do better in the event than the athlete who had won. His quest to win the decathlon at the following year's Kansas Relays became an obsession. After he graduated, Morris dedicated all the hours when he wasn't working as a car salesman to training.

Morris still had time for love, however. During his senior year, he met a petite brunette called Charlotte Edwards, who was reading home economics and hoping to become a teacher. 'Charlotte had several other guys who were crazy about her,' her sister later recalled, 'but she was fascinated with Glenn.' She and Morris were soon an item, and Edwards's fascination with her new boyfriend extended itself to helping him train for the decathlon. 'She really helped him,' he sister recalled. 'She would go to the track with him and time him, and then go home and prepare special meals.' Charlotte even regulated Morris's diet. 'I made him quit all starches except whole wheat bread and eat meat twice a day with stewed fruits,' she said. 'He lost ten pounds but said he was stronger than ever.' (It would appear that Charlotte's diet was a forerunner to the Atkins.) In fact, there were no limits to Charlotte's loyalty. No matter what the weather, she worked out with him for two hours a day, chivvying him along. 'I would start him on his distance runs,' she said, 'then dash across the field and shout at him after he rounded the turn, the time he was making.' Apparently, Charlotte also lost 10 pounds.

On 15 April 1936 Morris and Charlotte went to the Kansas Relays. It quickly became clear that all his training had paid off, because by the end of the first day Morris was leading the pack. In his last event, however, he pulled a muscle in his right leg, and he slept very little that night. Typically, the determined Morris did not let the injury affect his performance, and he came out the next day to win the discus and the hurdles. At the end of the decathlon, Morris found that not only had he won, he had smashed the American record with 7,576 points. Unless he performed spectacularly badly at the Olympic trials in June, then there was no doubt that he would be going to Berlin.

Another athlete for whom the Olympic trials seemed a formality was Eleanor Holm. The winner of the 100 metres backstroke at the Los Angeles Olympics when she was just eighteen, Holm was renowned not only for her swimming, but also for her looks and her body. 'She has the most beautiful physique I have ever seen,' said the impresario Florenz Ziegfeld. Ziegfeld was right – Holm's body was indeed a head-turner, and she had a face to match. Her smile was infectious, and she had a look about her that suggested that there was more to her life than hours spent in training. In fact, New Yorker Holm was more likely to be found in a nightclub than a swimming pool. After the 1932 Games she married the bandleader Arthur Jarrett, and she toured the country singing in clubs. She looked sensational, dressed solely in a white bathing suit, a cowboy hat and a pair of high heels, singing 'I'm an Old Cowhand (from the Rio Grande)'. 'I had never done any singing before that,' Holm recalled, 'but I was still on the sports pages, so I didn't have to sing that well. I always had a throaty voice.' Holm had also signed a $500-a-week deal with Warner Brothers, but by early 1936 she had played only a few bit parts. Hollywood wanted her to swim for the camera, but Holm refused, despite an offer of $750 a week, because she was all too aware that to do so would have violated her amateur status in the eyes of the all-powerful AAU.

If singing and acting did not come easily to Holm, then swimming most certainly did. 'I was a water rat as a child,' she said, 'I had no fear of water.' Holm's parents kept a holiday cottage on Long Beach, New York, and it was there that her mother taught her to swim. Holm was intrepid, and often she would swim too far out into the Atlantic, with the result that she would have to be rescued by a lifeguard. 'On the way in he would bawl me out and say, "Don't do that again," but he would also teach me how to swim on the way in. An hour later he'd be getting me out again. And he'd teach me on the way in again. I was no dope. I was getting free lessons.' Holm soon developed a fascination for the female divers of the Women's Swimming Association of New York, who would compete at the Olympic Pool at Long Beach. 'I used to sit there goggle-eyed watching them,' she recalled. Holm joined the Association, much to her father's chagrin. Her ability astonished everybody, and at the age of thirteen she won her first national title in the backstroke. At the 1928 Olympics in Amsterdam, Holm came fifth, although she was not disappointed. 'It didn't mean that much to me,' she said. 'I don't think I had the competitive will to win in '28. I thought, "This is great. This is wonderful." But when I saw that American flag go up, I got the spirit, and I said to myself, "Next time that's going to be for me." '

Holm trained hard for the next four years, and she even earned herself a reputation as a goody-two-shoes. 'I used to snitch on the girls if they kept me awake,' she recalled. 'I'd say to the coaches, "Did you know she was out last night? She didn't get in until ten o'clock." ' In view of her later behaviour, this was most uncharacteristic. When Holm won the gold medal at Los Angeles with a world record of 1:19.4, her demeanour changed, and she even took up smoking. Nights and early mornings in clubs also meant that Holm learned how to hold her drink, but no amount of carousing stopped her from training for the next Olympics. When she was singing with her husband at the Blackhawk club in Chicago, Holm would visit the Lakeshore Pool at three in the morning in order to train. All her efforts paid off, so much so that her confidence was supreme. 'When I was preparing for the [Olympic] try-outs, I would do a terrible thing,' she recalled. 'I used to walk into the locker room and light up a cigarette, and all of the girls would look at me and whisper, "How can she do that?

How can she smoke?" But I was just psyching them out, that's all.' Holm's oft-repeated quip to reporters of 'I train on champagne and cigarettes', although an exaggeration, was not so far from the truth. As her teammate Velma Dunn recalled, 'She could beat anybody else on the planet, even if she was plastered. She was a natural swimmer.'

It came as no surprise that Holm made the Olympic team – for her the try-outs were a formality. Nevertheless, her reputation had earned her at least one enemy, an enemy who was very powerful – Avery Brundage. 'I was everything Avery Brundage hated,' said Holm. 'I had a few dollars, and athletes were supposed to be poor. I worked in nightclubs, and athletes shouldn't do that. I was married. All of this was against his whole conception of what an athlete should be. It didn't matter to him that I held the world record.' Holm's and Brundage's paths were soon to cross, and when they did, the result would be explosive.

Another New Yorker who was to fall foul of Avery Brundage was Marty Glickman. Born in the Bronx on 14 August 1917, Glickman was the son of a cotton-goods salesman who had migrated from Romania. Although the Glickman family was Jewish, Glickman's father refused to allow the young Marty to speak Yiddish. 'He wanted to be an American,' Glickman recalled, 'so we only spoke English in our house.' Glickman's early childhood was one of playing games in the 'concrete jungle' of the Bronx. 'It was a happy, active life [. . .] We played games on the street or in a little courtyard leading to the apartment house.' Glickman found that he was a faster runner than any of his friends, and he was soon nicknamed 'the Fastest Kid on the Block'.

When Glickman was seven, the family moved to Brooklyn. Glickman continued to dazzle others with his speed, and by the time he went to high school he was on the baseball, basketball, track, swimming and football teams. In his junior and senior years, Glickman became the indoor and outdoor sprint champion of New York State, setting a state record in the outdoor 100-yard dash of 9.75 seconds. Nevertheless, times were tough for the Glickmans. During the Depression, Glickman's father lost his job, and when he started a new business, it went bankrupt. Embittered, he drank and gambled to excess, even frittering away Marty's bar mitzvah money. At one point, the family was so hard up that even buying a pair of long-coveted five-dollar trainers was a drain on the household's budget. Glickman remembered getting the trainers as being 'one of the great joys' of his life. As soon as he put them on, he ran all the way back home – some fifteen blocks.

In 1935, Glickman went to Syracuse University, New York, where his track career continued to prosper. His biggest rival was Ben Johnson, whom he faced in the 100 metres in the Metropolitan Championships in New York City in the late spring of 1936. When the gun went off, the two athletes rushed down the track, with Johnson in the lead. When they crossed the tape, Johnson had won, but when the two men turned round, they realised that they were the only ones who had raced – they had both made false starts. In the race proper, Glickman won. He beat Johnson again in the Olympic eastern regional finals in Boston. All that now stood in the way of Glickman becoming an Olympian was the final Olympic qualifiers to be held in July on Randalls Island underneath the Triborough Bridge in New York City. Glickman knew that to get to Berlin would require something special. He would be up against some of the fastest men on the planet – Owens, Peacock, Metcalfe, as well as the legendary Frank Wykoff and Foy Draper. There, he would also meet another Jewish athlete called Sam Stoller, with whom Glickman would be invariably linked to his dying day.

On 19 February 1936 Helene Mayer arrived back in Germany. She was hardly welcomed back with open arms. An edict from the Propaganda Ministry stipulated: 'The press is asked not to report her arrival. The only exceptions are permissible in the newspapers of Hamburg, Bremen, and Offenbach, which may carry the news because of special local interest. Commentaries about her "non-Aryan" descent and her chances for an Olympic gold medal are undesirable.' Mayer settled in quietly back home, no doubt noticing the changes that had taken place in Germany over the past four years – the 'Jews Forbidden' signs, the swastikas, the uniforms, the copies of *Der Angriff* affixed to public noticeboards. Forbidden from fencing at the Offenbach Club, Mayer trained in private, away from the eyes of her fans and journalists.

Meanwhile, her fellow Jew, Gretel Bergmann, was also in training. In March 1936 she was once again summoned to Ettlingen, where she found that she was treated 'just like everybody else'. Despite the fact that hundreds had now been eliminated, however, Bergmann was still in doubt as to whether she would be selected for the team. She knew she was capable enough – after all, she was the best female high jumper in Germany – but she had no inkling as to what the Nazis had in mind for her. 'I felt as if I were the main character in a mystery thriller,' she wrote, 'with the plot's creators unwilling to give the slightest hint about the outcome until the last possible moment.' A hint arrived all too soon. In May, Bergmann was dismissed from her school six months before she finished her studies. It was a blow, but Bergmann was used to blows. At a small, regional athletics meeting in Stuttgart, she got her revenge by equalling the German record of 1.60 metres. 'Had this happened under normal circumstances,' she noted, 'the stadium would have been in an uproar; now I could hear only some very scattered applause.' To have applauded a Jew would have been a brave move indeed. Nevertheless, Bergmann felt fired up by her per-formance, seeing it as one in the eye for the Nazis. ' "Okay you lousy bastards, how did you like my performance?" ' she recalled thinking. ' "How did you like it that this so-called miserable Jew equalled the German record, that this Jew beat your best by 20 centimetres, that this Jew put a crack into your image of Aryan superiority and that there isn't a damn thing you can do about it?" ' Naturally, Bergmann kept such thoughts to herself. She returned home and waited, waited for a letter to come from the Nazis, as she knew it would. And then, one morning in mid-July, it arrived.

Unlike Gretel Bergmann, the German wrestler Werner Seelenbinder had already openly taunted the Nazis at a sports meeting. Seelenbinder was not a Jew, however, but a member of that other group of people that the regime despised almost as intensely – the communists. Seelenbinder's opportunity had come after he won the 1933 German middleweight wrestling championships, held shortly after Hitler had come to power. At the prize ceremony, the first three wrestlers were presented with their belts and trophies, at which point the band struck up 'Deutschland über Alles'. As was now becoming customary, the

3,000-strong crowd rose to its feet, its arms shooting out in the fascist salute. Seelenbinder found his fellow competitors doing likewise, but he refused to salute, holding his trophy tightly and resolutely to his chest, his lips not moving. The crowd saw his action for what it was – an affront to Nazism.

The predictable knock on Seelenbinder's door came eight days later. The Gestapo took him to the dreaded Columbia House prison near Tempelhof airfield, where he was interrogated. The Gestapo would certainly have known that the twenty-nine-year-old Seelenbinder was a committed communist, as he had been a member of the KPD (the German Communist Party) since the late 1920s. Seelenbinder had competed in the 1928 and 1929 Spartakiads – workers' sports festivals – in Moscow, and it was there that the already left-wing young man became convinced that communism was the way forward. The son of an unemployed bricklayer, Seelenbinder had experienced his political dawning at the age of fourteen, when he took a job as a porter in a luxury hotel. He resented the wealthy guests, and resented even more having to kowtow to them, and he soon resigned to work in a factory as a joiner. He returned from Moscow preaching the communist gospel, and soon he and his fellow members of his workers' sports club in Berlin found themselves being harassed by the Nazis. Their hall was attacked twice by SA troops, and on one of these occasions Seelenbinder is said to have beaten off fourteen men single-handedly.

What the Gestapo did not discover about Seelenbinder was that he was employed as a courier for the Uhrig Group, an association of undercover Berlin communists under the leadership of Robert Uhrig, running messages between the group and the office of the Red Sports International in Denmark. Luckily, when he was interned in Columbia House, one of his captors was a wrestling fan, and put a sign on his door which read, 'German champion. Do not treat him badly!' After a few days, Seelenbinder was released, although he was banned from his club, which made it impossible for him to enter the Olympics. Seelenbinder's fellow athletes rallied to his support, and soon pictures of the champion were appearing in wrestling clubs up and down the country. With wrestling competitions being won by those vastly infe-rior to Seelenbinder, Tschammer und Osten's department found itself under increasing pressure to reinstate his membership, which they eventually did some eight days before the 1935 championships, believing that it would be impossible for him to win with such a short time to prepare.

Seelenbinder had been secretly in training, however, and once again he won the championship, much to the Nazis' disgust. He repeated the feat the following year, compounding Tschammer und Osten's anger, as he was now guaranteed a place on the Olympic team. At first, Seelenbinder wanted to boycott the Games, but his fellow members of the Uhrig Group convinced him that it would help their cause more if he competed and won a medal. Not only would Seelenbinder be able to do as he had done in 1933, refusing to salute when he was on the podium, but the group had another idea that would expose the cruelties of the Nazi regime to the world. After each event, the medal winners were to be interviewed on live radio. Seelenbinder could use this opportunity to reveal what was happening in Germany – the murders, the pogroms and the concentration camps. A number of technicians who worked on the radio station were members of the Uhrig Group, and they would ensure that the interview would be broadcast. Immediately afterwards, some Swedish sportsmen would attempt to get him to safety, although there would be no guarantee that the Gestapo would not get to him first. Seelenbinder agreed to the idea – knowing that if he were caught, then he would be executed. Nevertheless, he was determined to win – the Olympics would be his greatest chance to strike a blow against a regime he despised.

Salford in northern England was once described as the 'ugly illiterate scrawl of the Industrial Revolution'. When Bill Roberts was born there on 5 April 1912, the town was little better. Ranked as one of the unhealthiest places in Britain, it suffered an infant mortality rate for the under-fives of a shocking 50 per cent, with many dying from respiratory diseases such as tuberculosis and bronchitis. Others were claimed by scarlet fever and dysentery. The town, wrote one historian, was created not only by hard work and skill, but also by 'grasping greed and insensitivity to the appalling social consequences of industrialisation'. In his play *Love on the Dole*, the playwright Walter Greenwood described Salford as 'drab and sluttish'. 'A raving maniac could not have dreamed up a more shocking place had he been suffering from the most outrageous nightmare,' he wrote.

Roberts was born at the family's terraced house just a few hundred yards from the docks. His father was a pattern-maker, and although working-class, the family was reasonably comfortable. The outbreak of war in 1914 meant that Roberts' father was secure in his job, but times were still hard. Roberts was too young to remember the war, but he did recall the anti-German feeling on the streets. 'I can remember crowds breaking into a butcher's shop near our house because the owner was German,' he said, 'or at least he had a German name.' In fact, there were many families who bore German names in Salford, the descendants of immigrants of the previous century. As the war dragged on, many of these families were ostracised. 'You had to understand,' said Roberts, '[. . .] that didn't make any of it right, of course.' Roberts' other early memories were of the visit of King George V, and the Americans entering the war. Many of the troops arrived at Salford docks, and Roberts was there to see them. 'By then I was old enough to realise that it would make a difference to the war now that they were here.'

Roberts attended the Trafford Road School, and although he was a conscientious and bright pupil, he left at thirteen. The headmaster had found him a job in a timber yard, and Roberts knew that he had to take it. Timber was a vitally important business in the area, and Roberts knew that if he succeeded he would be secure. He started by being a Boy Friday, but his diligence saw him attending evening classes to learn all about the trade. By the age of sixteen, he was supervising grown men, wore a suit and tie, and even had his own car.

During his spare time, Roberts liked to go hiking and to indulge in his other love – athletics. His first significant athletic success was at the age of fourteen, when he won a running-backwards race at Salford Athletics Club. Running forwards also came naturally to Roberts, not least because he had spent most of his childhood running around the streets. Roberts joined the club, although it did not even have a ground. Even when he and his fellow members found somewhere to train, their efforts were hardly professional. 'We didn't know how to [train],' Roberts recalled, 'and in any case nobody that we knew in those days believed that you should train very hard [. . .] So we just ran round and round for a bit and did a few strides and some stretching, and that was it.'

By the time Roberts turned eighteen, he had found that his best distances were 220 yards and the quarter-mile. Soon, he was helping the club to win prizes in the relay, as well as winning the odd 220 yards on his own. The local newspaper noted that he showed 'much promise', but this was by no means delivered with an air of excitement. After all, Roberts was just another talented runner in just another small club. There were thousands like him in the country. Roberts persisted, however, and just as he had climbed the career ladder at the timber yard, he climbed the equivalent ladder in the athletics world. By 1932, he was still outside the 51.4 seconds required to enter the quarter-mile at the AAA Championships in London, but he continued to win prizes at lesser competitions, including the Lancashire quarter-mile title the following year. By 1933, he still wasn't good enough for the AAA Championships, but by 1934 he made the semi-finals. The final was won by Godfrey Rampling, an army officer to whom Roberts came second in the British Empire Games in August. Roberts' time of 48.6 was a vast improvement, and soon the press was beginning to take notice of the lad from Salford. The *Manchester Guardian* commented that his place was a surprise, and that he had 'the most wholehearted resolution'. This was quite correct – Roberts had honed what was a good talent into an exceptional one by willpower and hard work. The *Daily Telegraph* noted at the end of the year that 'this young man from Salford will certainly see Berlin'.

On 13 July 1935 Roberts once more found himself in the finals of the AAA Championships. As was becoming habit, he had come down to London with a third-class rail ticket costing him £1 17s 9d (some £85 or $150 in 2005). Given than he earned not much more than £250 a year (some £11,000 or $19,500 in 2005), even the ticket would have hurt his pocket. The only expenses that were met were the few pennies for the Underground fare. It was hardly surprising that there were so few working-class men among the Oxbridge students and army officers at White City. Money worries were at the back of his mind, however, as Roberts approached the starting line in the inside lane. Drawing the inside was bad luck, as that was the lane that got the most wear, and was therefore trickier to run on. Roberts dismissed his misfortune, and steeled himself.

A few seconds after the pistol went off, Roberts had already built up a commanding lead. His style was not pretty, with his head thrown back and his face in an agonised grimace. His strides were long and sweeping, although they were beginning to show the finesse of a world-class quarter-miler. He pushed himself as hard as he could, and the effort was rewarded by his crossing the line in first place, several yards ahead of the rest of the field. The only criticism came from the *Manchester Guardian*, which cautioned Roberts for 'squandering' his powers on every race: 'He should remember in next year's Olympic Games he will have run six quarter-miles in a week and that Berlin is hot in August. It is time for him to learn to economise energy and to win by what he must, not what he can.' This was surely nit-picking. All that now stood in Roberts' way between Salford and Berlin was the following year's AAA championships.

Three hundred and sixty-three days later, Roberts once more found himself in the quarter-mile final at White City. This time the stakes were the highest possible – places on the Olympic team. Luckily, Roberts was not drawn in the dreaded inside lane, but in lane four. Next to him in lane five stood Godfrey Rampling, who had recently rediscovered his form. In lane six was Godfrey Brown, a schoolmaster and perhaps the fastest of the six. Roberts knew that he was capable of beating both of them, but it would be tough. To his left in lane three stood Jack Whittingham, who was beatable. In lane two was the heir to a banking dynasty, Freddy Woolf, who could also be outrun, as could Oades in lane one. It would be Roberts' toughest race.

5

Getting Set

~

'LET ME SAY that I shall not resign from the International Olympic Committee. In opposing American participation in the Olympic Games in Nazi Germany, I have only been true to Olympic ideals and to American ideals of sportsmanship and fair play.' These words, written the day after the opening ceremony at Garmisch, were those of IOC member Ernest Lee Jahncke, and they were addressed to Count Baillet-Latour. Ever since the boycotters had been defeated at the AAU convention in New York in December 1935, the Louisianan's position on the committee had looked unstable. Baillet-Latour had insisted that he resign, but Jahncke had stayed firm. In his opinion, the boycott debate was still very much alive, not least because the majority at the AAU convention had been so slight. 'The issue is still open,' he informed Baillet-Latour, 'not only because of the circumstances under which the American Amateur Athletic Union gave its answer, but because great moral issues cannot be resolved by counting noses but only by an appeal to what is right and what is wrong.'

As far as Avery Brundage was concerned, the issue was very much closed and Jahncke was a figure from the past. 'The boycotters were badly whipped,' he wrote to a fellow AOC member, 'but the less said about it, the better. They should not be given any opportunities in the future to revive their agitation if we can help it. Jahncke's letter, of course, is filled with misstatements, which, if one is charitably inclined, might be forgiven because of his gross ignorance of the sport world in this country.' If one were charitably inclined towards Brundage, then his attitude might be forgiven not only on account of the AAU result, but because of the success of the Winter Olympics. Brundage would certainly have agreed with the words Gustavus Kirby uttered when he returned from Germany in the middle of February, telling them that the best sort of fact-finding committee on the state of Germany consisted of 'the athletes, the officials and the spectators who attended the Olympic Winter Games'. Kirby said that he had seen 'no discrimination whatsoever' and he was 'confident that not a single person at Garmisch will bring back a report other than I have'. Brundage returned at the end of February, and was even more effusive than Kirby. 'We've had sports fans to Olympic Games before,' he said, 'but I never saw an entire people dressed for sports and engaging in them the way the Germans did. Athletes, people and government are sports-minded on a national scale for the first time since the old Greek games.' Brundage was no doubt also delighted that he had met Hitler for the first time – Lewald and Diem had secured him a meeting immediately after the opening ceremony. A touch of the *Fuehrerkontakt* would have thrilled Brundage, and would have made him truly feel a player on the world stage.

Brundage was right about the Germans as sports fans. They were engaging in sports in the way that few other nations did, partly because their new masters were forcing them to do so. In fact, the Nazis saw sport as being essential not only for the body corporal, but also for the body politic. In the Nazi handbook *Sport and State*, commissioned by Tschammer und Osten in 1934, Hitler had written in the introduction: 'In the Third Reich it is not only knowledge which counts, but also strength, and our absolute ideal for the future would be a human being of radiant mind and magnificent body, that people may again find a way to riches through money and property.'

The Nazis looked back to Friedrich Ludwig 'Father' Jahn, who preached in the early nineteenth century a form of patriotism based on the body. Father Jahn popularised the Turners, gymnastic societies in which the participants engaged in highly regimented and coordinated movements. Instead of celebrating individualism, as English sport had done, the Turners were an exercise in creating solidarity. Their ethos was clearly very appealing to the Nazis. 'A new German physical education must be built on two powerful pillars,' declaimed *Sport and State*. 'The first was set solidly in the depths of German manhood more than 100 years ago by Friedrich Ludwig Jahn, the other was erected by the SA, when they gave their blood in the fight for the German state. In the future, it will not be possible to differentiate between the spirit of German physical education and the spirit of the SA.' The spirit of the SA was of course a violently military one, and *Sport and State* juxtaposed countless photographs of youths in sportswear alongside youths in uniform. For the Nazis, there was no differentiation between sports and militarism – the former was just the latter without rifles. In order to bolster the legitimacy of such an approach, *Sport and State* insisted that 'we should educate people in the way of the Greeks', because, the book claimed, 'Greek civilisation was a civilisation of force, like any great civilisation'.

One implementation of this 'force' was through the Kraft durch Freude (Strength through Joy) movement, of which millions of Germans were members. Attached to the Labour Front, Kraft durch Freude provided its members with sports and 'sensible amusements'. Every year, hundreds of thousands would be entrained to pleasure resorts, where they would undergo a kind of sporting indoctrination as they performed gymnastics in massed ranks. Athletics and other sports were also played, and any youth who showed an aptitude for a particular sport was given the opportunity and equipment to practise it. Kraft durch Freude was open to all ages, and it was by no means an informal affair – it was organised on quasi-military lines. Tschammer und Osten denied, however, that there was anything militaristic in the German approach to sport. 'The ideals of the founders were frequently misunderstood by other nations,' he wrote, 'for it was said of them that their motives were of a purely military nature. This was not the case formerly, nor is it the case now.' The Reichsportsfuehrer had clearly not read his copy of *Sport and State*, or indeed visited a Hitler Youth camp, where its boys trained under banners that shouted: 'Our duty is to die for Germany.'

There were many who disagreed with Tschammer und Osten. Among them was Ivone Kirkpatrick, who was on the staff at the British embassy in Berlin. Kirkpatrick saw Kraft durch Freude and the Nazi educational system as means of turning Germany's youth into tools of an aggressive state.

> The modern German is being brought up in a water-tight compartment, in which he has no opportunity of coming in contact with realities or with the opinion of the outside world. Like the Spartan, his life

and service is at the complete disposal of the state. [. . .] The methods adopted to inculcate these [spiritual and bodily] virtues are, as it happens and whatever the ultimate object in view, the methods which would be normally adopted to bring up a race of warriors. [. . .] The German schoolboy of today is being methodically educated, mentally and physically, to defend his country. He is being taught to die to protect his frontier. But I fear that, if this or a later German Government ever requires it of him, he will be found to be equally well-fitted and ready to march or die on foreign soil.

Brundage would have taken issue with such words. 'In 1930, German youth was undersized, anaemic and undernourished,' he said in speech. 'They were of poor colour. Today, they are strong and vigorous all because they are better athletes.' Brundage harkened back to a 'Golden Age' in Ancient Greece, in which 'physical soundness led to sound thinking'. He then drew an equivalence between the sporting health of a nation and its standing, using the example of Finland. 'It has the finest Olympic record per capita,' he said. 'It is a nation of athletes. What pleases those of us who are interested in sports is that the Finns carry the ideals from the playing field into other relations. At least little Finland is the only country that recognises its obligations to pay war debts.' The idea that athletic prowess is linked to sound financial management is a curious one, to say the least. Brundage pooh-poohed talk that Germany's zeal for physicality was in any way related to militarism. 'Perhaps some political leaders think healthy youth make better soldiers, but no one country can fail to profit universally, intellectually, physically, culturally and recreationally from clean wholesome sport.' Therein lay the flaw in Brundage's thinking. He felt that sport was an incorruptible divinity, or, as he said in another speech, 'sport is a religion'. What Brundage failed to recognise was that sport can be used for evil ends. It never occurred to him that the simple act of running around a track, or skiing down a mountain, might not always be taken at face value. If sport can be used to promote a nation's health and vitality, then it can also be used to promote ugly nationalism. Brundage's naivety was not to recognise that the Olympic Games were the perfect sporting vehicle to advance the appeal of something quite repugnant – in this case, Nazism. For the Nazis, Olympism and

Nazism dovetailed so neatly that, in the words of a memorandum from the Propaganda Ministry from October 1934, 'the Olympic idea is a cultural requirement of National Socialism, which concerns the entire German people'.

Brundage had more mundane and pressing matters to attend to, however, the most urgent of which was raising the $350,000 required to send the team to the Summer Games. According to Gustavus Kirby, the AOC's treasurer, however, the organisation was 'in a hell of a hole financially'. All the AOC had in the bank by the middle of March 1936 was $9,844, and all of this, according to Kirby, was earmarked. The boycott movement had certainly had its effect on fund-raising, and Brundage referred to how people would turn 'cold and fishy-eyed' when asked to contribute.

Brundage's solution was to go on the speech trail. He spent weeks lecturing businessmen on the glory of the Olympics, and reminding them that the Games were a great opportunity for America to take a stand against what really lay behind the boycott movement – communism. 'Shall we allow Communists, in whatever disguise and for whatever specious reasons, to trick any of our 400 athletes into such a course [i.e. non-attendance] for the Summer Games?' Brundage asked. Furthermore, he argued that sport itself would provide an essential bulwark against the threat of communism. To support this notion, he quoted Major J. L. Griffith, the president of the National Collegiate Athletic Association, who maintained that 'the countries subjected to regimentation are not the athletic nations, and I feel that our sports are a defence against it'. Presumably, Major Griffith thought Germany an unregimented society. 'Competitive sport', said Griffith, 'is the antithesis of the Communist principle. They cannot regiment the American people as long as we believe firmly in amateur athletics.' This was just what Brundage wanted to hear, and he even sent the statement out as a press release. Never mind that sport had no place in politics. So long as sport supported Brundage's own politics, then he was happy to break his own mantra. In short, Brundage was a hypocrite.

Brundage's idea was to raise the money through appealing to citizens directly. 'Truly American is our method of raising the American Olympic fund,' Brundage somewhat predictably claimed.

German-Americans constituted a particularly fertile group, but approaching them had its drawbacks. At a fund-raising dinner held by the German-American Bund at the Yorkville Casino in New York City in June, a hundred protesters gathered outside to voice their anger. The night was foul, driving rain literally damping their demonstration. Nevertheless, as the one thousand attendees arrived, the demonstrators marched up and down in twos, shouting 'Boycott the Olympics!', 'Hitler wants war!' and 'Defend American democracy: boycott the Nazi Olympics!' The attendees obviously viewed the protesters wryly, as some saluted them with a '*Heil!*' before going inside for their banquet. At the event, the German vice-consul, Friedhelm Draeger, told the guests that Germany under Hitler was 'a country united for peace'. The evening raised some $200, so it could hardly have been considered a huge success.

The man who received the $200 on behalf of the Olympic committee was none other than the German-American Dietrich Wortmann. It was Wortmann who in 1933 had vociferously opposed any AAU move to boycott the Games, and at the crucial meeting in New York in December 1935, it was Wortmann's hard lobbying which had helped Brundage secure the necessary votes. There were some who doubted Wortmann's motives, however, and it was openly suggested that he was nothing less than a Nazi. One of his accusers was Charles Ornstein, a Jewish member of the American Olympic Association whom Brundage and Wortmann wanted to expel for his pro-boycott stance. In April, Ornstein told the *New York Times* that the AOC was 'representative not of the sporting spirit of American tradition, but that it has adopted the color and tactics of Nazi Germany [. . .] Dietrich Wortmann was simply following the pattern of the man to whom he gives his allegiance – Adolph Hitler'.

This was robust criticism. Ornstein may well have been overreacting to his treatment and hurling convenient insults, but there was no doubt that if Wortmann was not a Nazi, then he was immensely sympathetic to the Nazi cause. Back in 1928, Wortmann had helped to found the German-American newspaper the *Deutsche Zeitung*, which was sympathetic to Hitler and hostile to the 'Jewish Bolsheviks'. The newspaper was circulated to various Turnvereins – German gymnasiums – in and around New York City, of one of which, the New

York Turnverein, Wortmann was a member. After the Olympics, this Turnverein was accused of being a hotbed of Nazism. In 1933, Samuel Dickstein, a congressman from New York, placed Wortmann on a list of 'smugglers, aliens, agitators, Hitlerites and propagandists' who Dickstein feared were trying to inveigle themselves into American society. It was Wortmann's April 1936 fund-raising letter to German-Americans, however, which attracted the most censure. Written on AOC headed paper, the letter cited the need for 'the united, moral and financial support of all German-Americans so that American Athletes, after competing at the Olympic Games in Berlin, return as apostles of truth and justice for the promotion of friendship between our great countries'.

Unfortunately for Wortmann, the letter fell into the wrong hands. A brouhaha erupted, in which private citizens wrote to Roosevelt himself, stating that the phrase 'apostle of truth and justice' could mean only 'promoters of Nazism'. On 16 April, one June Croll wrote to the president, stating that 'this is outright cooperation with Nazi efforts to utilise the 1936 Olympics for the spread in the United States of race hate, destruction of religious, trade union, and all civil liberties'. A few days later Stephen Early, assistant secretary to the president, wrote to the AOC demanding to know why it had approved the letter. Brundage did not reply until May, informing Early that Wortmann was 'a loyal and patriotic American citizen', who was only trying to foster a sense of goodwill. There is much to support Brundage's claim. After all, not only had Wortmann represented the United States in the Olympics, he had also worked extremely hard to improve the nation's weightlifting programme. Like Brundage, he was fanatical about the Olympic movement, and it may well be that Wortmann's only motivation was to ensure participation for the sake of the Games rather than for the sake of Germany. There can be no doubt, however, that his political sympathies, like Brundage's, dovetailed nicely with his support for an Olympics in Berlin.

Brundage and Wortmann were not the only members of the AOC who liked Hitler. Another was the treasurer, Gustavus Kirby, who wrote that the Fuehrer was 'alert, well-informed, understanding and sympathetic to those whom he knows and trusts and especially with and to the German people who he certainly considers as his children and for whom and to whom he is giving of his best'. Kirby, however, was convinced that the actions of the AOC had been instrumental in getting a fair deal for German Jews:

> [. . .] America's participation in the Olympic Games means not only the success of the Games, but also much to Germany and that there would be no American participation except for the change of attitude of the German government and the German Olympic Committee on the matter of Jewish participation and of anti-Jewish signs and all other propaganda in Germany.

Kirby was always careful to stress how much he respected the Jews, but it was clear that he felt a great deal of antipathy towards them. He let his full anti-Semitism slip in a letter to Brundage on 27 May. Kirby was clearly still exasperated by the 'rampant opposition' to the Games, and knew exactly who was to blame.

> Dear Avery,
> I take it that the fundamental difference between me and you is that you are a Jew hater and Jew baiter and I am neither; that you enjoy being hated and despised and threatened by the Jews and I don't: you have made no promises to the Jews and I have.
> You live in Chicago where the Jewish issue may be dead or gone; I live in New York, where, notwithstanding your thought to the contrary, Jewish opposition and Jewish action is [sic] still very much alive [. . .]
> I honestly believe [. . .] that the Jews ought to be everlastingly thankful to the American Olympic Committee, to the Amateur Athletic Union, and to me, for having both ameliorated and put off the evil day of their persecutions and I don't believe in persecutions – no more than I believe in boycott. That doesn't mean that I don't believe that countries ought to rid themselves of their undesirable citizens and inhabitants, for if I had my way right here in our own too true radically becoming U.S.A. I would chuck out thousand [sic] of our Reds, Jews and Gentile alike.

Although Kirby made some sort of nod to even-handedness with the inclusion of Gentiles in his great deportation, it was clear who the target of his mythical policy was. His suggestion that he didn't 'believe in persecutions' contradicted his desire to chuck out those who didn't agree with him or those who weren't 'thankful' enough. Like

Brundage, he believed the Germans really had displayed a volte-face with regard to the Jews, and it was impossible for either man to see why they were still complaining. It could mean only one thing – it was because they were damned Reds.

Brundage replied calmly to Kirby's spirited letter. 'I still think you are wrong about the Jews,' he wrote. 'Even with your forensic ability you are not going to convert them and argument only adds fuel to the flames. I find that good constructive publicity based on Americanism and the philosophy of amateur sport and the Olympic Games is more effective than debate on a dead issue.' In other words, Brundage had no wish to argue with anybody on the issue. He found it inconceivable that anybody might have a reasonable viewpoint regarding boycotting the Games. When it came to dealing with Kirby's confident assertion that he was a 'Jew hater', Brundage was brusque: '[. . .] I don't like the first paragraph of your letter. Anyone who has had anything to do with sport knows that hate is a poisonous emotion. Anyhow I am too busy to hate anyone and I certainly do not enjoy being hated.'

If Brundage's words are to be taken at face value, how then did Kirby come to the opinion that Brundage was indeed anti-Semitic, and, furthermore, have the confidence to express it so baldly? Brundage's words do stop short of an outright denial, and his attitude towards the Jews over the previous years could leave few in any doubt as to his true feelings towards them.

If the boycott movement was starting to die out in the United States, in Britain it was slowly coming to life. The Nazis could hardly have been shaking in their highly polished boots when the *Daily Worker* reported on 7 January 1936 that the Grafton Athletic Club in London was considering not allowing its athletes to go to the Games. The writer of the article urged Grafton to ally itself with a wider boycott movement being organised by the National Workers' Sports Association (NWSA), which had already enlisted the help of four athletics clubs, including that of the Post Office Stores (Holloway). Again, this was hardly something that would have threatened Lewald and Diem's sleep.

Over the next two months, however, the NWSA's campaign, led by its general secretary, George Elvin, soon began to gather pace. His efforts were helped by Sir Walter Citrine, the general secretary of the Trades Union Congress and the head of the International Federation of the Trade Unions, who wrote a widely circulated thirty-two-page booklet entitled *Under the Heel of Hitler – the Dictatorship over Sport in Nazi Germany*. Citrine outlined eloquently how the Nazis had politicised sport, broken the Olympic charter and discriminated against the Jews. He concluded by stating that '[. . .] individuals and organisations concerned with the development of the principles of international co-operation in every department of human activity may find themselves the unwitting agents of the Nazi tyranny, and unwillingly assisting it to destroy the foundations of freedom and democracy outside Germany'.

Elvin also drew much succour from the undergraduates at Oxford University. In February, the university's paper, *Isis*, also came out against the Games, declaring that '[. . .] sport has been subordinated to the needs of war. Germany has dragged down sport into the mire of politics. For us to participate in the Olympic Games [. . .] would be to acquiesce in that breach of faith and in that dragging down of sport into the mire of politics. Our duty is clear. We must lift sport out of that mire into which Dr Goebbels has thrown it.' Later that month, Elvin visited Cambridge University, where he addressed the Cambridge Labour Party. Unsurprisingly, its members passed a unanimous resolution calling upon 'all organisations concerned to refrain from participation'. If a handful of Oxbridge undergraduates, a trade unionist and the Post Office Stores (Holloway) Athletics Club were hardly the stuff of a nationwide boycott movement, for Elvin it was a start.

The NWSA's greatest opportunity to effect a boycott was at the Amateur Athletics Association's AGM on 21 March, at which 'fireworks' were predicted. One commentator suggested that the meeting would even match the temperature of the AAU's convention in December 1935. At the meeting, George Elvin moved the resolution 'that the spirit which prompted the organisation of the 1936 Olympic Games cannot be forwarded by participation in the 1936 Olympic Games in Berlin, and instructs the Association to withdraw its support, and to withhold the necessary permission to any members who may make application for a permit to participate'.

Watching Elvin speak to the floor that Saturday were Lord Burghley, the incoming president, and Lord Desborough, the outgoing president, as well as Harold Abrahams. All three were doubtless wondering, in the words of Evan Hunter, whether this was the start of the anticipated 'battle royal before the Summer Games'. Elvin knew that getting the motion passed would be hard work. His supporters inside the room would have amounted to no more than a dozen of the 200 assembled.

Elvin's most redoubtable enemy came in the form of Harold Abrahams, who spoke against the resolution. The fact that Abrahams was Jewish meant that his words carried extra weight, as the chief *raison d'être* of the boycott movement was of course to help Germany's Jews. Abrahams' clout was further enhanced by the fact that he was a former Olympian, and, as an experienced broadcaster, he spoke well in public. 'I know that there is not a single person in this room who does not deplore the conditions in Germany today; but, in spite of these conditions, I ask myself whether it is ultimately in the best interests of world sport and better world relationships that the AAA should pass this resolution and withdraw from the Games.' He then spoke of how the British Olympic Association and the IOC had, rightly or wrongly, decided to support the Games. He continued:

> [. . .] if I had been born in Germany, knowing myself as I do, I doubt if I should be alive today. But I still think the right thing is for us to show the German people what Great Britain believes to be real sport. After all, in my opinion, to isolate an individual because his behaviour does not meet with your approval never ultimately achieves anything. Countries are only collections of individuals, and to isolate Germany will never achieve what we all ultimately want, namely the furtherance of those ideals in sport – absolute freedom for all to participate – in which we all believe. [. . .] I [. . .] do not believe that any real good will come if this resolution is adopted; on the contrary, I believe that it will do harm.

Here at last was a cogent case for the need to participate. Rather than relying on Brundage-style *ad hominem* assaults and accusations of anti-patriotism, Abrahams had presented a reasoned and reasonable argument. Another difference between Abrahams and Brundage was that the Englishman was in no doubt as to the severity of the situation in Germany. Whereas Brundage wanted to participate in Germany because things were supposedly not as bad as they seemed, Abrahams wanted to participate because things *were* that bad. The weakness of Abrahams' position was his belief that showing the Germans 'real sport' would make any difference to the behaviour of the regime. Hitler did not listen to foreign diplomats and statesmen, so why would he listen to, say, Bill Roberts?

Elvin realised that the resolution would be defeated by a large majority, but Abrahams was decent enough to propose passing a resolution stating that the AAA acknowledged the conditions in Germany, but thought it in 'the best interest of world sport' to participate. Lord Desborough, the outgoing president, was not happy with this, and spoke forcefully against passing any resolutions at all. Eventually, a compromise was mooted: if Elvin withdrew his resolution, then the General Committee of the AAA would call a special meeting within the next two months if Elvin required it. This was the best result Elvin could have wished for, and so he accepted it. It bought him a little more time, perhaps enough to work on those who had their doubts about participation. According to the *Manchester Guardian*, there were 'many' in this position. Others doubted whether there was even a boycott movement at all. 'The British boycott [. . .] is now dead, killed or coffined by Mr Abrahams, according to whether or not one believes it was dead already,' said the *Jewish Chronicle*. Abrahams, however, did have his doubts about his position. He told the newspaper that although he had been invited to Berlin to accompany the British team, he would not go if he could be convinced 'that such action would do more harm than good to German Jewry'. His promise was not an empty one. 'I want you to understand,' he said, 'that this offer is made in all seriousness.'

On the following Monday, Elvin brought together some two thousand people at Shoreditch Town Hall at a meeting to 'arouse public opinion against the deplorable conditions of refugees from Nazi Germany'. Elvin found it easier to get a resolution passed at this meeting. The resolution declared that 'no time was to be lost for the cause of peace and progress if the entire annihilation of the Jews in Germany was to be prevented'. Elvin's father, the trade unionist H. H. Elvin, supported the motion, with a speech that anti-appeasers like Vansittart, Phipps and Churchill would have strongly approved of.

An appeal has been made in certain quarters that the great nations should participate in the Olympic Games, since otherwise the difficult European situation might be aggravated. But we should have no hesitation – now is the time for bold action and not for timidity. If the British Government desires peace and wants to save the minorities from persecution, it should hit hard at the prestige which Hitler is trying to build up in Germany.

Elvin spent the next two months attempting to rustle up some more support. His campaign was boosted by Sir Stafford Cripps, the Labour MP and former Solicitor-General, who, as president of the British Workers' Sports Association, promised to support Elvin's efforts. Emboldened, Elvin decided to ask for his special meeting of the AAA, which was subsequently scheduled for Saturday, 23 May. His confidence was increased by the number of messages of support he received from delegates who now realised that conditions in Germany were as bad as Elvin maintained. Elvin knew that although he had a very slim chance of winning, there was a chance that the result might be tight enough for him to continue his battle.

There can be no doubt that George Elvin was not on the guest list for the annual dinner of the BOA held on 19 May at the Dorchester Hotel. Assembled there in white tie were the great and the good of British athletics – Lords Aberdare, Burghley and Portal, as well as Sir Thomas Inskip, the minister for co-ordination of defence. Also seated with them at the top table was none other than Lewald, who had come over to Britain for the event. He was accompanied by Prince Otto von Bismarck, the chargé d'affaires at the German embassy. The toast was proposed by Sir Robert Horne, who welcomed Lewald, and then said, 'In these times of anxiety and trouble, might we not welcome the Games as a happy augury for Europe and the world, in which Germany plays so powerful a part?' Lord Portal replied to Sir Robert by saying that there was no need to consider sanctions in sport. 'Here we have a wonderful country,' he said, referring to Germany, 'which is offering hospitality and guaranteeing fair treatment. We will go to Germany with the esprit de corps and confidence of all right-minded Englishmen behind us. The contacts and the comradeship which we will establish will help enormously to restore the friendship we have always had in the past for a great nation like Germany.'

This was classic appeasing talk, but it got worse. Sir Thomas Inskip then rose, and said that he hoped one result of the Olympics would be to make his job a sinecure. 'I hope that Prince Otto von Bismarck, when he writes his next dispatch, will record that there are a great many warm feelings towards his country,' he said, 'and furthermore, that we would like bygones to be bygones and to march together in good will, in which alone lies the hope of posterity.' When Lewald came to speak, he told his hosts that Hitler had 'great enthusiasm for the Olympic ideal, and he promises that the whole German population will do their utmost to make the Olympic Games a festival of peace'. Barring a meeting of the Anglo-German Fellowship, it would be hard to imagine a gathering of greater appeasers.

The AAA delegates gathered at the London Polytechnic on Regent Street four days later. Once again, Elvin presented a resolution that advocated a boycott, declaring that participation 'would not be of service and value to sport, would not further friendship of the peoples, and would not assist the ennoblement of humanity, which were in the fundamentals of the Olympic idea'. This was perhaps a little too highfalutin for the delegates, and Elvin knew that his appeal had fallen on stony ground when all but one of the subsequent speakers spoke against the motion. D. G. A. Lowe, the honorary secretary of the AAA, made the point that not one of the 180 athletes invited to represent Britain had declined. When the vote was cast, the result was far worse than Elvin could have anticipated. Two hundred voted against him – a mere eight were in favour. If the British boycott movement was not dead before the meeting, then it was certainly dead after it.

Elvin's efforts, although valiant, were always doomed to fail. The primary reason was the appeasing mood of the times. If the politicians were not adopting a tough stance against Germany, then why should sportsmen? The Great War had ended only eighteen years earlier, and there were too many who had lost fathers, husbands, brothers and sons in the trenches. The predominant fear was that playing tough with Germany would lead to another slaughter. Far better to let Hitler have what he wanted and enjoy some peace. Many also doubted that conditions in Germany were as bad as they were being painted, and when it came to the Olympics, they were reassured by the promises that the Germans had made to the IOC concerning the treatment of Jews. In the magazine *World Sports*, Lord Aberdare informed readers that Lewald and von Halt had 'declared emphatically that the pledge given at Vienna had been loyally kept'. In addition, Aberdare wrote of 'letters from the Clubs of the Association of Jewish Ex-Soldiers, and from the Club of the Makkabikreis, the two important Jewish Associations, [that] prove conclusively that as a result of the assurance given to the IOC at Vienna, Jewish athletes have received an even better opportunity to display their worth than in previous years'. This was astonishing. Aberdare was actually suggesting that conditions for Jewish sportsmen were improving in Germany. But who would dispute him? After all, not only was Aberdare a peer, he was also a member of the IOC – two seemingly excellent reasons to believe what he said. Besides, caring about the plight of Jews in Germany was not something that many gave priority to – the world was in a depression, and for many the simple act of feeding one's own family was more of a concern. Those who did care about the Jews were often dismissed as communists and Jews, a charge that stuck because it was largely correct. As neither communists nor Jews were particularly adored by the British public, then it was hardly surprising to find that their concerns were of marginal importance. Had a figure from the right spoken against the Games, then the boycott movement might have stood a chance. The only likely candidate would have been Winston Churchill, but he was languishing in the political wilderness.

If it was not possible to boycott the Games, then there was another form of protest available to the Elvins and the Mahoneys – the grandly styled People's Olympic Games in Barcelona. This rival Olympics, which was to be staged from 19 to 26 July, was established by the Popular Front shortly after it had defeated the right-wing National Front in the Spanish general election. The Popular Front was not allowing Spanish athletes to go to Germany, and the idea of mounting an alternative Games in the city that came second to Berlin was therefore an attractive one. Its official object was 'to counter the Berlin games with a popular sports festival which does not hope for record feats, but intends to preserve the true Olympic spirit of peace and co-operation between nations'. Avery Brundage dismissed the event as the 'Communist Games', which was not entirely without foundation.

The organisers of the 'Olimpiada Popular' had a lot to achieve in a very short time. Whereas Lewald and Diem had the best part of five years to organise their Games, the Spanish had only a few months. Indeed, their invitation to the AAU in the United States was sent out only on 22 June – less than a month before the Games were due to start. The text of the invitation was both sincere and delightfully amateur:

> We regret that the time for preparation is so short, but it was only after the triumph of the Spanish Peoples' Front that the conception of our Olympiad became possible, and even then we unfortunately had no American addresses to write to. Now that we have managed to obtain these addresses we hope that you will do your utmost to attend the Games. [. . .] In the struggle against fascism, the broad masses of all countries must stand shoulder to shoulder, and Popular Sport is a valuable medium through which they may demonstrate their international solidarity.

Nevertheless, the organising committee was able to boast that over ten thousand athletes from twenty countries – including the Soviet Union, Canada, Poland, Palestine, Denmark, Norway, Sweden, France and Holland – were coming. Most of these athletes were not those who were going to Berlin. Instead, they came from workers' sports associations and similarly left-wing athletic clubs. The committee claimed that 1,500 athletes were coming from France alone, and that the French government had given 500,000 francs towards the expenses of their sportsmen. (The French were still vacillating about whether they would send a team to Berlin.) The figure of 10,000 seems ludicrously high when compared to Berlin's 4,000. No doubt the committee was doing what all good salesmen do, and claiming an inflated number of takers.

For British organisations such as the British Workers' Sports Association, the People's Olympics was a great opportunity to mount a small protest against Berlin. It hoped to send some forty athletes, led by George Elvin, and the grateful Spanish agreed to send at least £50 to help cover their costs. The AAA, however, was reluctant to allow any of its members – which included the BWSA – to go, as it feared that the Spanish Amateur Athletics Association had not given its blessing to the rival games. When it was pointed out by the *Daily Worker* that the Spanish AAA did in fact support the Games, the splendidly named G. H. Hogsflesh, the assistant secretary of the AAA, declared that a permit would be issued immediately.

Elvin's team consisted of some good, although by no means top-rate, athletes. Bernard Bamber had won the men's singles and doubles in tennis at the 1935 Paris Sports Festival. L. R. Pearce held Hampshire's record for the mile and the half-mile. E. G. Cupid was not only the Workers' European 100 yards title-holder, but also the Welsh champion over the same distance. Their leader himself could claim to be an international sportsman, as the heavily bespectacled Elvin had represented the BWSA at nothing less than table tennis at a match in Czechoslovakia. The team was due to leave on Friday, 17 July, but on Tuesday 14th they received some bad news. The AAA was withdrawing their permits. Apparently, the Association had been instructed by the IAAF to do so, as the Spanish AAA had still not recognised the Games. 'This is not the case,' Elvin fumed. 'I received assurances by cable and letter weeks ago that everything was in order.' Elvin telephoned the Spanish, who denied that they had not sanctioned the Games and cabled the British AAA to tell it so. A conspiracy theorist might deduce that someone at the British AAA was trying to stymie Elvin and his little band, but with an absence of evidence, we must assume a glitch. On the morning of the 17th, the team departed from Victoria Station amid a fanfare of bagpipes and cheered on by a hundred well-wishers. Elvin's father made a speech that urged the team to be spurred on by what he saw as the AAA's attempt to thwart them. 'Find incentive from such efforts to bring greater glory at Barcelona,' he enthused. 'Return proud of your efforts. Uphold the standards of fair play and prestige which our movement enjoys.' And with that, the train steamed out of the station. They were to return sooner than they had anticipated.

While the boycott movements were in their death throes, the diplomats were still discussing how to deal with Germany. On 17 June, Sir Eric Phipps wrote to the British Foreign Secretary, Anthony Eden, informing him that 'the Chancellor is in great form and has no intention of replying seriously to our questions'. Phipps was referring to the questionnaire that Eden had sent Hitler the previous month.

The questionnaire was intended to flush out Hitler's ambitions, by asking him a series of direct questions that the dictator would find hard not to answer directly. First, Eden asked Hitler whether he was in a position to negotiate what he called 'genuine treaties'. Second, Eden wondered whether Hitler drew a distinction between the Reich and the German nation. 'I had in mind that Hitler might regard himself as a protector, or even ruler, of German communities in Austria, Danzig or Czechoslovakia,' Eden wrote. 'If Hitler still had claims to make, the world had better know them.' The third question asked whether Hitler intended to 'respect the existing territorial and political status of Europe'. There were other subsidiary questions, but these three constituted the meat of the document.

Phipps told Eden that 'a very good source' had informed him that Hitler was 'rather disposed to answer with his tongue in his cheek' the question about future treaties. There was little hope that Hitler would answer the remaining two questions, as he resented them even being asked. Phipps reported, however, that Hitler continued 'to express feelings of admiration for Great Britain and the British people [. . .] what he really hankers after, however, is an Anglo-German understanding to the exclusion of third or fourth parties'. From Hitler's standpoint, reaching an agreement with the British did not seem that unlikely. 'The Chancellor's happiness would be complete,' wrote Phipps, 'if Labour came into office in England and based their policy on the letters which appear in *The Times*, especially those over several signatures. He reads these with particular satisfaction.' *The Times*, under the editorship of Geoffrey Dawson, was 'all for collaboration with Germany', much to the frustration of Anthony Eden, who saw the paper's position as an obstacle. 'If we are to pursue an effective foreign policy in Europe,' he wrote, 'it is essential that it should be made clear that *The Times*, with its defeatist leaders, does not represent His Majesty's Government.' Phipps was utterly contemptuous of Robert Barrington-Ward, the newspaper's deputy editor, with whom he had lunched in early June.

> I hardly got any chance for a private conversation with B.W.: but I had already heard that he was very pro-German. The weekend they previously spent with Bernstorff may have opened their eyes a bit; but probably an interview he had with Hess was even more useful.

Contact with full-blooded Nazis is invaluable in such cases. All foreign
editors and leader-writers in the 'Times' should be sent over here for
a little education. This is apt to wear off after a few weeks spent in our
fat, weak and comfortable little land, but it all helps.

Phipps's brother-in-law was equally depressed by Britain. 'Hitler has
never meant business in our sense of the word,' Vansittart wrote to
his brother-in-law in Berlin. 'The sooner the Cabinet realise that,
the better for this long misguided country.' But Vansittart and Phipps
did not represent the majority opinion in Britain. With an appeasing *Times* and a misguided cabinet, it was hardly surprising that
Hitler saw a chance to make an agreement with the 'comfortable
little land'.

The man Hitler thought best to negotiate any deal with the British
was Joachim von Ribbentrop. Since the occupation of the Rhineland, Ribbentrop had been working on arranging a secret meeting
between Hitler and the British prime minister, Stanley Baldwin. In
order to achieve this, Ribbentrop had engaged in what would now
be called 'shuttle diplomacy' between Berlin and London. Ribbentrop was not well received in Britain, however, partly because he displayed an obnoxious mixture of gaucheness and arrogance. At a
dinner held at Vansittart's house at the beginning of April, Ribbentrop startled the guests with his behaviour. According to the seating
plan, the German ambassador to Britain, Leopold von Hoesch, was
to sit at the place of honour to Lady Vansittart's right. Ribbentrop,
feeling unjustifiably slighted by this, sat at the ambassador's seat before
he could get to it.

Although Ribbentrop found little favour among the mandarins, he
gained a sympathetic ear in the form of Thomas Jones, a retired senior
civil servant who had kept in contact with many senior figures,
including Stanley Baldwin. Jones met Ribbentrop on numerous occasions, and he did not find him the 'ass' that Vansittart and Phipps
found. In the middle of May, Jones had flown to Germany to stay with
Ribbentrop at his home in the Dahlem area of Berlin, which had
once been used by Hitler, Papen and Goering as a secret meeting
place before the Nazis had come to power. Jones found the atmosphere in the house very congenial. 'One might be in Surrey or Sussex,
so English did it seem. There are three butlers, an adjutant in full

uniform, a private secretary, and a stenographer who speaks English and has studied at the School of Economics in London.' During their meeting, which took place on a Saturday morning, Jones noticed the plethora of English books lining the shelves in Ribbentrop's study, including Lytton Strachey's *Elizabeth and Essex*, T. E. Lawrence's *Revolt in the Desert*, and *Oliver Twist*. Ribbentrop lectured Jones on the need for Hitler to meet Baldwin, because Hitler was 'not the dictator in conversation', he maintained. After the meeting, Ribbentrop took Jones on a tour of the Olympic Stadium and the Olympic village. Ribbentrop clearly wanted to impress Jones with the new buildings, but Jones had his mind on his meeting with Hitler on Sunday.

Jones met the Fuehrer at 12.15 at his flat in Munich. Hitler 'made no attempt to impress or "aggress" his visitor' and instead seemed the model of bourgeois tranquillity, 'dressed in his Sunday best, all fresh from the laundry'. Jones told Hitler that it would be best if Germany replied to the questionnaire, which Hitler evaded by stating that what he 'wished most of all was to achieve some solid piece of security in Europe', so long as the British and the French fell in with Germany. Hitler told Jones that he greatly wished to see Stanley Baldwin, but Jones parried this by saying that Baldwin was a 'shy and modest states-man'. When Jones returned to London, Baldwin told him that he did not wish to see Hitler, because he 'did not fly and did not like the sea'.

Nevertheless, Ribbentrop was pleased with this tentative opening, and came to London at the end of May, bringing with him several invitations to the Olympics, which he distributed around sympathetic London society figures. On the evening of the 29th, the Conservative MP and socialite Henry 'Chips' Channon dined with Ribbentrop and his wife. Channon, who was an appeaser, had mixed feelings about the German couple.

> Frau von Ribbentrop is distinguished in the Berlin manner, that is she has intelligent eyes, appalling khaki coloured clothes and an un-powdered, un-painted face. How can the Germans be so silly about things that don't matter, or is it because their women are so unattrac-tive that the race is largely homosexual? He, Ribbentrop, looks like the captain of someone's yacht, square, breezy, and with a sea-going look [. . .] He is not quite without charm, but shakes hands in a over-hearty way [. . .]

Ribbentrop's nautical aspect was not matched by an ability to sail. He spent the weekend with Lord Londonderry in Northern Ireland, where he competed in a yacht race on Strangford Lough. Ribbentrop fell overboard, and had to be rescued with a boat hook.

Despite this *infra dig* mishap, Ribbentrop continued to woo all those he thought might help secure a secret meeting between Hitler and Baldwin. He lunched with Thomas Jones at the Carlton Club, where the genial Welshman told the German about Baldwin's reluctance to take to the sky or sea. Jones assumed that Hitler would not wish to visit Britain, with which Ribbentrop concurred, but he told Jones that he 'could arrange for Hitler to come quite close to our coast, two or three miles from Dover or Folkestone'. Jones then took Ribbentrop down to Kent, where he met Lord Lothian and Sir Thomas Inskip, the minister for co-ordination of defence, who had been present at the BOA annual dinner at the Dorchester a few days earlier. Ribbentrop impressed the two men, and they sat up until the small hours, discussing how the future of Europe might look if there was an agreement between Britain and Germany. Back in London, Ribbentrop met the editor of *The Times*, Geoffrey Dawson, and once again spent an evening with Chips Channon and his wife, who he invited to the Olympics.

Ribbentrop returned to Berlin in a mood of optimism. As everybody he had met was pro-German, he mistakenly assumed that this was the mood of the country, as well as that of the prime minister, telling Goebbels that Baldwin was 'completely on the German side'. Ribbentrop's bubble was soon pricked by Anthony Eden, however, who was adamant that no meeting between Hitler and Baldwin should take place, a suggestion that met with the approval of Baldwin, who found the whole matter of a clandestine rendezvous like something out of a spy novel. Thomas Jones wrote to Ribbentrop, telling him that the 'project of an open meeting must be regularised'. Ribbentrop was livid, not least because his failure to deliver the secret meeting put him out of Hitler's favour.

The German Foreign Secretary, von Neurath, now saw an opportunity to get rid of the meddling Ribbentrop, and he suggested to Hitler that Ribbentrop should be appointed ambassador to London to replace von Hoesch, who had died in April. This was a sly move by von Neurath, as he suspected Ribbentrop would be a failure in Britain. 'After three months in London, Ribbentrop will be done for,' he secretly told Papen. 'They can't stand him there and we will be rid of him for good and all.' Hitler agreed with Neurath, not because he wanted to get rid him, but because he still felt that Ribbentrop might be able to deliver an Anglo-German agreement. Despite much complaining from Neurath, Ribbentrop still kept control of his *Büro*. Other members of the Nazi hierarchy were far from delighted – Goering even told Hitler that Ribbentrop knew little about foreign countries apart from their national drinks. When Hitler replied that Ribbentrop knew a great many British lords, Goering replied, 'Yes – the trouble is, they know Ribbentrop.' The new ambassador received his formal letter of appointment just before the Olympic Games on 27 July, and Ribbentrop was even less pleased than his fellow Nazis. He had wanted to replace Neurath at the Foreign Ministry, but now he was being marginalised. Nevertheless, the Olympic Games would prove to be a great opportunity for Ribbentrop to show that, more than just an ambassador, he was a strutter on the world's stage. He and his wife were going to host a vast party at their house in Dahlem, and everybody who was anybody in Berlin during the Olympic fortnight would be invited.

Surprisingly, among them would be Sir Robert Vansittart, who had decided to come to the Games in order to give his brother-in-law some support. Recently, Phipps had been coming under attack in Britain for not pursuing a more appeasing line with Germany. At the end of June, Vansittart told him that

[. . .] since Ribbentrop's visit [to Britain] there had been a sort of intangible whispering campaign against you, based on nothing in particular but run, I think, by the ultra pro-German section in this country. You need not, of course, pay any attention to it. It represents nothing and, as you know, you have of course full support here.

Nevertheless Vansittart saw the matter as being sufficiently troubling for him to use the Games as an excuse to go to Berlin. As Phipps's wife was ill, Vansittart suggested that his own wife, Sarita, could 'play hostess' at the embassy during his visit, although his reason for being in Berlin was, superficially, 'a sporting one'. Nobody would believe this, of course, especially since Vansittart expressed no great desire to see the Games, telling Phipps that he would keep his ticket 'in reserve [. . .] in case I came'. For Vansittart, the real Games in Berlin would be diplomatic ones, in which the highlight would be the contest between him and Ribbentrop. 'The sporting events offered a very favourable opportunity to make contact with politicians and prominent men in the most diverse camps,' Ribbentrop was to write. 'I was also glad that Sir Robert and Lady Vansittart had accepted my invitation.' Ribbentrop's gladness could not have been more misjudged.

The weather in New York City during the weekend of 11/12th July 1936 was hardly ideal for the Olympic try-out finals – it was hot and humid. Indeed, it was said to have been the hottest week in many years, with the temperature reaching 36 degrees. All over the United States there had been forest fires and water shortages, and some 375 people had died because of the heat. (By 16 July that figure would climb to 4,137.) The try-outs were being held on Randall's Island, in a 22,000-seat stadium constructed under the recently completed Triborough Bridge. However, according to one journalist, the event had been organised 'about as systematically as the potato races at a church bazaar'. The stadium was half empty, and there were numerous technical difficulties with the loudspeakers.

The three heats for the 100 metres were held at around three o'clock on the Saturday afternoon. Both Jesse Owens and Marty Glickman were there, as was Owens' potential nemesis, Eulace Peacock. Owens, however, had recently had a piece of luck – Peacock was suffering from a bad hamstring injury. His right thigh was taped up, and although he had failed to qualify for the finals because of the injury, the AOC officials had given him special dispensation to come to Randall's Island. Peacock did his best in his heat, but it was hopeless – he limped in last. His long jump attempts were similarly feeble; he proved himself incapable of clearing 22 feet. Peacock's bad luck surely meant that Owens would be going to Berlin. With no serious competition to worry him, he easily made it to the 100 metres final that afternoon.

The final was supposed to have been held at 5.15, but the humidity had transformed itself into a thunderstorm. The wait made the finalists even more tense as they took shelter from the downpour.

Among them was Marty Glickman. 'I had been tense all week,' he recalled, 'unable to sleep much because of nerves and the heat.' Glickman waited in the locker room, which afforded him some coolness. Nevertheless, his nerves were so bad that when he finally walked out into the heat of the stadium he was almost sick with fright. It was hardly surprising. Glickman was in lane five, and to his left in lane four was Owens. To his right was Ralph Metcalfe, who had won the silver medal in 1932. His fellow Jew Sam Stoller was in lane seven.

'I trembled as I started digging a hole in the cinders,' said Glickman. 'We were called to our marks. I put my left foot in first, as you usually do, but my leg was quivering so much I couldn't get it in the hole. All the other guys were down in a crouch, almost ready to go. That was the only time this ever happened to me. It was agonising, and I was fearful I wouldn't stop shaking.'

The starter, noticing Glickman's nerves, told the runners to get up.

'Walk a little, Marty, jog up and back a bit, relax.'

Glickman did so and calmed down. Once more the athletes were called to their marks, ready to explode forward at the sound of the gun.

'I do not remember the gun, but we were running,' said Glickman.

For the first 25 or 35 metres, the boy from Brooklyn kept up with the boys from the Deep South. But then they pulled away, as if they were on 'a moving escalator at an airport'. He knew that he would never catch them, but he was hopeful that he might finish third. He looked out of the corner of his eye – the others were close behind, but he remained ahead. Stoller was miles back, having a terrible race.

Glickman crossed the line. I'm third, he thought, with visions of running in the 100 metre final in Berlin coursing through his brain. As he undid his shoelaces, he was interviewed by Ted Husing, the leading sports commentator. But before the interview could begin, Husing heard over his headphones that Glickman had come fifth, behind not only Owens and Metcalfe, but also behind Foy Draper and Frank Wykoff from the University of Southern California, whose coach could be seen lobbying the finishing-line judges. Although he would never be able to prove it, Glickman suspected the USC team of cheating. It meant that he was out of the 100 metres. There was some good news, however, his fifth place meant that he had made the team, as had Sam Stoller, but only as participants in the 4 x 100 relay. It was still a fabulous achievement, but the Fastest Kid on the Block felt robbed.

The swimming finals were held simultaneously at the Astoria Pool in Long Island. One of those who entered was Iris Cummings from Los Angeles, who had recently won the national championships in June at Manhattan Beach on Long Island. A lack of money meant, however, that she could not return to the West Coast, and the seventeen-year-old Cummings had to spend a month staying with her grandmother in Philadelphia, where she found it hard to train. 'I had to swim after hours,' she recalled, 'because the pools wouldn't let someone in who just wanted to swim laps. These circumstances were not at all conducive to training. You just had to get by.'

The training paid off, and Cummings came third in the finals, which was good enough to get her on to the team. She was soon to find, however, that her place was not secure. At the beginning of the following week, all the third-placed athletes were summoned to a Manhattan hotel, where they were told by Daniel Ferris of the AOC that because of a shortage of funds, their places were in question. 'All you people go on your little horses and go home and try to raise some more money,' Cummings recalled Ferris saying, although perhaps not in so condescending a manner. Cummings came back to the hotel a few days later, and was told that she would be able to go, although many of the 'alternates' – athletes who would replace those who were injured – were not able to go. Cummings was escorted to Berlin by her mother, who 'scraped up enough money to go over there for a week'.

The athletes were made to understand that the boycott movement was to blame for the lack of money. Like many swimmers, Cummings was particularly aware of the boycott issue, because Charlotte Epstein, the Jewish coach of the Women's Swimming Association of New York and the most likely candidate to be the Olympic coach, had decided not to go to Berlin. 'She trained Eleanor Holm, among others,' Cummings recalled, 'and she told them, "You're on your own. I cannot do it."'

Epstein was one of the very few Americans to boycott the Games. She was joined in her decision by three other Jews, Milton Green, Norman Cahners and Herman Neugass. Of these, Green was the most distinguished – he jointly held the world record of 5.8 seconds in the 45-yard hurdles and had been selected to compete at Randall's Island. Cahners, Green's room-mate at Harvard University, had also been selected, but the two were dissuaded by their rabbi, who told them what was happening in Germany. According to Green, the meeting was a 'shocker'. 'He suggested the boycott,' Green recalled, 'and we talked it over with our families and decided.' Their coach tried to change their minds, but he failed. In this, he was no more successful than the Olympic coach Lawson Robertson, who asked sprinter Herman Neugass to reconsider his boycott. Neugass had decided not to try for Berlin in December 1935, after he heard about that year's Nuremberg Laws. He wrote to the *New Orleans Times-Picayune*, saying that he had been informed by an 'unimpeachable authority' that the Germans were discriminating against the Jews.

Other Jews around the world boycotted the Games as well. Three female Austrian swimmers, who were members of the Austrian Jewish sports association called 'Hakoah' (Strength), decided not to go. One of them, Ruth Langer, was only fifteen, yet she was already the Austrian champion in the 100 metre and 400 metre freestyle. Because of their refusal to go to Berlin, the Federation of Austrian Swimming Clubs banned Langer and her two teammates from competing for life, and stripped them of their records 'due to severe damage of Austrian sports' and 'gross disrespect for the Olympic spirit'. In Denmark, Abraham Kurland, the winner of the silver medal at Los Angeles for Greco-Roman wrestling, also boycotted the Games. 'Many people wrote to him and called him up, telling him not to go,' his brother Simon Kurland recalled. 'My family and I also told him that he shouldn't go. At first, he wanted to, but then he got lots of information about the Jews in Germany. He received letters from Germany, many of which were anonymous. That's when he decided not to go.' In Canada, two Jewish boxers, Yisrael Luftspring and Norman Yack, told the *Toronto Globe* that they would not be trying for Berlin because 'we would have been very loath to hurt the feelings of our fellow Jews by going to a land that would exterminate them if it could'. Jews had also boycotted the Winter Olympics. Perhaps the most notable was Philippe de Rothschild, who had competed in the bobsleigh at the 1928 St Moritz Games.

★

Saturday, 11 July was as wet in Britain as it was in New York City. There were thunderstorms all over the country, and many boats had been struck by lightning. By the time the final of the 440 yards was due to start at 5.15, the cinders on the track at the White City stadium in West London were not only sodden, but also worn and rutted by the afternoon's previous competitors. Bill Roberts took his place in lane four next to Godfrey Brown in lane five, and Godfrey Rampling in lane six. The eyes of the stadium were on this trio, as they were the best in the country. As he crouched down, however, Roberts knew that if he finished outside the top three places, then he was unlikely to be getting a train ticket to Berlin.

After the starting pistol went off, Brown powered into an early lead, his relaxed running style belying his immense power. Roberts ran close behind him, with Rampling narrowly in third place. Roberts knew that he not only had to beat Brown, but that he also had to stop being beaten by Rampling. At the start of the last 200 metres, Roberts put the pressure on Brown, gradually closing the gap. But Brown was too strong and staved off the assault from the 'Salford Lad'. The attempt was to prove costly to Roberts, because his pace started to diminish. Rampling saw his chance just a few metres away from the finishing line, and with a supreme effort he swept past Roberts to take second place. Roberts had done enough by finishing third, yet his time of fifty seconds was well short of his personal best. The sogginess of the cinders could be blamed, but so too could Roberts' inexperience. His tactics left something to be desired, but for the time being he could justifiably congratulate himself that he was on his way to Germany to represent his country in the Olympics. Despite his achievement, Roberts' employers would not give him the two weeks off in August. The time therefore had to be regarded as his annual leave – a problem not shared by his fellow relay runners, who were to be Brown, Rampling and Woolf. Nevertheless, as a result of the imminent events in Berlin, the men would share a bond that transcended class barriers and would last until the ends of their lives.

The letter that sealed Gretel Bergmann's fate was dated 16 July 1936. There was nothing personal about it, nothing anodyne. It was simply a standard form letter, one issued to thousands of aspiring German

Olympians. It told Bergmann that because of her 'mediocre perfor-
mances', she had not been selected to compete in Berlin. An insulting
panacea came in the form of an offer of a standing-room ticket for the
Games, which Bergmann declined. 'I read it again and again and again,'
Bergmann recalled. 'And then, instead of tears, a stream of invectives
came pouring out of my mouth.' Two years of highs and lows had come
to this point. Her dream of competing in order to show the Nazis what
a Jew was capable of had come to nothing, her efforts stymied by an
Olympic committee conspiring with a despicable regime. Seeking soli-
tude, Bergmann travelled to Baden-Baden and stayed under an assumed
name. What was she to do now? There was only one thing she could
do, and that was to leave Germany. She made the decision, she said, in
less time that it took her to decide what to wear when she got up.

She returned home, and booked an appointment with the American
consul-general in Stuttgart, who encouraged her to migrate to the
United States. A rich friend of her father who had moved there had
promised to sponsor her, and so, just before the Olympic Games started,
Bergmann found herself posting a letter asking whether she could take
him up on his offer. It would be several weeks before she heard back
from him. In the meantime, she had to endure the fact that the mysterious Dora from Ettlingen and Elfriede Kaun, neither of whom were
aware of the truth, would be competing instead of her. 'We were told
that Gretel Bergmann was injured,' Kaun recalled, 'and we were told
that her place would be kept open until she was fit enough to join the
competition. I was a friend of Gretel's, and so I started writing letters
to her, but I never got an answer. I wanted to know what happened,
and how she was, but I never heard.' Kaun said she never guessed that
the Nazis were lying: 'We never suspected anything because her place
was always kept open.' The Nazis had timed their letter to Bergmann
well. By the time the news got out that she was not competing, the
American team was already on the high seas. There was no way they
would turn round, not for the sake of one Jewish girl.

As well as ensuring that as few Jews as possible would appear on their
team, Lewald and Diem had been working hard since the beginning
of the year to guarantee the success of the Games. One aspect of the
coordination they did not need to worry about was the propaganda

for the event, as this had been taken over by Goebbels' Propaganda Ministry in January. This raised eyebrows around the world, not least in the editorial pages of the *New York Times*, which commented wryly that 'from the Nazi standpoint a man can do 100 meters under 11 seconds in a manner that is beneficial to the State or inimical to the State'. In fact, the German state was exerting such a stranglehold over the GOC that its list of members reads like a Who's Who of the Third Reich; many of them were to find notoriety as the worst disciples of Nazism. The list included the loathsome chief of the Reich Security Head Office, Gruppenfuehrer Reinhard Heydrich, who was later to become Protector of Bohemia and Moravia until he was assassinated by SOE-trained Czech agents in 1942. His former deputy and fellow GOC member, Police General Kurt Daluege, succeeded Heydrich as Protector, and was responsible for the brutal reprisals that followed Heydrich's killing. Daluege was hanged by the Czechs in 1946. Lieutenant General von Reichenau was to earn his reputation as a liquidator of Jews on the Russian front, for which he would have been tried at Nuremberg had he not died in a plane crash in 1942. His fellow army officer, Lieutenant General Keitel, also sat on the committee. It was Keitel who was to issue the infamous 'Night and Fog' decree in 1941 that enabled the Nazis to execute without trial, and for which Keitel was hanged at Nuremberg.

As the mighty stadium neared completion and the boycott movement died down, Lewald and Diem could start to reassure themselves that the Games were definitely going to take place. A physical manifestation of the coming of the Olympics was the transportation of the massive 30,000-pound bell from Bochum, north of Cologne, to Berlin – a journey of well over 300 miles. The bell, the rim of which was inscribed with '*Ich rufe die Jugend der Welt*' ('I call the Youth of the World'), took several weeks to make the journey to the bell-tower on the Mayfield next to the Olympic Stadium. It was mobbed all the way, cheered by schoolchildren and saluted by SS and SA men. At seven o'clock on the morning of 11 May, the bell was hoisted to the top of its 75-metre home, from where its first peals – pitched in E minor – rang out on 20 May. The procession of the bell also anticipated another piece of theatre that would take place in July – the Olympic torch relay from Olympia to Berlin. This was the idea of Carl Diem, and for the past year the timetable for the 2000-mile run, which would involve 3,075 runners, had been worked out in great detail.

There was a piece of the Olympic jigsaw that was not fitting into place, however, and that was Pierre de Coubertin. Unlike the bell, and much to the concern of Lewald and Diem, the penniless baron had so far not given the Games of the XIth Olympiad his ringing endorsement. Coubertin was noticeably non-committal about the Games, despite the fact that Lewald wrote him the most oleaginous of letters. During the Winter Games, Lewald told Coubertin that 'all those who are working for the Olympic Games have spoken of you over and over with so much hearteness [sic], thankfulness and respectfulness'. Lewald knew, however, that smarminess would not be enough to woo Coubertin. What Coubertin wanted more than anything else – apart from money – was recognition. In the same letter, Lewald broached a subject that the IOC had discussed on previous occasions – the awarding of the Nobel Peace Prize to Coubertin. In December, Lewald had told Coubertin that he was asking the Norwegian members of the IOC to have a word with the peace prize's Norwegian awarding committee, and now, in February, he was able to report a small piece of progress.

> As I have been informed by the German minister in Oslo, the Nobel prize was not presented for the last two years, thus it can be very well taken into consideration to present the Nobel Prize for 1936 to you as well as to the Prince Charles of Sweden. After the successful closing of the Winter Games here and the main Games in Berlin I believe that the Nobel Prize will certainly be handed over to you.

It was clear to Coubertin that Lewald was going to be the man to deliver the prize. Although he had so far stopped short of asking Coubertin to endorse the Games, there was enough implication in his letter to make Coubertin realise that this was the price of his prize.

The Germans had another reason for wanting Coubertin to win the prize. In 1934 Carl von Ossietzky was nominated for the 1934 peace prize. Ossietzky was an anti-Nazi journalist who had been imprisoned in February 1933, and subsequently locked up in concentration camps in Sonnenburg and at Esterwegen-Papenburg, where he was forced to do heavy labour, despite having suffered a heart attack. Unfortunately, the nomination for the 1934 prize arrived too late, but when 1936 came and Ossietzky was still incarcerated, it looked likely that he would win the prize for 1935. There was little the Nazis could do about it, but if Lewald, through the IOC, could persuade the awarding committee to present Coubertin with the 1936 award, then the glory of the prize would be reflected on to their Olympics.

By May, Lewald had still not received his endorsement from Coubertin, and so he and Hitler took advantage of Coubertin's impecuniousness and they bribed him. On 25 May, Lewald wrote to Coubertin at his house in Geneva.

> You have not ignored that at Garmisch-Partenkirchen an initiative was taken to put at your disposal – as a sign of profound respect for your life's work, and to ease your worries – some moneys which you will able to dispose of entirely at your discretion, particularly with respect to your family. I have spoken to several people who, in view of the Modern Olympics in Berlin, wish to express their respect and admiration. To my great joy, I have just learned from our Fuehrer and Chancellor who, as you know, enthusiastically defends the Olympic ideal and who infinitely regrets that you are not able to come to help with the Games, has put at my disposal a sum of RM 10,000 – or 12,300 Swiss Francs with a plea to send it to you. It is unnecessary to assure you that this action should never be mentioned in public, and in case there is any question from Baillet-Latour I would respond that Germany, in its capacity as the organiser of the Modern Olympics wishes to contribute to the Coubertin Foundation.

It is hard to put a precise modern figure on the two sums, as the two currencies had a different purchasing power. In 1936, however, 10,000 Reichsmarks had the purchasing power of some $350,000 today, although 12,300 Swiss francs had a value equivalent to around $550,000. If one takes the average, the sum being offered to the poverty-stricken Coubertin was around $450,000. To a man who was having to sell his furniture, the sum was too tempting to resist. There can be little doubt that the money was indeed a bribe, otherwise Lewald would not have urged Coubertin to lie to Baillet-Latour, nor would he have insisted that the money was for the ageing baron's personal use. The conspiratorial nature of the offer was enhanced by the fact that Lewald, upon Coubertin's acceptance, was discreetly going to ask Hjalmar Schacht, the president of the Reichsbank and an old friend of Lewald, to obtain the authority to transfer the money.

As soon as Coubertin accepted the money, Lewald's tone changed from oiliness to one of outright bossiness and censure. Now that the Frenchman had taken the Nazi shilling, and indeed was unable to reveal that he had done so, he was effectively blackmailed into doing whatever Lewald asked of him. At the end of June, Lewald curtly informed Coubertin that his idea of giving a short address to the athletes at the Games 'could not be realised'. He then reprimanded Coubertin for even suggesting it.

> This would not only be an infringement of the regulations of the Olympic Charter, in which it is expressly stated that only the president of the Organising Committee is able to say a short address. It is you yourself who created this regulation and Baillet-Latour is its most faithful and ardent defender. But also, it would not be appreciated in Germany if the first speech made in the monumental new stadium was in French and not in German.

Lewald was also angry with Coubertin over another matter. 'I cannot hide from you my extreme surprise that in your message that you have drafted for the relay of the Olympic torch, you have not given a single mention of the fact that the idea for the torch relay is a purely German idea; it is our friend Diem who briefly mentioned it to me during our voyage trip to Athens in May 1934.'

The idea for the torch relay was indeed Diem's, but Lewald's nationalism was boundless. For the next page and a half, he repeatedly stressed how the organisation of the relay had been German, and how the costs had been borne by the Germans. 'You have probably not given enough thought to how much has gone into realising this idea,' Lewald admonished the old baron, before once again telling Coubertin that it was Germany who had done all the hard work.

Now that Coubertin was in their pocket, the Nazi takeover of the Olympic Games was complete. Not only were the Games being organised by the regime, but they were also being run according to Nazi rules and not those of the IOC. Four thousand athletes would shortly be attending a celebration not only of sport, but of fascism. There was nothing the IOC could do, even if it had wanted to, which it most certainly did not. Coubertin may well have registered some sort of protest, but the bitter old man was greedy for his Nobel Peace Prize and compromised by a huge pile of Reichsmarks. The only place where the true flame of Olympic idealism would burn would be in Barcelona, but events in Spain were beginning to move faster than any athlete.

6

Iberian Interlude

~

THE TABLE-TENNIS-PLAYING George Elvin and his band of worker athletes arrived in Barcelona at 6.30 on the evening of Saturday, 18 July. They were met at the station and driven to the Montjuich stadium before being taken to their hotel just off the city's bustling Las Ramblas thoroughfare. After supper, some members of the team went for a stroll, and found that the atmosphere was somewhat disconcerting. Policemen were stopping cars and questioning the drivers. Several Catalonians approached them and warned them in simple English, 'Plenty revolution soon,' accompanied by hand signals imitating the firing of guns. The warnings were made for good reason. Over the past week, the relationship between the left-wing Republican government and the right-wing rebel Nationalists had disintegrated into violence. By the evening of 17 July, the cities of Pamplona, Saragossa, Oviedo, Salamanca, Avila, Segovia and Cadiz had been captured by the rebels, who controlled large parts of the army. That Saturday saw more fighting, and by the time the athletes were taking their post-prandial constitutional, the rebels controlled one third of Spain. It looked certain that Barcelona would be attacked shortly. Naturally, the worker athletes' sympathies lay with the government, but for the time being there was nothing they could do except go to bed.

At two o'clock that morning, the government broadcast over the radio that all 'good citizens and communists' should be prepared to help the government fight against the rebellious army. As it grew light at about half past four, the team was woken by the sound of gunfire coming from Las Ramblas and the streets around it. Aircraft could also be heard. One of the team members was A. R. Northcott, the president of the Acton Labour Party Sports Section, who was due to play chess at the Games. As the firing sounded distant, Northcott was

147

not unduly alarmed, and went back to sleep until 7.30. 'This time the firing was close at hand,' he recalled, 'one rifle at least apparently being fired on the roof of our hotel.' As well as rifle fire, machine-gun fire and 'big gun fire' could be heard, which suggested that the rebel-controlled army forces were near by. This time, Northcott stayed awake, and he and the rest of the team spent the day incarcerated in the hotel, rushing from window to window to watch the action unfold on the streets below. The team saw one fighter being killed; although what made the situation even more alarming was that some Nationalists were holed up in the church – the Eglise Elpi – next to the hotel. Many priests despised the communist-led Republicans and let their churches be used by the rebels as strongholds and sniper points. As it grew dark, the hotel management informed the team that it had run out of food. Two of the athletes, Ted Harding and E. G. Follett, bravely volunteered to get some from a nearby hotel. As they ran through the streets, they were often stopped by trigger-itchy Republicans on the hunt for Nationalists. The two men made it safely back to the hotel, although not without having to explain themselves several times.

On Monday morning, the team was once more woken by gunfire. More shooting was coming from the tower of the church, and Northcott and a few others went up to the hotel roof to investigate. 'We were ordered down in view of the danger,' he said. 'We were there long enough to confirm that the firing was coming from the church tower and to hear the sing of his bullets.' Throughout the day, the party watched as cars sped past, many of them daubed with 'CNT' (Confederation of Workers) and 'FAI' (Federation of Anarchists), out of the windows of which young fighters brandished rifles. In the after-noon, the team saw Republican forces approaching the church. 'Parties of two or three men were inspecting its surroundings, evidently trying to find an advantageous point to retaliate,' said Northcott. Soon, the sound of a door being broken could be heard, and then, much to the worry of all, flames and smoke started issuing from the windows. A short while later, the team heard cheering coming from the front of the church, and failing to hear any more firing they assumed the sniper had either been burned to death or had been shot. The fire soon spread out of control, however, and given the absence of the fire brigade, the team realised they would have to fight the blaze themselves.

The team members formed a human chain and passed buckets of water along it. While they did so, the female members packed, getting ready for a quick getaway. Eventually, the fire brigade arrived and quickly got the blaze under control, although as one athlete described it, only 'after the preliminary work was done by us'. During the commotion, the team made a grisly discovery – the burned body of the priest, who had supposedly been one of the snipers. 'His body had fallen to the floor, and so badly was it burned, that it was completely beyond recognition,' said R. G. W. Hopkins, who had come to Barcelona to compete in the triple jump. 'Only a limb or two and some ribs could be distinguished.' Despite the drama of the situation, the team members went back inside, and either played the piano or some cards or wrote letters back home. 'To look at us then you would have thought that nothing had happened,' said Hopkins.

On Tuesday, the team was finally allowed out of the hotel. It appeared that the Republicans had beaten off the rebel insurgency, although there were many armed men – and women – patrolling the streets. Northcott recalled seeing the evidence of the past two days' violence, including the charred body of a rebel next to a burned-out church on Las Ramblas. The news of gutted churches spread around the world, causing a great amount of controversy. Commentators loyal to the Republicans said that the churches were destroyed as a tactical measure, whereas Nationalist sympathisers said that the government was waging war on good Christians. Northcott also saw a great many bullet holes in walls, and in Cataluña Square he counted seventeen dead horses and mules, which were already starting to stink in the heat. There was broken glass everywhere, and branches had been ripped off trees by bullets. Nearly every side street had a barricade across it, consisting of granite stones ripped up from between the tramlines. All of them were manned by grinning government supporters.

Back at the hotel, the team found that the organisers of the Games had not given up, and a truncated event was planned to run from Friday to Sunday. In order to prepare for this, the British contingent and those from several other countries were asked to march the 2½ miles through the streets to the stadium. Led by a band of bagpipers, they were cheered all the way, and at the stadium the athletes spent a few hours limbering up and getting some exercise. It looked as if the ancient Olympic ideal of holding the Games during a time of war was going to be lived up to. The organisers had been more than a little optimistic, however, 'When we tried to leave the stadium we were allowed to use only one exit,' said Northcott, 'and found that this was because firing had recommenced in the city.' The athletes had to rush through the streets in twos and threes, halting in doorways while gunfire clattered around them. Rebel snipers had started firing on them, and it was only through a mixture of luck and fast running that all the members of the team made it back to the hotel safely, no doubt cursing the organisers of the Games for putting them at risk.

On Wednesday, the fighting died down once again, and some of the athletes tried to send telegrams home, only to join a queue 100 yards long outside the post office. Other athletes went down to the docks, where they were rewarded with the sight of a British cruiser, HMS *London*, commanded by Rear Admiral Max Horton, a submarine hero from the Great War. The ship represented a means of escape, and when the athletes returned to the hotel, they were advised by the British vice-consul that they should get on board. Many members of the team did not wish to leave, however, because they did not want to let down the Games' organisers. Their wishes could not be granted, as later that day everybody under the age of twenty-one was ordered to leave the city as soon as possible. Apparently, the sixteen-year-old Miss J. Crew burst into tears when she heard the news.

Nevertheless, the British team did manage to demonstrate their solidarity for their fellow workers on Thursday. That morning, a large group of Republican fighters assembled to march the hundred miles to Saragossa, where they hoped to deal with the Nationalists as effectively as they had in Barcelona. For a short while, the British team marched with the column – accompanied by the ever-present bagpipers – with George Elvin even taking a ride in an armoured car. 'The departure of the militia was a wonderful sight,' said Hopkins, 'although they had no uniforms as they passed down Las Ramblas. We had great admiration for the women who served side by side.' Northcott thought he detected a 'spirit of elation underlying the surface at the defeat of the rebels', a spirit that was no doubt enhanced by the speeches made by the team leaders, including George Elvin.

By early afternoon it was time for the British to go home. At three o'clock the team boarded the *London*, where they spent the night. At 7.15 the following morning they were transferred to a destroyer, HMS *Gypsy*, which took them and around 150 other British refugees to Marseilles, a voyage that lasted seventeen hours because of thick fog. 'The British Navy was a godsend,' said one Scottish athlete. Northcott said that the crew of the *Gypsy* 'went out of their way to make all the refugees comfortable and happy'. At Marseilles, the team found themselves in for a shock when they read their first English papers, which reported that Barcelona was 'in the hands of a riotous mob'. Indeed, many British papers sided with the rebels, and it was only socialist papers such as the *Daily Worker* which spoke up for the Republicans. In fact, the *Daily Telegraph* reported one eyewitness account from an anonymous Englishwoman, whose husband had viewed the athletes with suspicion: '[He] kept muttering to himself as each lorry-load arrived, that never had he seen such a tough-looking lot and he did not believe there was one single athlete among them. He thought it must be some sort of publicity stunt . . .'

Elvin and his team arrived back at Victoria Station at eleven o'clock on the morning of Monday, 27 July. It had been an eventful ten days. 'Never have I seen such remarkable enthusiasm,' Elvin said, 'and we are proud to have been there to see comrades in the struggle against the murderers employed by Spanish Fascism and reaction.' For communists like Elvin, the events were nothing less than a new and exciting chapter in the struggle against fascism, and another chance for the workers of the world to rid themselves of their chains. 'Every worker, every organisation, every lover of freedom and progress should rally to the side of the Spanish workers,' he declaimed. Fascism, in Elvin's words, had been given 'such a terrific kick in the pants'.

Although there were no Games for the little British team to compete in, the events in Barcelona were a game of sorts for its members. Nobody had been hurt, and their smiling faces back at Victoria Station bore the looks of those who had been on an awfully big and exciting adventure. As Elvin said, 'the team has had a remarkably interesting experience – one that they would not have missed for anything in the world'. For the Spanish, it was the beginning of three years of civil war that would claim 500,000 to 1,000,000 lives, with atrocities carried out by both Republicans and National-ists. But on that platform on Victoria Station that Monday morning in July 1936, men like George Elvin could raise their right fist in the workers' salute and feel that they had done their bit for their beloved workers.

7

Going There

~

A T 10.30 ON the morning of Wednesday, 15 July, the 384-strong
American team boarded the SS *Manhattan* in New York harbour.
Smartly dressed in straw boaters, white trousers and skirts, and blue
blazers emblazoned with the Olympic shield, the team waved back at
the thousands of well-wishers assembled on Pier 60, who were chanting, ' "Ray!" Ray for the USA! A-M-E-R-I-C-A! "Ray!" ' Aeroplanes
and airships circled over their heads, while in the water a whole flotilla
of tugs waited to escort the ship out of the harbour. It was a truly patriotic occasion, right down to the *Manhattan's* two funnels, which United
States Lines had painted red, white and blue. At twelve o'clock, the ship
set sail, accompanied by the whooping tugs. The athletes, many of
whom had never sailed on a boat, or even left the United States, stayed
on deck as long as possible to watch as Manhattan island retreated. The
temperature was fearsomely hot, although a welcome stiff breeze
started to cool them down.

The athletes were billeted in two and threes in third class, and many
of them found their accommodation cramped but adequate. Jesse
Owens was installed in Cabin 87 on Deck D. Although it was small,
it was a respite from the newsmen who had crowded on board before
the boat set sail, all of whom had frantically jockeyed to gain a few
words with America's – and perhaps the world's – most celebrated
athlete. Charles Leonard, who was competing in the pentathlon,
found his berth very small, but at least it had a porthole. The female
sprinter Helen Stephens also had a porthole, but she found something
else in her cabin which unsettled her. Before the ship had even pulled
out of the harbour, Stephens discovered some boxes containing literature and letters. They were 'about the Jewish people wanting us to
take a stand against competing against the Germans in the Olympics',

she recalled. 'They were wanting us to stage a protest of some type. I turned this material over to my coach, and I think she turned this over to the Olympic officials.' One of the letters Stephens received suggested that she should make her protest by remaining on the starting line when the gun went off for the 100 metres final. The boycott movement, it seemed, was not quite dead.

Rather than concerning themselves with such matters, the athletes were more worried about whether they were going to get seasick. 'Almost everyone was [. . .] hoping to gain sea legs rapidly, and <u>stay well</u>,' Charles Leonard wrote in his diary. What was also important was the issue of food, and the athletes found within an hour of departure that they were being saddled with a special 'training menu'. The lunch menu that day consisted of roast beef, baked potatoes, stewed knob celery, tomato salad and baked apple. Dinner that night featured chicken soup, roast chicken with gravy and cranberry jelly, mashed potatoes, fresh peas, ice cream and candy. Apparently, this wasn't good enough for the athletes, and within twenty-four hours they were able to enjoy the regular ship's fare, which, according to Leonard, provided 'a good bit more variety and essential quality and is greatly appreciated'. The ship's fare obviously went down well, as many of the athletes put on weight during the ten-day voyage. 'The selection on board was beyond words,' wrote 5,000 metre runner Lou Zamperini, 'plus it was free. At mealtime each table was laden with not just a basket of sweet rolls, but with *six* kinds of sweet rolls.' By the end of the voyage, Zamperini estimated that he had gained ten pounds. He had probably also eaten a sizeable proportion of the 1600 pounds of peanut brittle on board. Clearly, he had not read Brundage's recollections of sailing on the *Finland* over to the 1912 Stockholm Games. 'Exposure to the unlimited menus on shipboard was fatal to some,' he wrote, 'and several hopes of Olympic victory foundered at the bounteous dinner table.'

Glenn Morris also put on weight – some 8 pounds. To make matters worse, the cold, wet conditions of the mid-Atlantic gave him a chill. 'I caught a cold which settled in my muscles,' he recalled, 'and I was too tensed up to work out for two days.' Even if an athlete had not succumbed to a cold or seasickness, it was hard enough trying to stay in shape on board. Although the runners could run up and down the deck, even as it pitched and rolled in high seas, for the swimmers and divers, practising their technique was somewhat tricky. Although there was a small pool – 'watered directly from the icebergs', wrote Leonard – the boat was not stabilised, so it was impossible for divers such as Velma Dunn to train effectively. Even swimming was a problem. 'They tied a rope around our waist so we swam in place,' Dunn recalled. 'Because the boat was pitching, you'd get two feet of water at one end, with eight feet at the other, and then at the next moment it sloshed the other way. It made for interesting training.' Charles Leonard found training sessions in the pool just short of torture. 'We swim against belts anchored to the side of the pool and very nearly drown in a congealed condition at least twice a day,' he wrote. 'That's [coach] Dick Mayo's minimum requirement.' Mayo would stand at the side of the pool, well wrapped up in thick woollens, while Leonard and his fellow pentathletes would sink to the bottom of the icy water, his shouts of encouragement often ignored.

For the other passengers, the athletes added a novelty to the cruise, although their presence could often be an obstacle. George F. Kennan was a diplomat at the United States embassy in Moscow who was travelling back to Europe with his family after the birth of his second child. 'For a week we dodged the motions of gum-chewing supermen with crew cuts,' he wrote, 'and a variety of hefty amazons, as they practiced their particular skills on deck.' The athletes had the run of the ship during daylight, but the first- and second-class passengers did not seem to mind too much to find that their deckchairs had been pushed out of the way to make space. Charles Leonard and his pentathletes even managed to get some target practice in, shooting across the forward deck and out to sea. 'Makes some of the passengers nervous,' Leonard noted in his diary. 'First class didn't bargain for this when they agreed to passage with the Olympic team. However, we have CAPTAIN'S approval – at sea his word is law.' With the wind and the pitching of the ship, their scores were not great. At least Leonard could get some sort of practice. For those involved in sports that involved throwing objects, training was impossible. 'One soon reduces to zero the number of javelins, shot, hammers and discus if one throws them out to sea,' Leonard commented wryly in his diary.

As well as working out, there was much time left over for the team members to get to know each other. They were a snapshot of American society, coming from all backgrounds and races. One feature that was remarkable about the mini-society that developed on the boat was the lack of racial segregation. Back on the mainland, it was unthinkable in many states that blacks and whites should share a table, but on board the *Manhattan* things were different. 'Everything seems to be harmonious so far,' wrote Leonard in his diary on 16 July. 'The Negroes of the team eat, live and associate with all others – no distinctions are made. It's the only way the team can function – most people realise that.' In fact, the only distinction that anyone could note was that the African-Americans were more susceptible to seasickness, Jesse Owens being no exception. Owens was, however, involved in a minor racial incident, although ironically it was he who was responsible for it. On the first night, Owens found that he had been sat next to three white Southerners – the hurdlers Glenn Hardin and Forest 'Spec' Towns, and the shot putter Jack Torrance. Unable to cope with sitting next to what he assumed to be a bunch of rednecks, he moved tables, and was light-heartedly ribbed for the rest of the voyage by Towns for his prejudice against white Southerners. Nevertheless, Owens charmed everybody on board, with many of the other athletes asking for his autograph. He was even voted the second-most popular shipmate, behind Glenn Cunningham, the long-distance runner from Kansas. He was more successful in the 'best dressed' category, in which he came first, largely for the nattiness of his immaculately tailored blue pinstripe suit. What his fellow athletes didn't realise was that it was Owens' only suit.

It appears that Owens' charm worked on at least one woman on board. On the night of Wednesday 23rd, Helen Stephens turned in early, at around nine o'clock. Finding she couldn't sleep, she got up and went for a walk on what she thought to be an empty deck. After a while, she became aware that she was not on her own, a sense reinforced by giggled whispers and 'muffled sounds' coming from a lifeboat. Edging closer, she noticed that the canvas covering the lifeboat was moving in a suggestively rhythmic way. She stepped back into the shadows and waited. After several minutes, a man got out of the lifeboat, a man Stephens instantly recognised as Jesse Owens.

Helen waited for him to disappear, and just as she started to leave the other occupant of the lifeboat emerged and walked past her, even whispering 'Good morning' to her. As Stephens could not identify the woman, it has to be assumed that Owens' lifeboat paramour was not a member of the team.

For the majority of the athletes, the evenings were spent indulging in far more innocent pastimes. One night, the pentathletes organised a casino night, complete with paper money. 'One of the track Negroes broke our bank eventually,' Leonard recalled, 'but didn't come close with his paltry 39,000 against the 102,000 of one of his contemporaries.' The athletes had to retire to bed because their coaches were grumbling about the lateness of the hour, a grumble that was repeated on many an occasion. On another night, the athletes held a contest as to which of them was the most handsome man and which the most beautiful woman. The man was Glenn Hardin, but as he didn't pick up his prize it was instead awarded to the second-placed Glenn Morris. 'Glenn was perhaps the most handsome man on the team,' said Marty Glickman. 'He had a lean, smooth-muscled body, and hawk-like features, almost like an Indian.' What Morris seemed to lack was Jesse Owens' charm. 'He was rather quiet, even aloof,' Glickman recalled. 'He wasn't one of the boys [. . .] The word "respect" comes to mind, rather than "well-liked".' The most beautiful woman was judged to be Joanna de Tuscan, a fencer from Detroit. This result annoyed Eleanor Holm, who had been used to being fêted as a great beauty. According to Adolph Kiefer, she didn't even make the top three places. 'I remember her storming off, shouting, "You're all jealous of me!" She wasn't one of us – she wasn't the Olympic ideal.'

Kiefer was right – Holm was not like the other athletes. Years spent in Hollywood and on the cabaret circuit had given her a sophistication utterly lacking in the rest of her teammates. While the athletes socialised among themselves, indulging in sophomoric activities such as fake weddings, Holm could be found drinking champagne with the first-class passengers, who included William Randolph Hearst Jr, the playwright Charlie MacArthur and his wife the actress Helen Hayes, and several journalists. As well as having a healthy appetite for champagne, Holm also had a taste for some of the men on board. 'She spent her time chasing boys,' Kiefer recalled. 'I remember a fight on the deck between Holm and Dick Degener's wife. They were scratching and biting each other. "You stay away from my husband!" Mrs Degener was shouting.' It would seem that Degener – a bronze medal winner in springboard diving at the 1932 Games – was not the only target of her affections. According to Lou Zamperini, there was speculation that Holm and Hearst were an item, 'but whatever her association was, I don't know', he recalled.

Holm soon earned herself a reputation as a hard partier. At 6 a.m. on the morning of Saturday 18th, her inebriated form was seen being carried to bed. She had sufficiently recovered by Sunday to spend another night on the razzle in first class, despite the protestations of the swimming team's chaperone, Mrs Ada T. Sackett, who told her to go to bed. Holm refused. 'Look,' she replied, 'it's my third Olympic team. I don't think you've been on any before. I know what I'm doing. And what are you doing up here? Why aren't you downstairs watching the athletes?' A shocked Mrs Sackett reported the incident to Avery Brundage, who reprimanded Holm the following day, reminding her of the contents of the AOC handbook, which stated: 'It is understood of course that all members of the American Olympic Team refrain from smoking and the use of intoxicating drinks and other forms of dissipation while in training.' Brundage told Holm that if she continued in this way, then he would throw her off the team. Holm regarded this as an empty threat. She was a dead cert to win gold – there was no way she was going to be expelled. Besides, as Velma Dunn said, 'She could beat anybody else on the planet, even if she were plastered.'

On the night of Wednesday, 22 July, Holm called Brundage's bluff by getting horrendously plastered up on A deck. 'Holm was daring Brundage,' recalled Iris Cummings, 'and she was going to stand up to him, no matter what.' According to Holm, the journalists threw a 'humdinger of a party – everybody got pleasantly soused'. At some point in the small hours, Holm was discovered by Mrs Sackett in the arms of a young man. Early the next morning, a slumbering Holm was woken up by Sackett and the ship's doctor, J. Hubert Lawson, who diagnosed Holm as having 'acute alcoholism'. This was clearly nonsense – Holm was merely hung over. Nevertheless, her condition did not stop Dee Boeckmann, the coach of the women's team, parading all the female athletes into Holm's cabin to show them a barely living embodiment of the perils of demon drink. Worse was to come. Later that day, Holm was summoned to see the team manager, Herbert Holm (no relation), who informed her that the AOC had decided to throw her off the team. Not only had she broken the rules by getting 'dissipated' but she had also been gambling – the night before Holm had won $100 at craps.

Holm was disconsolate. 'I'll never touch another drop again if I'm given another chance,' she sobbed. A rumour reached her that if she apologised, then there was a chance that she might be reinstated. 'Of course, all the newspapermen grabbed me right away and said "Don't you do that; whatever you do, don't do it." And I said, "Don't worry. I won't." ' Holm didn't apologise, and neither did Brundage back down – as far as he was concerned she had not shown sufficient team – or indeed Olympic – spirit. Two hundred and twenty members of the team disagreed with him, and signed a petition calling for Holm to be reinstated. The petition was ignored. Nevertheless, many of the athletes thought it right that Holm had been thrown off. 'I agreed with the decision,' said Adolph Kiefer. 'Her behaviour interrupted the whole proceedings, and it lacked discipline. Without discipline, you don't have a team.' Charles Leonard concurred. 'I thought it was fair enough,' he said. 'I don't think any person should raise himself or herself above the average.' Velma Dunn thought differently. 'Her friends were up on first class,' she said. 'What would you do?' Dunn was fond of Holm, who would spend time helping her fellow athletes rather than getting on with her own training. 'She was *really* a nice girl,' said Dunn. 'I think she should have stayed on the team.' Others, such as Lou Zamperini, thought Brundage's decision revealed a double standard. 'What killed me was that most of these athletes, after sweating all day, liked to have a glass of beer,' he recalled. 'On the deck there was a little opening where you'd go and buy [one]. I'd say most of the athletes that I saw would just take a workout, and then while walking the deck they'd stop and have a glass of beer.' Zamperini felt that Holm was dismissed because of a combination of factors. 'I think the Olympic committee probably just tied the first class, the dancing, the champagne and her association with Hearst together.'

But Brundage got his way. In order to add insult to injury, he even ordered her to go back home as soon as she arrived in Germany. Holm's antics on A deck had won her several friends, however, including Allan Gould of the Associated Press, who offered her a column in which she could report on the Games. It was clear that Holm was not hired for her writing talents, but rather for her notoriety. She had no objections. 'I had some mighty fine writers doing it for me – writers like Paul Gallico, Allan Gould and Tom Walsh. I had the best time ever doing my column.' Brundage was furious that Holm was still around, but for once there was nothing he could do.

The *Manhattan* arrived in Hamburg late in the evening of 24 July, after cruising sedately up the Elbe. The athletes looked out over the low, flat countryside, admiring the gently pastoral scene of cattle, windmills and quaint old buildings. George F. Kennan recalled how the stillness of the summer evening was broken by the athletes, who, 'oblivious of linguistic differences, hurled wisecracks and frivolities at the bewildered Germans along the riverbank'. Before the team disembarked the following morning, Avery Brundage made a speech, or rather gave a lecture. 'I understand that stories have been printed in various papers that there have been wild parties – high jinks on the high seas. It is an outrage that this team should be so slandered [. . .] Some people will believe these sensational stories, so when you write home, I want you to correct them.'

There was no doubt that Brundage was worried about negative press publicity before the Games had even started. He may have been an arrogant man, but he was not so pig headed that he thought that he would get the better of the glamorous Eleanor Holm in a scrap in the public prints. Then, with the disgraced backstroker in mind, he continued his lecture.

We are a free and easy people who scorn discipline. Other nations are taught to respect it. I hope you will not be outdone in politeness and courtesy any more so than you are on the field [. . .] I won't have the opportunity again to address you. Remember we are represent-ing the grandest country in the world and we are here to win for the honour of our country and for the glory of sport. Good luck to you all.

The Olympic Stadium viewed from the north, the swimming stadium in the foreground. The Marathon Gate, through which Hitler entered for the opening ceremony, is on the western edge of the stadium.

Theodor Lewald (left) president of the German Organising Committee, and its secretary, Carl Diem. Both men's Jewish connections would allow them to be manipulated by the Nazis.

Baron Pierre de Coubertin (left) the founder of the Modern Olympic Games, and Count Henri de Baillet-Latour, the president of the International Olympic Committee. The two men would prove both incapable and unwilling to stop the Nazis making the Olympics their own.

Karl Ritter von Halt, one of the German members of the IOC, and a friend of Avery Brundage.

Hans von Tschammer und Osten, the *Reichssportfuehrer*. Although well-liked abroad, he was one of Hitler's oldest allies.

Avery Brundage (left), head of the American Olympic Committee, meeting the pro-boycott head of the American Athletic Union, Jeremiah T. Mahoney. Never was a handshake more insincere.

Avery Brundage (left) being escorted by Karl von Halt during his inspection of Germany in 1934. Brundage was to claim to have seen no signs of anti-Semitism during his visit.

Sir Robert Vansittart (left), the permanent under-secretary at the British Foreign Office with his brother-in-law Sir Eric Phipps. Both men were virulent anti-appeasers.

'How extraordinarily interesting': Britain's ambassador to Berlin, Sir Eric Phipps (right) talking to the German ambassador-designate to Great Britain, Joachim von Ribbentrop. He is wearing the uniform of an SS General.

Above: Jews – Admission Forbidden! The sign at the Winter Olympics that proved to the world that the Games had done nothing to stop the persecution of Jews.

Right: Adolf Hitler signing autographs at the Winter Olympics in February 1936. His minister of propaganda, Josef Goebbels, is to his right.

Below: Garmisch-Partenkirchen, the Bavarian village that hosted the Winter Olympics, struggled to cope with the volume of visitors.

Sonja Henie, the outstanding 23-year-old
Norwegian figure skater whose star came close
to outshining Hitler's at the Winter Olympics.

Cecilia Colledge, the 15-year-old
British girl who almost removed
Henie's crown in a thrilling contest.

With three gold medals and one silver, the Olympic achievements of Norwegian speed skater
Ivar Ballangrud are comparable to those of Jesse Owens.

Birger Ruud of Norway, one of the most impressive Alpine sportsmen of the last century.

Ernst Baier and Maxie Herber, German gold medal winners in the pairs figure skating. The music for their performance was specially composed to ensure synchronicity between skating and music.

The *Hindenburg* flying over the Brandenburg Gate in the centre of Berlin on the morning of the opening ceremony.

The swastika and the Olympic rings made easy companions on the crowded Berlin streets. Such displays were not purely the result of genuine enthusiasm – the Nazis ordered homeowners to fly the flags.

The patron of the Games of Berlin at the opening ceremony. To his right stands Count
Baillet-Latour.

'Imagine you're sprinting over a ground of burning fire': Jesse Owens at the start of the 200 metres final.

Jesse Owens and the German Carl 'Luz' Long. Owens would embellish the significance of their duel in the long jump in later years.

A tracksuited Cornelius Johnson competing in the high jump. Johnson won the event, and had more grounds to feel snubbed by Hitler than Jesse Owens ever had.

'Pistol-shooting is a gentlemanly game': The dapper Charles Leonard competing in the rapid fire pistol shooting in the pentathlon.

Son Ki-Jung and Ernest Harper of Great Britain at the halfway point of the marathon. Son resented having to run under the Japanese flag which flew over his Korean homeland. Note Son's split-toed running shoes.

Helen Stephens of the Unites States winning the 100-metres final. In second place, at the far left, is Stella Walsh. In third, second from left, is Kathe Krauss. The gender of all three women would be subject to many doubts.

English Walkyries and the SS: Unity Mitford (left) and her sister, Diana Guinness. Unity was in love with Hitler, Diana saw him as a source of funding for the British Union of Fascists, led by her lover, Sir Oswald Mosley.

Leni Riefenstahl, the German filmmaker, flirting with American decathlete Glenn Morris in the centre of the Olympic stadium. Their relationship would go several stages further.

The Fulton Flash and The Fuehrer: Helen Stephens did not accept Hitler's offer of a weekend in the mountains.

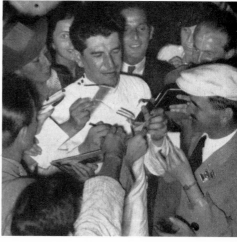

Marty Glickman (left) and Sam Stoller, two Jewish members of the United States' 4 x 100 metres team who were mysteriously dropped shortly before their event.

The Jewish Hungarian fencer Endre Kabos surrounded by fans. Kabos had given up fencing owing to the anti-Semitism in his own country, although his return to the sport was triumphant.

Helene Mayer, the silver medal winner in the fencing, performs a Nazi salute despite the fact that her Jewishness had almost deprived her of a place on the team.

Left: Dorothy Poynton Hill, the United States diver. She kept her imminent sponsorship deal with Camel cigarettes a closely-guarded secret throughout the Games.

Right: Dorothy Poynton Hill (right) always struck the right pose. Note the shoes. To her right is fellow American Velma Dunn and German Käte Koehler.

Below: 'You flip out and reach out as far as you can': Adolph Kiefer of the United States displaying his gold-medal winning form.

Above: Decathlete Glenn Morris and backstroker Eleanor Holm in a studio shot to publicise the execrable *Tarzan's Revenge*. Holm's antics on the ship over to Germany saw her dropped from the Olympic team.

Right: Hendrika Mastenbroek and her coach, 'Ma' Braun, who would covet the Dutch quadruple medal winner as a daughter.

Below: Bill Roberts (far left) takes the baton from Godfrey Rampling at the start of his leg of the 1600-metre relay. He would be mercilessly challenged by O'Brien of the United States (centre, white shorts).

Above: German wrestling champion Werner Seelenbinder (right) in his match against Axel Cadier of Sweden. Seelenbinder, a Communist, was determined to win a place on the podium in order not to perform the Nazi salute.

Left: Robie Leibbrandt, the South African boxer who would later work as a Nazi agent in a mission to assassinate his country's leader.

Below: Owens' name would appear three times on the tablets at the stadium's Marathon Gate. He won the 100 metres, the 200 metres and the long jump. His fourth gold medal was won as part of the United States' victorious 4x100 relay team.

The team would need it. Tired, still a little seasick, suffering from colds, overweight, dogged by scandal and missing home, its members had only a week to recuperate from what had been quite a trip.

For the British, going to Berlin was a far less eventful affair. Lacking a certain amount of Brundagian discipline, the team members assembled in dribs and drabs at Liverpool Street Station in London on the evening of Wednesday, 29 July in order to catch the 8.30 train to Harwich, from where a boat would be caught to the Hook of Holland. The station was crowded, not only with well-wishers, but also with tourists setting off for holidays in Austria and Germany. Rushing around were stout, elderly British Olympic officials, instantly recognisable by their newly designed British Olympic tie, which was regarded as 'the most complicated tie in the history of haberdashery'. It featured a blue background, on top of which were red and white stripes. Between each group of red and white, however, came a group of stripes in the Olympic colours of pale blue, yellow, black, green and red. The London correspondent of the *Manchester Guardian* was withering. 'A member of your London staff who is entitled to wear the tie received it yesterday, extracted it eagerly from its envelope, looked at it in a dazed way while his wife said what she had to say; and then shut it up in a wardrobe. It may be all right in Berlin, but it will not do for London.'

Eventually, after much chivvying by the officials, the athletes got on the train. Outside the station, a chocolate seller had been monitoring their arrival, and was worried that there was no sign of Jack Lovelock, the New Zealand miler. A Rhodes Scholar at Oxford, where he read medicine, Lovelock had competed in the 1932 Olympics and had come seventh. The following year, however, he set a new world record in the mile of 4:07.6, and in 1934 he won gold at the British Empire Games. An intensely private man, Lovelock approached running as a science, and kept a diary in which he recorded medical and dietary observations. On 15 June 1935 Lovelock ran in the 'Mile of the Century' at Princeton, although he was suffering from an inflamed knee. Before the race he injected himself with a vaccine prepared by none other than Alexander Fleming, the discoverer of penicillin. Wearing his distinctive black shirt with a large silver fern, Lovelock won the race, cheered on by a crowd consisting of what he somewhat unkindly described as 'kind, but thoughtless enthusiasts'. By the time the train had left, the chocolate seller had still not spotted Lovelock, but then the New Zealander was a small, frail-looking man, and may well have slipped on to the train unnoticed, obscured by the tourists with their bulky luggage.

Lovelock was fortunate not to suffer the fate of Edgar Howitt, who had been selected as stroke for the British coxless four. His teammate from the London Rowing Club, Martin Bristow, recalled how the four men had all applied for extra leave from their employers or tutors, and all had been granted it except for Howitt, who worked at Cable & Wireless. 'His boss said no. "You've had your leave, that's it." ' A fellow member of their club then came up with a solution that looked infallible. 'This chap was called Bradshaw,' Bristow remembered, 'and he knew Stanley Baldwin, the prime minister. So Bradshaw had a word with Baldwin, and Baldwin had a word with the chap at Cable & Wireless, and still he said *no!*' Despite this failure, the captain of their club, Peter Jackson, thought he might succeed where the prime minister had failed. 'He went to see the Cable & Wireless man and told him that Howitt had to have more leave. Jackson's trump card was to say that all this would look very bad in the press if it came out. Quick as a flash, the boss said that if it gets into the papers, Mr Howitt will be dismissed. As a result, Howitt couldn't come. He couldn't leave his job as he had no means of his own.' Howitt was replaced by a stroke from Oxford, whose different rowing style would have a huge impact on the four's chances of success.

The train arrived at Harwich just before ten o'clock, and the team boarded the boat for the Hook of Holland. The lateness of the hour, the fact that the female team members were coming over separately and the shortness of the voyage meant there was no time for the high jinks that had been so prevalent on the *Manhattan*. However, the team members were permitted to drink alcohol, although there is no record that there was a raucous party on board. Even without alcohol, it would have been a bleary-eyed team arriving at the Hook of Holland at six o'clock the following morning, there to catch the North German Express to Berlin at 7.21 a.m.

On the train the athletes may have had a chance to peruse one of the leaflets that had been distributed to those visiting Berlin. One of them succinctly summed up the state of Germany.

You will be shown

1) The Reichstag, partly 'burnt out' in 1933.
2) Happy workers cheering the National Leaders at popular demonstrations.
3) Jews, sitting in their cafés unmolested (for the period of the Olympic Games), enjoying their glass of beer as well as any Aryan.
4) Contented women nursing their children in houses especially painted up for the Olympic Games.
5) Busy factories, and signs of plenty of work and attention for the conditions of workers.
6) Eggs and butter in the shops, hoarded up by instructions for the last few weeks.
7) Many new and magnificent buildings like the new Air Ministry.
8) The peaceful unity of the nation.
9) Impressive libraries from which all literature of writers such as Heinrich Mann, Einstein, Ernst Toller, have been removed.
10) The magnificent buildings of the Olympic village and district which will be used as a military centre after the Olympic Games

But ask to see

1) The oath, under penalty of treason, which every guide was asked to take; the secret rules laid down to Chambermaids, Waiters, Porters etc whom you will meet in Berlin.
2) Columbia House, and other prisons with their torture chambers.
3) The leaders and other members of the old Trade Union Movement who have not yet 'been shot while attempting to escape'.
4) Jewish surgeons, after years of training to save life, are denied not only hospital appointments, but also general practice because they are Jews; Jewish teachers and scientists who have lost their positions because they are Jews.

5) The women and baby hostages still languishing in concentration camps and prisons – their only offence being the fact that their menfolk were Pacifists, Socialists or Communists.

6) Koepenick, near the Olympic Regatta Course, where in the summer of 1934, 12 Social Democratic civil servants and one MP (Stalling) were murdered; and Lichterfelde where in the SS Barracks hundreds of Nazi boys were shot on June 30, July 1st, 2nd and 3rd 1934; the Bernerstrasse where there is a women's political prison.

7) The daily sittings of the political tribunal at Bellevuestrasse 14, only to see whether heavy sentences are being passed there hourly on a continuous stream of men and women who do not think like Hitler.

8) Ossietsky, a great German writer: dead; Ernst Thaelman the leader of the German Communist Party and Edgar Andre [a communist trade unionist] who lies in Hamburg under sentence of death.

9) Great religious leaders of the Catholic and Protestant Church whose sermons have been seized by secret police.

10) The budget of working class houses, especially those where there is no unemployment pay and no relief and their conditions in 1932 before the Nazi regime.

Despite the error concerning Ossietzky – he was in fact alive – the leaflet was largely accurate. For the duration of the Games, the regime was desperate to show a public face that did not match its rotten heart. The list of cosmetic changes the Nazis put in place was typically thorough. Local officials had to ensure that all the main streets in all villages were free of rubbish; houses on main roads or whose backs looked on to railway lines had to be whitewashed or painted; front gardens had to be kept in order; empty buildings were to be let cheaply; convict labourers had to be employed away from main roads; concentration camp inmates were not to work on the land; visiting Jews were to be 'treated just as politely as Aryan guests'; anti-Jewish signs were to be removed; display cases showing the rabidly anti-Semitic *Der Stuermer* were closed; taxi drivers had to wear uniforms; all flats and houses on main thoroughfares in Berlin had to display Olympic and Nazi flags – and so on. The orders were rigorously implemented. In Berlin, the streets were patrolled every morning to ensure that the flags and decorations had not been damaged by the weather or vandalism. On the Bismarckstrasse in Berlin, one Jewish woman refused to hang up any flags because her son had been forbidden from swimming in the local baths. The Nazis ignored her, and brought their own flags and illuminations which they hung up despite her protestations. For those good citizens who did want to display the flags, expert advice on how to hang them was available from the district Nazi Propaganda Office. As if to emphasise that the changes were merely temporary window dressing, the orders concerning the treatment of foreign Jews stated, 'The fundamental attitude of the German people towards Judaism remains unchanged.' The *New Statesman* noted how 'the flags in the Berlin streets and the appliances in the Hamburg prison are all part and parcel of the same system', referring to the location of Darré's incarceration. 'Terrorism for the few and megaphone propaganda for the many provide the essentials in this new technique of government.'

Indeed, it was not only rubbish which was cleaned up, but people too. Two weeks before the Games, the Sinti and Roma were arrested and sent to a special 'Gypsy Camp' that had recently been established in the Berlin suburb of Marzahn. The arrests began at 4 a.m. on 16 July, and nearly six hundred men, women and children were rounded up. The men were allowed to work during the day, but at night they were locked up with their families in the camp, which was situated next to a sewage works and a cemetery, leaving the Gypsies in no doubt as to how the Nazis regarded them. They were even subjected to 'race-hygiene examinations'. Marzahn would grow into a de facto concentration camp, and it was from here that Gypsy families were deported to the death camps in the east. The other people the Nazis cleared up were the prostitutes, who were banned from the centre of Berlin. Over two thousand prostitutes, bar hostesses and dancing girls were forcibly examined for venereal disease, and some 350 were found to be in need of treatment. Beggars were also hidden away, with 1,433 arrested in June alone, incarcerated in the 'Municipal Work and Detention House'. The one group that was tolerated, however, was homosexuals. On 20 July, Himmler issued an order to the Gestapo that forbade them 'from taking any action, even questioning or summons, against any foreigner on the grounds of §175 without my personal authorisation during the next few weeks'.

The fate of Gypsies, beggars and prostitutes was far from the minds of the athletes as they drew into Friedrichstrasse Station in Berlin at 4.30 p.m. There was no sign of any repression on the platform, merely the portly figure of Lewald, who welcomed the British as 'the finest team that Great Britain has ever had'. Lord Burghley replied by expressing his hope that 'these games will do much to cement greater friendship not only between our two great nations but among all the nations gathered together here for the glory of sport'. The team was then ushered outside into the waiting buses, no doubt grateful that the lateness of the hour meant that they did not have to endure the normally obligatory glass of welcoming sherry at Berlin City Hall. Instead, they were taken straight to the Olympic village.

The Americans had enjoyed no such luck since they had arrived in Germany. As soon as they had disembarked they were subjected to countless speeches and welcoming committees. At the docks in Hamburg, thousands had gathered in a slight drizzle to welcome them, and as they were driven to the City Hall, thousands more cheered them along the flag-lined streets. There was one member of the team, however, who was singled out for particular attention, and that was Jesse Owens. The crowds shouted, 'Yessay Oh-vens! Yessay Oh-vens!', and it took a while for Owens to realise that they were chanting for him. Owens could have been forgiven for expecting his reception to be anything but warm. In the German newspapers, the rise of 'der Negerfest' had been written about for weeks, and pictures of Owens were reproduced next to that of an ape, indicating that Owens' phenomenal speed was because of his 'animal qualities'. Despite the Nazis' best efforts to knock him down the evolutionary ladder, the German public adored 'Yessay'. At the City Hall, which Charles Leonard described as a 'grand place harboring leather walls, inlaid floors, heavy paintings and marble statuary', the athletes were serenaded by oompah bands and orange juice and sherry. 'The o.j. is of unknown quality,' wrote Leonard, 'the sherry the best I've ever tasted.'

Velma Dunn found Hamburg a 'beautiful' city. 'Canals, lakes and rivers line almost every block,' she wrote to her mother. 'On all the buildings there are window boxes, mostly filled with red geraniums. It is certainly a colourful sight.' The authorities had clearly done well to ensure that Hamburg looked its best, as had the railways, which had festooned the deluxe train that was to take them to Berlin with countless swastikas and Olympic rings. The train journey to Berlin took three hours, and the young Velma Dunn soon noticed some small differences between Germany and the United States. At lunch, they were served 'very peculiarly'. 'One waiter brings a fork to everyone,' she wrote. 'He is then followed by a waiter with knives. Another with spoons etc. They serve the food that way, too. One waiter serves the meat, another a vegetable, etc. Quite a novel way of serving, but I prefer the usual method. The straws in the milk were made of a form of cellophane.'

Nothing could have prepared the Americans for their reception in Berlin. In contrast to the quietness of the British welcome, the Americans were once more fêted by thousands of their hosts, who had crammed on to the platforms of the Zoo Station and the streets outside. Wearing their Olympic uniforms, the team was taken aback by the enthusiasm of the crowd and the abundance of swastika and Olympic flags. Outside the station, they were loaded on to open-top cars and charabancs, and driven to the City Hall. 'It was like a Broadway parade,' Marty Glickman wrote to his parents. 'Men who had been with former Olympic teams said that this was by far the greatest reception ever given to an Olympic team.' The Berliners were heeding the words of *Der Angriff*, which had instructed them to be 'more charming than the Parisians, more easygoing that the Viennese, more vivacious than the Romans, more cosmopolitan than London, and more practical than New York'. Once again, Velma Dunn was noticing the differences between the Germans and the Americans. 'There certainly was no resentment against America shown,' she wrote. 'The people here seem so genuine. They wear absolutely no lipstick or makeup. Most of them wear their hair in a big knot at the back of their heads.' Charles Leonard was somewhat disappointed by the *junge Frauen*. 'Some of us sat on the rolled back tops to answer the cheers of the multitude – also to see and wave to the pretty girls of which there are few. Most of those we saw were plain – no rouge or lipstick with straight hair and wearing low heels. <u>Plump</u> too.'

Nevertheless, the reception for the African-American athletes was not that rosy. Iris Cummings recalled an altercation at the station. 'We were in a long line of people,' she said, 'and they [her fellow American athletes] had the girls in a group, and our basketball players and other tall men got in the way and circled around us a few times.' At first, Cummings was unsure of why she and the other female athletes were being protected, but she soon found out. 'There was hassle between the German police and our negro boys. That's what our teammates told us, but we couldn't tell. I heard there was a heap big meeting about it, and it got to Avery Brundage who went to the German committee and he said that we would go home if they didn't put a stop to this.' However, Cummings's story does seem a little unlikely. Had there been such a scene at the station, then the American press would certainly have picked up on it, and a scandal would have ensued.

At the welcoming drinks at the City Hall, each team member was presented with a book about the new Germany, intended as propaganda, although their effect was somewhat diminished by the fact that they were not written in English. 'They have lovely pictures,' Dunn noted, 'but I don't have any idea what they are about.' The book featured pictures, including one of a benign-looking Hitler digging into some sand and cement, accompanied by the caption: 'It was necessary to rebuild Germany from her very foundations. As a first step, employment had to be provided for millions of diligent workers who had been unwillingly condemned to idleness. The Fuehrer, as the first worker among his people, opened the employment campaign.' The athletes would also have been able to see a book of photographs of Berlin by Heinrich Hoffman, which featured an introduction in English written by Goebbels. There was no doubt that the propaganda minister and the Gauleiter of Berlin saw the Games as an opportunity to promote the regime.

> National Socialism as an idea has cast a spell upon the whole world, but for a foreigner to become truly acquainted with the Germany of National Socialism without seeing Berlin is an utter impossibility [. . .] May all foreign visitors to this city, in the rhythm of her life, in the tempo of her work, and in the enthusiasm with which she devotes herself to Adolf Hitler and his idea, catch a breath of the spirit with which the new Germany is inspired.

If proof were required that the Nazis were using the Games as a show-case for the 'joys' of Nazism, then here it was.

After the reception at the City Hall, the male athletes were driven to the Olympic village, which lay near the village of Doeberitz, some 20 miles west of Berlin's centre, and 10 miles west of the Olympic Stadium. Not one of them was unimpressed by the 136-acre site, which featured some 140 single-storey houses, each of which accommodated around twenty athletes. The village, which included a practice track and a swimming pool, was set in rolling parkland, complete with specially planted firs, silver birch, larch and pines. Every comfort and convenience the athletes could require was attended to – even a lakeside sauna was provided. There was also an assembly hall – the Hindenburg House – at which entertainments were staged, although Charles Leonard described them as 'rather poor vaudeville – little talking as the audience is not bilingual'. 'Athletes', he added, 'are not particularly adept at languages or else they might be teachers.' The Hindenburg House was, however, a good place for the athletes to socialise in and to observe each other's national characteristics. Dhyan Chand, the captain of the Indian hockey team, captured the multi-national flavour of evenings at the Hindenburg House.

> Every evening after dinner, we used to pass two hours in the house, with our sweatsuits on or any other informal dress, cheering, clapping and joking. The Italians were the most noisy and none could beat them in this respect. A sight of a pretty girl dancing gracefully was always enough to rouse our Italian friends to the highest pitch of enjoyment, which sometimes appeared carried too far to our Eastern minds.

Some of the entertainments laid on by the Germans at the village were rather more edifying, however. João Havelange, who was swimming in the 400 and 1,500 metres freestyle for Brazil, recalled how the Berlin Philharmonic Orchestra would play at the village. 'The orchestra came at least three times,' he recalled, 'with at least some seven hundred musicians. It was a dream for me to listen to them.' It is unlikely that the orchestra would have been so large, but the logistics involved in transporting an orchestra at all are great enough to suggest that the Germans wanted to make the athletes' time at the village as pleasant as possible.

The Germans also found another means of promoting their country, by naming each house after a German town or city, featuring paintings and photographs of the town on its walls. The Australians were bemused to find they occupied a house called 'Worms', and the British now occupied the Rhineland cities – Emden, Durisberg, Krefeld, Aachen, Düsseldorf and Solingen. Whether they had been placed there in ironic reference to the events in March is not known, but there can be little doubt that had the Germans placed their athletes in these houses, there would have been some form of protest. The Germans were sensitive enough, however, to keep the village free of swastikas.

'The Olympic village was really a sight to behold,' Lou Zamperini recalled. 'They had everything there. They had wild animals running over the grounds [. . .] They had green grass mowed like a golf course. The buildings we lived in were like motels. There were no bathtubs, only showers. I think Hitler had all the bathtubs taken out of Germany because he didn't feel that they were sanitary. So we had showers.' Zamperini also commented on how pristine the place was. If an athlete dropped an apple core or a banana skin to the ground, a German would run over and swiftly deposit it in a bin. There was plenty of food, provided by a huge household block that boasted forty different kitchens specialising in cuisines from all over the world. The variety of food offered was staggering, ranging from *empanada à la creole* for the Argentinians, macaroni for the Greeks, cabbage dishes for the Poles, black beans for the Mexicans, raw eggs for the Luxembourgers, blueberry consommé for the Finns, steaks for nearly every nation, and for the British, Horlicks. According to Alfred Proksch, a pole vaulter from Austria, the Germans even provided kosher food for the Jewish athletes, but there is no record of this in the official Olympic Report. Most of the athletes found the food highly satisfactory, except for the Indians, for whom the German version of curry, according to Dhyan Chand, 'could not satisfy our palates'. 'We were unanimous in the opinion that it was very difficult to cater for Indians abroad,' he wrote. 'There is not only divergence in the choice of dishes and their mode of preparation, but also in the choice of meat.'

What every athlete from every nation noticed was the plethora of men in uniform. Each team had an army officer assigned to it, who was able to speak the relevant language and attend to the needs of the athletes. The officers integrated closely with the teams, even eating with them and accompanying them to practices, which gave rise to some suspicions. 'I think our escorts are a bunch of spies,' wrote Charles Leonard, 'who report to the German team their observations, including our times, styles in fencing and so on.' Leonard had no evidence to support what he suspected, but he was not the only athlete who thought the Germans were using their positions as hosts to give themselves an advantage. Martin Bristow recalled how his team was deprived of an important piece of kit. 'Our boat went by train,' he said, 'but there was a delay in its arriving. It was said that the Germans held up the boat deliberately so we couldn't train.' The British cyclist Harry Hill said the British team's bicycles and clothes were also delayed by twenty-four hours, which cost them a vital day's training on a course they had never ridden on. It is more likely that the British were simply the victims of bad luck rather than singularly unsporting play. Suspicions directed at the host nation are a staple of any Olympics, and the XIth Olympiad was to be no exception.

As well as the army officers, several other types of men in uniform walked around the village, and were quick to salute the athletes with a '*Heil Hitler!*' Many of the visitors found this highly amusing, and saluted back sloppily with a jocular '*Heil Adolf!*' or, in the case of the British, with a '*Heil* King Edward!' The Germans took this mickey-taking in good measure – 'nobody got mad', said Zamperini. Also dressed in uniform were members of the Honorary Youth Service, which consisted of 185 boys and seventy girls who were there to help the athletes with small matters such as how to post letters home, as well as to guide them around the city and its attractions. 'They have all been in training for two years and have learned English fluently,' Velma Dunn wrote to her mother, 'and have been taught the American mannerisms and customs. They are a lovely group of girls. They meet us at breakfast time and are near us until after dinner at night.' Dunn was right to take the girls at face value. If the SS Main Security Office had had its way, then the boys and girls would have been used as agents to monitor the athletes, and also to try to indoctrinate them politically. The Gestapo rejected the plan, as it was felt that the best means of diffusing political propaganda was for the Youth Service to be as apolitical as possible.

There was a dark side to the village, however. The commandant was Captain Wolfgang Fuerstner, a brilliant young army officer, who had designed the village, transforming it from a drab army barracks into a place many of the athletes did not wish to leave. Fuertsner was also responsible for the formation of the Honorary Youth Service. Just before the Games, however, it was discovered that Fuerstner had a problem similar to that of Lewald – he was partly Jewish. He was immediately stripped of his citizenship and demoted to assistant commandant – sacking him would have created a scandal the Nazis could have ill afforded. As a result, Fuerstner knew that he was living on borrowed time as an army officer – after the Games he would surely be dismissed, a fate that he found hard to face, as he loved the army.

While the male athletes enjoyed the luxuriousness of the village, their female counterparts were housed in the relatively austere 'Friesian House', which was only a block away from the stadium. The reason for the sexual segregation and the Friesian House's proximity to the stadium was because the organising committee felt that 'after long and intense training, women are very highly strung immediately before difficult contests'. The large red-brick house was administered by the fearsome figure of Baroness Johanna von Wangenheim, who Iris Cummings remembered as being very tall, with grey hair gathered in braids. Although the committee claimed that the house was as good as any first-class hotel in the city, its occupants were rather less complimentary. 'It was pretty plain,' said Cummings. 'There were no pictures or anything, but it was adequate.' The athletes shared twin rooms, complete with basic furniture such as cupboards and chairs. The beds, however, left something to be desired. 'The beds are very peculiar,' wrote Velma Dunn, who was rooming with Cummings. 'Everything had been so nice that when we went to bed last night we expected soft beds. We jump in and they are as hard as rocks. I guess that is the German custom. We have two pillows. The top one feels like hard straw and the other is very soft.' Dunn also moaned about the bedding, which had a tendency to slip off frequently during the night.

The overall effect, then, was spartan rather than luxurious, an impression particularly reinforced by the quality of the food. 'We got boiled potatoes and cabbage!' said Cummings. 'This was before they flew some food out for us. We maybe got a few beets, and everything was boiled. As Californians, we were so spoiled, as we lived off fruit and orange juice. There were some rather vociferous complaints from

Dorothy Poynton, and she was shouting off because she couldn't get the food she wanted. I didn't care for it, but I ate it.' Americans such as Poynton, who had won silver at Amsterdam and gold at Los Angeles for diving, were more fussy than their European counterparts. Halet Çambel, a nineteen-year-old Turkish fencer, recalled that the women 'had very good breakfasts, with grapefruit'. Domnitsa Lanitis, a twenty-two-year-old Greek sprinter, bemoaned the lack of Greek food, but said that 'the food was good' and 'everything was comfortable'. Dorothy Odam, a sixteen-year-old British high jumper, also thought the food rather good. 'Perhaps I had such plain food at home,' she said. 'I had a nanny who cooked so plainly, and the food at the Friesian House seemed rather nice. I wasn't used to anything better.' The Americans did like some of the food, however. Velma Dunn recalled wolfing down Melba toast with lots of butter. 'I remember thinking that butter must be cheap,' she recalled, 'because there was lots of it.' In fact, butter was anything but cheap. The liberal quantity given to the athletes was nothing more than an example of propaganda. Butter cost 1.60 Reichsmarks per pound ($8.48 or nearly £5 in present-day terms). Like eggs, butter had been hoarded in order to convince visitors that such foodstuffs were in plentiful supply. While the visitors to Berlin enjoyed unlimited butter, the Berliners had to make do with lard and margarine, which was privately referred to as 'Hitler-butter'.

Also in abundance at the Friesian House were Germans in uniforms. 'The biggest thing that I noticed right away was that every man and boy was in uniform and it was all "Heil Hitler",' recalled Velma Dunn. 'We were not used to that.' The militarism could be heard as well as seen. 'We woke every morning to the sound of marching feet,' Dorothy Odam said. 'When I got to the window, I could see young people with shovels held like rifles over their shoulders. I learned that they were Hitler Youth.' In the main, both the female and male athletes regarded the uniforms, the swastikas and the regimentation with amusement. As Lou Zamperini was to write, 'in 1936 we still thought of Hitler only as a dangerous clown'.

Making light of the Nazi regime was common among the rowers, who were accommodated in a place that was now the Koepenick Police Officers' School near the Grunau regatta course. 'It was impressive, comfortable and bare,' said Martin Bristow. 'But there was good service and good food. However, there was a picture of Hitler in the dining-room, and we used to throw bread pellets at him. The waiters accepted it, but it must have been very hard for them. There were no repercussions or protest of any sort.' Such undergraduate tomfoolery was confined to the dining room. 'When we got out on to the street, we didn't laugh at the police – we weren't that badly behaved!'

Not all the visiting athletes, however, regarded the regime with such amusement. Some, such as the South African boxer Robey Leibbrandt, were ardent supporters of the Nazis. Leibbrandt's father, Meyder, was of German descent and had fought against the British during the Boer War. His twenty-three-year-old son had a profound hatred for the British, compounded by the fact that his mother, Susan Joyce, was of Irish descent. Her cousin was none other than William Joyce, who was later to find infamy during the war as Lord Haw-Haw. Leibbrandt was a phenomenal boxer in the light heavyweight class, and by the age of nineteen he had become the South African champion. He looked the part too – his chin square, his hair closely cropped, his eyes staring menacingly from under a broad brow. Owing to a broken thumb, Leibbrandt missed the 1932 Games, but his chance for international glory beckoned at the 1934 Empire Games in Britain. He was not to disappoint, because in his bout with the British champion, George Brennan, Leibbrandt knocked out his opponent in the first round. The result was declared void, however, because the judges deemed that Leibbrandt had punched low. Despite the result, Leibbrandt managed to win bronze, although his hatred for the British was magnified.

By 1936, Leibbrandt's boxing ability and his political beliefs had brought him to the attention of German agents in Cape Town. One of these agents approached him, and found the boxer to be a potentially useful figure. The agent's report was glowing:

> With more than 100 fights under his belt – 90 per cent won by knock-outs – he must be one of the favourites in Berlin to win the title. This will make a hero for South Africa and so much more valuable for our cause if we can influence him the right way.
>
> He speaks German well and although he admires our leader and country, he must be educated in the theory of National Socialism.

Proof of his sentiments is contained in a letter written to a mutual friend and shown to me. Leibbrandt wrote, *inter alia*: 'I will now go to Germany to see that legendary figure, Adolf Hitler.'

[. . .] I am convinced that here we have excellent material. With the right approach, he can be a great asset to our cause in his country.

The Olympics proved an ideal opportunity to woo Leibbrandt. Although there is nothing to suggest that the German officers attached to the teams had orders to assess the athletes as suitable agents, the officer with the South African team, Lieutenant von Vietinghoff, was certainly aware of Leibbrandt's political sympathies, and had been ordered by Ernst Bohle of the Auslands organisation – which was tasked with spreading Nazism overseas – to pay the boxer special attention. What Vietinghoff found was a man who displayed an asceticism similar to Hitler's. Not only was Leibbrandt a vegetarian, an almost unprecedented diet for an Afrikaner, let alone an Afrikaner boxer, but he also insisted on sleeping on a bare wooden board. In fact, Leibbrandt was a 'physical culture fanatic', as one South African newspaper described him. He would get up at five every morning, and run along the steep road near the village, rather than on the level practice track. In his first spar, he had knocked out his professional partner in less than a minute. 'He is mauling his sparring partners like a sadistic tiger,' it was reported. Had Leibbrandt wanted to become a German citizen, then doubtless he would have been readily accepted, and then picked up by either the SA or SS. It was Vietinghoff's task, however, to introduce Leibbrandt to those who wanted him to go back to South Africa to further the reach of Nazism. He would find the boxer to be more than receptive.

One German who Robey Leibbrandt would not have liked was Werner Seelenbinder. Since winning the championship earlier in the year, the wrestler had been devoting every spare hour to training, determined to win a medal, not just for himself, but for the chance to make that vital live radio broadcast to the world. If everything went well, then Seelenbinder's words would be transmitted to the world on the evening of 9 August. All around Europe, people would be tuning into their wirelesses that Sunday, people whose attention would be grabbed by an athlete spouting not just the normal sporting platitudes, but instead denouncing Nazism and its evils.

A few days before the Games were due to open, however, the Gestapo struck. They arrested over ninety worker-sportsmen, including many members of the Uhrig Group. Also seized were many of the radio technicians who were going to ensure that Seelenbinder's speech was aired. Now that they were incarcerated, Seelenbinder knew that his words would never be heard. He was not only dejected, but also frightened and confused. Why was he the only such worker-sportsman not to be arrested? Was the Gestapo trying to make it appear that he had betrayed his comrades? When would he be arrested? Only after he had won a medal? Seelenbinder knew there was nothing he could do but to continue to train. Even though he would not be able to make his speech, he would still be able to refuse to salute when he stood on the podium. All he had to do now was make sure he got on it. The competition would be tough, but Seelenbinder knew that he had a good chance.

It was not just sportsmen and diplomats who were travelling to Berlin that July. As well as thousands of ordinary tourists – some estimates put the number as high as 1,200,000 – there were many society figures from all over the world who were attending the Games. Many went to Berlin not to enjoy the sports, but more to revel in fascism *en fête*, there to join their fellow travellers and others whose sympathies for Germany transcended a mere love of peace. One of these was Diana Guinness, the third of the six daughters of Lord Redesdale, who was sympathetic to the German cause. Redesdale's daughters would soon be celebrated as the 'Mitford Girls', noted for their combination of beauty, charm, intelligence and effervescence. Of the six, Diana was considered the most beautiful, a classically cool blonde, her face exquisite and normally set in an expression that combined repose and aristocratic hauteur. Diana's eldest sister was Nancy Mitford, who had published three novels, including *Wigs on the Green*, which satirised the blackshirted antics of Diana and Unity Mitford, the fourth sister, who had developed a passion not only for Nazism, but also for Hitler himself. Diana had a similar love of fascism, but her attachment to the cause was not just political, but also romantic. Her lover was Sir Oswald Mosley, the leader of the British Union of Fascists (BUF). Her marriage to Bryan Guinness had ended three years earlier, and since then she had been living openly as Mosley's mistress. Mosley had founded the BUF in 1932, and although he claimed that its membership was as high as 50,000, it had enjoyed no electoral success. Nevertheless, what it had attracted was a significant amount of attention, not least for its public meetings, which often ended in violent battles between the Blackshirts and communists.

Mosley saw Germany as an ally, a message he often preached. On 22 March, at the Albert Hall in London, Mosley had advocated '[. . .] the closest possible friendship with Germany, a nation with a blood brotherhood. Germany is a nation with us, which can and will maintain for all time the peace of mankind. Why should we not have peace with Germany? What interests come between us?' A voice from the audience was heard to murmur 'Hitler', but Mosley ignored it and carried on, saying that Germany and Britain had 'almost every interest the same'.

Although Mosley was wealthy, one of his biggest problems with the BUF was raising money. Financial support for his British brand of fascism had dwindled, particularly after the Night of the Long Knives in Germany at the end of June 1934, which saw Hitler murder as many as four hundred of his political enemies, including the leader of the SA, Ernst Roehm. The brutality, it could be said, had helped to give fascism a bad name. Mosley had to look abroad for money, and in January of that year he had visited Mussolini in Italy. He returned with £20,000 (today worth approximately £900,000 or $1.5 million) in the gangsterish form of used notes in different currencies. It was not the first donation the Italians had made – since 1933, the BUF had been receiving some £60,000 a year, always in the form of used notes. The money was soon exhausted, however, and by 1936 an increasingly desperate Mosley was forced to look elsewhere. Germany was a likely source of income, and although Mosley himself had met Hitler only briefly once, Diana had done so on several occasions. His lover, then, became the ideal vehicle through which the British fascist leader could beg secretly for more funds.

Diana had first met Hitler with her sister Unity at the Osteria Bavaria restaurant in Munich in 1935. Unity's obsession with Hitler had seen her stalk the Fuehrer, to the extent of sitting in the restaurant on numerous occasions, waiting for the day when the subject of her yearnings would ask the mysterious English girl to come and join him. On 9 February 1935, he did so, and soon Unity fell under his spell. After the initial meeting, she wrote in a letter to her father that she was so happy that she 'wouldn't mind a bit dying'. 'I suppose I am the luckiest girl in the world [. . .] you remember that for me, he is the greatest man of all time.' By the time Diana met him, her sister and Hitler enjoyed a rapport that verged on the flirtatious, with Unity addressing Hitler in a familiar way that bordered on insubordination and which astonished the Fuehrer's lackeys. Like her sister, Diana found Hitler good company. 'He was extremely polite to women,' she recalled, 'he bowed and kissed hands as is the custom in Germany and France, and he never sat down until they did.' As well as coming across as the respectable bourgeois, Hitler 'could be very funny; he did imitations of marvellous drollery which showed how acutely observant he was'. Diana and Unity's friendship with Hitler blossomed very publicly. He invited them to the party rallies in Nuremberg, and later the Olympic Games, during which the two women would stay with the Goebbels family in Berlin. Soon the relationship between the Mitford sisters and Hitler was the talk of Mayfair. Was Unity Hitler's lover? Everyone knew who Diana's lover was, and a gossipy need for social symmetry wanted to pair the two sisters off with the two fascist leaders. It is unlikely, however, that Unity's relationship with Hitler ever mutated beyond a schoolgirlish infatuation. For Hitler, Unity and Diana were English versions of Wagnerian Rhine maidens, their features pressed from the archetype Aryan cast. He liked their company, and saw them as a conduit into British society.

On 19 June 1936 Goebbels took Diana and Unity to see Hitler. This time, the visit was not a social call, but an appeal for funds. Diana baldly told the Nazi leader that Mosley required £100,000 (today worth £4.1 million or just over $7 million) to continue his activities. Hitler may have liked Diana and Unity, but his attitude to Mosley was lukewarm. He rightly suspected that Mosley's star was dimming, but he nevertheless told Diana that the BUF could have £10,000, which was still a considerable sum.

Mosley was disappointed, and he asked his lover to request more funds during the Olympic Games. Diana knew that it would be difficult, but Mosley was hoping that her charm would appeal to the Nazis.

The Goebbels family occupied a lakeside villa on the Schwanenwerder outside Berlin. The house had belonged to a Jewish family that had since emigrated, and it had been given to Goebbels by Hitler. Diana warmed to her hosts, becoming fond of Magda Goebbels and her seven children, one of whom was the product of her previous marriage. She found their father 'intelligent, witty and sarcastic' with an 'exceptionally beautiful speaking voice'. Diana knew that she had to be as gracious a guest as possible in order to raise more money, but she also had another favour to ask of the Nazis, one that would eventually cause a scandal when it was discovered in Britain.

The British did not have the monopoly on German sympathisers travelling to Berlin that summer. The Americans had them too, and none was more famous that the aviator Charles Lindbergh, who had become a national hero after successfully flying across the Atlantic non-stop in May 1927. Two years later, he married Anne Morrow, the daughter of the diplomat Dwight Morrow. Their first child, Charles, was born in 1930, but was kidnapped on 1 March 1932 when he was just twenty months old. The ten-week hunt for the child made sensational news, and when the child's body was found on 12 May, the nation mourned along with the parents. It was not until September 1935 that a suspect was found, in the form of a German immigrant called Bruno Hauptmann, a former robber and carpenter living in the Bronx. The subsequent trial made for even more sensational news, and Hauptmann was found guilty and sentenced to death. There were doubts about the safety of his conviction, but in the public mind the German was guilty. In December the Lindberghs, tired of the publicity, fled the United States and made a temporary home in Kent in south-east England. There, they were able to live relatively undisturbed, apart from one occasion when some newspaper reporters threw stones at Lindbergh's dog when his master refused to be interviewed or to pose for photographs.

In June 1936 Lindbergh received a letter from Major Truman Smith, the military attaché at the American embassy in Berlin.

My dear Colonel Lindbergh
[. . .] In a recent discussion with high officials of the German Air Ministry, I was requested to extend to you in the name of General Goering and the German Air Ministry an invitation to visit Germany and inspect the new German civil and military air establishments.

Lindbergh readily accepted the offer, telling Major Smith in his letter of acceptance that he would be 'extremely interested in seeing some of the German developments' in aviation. 'I hope that General Goering does not feel it necessary to provide any special entertainment as far as I am concerned,' he added. The appeal was made in vain. There was no way that the Nazis would allow such a distinguished figure to visit Germany incognito. The moment a gleeful Goering heard of Lindbergh's acceptance, he said, 'He will be my guest at the opening of the Games.' Lindbergh was to become yet another whom the Nazis used to help legitimise their regime.

When the Lindberghs landed in Berlin on the afternoon of Wednesday, 22 July, they were met by a welcoming committee that was anything but inconspicuous. Not only were all the American naval and military attachés present, but there were also officials from the Air Ministry, Lufthansa, the Air Clubs of Germany, as well as Colonel Gustav Kastner, who greeted Lindbergh with a Nazi salute, before announcing that he would be the aviator's guide during his stay. Lindbergh spent the next few days enduring a hectic schedule of lunches, dinners and tours of aviation facilities. At one lunch, General Erhard Milch, the state secretary of the Reich Aviation Ministry, told Lindbergh that the Germans were planning to build an air force 'second to none in the world'. Such preparations were of course directly contrary to the terms of the Treaty of Versailles, but by now, after the occupation of the Rhineland, Germany was becoming far less coy about its rearmament. According to *The Economist*, Germany had spent some 10–12 billion Reichsmarks (today worth some $330 billion or £190 billion) directly or indirectly on rearming from 1933 to 1935. From what Lindbergh could see, Milch was telling the truth, as factories, squadrons and airfields all put on their best show for their guest. 'Obviously Germany was preparing for war on a major scale with the most modern equipment,' Lindbergh later wrote. 'In Nazi Germany, for the first time, war became real to me. The officers I met were not preparing for a game.'

According to one observer, Lindbergh was enjoying his time in the limelight. The German press was highly sycophantic, unlike the stone-throwing British and intrusive Americans. 'The Colonel seemed completely spellbound by the honours showered upon him since his arrival in Germany,' wrote the anti-Nazi journalist Bella Fromm, a columnist on Berlin's *Vossiche Zeitung*. 'It was obvious he enjoyed the limelight. His words lead to the conclusion that he not only thinks highly of German aviation, but also sympathises with the new Germany [. . .] One officer with an especially sharp tongue said: "If they had a National Socialist party over there and an SA and an SS, Lindbergh would certainly run around as *Gruppenfuehrer*".'

One of the highlights of the tour was a formal lunch held by Goering on 28 July at his official residence on the Wilhelmstrasse in Berlin. Lindbergh recalled how he and his wife sat with several German and American officers and their wives in a sumptuous room, decorated with elegant mirrors and madonnas.

> After the meal was over, Goering, white-uniformed, bemedaled, and gold-braided, escorted me to a side table, where he opened a photograph album. 'Here are our first seventy,' he said, turning the pages. Each page contained a picture of a military airfield. From the inspection trips I had made through German factories, I knew warplanes were being built to fill those fields.

As well as showing off his airfields, Goering was also said to have shown Lindbergh his latest lion cub. Goering was inordinately fond of cubs, although when they reached maturity they had to be returned to the zoo. Goering led Lindbergh by the arm down to the basement, where the American patted the cub without flinching, a display of fearlessness that impressed Goering enough to invite Lindbergh hunting. According to another account, Goering then cuddled the cub, whereupon it decided to relieve itself all over the

Reichsmarschall's bemedalled tunic. Goering's behaviour did not dissuade Lindbergh from meeting the head of the Luftwaffe once more. The venue for their next encounter would be in Goering's box at the Olympic Stadium for the opening ceremony of the XIth Olympiad.

8

The Opening

~

AUGUST IN BERLIN is normally dry and warm, but in 1936 the weather was anything but. Theodor Lewald and Carl Diem must have been cursing when they looked out of their bedroom windows in the early hours of Saturday, 1st August. An intermittent drizzle was falling, and with a heavily grey sky it looked as though the precipitation might get heavier. This was certainly not 'Hitler weather', the tongue-in-cheek epithet secretly used by Germans to describe sunny days. Five years of hard work, five years of detailed organisation, extensive travelling, diplomatic manoeuvring and political wrangling, would now be rewarded with a wash-out of an opening ceremony. It would hardly be the most auspicious of starts.

Nevertheless, rain or shine, the show had to go on. The hours leading up to the ceremony in the stadium at four o'clock were packed with rite and ritual. Church services were attended. Special guards were mounted. Battalions of honour were inspected. Wreaths were laid at war memorials. Military bands oompahed through the streets. Nearly thirty thousand members of the Hitler Youth and the German Girls paraded in the Lustgarten. Uniforms were in abundance, with one observer estimating that he had passed through some 700,000 of them on his way to the stadium – SA men in brown, SS men in black, soldiers in grey-green. Any visitor to Berlin could be in no doubt that exactly twenty-two years after the outbreak of the Great War, Germany was once again a mighty military power. It was as if the country were mobilising, not putting on a sporting pageant.

Although the timetable was exhaustive, and much of it had been rehearsed, there was still plenty of room for error. The most unreliable participants were the athletes themselves, who lacked the discipline of the highly regimented youth groups. At precisely 1.15, 170 buses turned up at the Olympic village to transport the athletes to the stadium, depositing them on the huge May Field to the west of the complex. They now had some three hours to wait before they would march into the stadium, and with the drizzle and the coolness, for some the time passed slowly. 'It was very boring,' recalled Dorothy Odam. 'We were all lined up outside in alphabetical order. However, we were all very smart, well dressed, and well disciplined.' The athletes were not provided with any food, but Odam remembered some drinks being brought round. While she found the wait boring, there were others who revelled in the anticipation. 'The air of excitement and noise among the teams drove our tiredness away,' said Pat Norton, a female Australian backstroker. 'Everyone was very excited and talked to each other,' recalled Elfriede Kaun.

Above the stadium drifted the mighty *Hindenburg* airship, its tail fins emblazoned with swastikas, the Olympic flag fluttering below it. The *Hindenburg* was yet another symbol of the re-emerging might of the new Germany. Along with her sister ship, the *Graf Zeppelin II*, the airship was the largest aircraft ever built. At 245 metres long it was three times the length of a jumbo jet. In July, it had completed a record double crossing of the Atlantic in 5 days, 19 hours and 51 minutes, its most recent return trip bringing with it another symbol of German might, the boxer Max Schmeling. Schmeling had sensationally defeated Joe Louis in New York City, a victory embraced by the Nazis as further evidence of Aryan superiority. Louis's defeat had been emphatic – the German had knocked him down in the fourth round, and knocked him out in the twelfth. When the *Hindenburg* landed at Frankfurt Airport on 26 July, the ground was thickly covered with well-wishers. Not one of them, however, was more effusive than Hitler himself, who received Schmeling and his wife at the Chancellery later that day. 'Hitler wanted to be told of the fight in full detail,' Schmeling wrote. 'It was clear that he had already been well informed by the press accounts. For example, he asked me if I had known even before the fourth round whether I would "beat the Negro". ' Schmeling then produced a film of the event, which Hitler ordered to be broadcast as a feature throughout Germany, nationalistically entitled *Max Schmeling's Victory – a German Victory*.

At exactly 3.18 on the afternoon of the 1st, Hitler left the Chancellery for the Olympic Stadium. Hundreds of thousands lined the streets as their Fuehrer passed, all of them craning their heads to catch a glimpse of him over the helmets and caps of the 40,000 troops who guarded the way. Wearing a military uniform, Hitler stood in the front footwell of his large black Mercedes-Benz, acknowledging the cheers of his people with a right arm set in an almost permanent salute. For those who were in the motorcade, the effect of the cheering masses was something to witness. The British journalist George Ward Price had ridden in the back of Hitler's car earlier in the year in Breslau, and the experience was similar to what was now happening along the Unter den Linden.

> We drove [. . .] for forty minutes at little more than walking pace through the streets of the city, lined with dense crowds from which went up an unceasing roar of 'Heil! Heil! Heil!' It beat upon our ears like the surge of the sea. Every window was hung with flags and crowded with onlookers. Hitler remained on his feet all the time, raising his arm in salute and smiling right and left. I studied the serried ranks on either side. All ages and types of people wore the same expression of ecstatic delight.

The experience of being part of the adulatory crowd was no less intense. The American novelist Thomas Wolfe was in Berlin during the Games, and he saw how a collective mania infected the crowds as they waited for their Fuehrer.

> At last he came – and something like a wind across a field of grass was shaken through that crowd, and from afar the tide rolled up with him, and in it was the voice, the hope, the prayer of the land. The Leader came by slowly in a shining car, a little dark man with a comic-opera moustache, erect and standing, moveless and unsmiling, with his hand upraised, palm outward, not in Nazi-wise salute, but straight up, in a gesture of blessing such as the Buddha or Messiahs use.

Wolfe, like every other visitor, also remarked on the abundance of uniforms. Later that month he sent a postcard of the guard at the Brandenburg Gate to his editor. On the back he wrote, 'We can never learn to march like these boys. – And it looks as if they're about ready to go again.' Not every German, however, was caught up in the intense feelings of national pride. That month, Helmuth von Moltke, a young lawyer who had a passionate hatred of Nazism, wrote to his wife Freya, telling her that 'Berlin is frightful! A solid mass is pushing its way down the Unter den Linden to look at the decorations. And what people! I never knew the likes of them existed. Probably these are the people who are National Socialists because I don't know them either!' Moltke would later become a founding member of the Kreisau Circle resistance group, and he would be hanged in Berlin in January 1945.

At 3.50, Hitler arrived at the Platz am Glockenturm in the shadow of the monolithic bell-tower that lay on the western edge of the May Field. The dictator stepped briskly out of the car, and inspected an Honour Battalion that was assembled before the tower. So far, an ignorant observer would have assumed that Hitler was on his way to a party rally, not a sporting event. He then walked on to the May Field, past a row of cannon, until finally the ceremony began to reveal a hint that this was not a military or political occasion. The Olympic fanfare started up, and Hitler was greeted by Baillet-Latour and Lewald, both of whom were dressed as though they were nineteenth-century statesmen, wearing tailcoats and top hats. Around their necks hung the heavy gold chains of Olympic office. At an earlier event, Goebbels had described them as resembling 'flea-circus directors'. Other members of the IOC and the GOC flanked them, as did numerous army, SS and SA officers. The procession of around one hundred men, led by the Fuehrer, formed roughly into four columns and walked past the waiting athletes to the Marathon Gate, which was – and is – the western entrance to the stadium. As they passed the athletes, the entire May Field fell eerily silent as thousands of pairs of eyes looked at Hitler. 'He was clad in brown,' wrote Dhyan Chand, 'an athletic figure, and trod the ground with a firm step. Occasionally he looked sideways and his face was serious, but not stern.' Other athletes, such as Pat Norton, were less impressed. 'It was my first direct look at the man who was the talk of the world,' she said, 'and a more uninspiring person would be hard to find.' Percy Oliver, an Australian swimmer, recalled how Hitler paid the Australian contingent special attention. 'Hitler came through the centre of the teams and then he came to us. He then walked up and down our ranks specifically. I have no idea why. Perhaps it was because of our record during the war.' The silence continued until the procession reached the stadium, where a group of white-shirted Hitler Youth near the entrance started shouting, '*Heil Hitler!*' At this moment, the whole May Field erupted into cheers, a sound that rushed into the massive bowl of the stadium, causing the 100,000 spectators to rise to their feet as one, raise their right arms in salute and cry out '*Heil Hitler!*' 'As he went into the stadium you would have thought God had come down from heaven,' said British hurdler Violet Webb. It was no wonder that Dorothy Odam regarded the moment as being one of 'mass hysteria'.

From the point of view of the three men at the front of the procession – Hitler, Baillet-Latour and Lewald – the moment must have been extraordinary. The Olympic Stadium is larger on the inside than it is appears from the outside as it sinks some 12 metres into the ground. The effect is like entering an almighty and partially subterranean cave, which in 1936 was full of people looking directly at one man, who walked purposefully past the as yet unlit brazier, down the steps to the ground level, accompanied by an oceanic roar of '*Heil Hitler!*' which drowned out Wagner's 'March of Allegiance'. Before Hitler reached his seat on the south side of the stadium, his progress was interrupted by a five-year-old girl dressed in a simple white dress with flowers in her blonde hair. This was none other than Gudrun Diem, the daughter of Carl Diem. An avuncular grin stretched across Hitler's face as he stooped to receive the bouquet he was being offered by this small example of Aryan femininity.

By the time Hitler reached his seat at 4.05, there was no doubt that he was already the star of the Olympics. These were his Games now, not Baillet-Latour's, and most certainly not Coubertin's. As if to reinforce the Nazification of the Games, the orchestra struck up with 'Deutschland über Alles' and the Horst Wessel Song, both of which had heralded the start of the Winter Games back in February. Despite the inappropriateness of both songs, the spectators heartily sang along, and, according to Dhyan Chand, 'not an eye was left dry'. After the last words of the Horst Wessel song had died down – 'Comrades shot by Red Front and reaction / Still march with us, their spirits on our ranks!' – the order was given for the flags of the competing nations to be raised. With a cry of '*Heisst Flagge!*', two sailors at each flagpole slowly drew them up, an act that was accompanied by the vast chimes of the bell sounding from the other side of the May Field.

At 4.15, the athletes were finally allowed to enter the stadium. Led by the Greeks, as is the Olympic tradition, the march took some forty minutes. The differences in the manner in which the teams presented themselves were just as great as the differences in the way the crowd reacted. Despite the ambiguity of the gesture, the Greeks made the Olympic salute, to which Hitler responded in kind, his arm stretched out to the right. Hitler often saluted in this way, however, so it was not clear whether his salute was Olympic or Nazi. Perhaps in his mind such a distinction was an irrelevance. As the Greek team passed, an elderly figure broke ranks and climbed the stands towards Hitler. It was none other than Spiridon Louis, the winner of the Olympic marathon from 1896. Now sixty-three and looking weathered by the Greek climate, Louis made his way with difficulty, but he eventually reached Hitler and presented him with an olive branch from Olympia. Hitler clearly did not keep the branch, for he would successfully invade Louis's homeland just over four and a half years later. Louis was not to witness his country's occupation, as he died on 26 March 1940.

When the French team passed Hitler's box, they made an Olympic salute, at which the crowd went wild, believing their neighbours and former enemy had made the fascist salute. 'Never was the war threat on the Rhine less than during these moments,' noted one French journalist. 'Never were the French more popular in Germany than on this occasion.' The cheers for France exceeded those made for the Austrians and the goose-stepping Bulgarians. Hitler, however, was clearly not happy with his people's reaction, and looked on sourly at the French in their black berets. 'In the prolonged applause Hitler sensed a popular mood,' wrote Albert Speer, 'a longing for peace and reconciliation with Germany's western neighbour. If I am correctly interpreting Hitler's expression at the time, he was more disturbed than pleased by the Berliners' cheers.'

Following the French were the British, who had elected not to salute at all, and merely made an eyes-right at Hitler. There had been much discussion among the team about whether to use the Olympic salute, but the experience at Garmisch, in which the Britons' salute was mistaken for a fascist one, was informative. The crowd went quiet, regarding the lack of any form of salute as a sign of disrespect to them and their leader. There was some small applause, but it was insignificant compared to the reception that had been given to the French. Many of the other British dominions, such as India and Australia, refused to salute – 'We just didn't think it the right thing to do,' recalled Percy Oliver – although the seven-strong Bermudan team doffed their white solar topees and made the fascist salute with their right arms.

The United States was one of the last teams to enter the stadium. 'We were a total disgrace,' recalled Joanna de Tuscan. 'About thirty or forty non-members of the team, fat, with cigarette ashes on their clothes, marched at the head of the team.' Marty Glickman felt that the word 'marching' was inappropriate to describe how the Americans proceeded. 'American athletes don't march very well,' he wrote. 'We kind of moved in our usual loose-gaited walk.' At the team's head was Avery Brundage, who was neither fat nor a smoker, and was one of the few who really did march. Brundage would have been especially proud that day, not just because he had managed to get the team to Berlin, but also because he had just achieved one of his greatest ambitions – he had been made a member of the IOC. Two days earlier, at the thirty-fifth session of the IOC, Ernest Lee Jahncke was expelled by a vote of 49 to 0. Although William May Garland did not vote, he expressed his disapproval of Jahncke. General Sherrill also did not vote, because he had died on 25 June. There was no doubt, however, as to which of the two members Brundage had replaced. The minutes of the meeting state emphatically that Brundage had been elected by a unanimous vote 'en replacement de M. Lee Jahncke'. Finally, after years of battle, Brundage had got his prize.

As the Americans marched past Hitler, they removed their boaters and clutched them to their hearts. Whereas other flags were dipped in honour of the Fuehrer, the Stars and Stripes remained resolutely aloft, which caused a murmur of discontent around the stadium. Marty Glickman recalled the moment when the team passed Hitler. 'We looked up at the box where he was flanked by Goering and Goebbels and Hess and Himmler and the rest of the Nazi hierarchy,' he wrote. 'And you could hear the comment run through our crowd as we were walking in, "Hey, he looks like Charlie Chaplin". And indeed he did.'

Others were more respectful of Hitler, some to the extent that they regarded him almost as a god. The South African Robey Leibbrandt was probably more fanatical in his regard for the man than any German. 'I looked straight at him,' he recalled. 'Suddenly I was seized by a strange sensation. I still don't know if it was his humble uniform or his magnetic personality that fascinated me, but it was as if I was taken over by a hypnotic force. I stopped hearing the march music and marched on mechanically.' Leibbrandt was leading the team in, and instead of shouting his commands in English, as had been agreed, he did so in Afrikaans. The Nazi-loving Leibbrandt had a theory as to why. 'At the sight of Hitler the German-Irish blood pumped turbulently through my Afrikaner heart and gave the orders in my mother tongue. Perhaps I wanted to impress the Fuehrer. I wanted to tell him in the language of General de Wet [a notable Boer leader who had died in 1922] that the descendants of a heroic people were marching in front of him. I knew that Adolf Hitler held General de Wet and the Boer people in very high esteem.'

The last team to enter the stadium was that of Germany. Predictably, and reasonably enough, the spectators leaped to their feet and saluted the team, immaculately dressed all in white, and wearing yachting caps. Once again, 'Deutschland über Alles' and the Horst Wessel Song were belted out. As the athletes passed Hitler's box, their salutes were performed immaculately, even by Werner Seelenbinder. He knew he had to be patient, but it still pained him to have to raise his right arm. His moment of protest would soon come.

At five o'clock, the words of Coubertin were broadcast around the stadium. Claiming he was too ill to make the trip to Berlin, he had instead made a recording in French. 'The important thing at the Olympic Games is not to win, but to take part, just as the important thing in life is not to conquer, but to struggle well.' This was hardly a sentiment that Hitler would have agreed with, but then the dictator would not have cared. The recording represented a few seconds of lip-service to the Olympic ideal, spoken by a frail old man who had been bought up by the Nazis. Besides, as soon as the recording had finished, Lewald stepped up to a rostrum erected on the side of track, and started to make a speech that was to last twenty agonising minutes. The rostrum was decorated with a vast German eagle clutching the

Olympic rings. The symbolism could not have been clearer – the Olympic movement had fallen prey to Nazism, its rings helpless under the eagle's talons.

While the crowd fidgeted, Lewald pompously droned on about the nobility of the Olympic movement. This was his moment, and he was going to make it last as long as possible, even if it meant that he overran the timetable. Lewald also spoke about peace.

> In spite of the keenness of the contest and the ardour of the struggle, may harmony and friendliness, understanding and comradeship prevail between you all, so that a shining example may be created of that ideal, emphasised again and again by our Fuehrer and Chancellor, of friendly cooperation between all the peoples.

Quite when Hitler had re-emphasised the need for such an ideal was unclear, but Lewald was doubtless sincere. Despite the pacts he had made, the underhand dealings he had indulged in, Lewald was a believer in Olympism. He really did believe that it was a panacea for mankind, and if he had to transgress morally in order to impose what he saw as a morally perfect order, then so be it. Such an attitude, of course, was identical to that of Hitler, whose turn it now was to speak. For once, he was brief. 'I announce as opened the Games of Berlin, celebrating the eleventh Olympiad of the modern era.'

The Olympic flag was then hoisted, and for many the most spectacular part of the ceremony took place – 20,000 pigeons were released into the air. There was, however, a comic side to what should have been an uplifting spectacle. Just after the birds took flight, a terrific artillery barrage rang out, frightening the birds and causing them to deposit guano all over the athletes. 'Those pigeons circled right overhead and dropped on us,' said Lou Zamperini, 'and you could hear it falling on our straw hats, splat, splat. Everybody tried to stand at attention, but it was pretty hard. The poor girls got it in their hair.' The Americans were obviously unlucky, for no members of the British team were hit. As the pigeons circled and left the stadium, the orchestra, conducted by Richard Strauss, played the 'Olympic Hymn', the music which Strauss had specially composed for the German Olympic Committee in December 1934 in his home in Garmisch. Strauss was not proud of his collaboration with the Nazis.

'I while away the dull days of Advent with the composition of an Olympic hymn,' he wrote to his friend, the Austrian-Jewish librettist Stefan Zweig. 'Yes, the devil finds work for idle hands.' Neither was it just the Nazis whom Strauss loathed. 'This common lot,' he wrote to Zweig. 'I, of all people, who hate and despise sport!' Strauss's association with the Nazis would forever taint his reputation, but many maintain that his behaviour was simply a means of ensuring the safety of his daughter-in-law, Alice, who was Jewish.

As the last notes of the hymn faded, a solitary figure appeared at the eastern entrance to the stadium. Dressed in a white vest and white running shorts, the figure was the epitome of Germanic manhood – tall and muscular. In his right hand he held a piece of Krupp steel, out of which blazed the Olympic flame. The athlete was a middle-distance runner called Fritz Schilgen, who was the 3,075th person to have carried the torch the 3,075 kilometres from Olympia, where it was lit on the morning of 20 July. The rays of the sun had lit the flame, their heat focused by a glass on to the torch. An extra element of ritualism was added by the presence of twelve Greek girls, all dressed in short athletic skirts – vestal virgins guarding the fire of Zeus. A hymn was chanted, and musicians played on ancient instruments. It was a moment of pure theatre, all of which was watched by a heaving throng of Greeks, who cheered on a local runner, Constantine Condylis, who was to take the torch for the first kilometre. Behind him travelled a car laden with spare torches and runners in case of any accidents.

Also motoring along was Leni Riefenstahl, the German film-maker who had been commissioned to make a film of the Olympics. A former actress, Riefenstahl had famously directed and produced a film of the Sixth Nuremberg Nazi Party Congress. Called *Triumph of the Will*, the film was seen as a homage to both Hitler and the Nazi movement, featuring the Fuehrer and his massed hordes in strikingly composed shots, set to stirring martial music. Riefenstahl was therefore the obvious choice to film the Games. When she was approached by Carl Diem from the Olympic Committee, however, Riefenstahl had her reservations about whether the project was feasible. 'I had sworn to myself that I would never make another documentary,' Riefenstahl recalled. '"Impossible," I said. But Diem persisted.' The director eventually gave in, realising that the film had great potential. 'In my mind's eye, I could see the ancient ruins of the classical Olympic sites slowly emerging from patches of fog and the Greek temples and sculptures drifting by [. . .]' Riefenstahl signed a contract, and soon found herself immersed in innumerable technical and bureaucratic difficulties. 'We had to struggle against a mountain of red tape, months before the Games even began. The main issue was the location of the cameras. Actually, any camera inside the stadium was disruptive. I had to muster a lot of patience and self-control not to give up in my fights with the officials.'

In Greece, Riefenstahl found that the picture she had in her mind's eye was at odds with the reality. The scruffy Condylis in his vest and shorts did not typify the noble figure of antiquity she desired. Furthermore, the crowds got in the way of her cameras, and her attempt to follow the progress of the torch was thwarted by local officials. There was only one solution. Riefenstahl created her own idealised version of the truth and filmed her own beginning to the torch run, using the naked figure of the fourth runner, who was the handsome nineteen-year-old son of Russian émigrés. The resulting footage, while undoubtedly beautiful, is complete myth. No matter – for Riefenstahl, and indeed for the Nazis, the purpose of the film was to make explicit the supposed link between Germany and Ancient Greece. The Reich was not only the present home of the Olympics, but the true repository for all the virtues of the Ancient Greeks. As Lewald had said in his speech in a typical piece of Nazi cod history, the Olympic torch created 'a real and spiritual bond between our German fatherland and the sacred places of Greece founded nearly 4,000 years ago by Nordic immigrants'.

Riefenstahl also glossed over the effect the torch had on the countries it passed through, most markedly in Austria, where it became a symbol of controversy. The torch arrived in Vienna in the early evening of 29 July, where it was joyfully greeted by 10,000 Austrian Nazis, who welcomed it with shouts of '*Heil Hitler!*' and, predictably, the Horst Wessel Song. The Nazis also demonstrated against the Jewish members of the Austrian Olympic team, which had gathered to see the torch. They shouted 'Perish Judah!', and as matters threatened to get violent, the police made over five hundred arrests. Such events made a mockery of Coubertin's proclamation to the torch runners, that through the run '. . . there will be established the vigorous and well-considered Peace appropriate to a sporting epoch of high ambition and strong will'.

The torch reached Germany at the Czech border at 11.45 on the morning of 31 July, and was greeted by some fifty thousand Germans. Some thirty hours and thirty minutes later, it arrived in the Olympic Stadium, which fell into a hush as Fritz Schilgen made his way around the southern half of the track, passing in front of Hitler's box. He then ran up the steps towards the Marathon Gate, and paused before he reached the brazier. The crowd remained silent until finally Schilgen lifted up the torch, igniting the flame. Once again, the stadium filled with the huge roar of 100,000 cheers. With the arrival of the flame, it felt as though the Games had finally begun. There was one more piece of ritual however – the taking of the Olympic oath. This was performed by Rudolf Ismayr, a weightlifter who had won gold at the 1932 Games. Gripping a flag, Ismayr declaimed the oath loudly and clearly. 'We swear that we will take part in the Olympic Games in loyal competition, respecting the regulations which govern them and desirous of participating in the true spirit of sportsmanship for the honour of our country and the glory of sport.' The only mistake Ismayr made was that he clutched the wrong flag. Instead of holding on to the Olympic flag, he instead held a swastika. It was a small mistake, but a telling one.

9

The First Week

~

THE FIRST ROUND of the 100 metres heats started at 10.30 the following morning. There were twelve heats in total, and Jesse
Owens had the misfortune to be drawn in the last one, which was due
to be run just before noon. With the second round of heats starting
at three o'clock, Owens would have little time to take the forty-five-
minute bus ride back to the village, eat his lunch and then return to
the stadium. Owens sat in the warmth of the dressing room – there
was no point in exposing himself to the somewhat autumnal conditions outside. There was a chilly wind blowing from the north-west,
making the air feel cooler than its actual 18 degrees. While he waited,
his coach, Larry Snyder, warned him about what reaction he might
expect from the crowd. 'Don't let anything from the stands upset you,'
said Snyder. 'Ignore the insults and you'll be all right.'

Snyder's hunch could not have been more wrong. When Owens
entered the stadium, he was the subject of much good-natured
curiosity. Although the Germans had had weeks of derogatory articles about *der Neger* forced on them by the Nazi press, they were fascinated by this man, who had performed astonishing feats on the
other side of the world. After all, Owens was, in the words of one
observer, 'a charming creature, courteous and modest, and entirely
unspoilt by the fact that he is already the most-discussed athlete
in Berlin'. While Owens waited for his heat, he chatted with
Germany's mighty Erich Borchmeyer, who would be a serious rival
for the gold. Borchmeyer reminded Owens that the two men had
once met, in Los Angeles in 1932, when they had run the 100 yards
in the Coliseum. Owens had won the race, and Borchmeyer, in a
display of respect, had asked Owens for a signed photograph. 'I still
have that photo,' the German told Owens. 'I always keep it. One day

I shall show my children.' Unfortunately, the men could not talk for much longer, as Borchmeyer's English was weak, and Owens' German was non-existent.

Just before 11.55, the athletes went to their marks. They got set, and then they were off. With a field of five men, it was an easy race for the American, and he breasted the tape in a time of 10.3, which equalled the world and Olympic record. Sasaki of Japan came second, a full seven-tenths of a second behind Owens, or some 7 metres. If Owens had been a 1,500 metres runner, then his margin of victory would have been just over 100 metres. As soon as the race was over, Owens hurried back to the Olympic village and grabbed a rushed lunch, returning just in time for the second round of heats. By three o'clock, the weather had worsened, and that morning's tail wind of some 6 kilometres per hour had increased to just over 8 kilometres per hour.

Owens walked to the start of lane two and removed his tracksuit. He tucked his vest into his shorts, partially obscuring the large black '733' stuck to the front of his vest. And then the crowd began to shout. It was a shout he had heard in Hamburg, and now he was hearing it again. Far from being racially abused, the African-American was being lionised. 'Yess-say! Yess-say! Yess-say! Ovens! Ovens! Ovens!' 'Ovens' placed his hands on his hips, and nervously transferred his weight from one foot to another, looking down the lane to the finishing tape. The competition to his right was hardly awesome, but Owens knew there were no certainties. A trip, a stumble, a pulled muscle, a late start – all might see him spend the rest of the afternoon back at the Olympic village, imagining the headlines on the sports pages around the world the following day.

The athletes went to their marks. Owens breathed out calmly. The starting pistol fired. Owens made a good start, but it was no better than that made by the Japanese Yoshioka, who was sporting a white headband. The two men ran abreast for the first 30 metres, and it looked as though Owens would be pushed all the way to the tape. But then something extraordinary happened, something that very few of the 100,000 spectators had ever seen in the flesh. It looked as if an invisible force suddenly pulled Owens ahead of the pack. There was no sign of any particular effort, no grimacing, no wild exertions, just an increase in speed that seemed magical. Owens reached the line in a new world and Olympic record of 10.2 seconds. He was going so fast by the end of the race that he nearly plunged into a camera pit some 65 metres beyond the finishing line. It was only his quick reactions which made him step aside and avoid a catastrophe. The crowd loved his performance, and once more chanted his name.

The only people who were fuming were the Nazis, who were shocked not so much by Owens' success – after all, wasn't he an animal, not a human being? – but by the crowd's reaction to him. So far, the German people had cheered on not only the French, but now a 'Neger' as well. The Games were not going exactly to plan. That afternoon, however, saw some Nazi face being saved as Germany won two gold medals. Tilly Fleischer won the women's javelin with a new Olympic record of 45.18 metres, and Hans Woellke projected his shot 16.20 metres, which broke the Olympic record by 20 centimetres. In the 10,000 metres final held at 5.30, Aryan 'superiority' was again confirmed by the Finnish triumvirate of Ilmari Salminen, Arvo Askola and Volmar Iso-Hollo, who took gold, silver and bronze respectively. The Nazis were thrilled by these victories, and in the excitement Tschammer und Osten summoned the victors to Hitler's box so the Fuehrer could congratulate them personally.

While the Aryans were receiving Hitler's best wishes, the final of the high jump was taking place. Over the course of the day, nine competitors had been selected to jump in the final, all of whom had cleared 1.94 metres. The two favourites were African-Americans Cornelius 'Corny' Johnson and Owens' old friend David Albritton, both of whom had set an unofficial new world record back on 12 July of 2.07 metres. As well as facing their fellow American, Delos Thurber, Johnson and Albritton were up against Kotkas and Kalima from Finland and Weinkoetz from Germany. Three Japanese had also made the finals. Of these seven men, Kotkas, the European champion, represented the biggest danger to Albritton and Johnson. A giant and muscular blond, he looked so heavy it was hard to imagine him attaining any great height. Nevertheless, his enormously powerful legs were able to lift him well within striking distance of the two African-Americans. Albritton was nursing an injured ankle, however, so it looked as if Johnson was going to steal the gold.

The difference in the jumpers' composure and styles was enormous. While the other athletes received intensive rub-downs and pep talks from their trainers, Albritton and Johnson lay or sat back on the grass contentedly, looking for all the world as if they were lazily waiting for a couple of women to unpack a picnic. With the bar set at 1.90, none of the nine had any trouble in clearing it, with both Johnson and Albritton doing so in their tracksuits. Of the two men, Albritton had the more graceful style. One of the first to use the straddle technique, he would approach the bar from the left, and launch himself off his right foot to roll over the bar. Johnson, however, used his immense power and height – he was 6 foot 5 inches – to more or less hurdle it.

Weinkoetz, Kalima and two of the Japanese tipped the bar at 1.97. So too did Albritton at his first attempt; he then removed his track-suit for his second attempt, at which he was successful. Kotkas, Thurber and Johnson cleared the bar on their first attempts, with Johnson resolutely – perhaps cockily – still in his tracksuit. At 2.00 metres, Yata from Japan went out, with both Kotkas and Albritton scraping through on their third attempts. Thurber managed to get over on his second, although at 2.03 he went out, as did Kotkas and Albritton, who nudged the bar with his groin on his final try. Johnson had no problems, however, although by now he had finally removed his bulky tracksuit to sail over on his first attempt. Johnson had therefore won gold, and over the loudspeaker system he could hear the words 'Champion Olympique Protocolaire'. The bar was now set for a world-record-busting height of 2.08, but with the light fading and a gentle rain starting to fall, he was unable to clear it. Nevertheless, 2.03 represented a new Olympic record. For the United States, the high jump had been a great success, as they had taken gold, silver and bronze.

Had Cornelius Johnson been wanting to meet the Patron of the Games, however, then he was to be disappointed, as Hitler had left after his congratulatory session with the Finns and the Germans and before the high jump victory ceremony. The Chancellery later main-tained that Hitler had to leave both because he had an appointment and also because he did not wish to cause a traffic snarl-up if he left later. Others claimed it was because Hitler had no wish to find himself congratulating a 'Neger'. Many, such as Arthur Daley of the New York

Times, fancied the latter theory. 'The fact remains that his abrupt departure after reviewing virtually the entire afternoon program caused the wagging of many tongues,' he wrote. 'Press box interpreters of this step chose to put two and two together and arrive at the figure of four.' It is impossible now to know the truth, but what is certain is that if Hitler directly snubbed anybody during the Games, then it was Cornelius Johnson and not Jesse Owens. It was not as if Johnson particularly cared, however, 'There's nothing in the program stating that we winners are to be received by him,' he said. 'I'm not kicking.' The following morning, Hitler found himself being taken to task by Baillet-Latour, who insisted that as the German leader would be unable to congratulate all the athletes, then it would be less discriminatory if he congratulated none at all. With a few exceptions, it was a request to which Hitler agreed.

At 3.30 the following afternoon, Jesse Owens stood at the start of lane six for the first of the two heats for the semi-finals. The fastest three athletes from each race would go through to the final. Owens looked down at the track. It was soggy and heavy from the two rain showers that had passed over the stadium at lunchtime. Earlier, he had found that his world record had been disallowed – the tail wind had been too strong. Judging by the quality of the track, there was little chance he was going to threaten the record today. Owens jogged gently on the spot, the waistband of his shorts brought up high, revealing his long legs, which Leni Riefenstahl's camera caressed. The secret behind Owens' speed lay in the fact that his body was perfectly proportioned – there was not one single flaw in its constituency. Whereas other athletes may have had longer and larger limbs, Owens' entire form was sculpture-perfect, possessing a harmony that enabled his body to work so brilliantly. It was this quality which gave Owens' running style that sense of magic. 'He was', said Lou Zamperini, 'athletic perfection personified.'

Owens' start that afternoon was good, but not great. Against him was his fellow American, Frank Wykoff, and Strandberg of Sweden, both of whom were strong, and were proving so as they sprinted up to the 30-metre mark, at which point Owens was running third, perhaps even fourth. It took Owens another fifteen strides to rectify the situation, and at 60 metres he was ahead. When he was just under

10 metres from the finish, Owens snapped a quick look to his left. There was no one there. Just under a second later he had broken the tape in a time of 10.4 seconds, which for him was comparatively slow. Wykoff and Strandberg finished second and third, both of them one tenth of a second behind Owens. In the other semi-final, Owens' fellow African-American Ralph Metcalfe beat Martinus Osendarp of Holland and Erich Borchmeyer in a time of 10.5 seconds.

Just under an hour and a half later, Jesse Owens had won his first gold medal. Ralph Metcalfe, who had so nearly beaten him, was second, and in third place came an ecstatic Martin Osendarp, who had just beaten Borchmeyer. Although the crowd – and indeed Hitler – had wanted the home-grown Borchmeyer to win, Owens' victory was a popular one. Nevertheless, Hitler, mindful of Baillet-Latour's words the previous evening, did not congratulate Owens, which started the apocryphal tale that he had snubbed the athlete. Owens was later to claim, however, that he and Hitler waved at each other, a claim supported by John Woodruff, the gold medal winner in the 800 metres. 'I do recall seeing Jesse while still on the track,' said Woodruff, 'waving and exchanging salutes with Hitler in his box.' Curiously, this friendliness between Hitler and Owens was spotted by nobody else that day, and the story appears to be apocryphal.

There is no doubt that Hitler was far from delighted with Owens' victory. Domnitsa Lanitis recalled sitting near the dictator when Owens won. 'He was annoyed when the Negro was winning,' she said. 'I saw him annoyed. He was furious with Jesse Owens.' Baldur von Schirach, the Reich Youth Leader, witnessed a similar reaction while he was sitting with Hitler in his box. ' "The Americans should be ashamed of themselves, letting negroes win their medals for them. I shall not shake hands with this negro." ' Albert Speer's memoirs confirm this reaction. 'He was highly annoyed by the series of triumphs by the marvellous coloured American runner, Jesse Owens,' Speer wrote. 'People whose antecedents came from the jungle were primitive, Hitler said with a shrug; their physiques were stronger than those of civilised whites. They represented unfair competition and hence must be excluded from future games.'

In truth, Hitler was able to hide behind Baillet-Latour's edict. It let him off the hook. There would be no photographs of a humiliated

Hitler greeting a black man, displaying a smile the world knew to be false. Had Baillet-Latour not insisted that Hitler was not to congratulate the victorious athletes, then his refusal would indeed have been a snub. In order to clarify Hitler's position, the Chancellery released a statement the following day.

> As the Fuehrer and the Chancellor of the Reich could not be present at all of the final competitions and was therefore unable to receive the winners of different nations, receptions of the winners after the individual finals in the Fuehrer's box will no longer take place; only German winners will be introduced to the Fuehrer in the case of his being present at the victory of a German in the final.

Hitler's position may have been unfair, but at least it was honest. Nevertheless, there were some around him who were brave enough to suggest that he should meet the man of the moment, among them Tschammer und Osten, who told Hitler that he should do so 'in the interest of sport'. Schirach also appealed to Hitler, who snapped back ferociously, telling the Reich Youth Leader that there was no way he was going to be photographed with Owens.

Even if Hitler had not technically snubbed Owens, there were many who felt that the accusation that he had had the ring of truth to it. One of them was Peter Gay, a young Jewish boy who was growing up in Berlin. His father had bought some tickets in 1932 on a visit to Budapest, and the two of them had watched Owens' performance with the usual astonishment. Of the 'snub', Gay was to claim that it was '*morally* true'. 'The swine who were ruining our lives could not have behaved differently,' he wrote. 'Whatever did happen, there was no denying that Owens had done his bit to puncture the myth of Aryan superiority.' As many commentators back in the United States agreed with Arthur Daley and Peter Gay – that the accusation concerning the snub *felt* true, and if it wasn't true then it was so close to the truth as to be indistinguishable – the myth was therefore born. For the majority of newspaper readers, there was no point in questioning a story that involved a man who didn't like black people refusing to shake the hand of a black person. After all, refusing to touch black people was the reason for segregation in the Southern states. Nevertheless, endemic racism in American society did little to dampen the outrage that the German leader had snubbed America's new golden boy.

There were some who saw much hypocrisy in all the brouhaha. Among them was an African-American from New York called Henry A. Slaughter. His letter to the *New York Times* on 8 August was a powerful reminder that all was not well back home.

Reams of inanity have been prevalent in the press recently as a result of the failure of Reichsfuehrer Hitler to greet and congratulate Jesse Owens for his Olympic triumphs. Writers who previously had never mentioned fair play and Negro in the same columns jumped on the band-wagon for a short ride in the reflected glare of the publicity that sought out this unusual athlete.

One unfamiliar with the facts would assume that this situation was an uncommon one, and that Jesse Owens was being subjected to some strange and novel treatment; that the countless words written by numerous American columnists, commentators and reporters were the sincere indignation of honest, fair-minded people. On the contrary, however, it is in truth the epitome of hypocrisy.

It is, to the thinking Negro, more detestable than the honest though deplorable actions of Hitler. In face of the entire world, he had the courage to align his conduct with his philosophy and pursue a consistent policy both in words and in actions. This consistency, however, is surpassed only by the rank inconsistency and hypocrisy of the press and of a large part of the public in our own country.

Have all forgotten that this same Jesse Owens in sections of his own country would fail to be congratulated only because he would not even be allowed to participate in officially sanctioned AAU competition? Is it a startling revelation that the Owens who was only snubbed in Berlin is denied the privilege of rising to the full height of his ability in the social, political and economic fields of his homeland?

The writer, speaking for only one of America's millions of Negroes, would welcome tolerance in fact rather than meaningless words.

Ironically, Owens and his fellow African-Americans were being treated better in Germany than they were in the United States. As M. N. Masood, the vice-captain of the Indian hockey team, was to observe, 'they were members of a coloured race, but no one in Germany seemed to think of it. They were sportsmen, and that was all that was necessary'.

If Hitler wanted to use the Games to promote his own ideology, then there were those who wanted the athletes to use their positions to denigrate Nazism. On the afternoon that Owens won his gold medal in the 100 metres, a J. M. Loraine in Britain decided to write to the new hero of the Games, outlining a way in which the sprinter could draw attention to the iniquities of Hitler's new order.

> [. . .] when you go up to receive, as you surely will, your Olympic prize you will have the opportunity to be remembered by posterity not only as a great runner but as a great <u>MAN</u>, if, remembering all the filthy abuse poured out by Herr Hitler and his gangsters upon 'Niggers', Jews and others whom he calls 'Subhumans', you refuse with a grand and dignified gesture to be crowned by him or any of his henchmen, saying that you were proud to represent your country and that you enjoyed the contest with your fellow athletes, but that you would not feel honoured but only insulted by a tribute from the blood-stained hands of race-persecutors.
>
> If you make this fine and honourable gesture with the eyes of all the world upon you, you will earn the admiration and gratitude of every liberty-loving man and woman and your words will reverberate around the world.

It was certainly not in Jesse Owens' character to take such a stance. He was too retiring, too modest and unsure of his position to start lambasting the Nazis on the world stage. Unlike Werner Seelenbinder, he was not a political creature. Nevertheless, Owens never got a chance to read the letter, because it was intercepted by the Gestapo at the Charlottenburg Post Office No. 2, the sorting office that served the Olympic village. Had Owens – and indeed the other athletes – known about this, then there would have been a furore. A copy of this letter was sent to the head of the Reich Security Main Office, Reinhard Heydrich, who had asked for the Gestapo to monitor the mail of any medal winners who were coloured. By the end of the Games, the Gestapo must have had to open a separate section to deal with the volume of correspondence sent to Owens.

Other letter writers were more successful in getting their pleas through to the athletes. Dorothy Odam, the sixteen-year-old British high jumper, received a letter at the Friesian House from the inmate of a concentration camp. 'It was about the atrocities and what was going on,' she recalled. 'About how terrible the camps were. I was a bit frightened by it. The writer asked me to show the letter to somebody in England. But imagine being caught going out of Germany with a letter like that.' Odam decided to hand the letter to one of her German chaperones, who took it away and asked Odam not to mention it. 'I felt that it had nothing to do with me,' she said. 'I thought it was a thing that I shouldn't have personally with me or take home to England. Who would I have given it to?' Odam suspected that many other athletes received similar letters. Although her letter no doubt ended up in a Gestapo file, it at least made the teenager aware of the real Germany. 'It did bring in the fact that there was something going on behind all the strutting and the *Heil Hitlers*.'

Odam was right – she was not the only athlete to receive such a letter. Pat Norton remembered how Jeanette Campbell, an Argentine 100 metres freestyler, received a letter from a man from Holland two weeks before the Games started, stating that two of his friends had recently disappeared in Germany. 'He asked would we rally the women competitors together and demand their release or the women would boycott the opening ceremony,' Norton recalled. 'She read the letter to us and there was considerable discussion about what we should do. Finally, Jeanette decided it was asking too much of her and decided to let the matter drop. We had heard stories before arriving in Berlin of missing people, but what was speculation was now a reality.'

Sometimes the communications were made verbally. Doris Carter, an Australian high jumper, recalled how some of the girls who worked at the Friesian House feared for their lives. 'Several charming girls [. . .] whispered to us that they were afraid,' she said. 'They were quarter Jewish and they had heard several of their Jewish friends had disappeared.' It was not just the young women who spoke of their fears. Both Baroness von Wangenheim and Fräulein Weimbeir, who was the officer in charge of the female guides, mentioned their dislike of the regime. 'They both said that they really didn't approve of the way things were,' said Carter, 'but had no option but to go along with it.'

Although she was only fifteen, Iris Cummings was also sensitive to what was going on behind the razzmatazz of the Games. 'I got a feeling for the subterranean disapproval of Hitler,' she said. Cummings recalled how her mother and the mother of Marjorie Gestring, the prodigious thirteen-year-old American springboard diver, had made friends with a German woman, who accompanied them to the stadium. 'This lady was afraid to go,' said Cummings, 'and asked if she could stand between my mother and Mrs Gestring, because when they [the German spectators] all stood and sang the national anthem and went "*Sieg Heil! Sieg Hiel!*", she would not salute.' The woman – who was not Jewish, but simply hated the regime – was so afraid that she hid behind the Americans, down under her seat and as low as she could get. 'At the end of the row there were Gestapo in uniform,' said Cummings, 'and they noticed who saluted and who didn't.' The woman hid on a number of occasions, and Mrs Cummings and Mrs Gestring helped to conceal her each time. It is unlikely that there were uniformed Gestapo men stationed at the end of each row, but such is the nature of police states that it requires only a minority of the population to be informers in order to make the majority fearful and therefore behave as the regime wishes. Two German spectators who did feel safe were Peter Gay and his father, who were sitting among the Hungarians. 'It meant that my father and I could simply blend in with our surroundings,' Gay wrote later, 'so that we did not have to give the Nazi salute when the Fuehrer appeared or a German was awarded a gold medal.'

Cummings also remembered meeting another German who was fearful of the regime. One day, she and Velma Dunn went to a teahouse on the Unter den Linden, where there was a small, all-female orchestra playing. 'They were playing violins and strings,' said Cummings, 'and I liked the music. We went there several times. After the first time, I noticed one of the girls, the leader of the orchestra, making eye contact. We spoke to each other.' The girl's name was Irmgard Schnell, and she gave Cummings her address. 'Before we left, she came to us and made it very clear that she was terrified for her life. It wasn't because she was Jewish, but she was one of those who didn't salute and didn't agree. She was trying to figure out how she was going to survive.' Cummings and Schnell exchanged letters over the next three years until the war came, at which point they stopped. Cummings never knew what happened to Schnell.

★

Not all the sporting action was confined to the Olympic Stadium. The competitors in the modern pentathlon found themselves seeing a lot more of the German countryside than many of the other athletes. Among them was Charles Leonard, who found that he was enjoying the company of his fellow competitors in the week leading up to the Games. 'Our most pleasant contact so far has been the Belgian team,' he wrote in his diary on 30 July, 'two of whom sing *Home on the Range*, have a sense of humor and speak passingly good English.' He also noted that the Swedes were 'a funny lot' who believed that the pentathlon medals were theirs by right, as they had won the event so many times. This was certainly true, as the Swedes had won gold in the modern pentathlon in every Games since 1912. The Dutch were 'stolid, good fellows,' but the Swiss, Finns and French appeared to keep to themselves. Meanwhile the British were 'of course sporting chaps'. With a few exceptions, nearly every competitor was a young army officer, and so the men had not only sport in common, but the military as well.

The first event in the pentathlon was the 5,000-metre cross-country riding, which took place on the morning of Sunday, 2 August. The competitors had walked the course just south of the village on the Friday morning, and had spent Saturday having what Leonard called a 'strategy conference'. As none of the teams had brought their own horses, a draw was held for the forty-two horses that the Germans had supplied. Leonard drew the twelfth horse, a large, blazed-face bay, which he had a mere twenty minutes 'to get to know' before the competition. Leonard found that the horse was good at jumping, easy to handle, but not particularly fast. Nevertheless, 'he spoke horse language,' Leonard wrote, '<u>not</u> German'. The young lieutenant found the course not particularly difficult, with twenty hazards in total, many of which were fences, water jumps and water and ditches combined with fences. The terrain was varied, with a mixture of hills, sand and some swamp, none of which was absurdly tricky. It was more of a race than a cross-country, Leonard realised, albeit only after he had finished in fifteenth position with a time of 9:47. 'I should have pushed my horse harder on the back stretch, but I jumped cleanly.' The winner was Italy's First Lieutenant Silvano Abba, who completed the course in 9:02.5, and in second came the favourite, First Lieutenant Gotthardt Handrick from Germany, with a time of 9:09.6. Handrick had been lucky – riding was not his strongest sport, but he had drawn a good, fast horse, which Leonard regarded as probably being the best of the stable. 'Breaks of the game,' he wrote. There was no suspicion – nor was there any evidence – that the Germans had cheated.

In the fencing the following day, the forty-two competitors all had to fence each other for a five-minute draw or a one-touch bout. It was an exhausting day, as epée fencing makes great demands not only on the physique, but also on the brain. The fencing started outside, but the rain forced the competitors into the grand cupola hall in the House of German Sport at the main Olympic complex. Leonard came tenth, winning twenty-two of his bouts, and had the pleasure of 'sticking' Handrick, nicking him with a 'squat shot'. 'You should have seen his face,' Leonard wrote in a letter back home. Handrick, however, finished second in the fencing, and was beginning to look unbeatable. But Charles Leonard was about to play his strongest hand – the rapid-fire pistol shooting.

Leonard had been brought up with guns. His father had bought him, aged six, a .22-calibre rifle with a 20-inch barrel. 'He put a military sight on the back of it,' Leonard remembered, 'so I could get a really good sight picture. He gave me preliminary rifle instruction until it came out of my ears. He even built a twenty-five-foot range in our basement.' Leonard was an exceptionally fine shot, but until the Berlin Olympics nobody knew quite how fine. The rules of the pistol shooting were complicated, and involved shooting four series of five shots into a 1.65-metre silhouette positioned at a distance of 25 metres. The silhouette had a ringed target set over it, with the scores ranging from 1 on the outside of the ring to 10 for a bull's-eye, which was about five inches in diameter and lay in the equivalent of the silhouette's solar plexus. The silhouette was visible only for three seconds, however, which allowed very little time to aim and let off five shots. The silhouette then disappeared for ten seconds, during which time the shooter had to reload before it reappeared. The theoretical maximum number of points that could be achieved was therefore 200 – twenty bull's-eyes. Nobody had ever achieved that score before.

When Leonard arrived at 9 a.m. on the morning of Tuesday, 4 August at the range of the 67th Infantry Regiment at Ruhleben, he looked more like a dandy from the pages of F. Scott Fitzgerald than a sportsman. He wore a neatly ironed white shirt, complete with a starched detachable collar with wing fasteners, a silk tie, a sleeveless cricket jersey, dark woollen slacks, highly polished black shoes and a double-breasted, brass-buttoned blue blazer. A black beret added a touch of the Maquis to the appearance. 'Pistol shooting is a gentlemanly game,' he recalled. 'You don't have to lie down on mats.' Leonard was carrying a .22-calibre Colt on a .38-calibre frame, which made it a little heavier than the normal .22. Leonard's only concession to the fact that he was about to take part in a sport rather than charm women at a garden party was to remove his jacket before he started shooting. Indeed, the few women present in the stand would doubtless have been drawn to him – Leonard was a handsome man.

Nevertheless, looks do not win competitions, and Leonard had some shooting to do. As usual over the Olympic fortnight, a slight breeze was blowing, which occasionally disturbed the shooters as it blew from behind them. Four athletes shot at four separate silhouettes simultaneously, with each of the marksmen shielded from the others and the sun in small wooden open-backed cabins. At the back of each cabin stood the off-putting presence of a German army officer, and behind him were more officers, sitting at tables and keeping the scores. Behind them were the stands, packed chiefly with even more army officers. This was hardly the most civilian of events.

Leonard started shooting as soon as the first silhouette popped up, doing just as his father had taught him – holding the pistol firmly but not too tightly, watching the sights and squeezing the trigger. His first five shots hit the bull's-eye. A lucky start, he thought. The silhouette disappeared, and Leonard smoothly reloaded the Colt with five more rounds. The silhouette came back, cutting a slightly comical figure with its helmet and slightly effeminate mouth. Leonard shot five more times, and scored another fifty points. This was too good to be true. So far he had a perfect score. The officers in the stands leaned forward, the wood creaking under their combined bulk. With the third and penultimate series, Leonard hit inside the 10 ring another five times. He had 150 points. He reloaded for the final time, doing his best to stop his hands shaking. Leonard then lifted his pistol, aiming with his right eye, his left eye partially closed, waiting for the silhouette to spring back. When it did so, he fired. His first shot hit the bull, as did the second. He was on 170 – already a good score. The third shot brought him to 180. With just over a second of time left, he let off his fourth shot. Another bull's-eye. He had just one shot to go.

If Leonard had scored 190, then he would have been placed around fifth or sixth in rapid-fire pistol shooting. Instead, he came first, unassailably so. His final shot had brought his score to a perfect 200 points. It was a stunning achievement, and it put Leonard in sight of a medal. Unfortunately, Handrick had scored 192 points, which was enough to keep him in the lead. Nevertheless, with the swimming and the running to go, both events in which Leonard was strong, there was a chance that Handrick's lead could be snatched. After the shooting, Leonard found himself being mobbed back at the village by those wanting to know the secret of his success. 'I have explained about my pistol and what I do many times – grips, squeeze, kind of sights,' he wrote in his diary the following Monday. 'They were most surprised to find it has almost 3lb pull, they expected a hair trigger.' Many asked him whether his performance relied on something medicinal to steady him. 'I do <u>NOT</u> use dope,' Leonard wrote angrily.

The fact that his fellow athletes asked Leonard about dope indicates that performance-enhancing drugs were not the taboo subject in the Olympic village that they are today. Presumably, had Leonard admitted to taking dope, there would have been little or no fuss. The reason why he was angry with the suggestion was that taking dope would have been an ungentlemanly thing to do, rather than something illegal. Doping had been present in sports since the Ancient Olympics, in which competitors had eaten beef in the belief that it magnified their strength tenfold. As new drugs were developed, the world of sport quickly started to abuse them. In the nineteenth century, morphine was used in endurance sports. The Welsh cyclist Arthur Lindon was the first sportsman known to have died from abusing the drug. In the 1904 Olympics in St Louis, the marathon runners used immensely dangerous substances to give themselves an edge. The winner that year was the American Thomas Hicks, who is said to have taken a couple of milligrams of strychnine washed down with brandy and raw eggs to push himself to victory. It was considered somewhat miraculous that he didn't die – had he taken a third milligram of strychnine, then he would have done. Drug abuse certainly took place at Berlin, but its extent is a matter of conjecture. The drug used would have been amphetamine – probably in the form of Benzedrine, which was developed to be taken via an inhaler in the late 1920s. Amphetamine – now commonly referred to as speed – would have given tired athletes a much-needed boost, and as such it would have been used in sports that required successive days of intense competition, such as the pentathlon and the decathlon.

If taking drugs was one form of cheating, then pretending to be a member of the opposite sex was another. The question of men – or hermaphrodites – passing themselves off as women became an issue at the final of the women's 100 metres at four o'clock on Tuesday, 4 August. Lined up were six women, of whom half were regarded as being singularly unfeminine by their fellow athletes. Helen Stephens – the so-called Fulton Flash – was the favourite to win the race. Brought up on a farm in Missouri, the world record holder had endured a rough childhood which had seen her being raped when she was just nine by a sixteen-year-old relative, an experience that turned her away from men. Had this been common knowledge, then nobody would have suspected that she was a man, but because of her large and somewhat manly frame and her deep, husky voice, everybody assumed she was male. During the crossing on the *Manhattan*, Velma Dunn wrote to her mother that Stephens had given her 'the surprise of my life'. 'She is a huge girl, about 6ft tall and very large boned. She acts very mannish and talks lower than most men.' Stephens's low voice was perhaps not the function of some hormonal imbalance, but rather the result of a bizarre childhood accident. When she was about ten, she was playing with the family's pet dog – 'Doogie' – with a piece of wood carved into an arrowhead. Stephens held the wood in her mouth, tempting Doogie to snatch it from her. When the dog leaped towards her, Stephens jumped up to escape, but her foot caught on something and she tripped. The arrowhead lodged in her throat, puncturing her larynx. Her attempts to extricate the wood with a piece of string attached to it caused her immense agony, and the object was subsequently removed in surgery. Stephens was mute for a month, but when her voice returned, it sounded like that of a large fifty-year-old man with a sixty-a-day cigarette habit.

Nevertheless, Stephens could do little to convince people she was anything but a man. Dorothy Odam recalled standing in the post office at the Friesian House, and hearing men's voices behind her. 'You would turn round because there were not supposed to be any men there,' she said, 'and it was Helen Stephens and Stella Walsh. She was definitely a man.' Stella Walsh's real name was Stanislawa Walasiewiczówna, a mouthful of ten syllables that had been pollarded into three since she moved to the United States when she was two years old. In 1932, she had won gold at the Los Angeles Olympics, although she had to compete under the flag of her native country, Poland, as the United States had not allowed her family to become American citizens. The third athlete who possessed some masculine qualities was Kathe Krauss, who was regarded as being a man by another of the 100 metres finalists, Marie Dollinger. Elfriede Kaun recalled how Dollinger said to her in 1986, 'You know, I was the only woman in that race!' This is unfair on the other two competitors, Annette Rogers and Emmy Albus, both of whom were clearly women, but it is easy to see in photographs why Dollinger should have suspected Krauss of being a man.

Dollinger's comment may well have been inspired by her coming fourth in the final, beaten by the three 'men'. As was predicted, Stephens won the race in a world record beating 11.5, which was disallowed because of a tail wind. Walsh came second in 11.7, and Krauss was third with 11.9. The three women certainly made a curious sight on the winner's podium, with the gigantically tall Krauss dominating the podium in her white tracksuit and doing a Nazi salute. Behind her, Stephens saluted in the traditional style, with her right hand raised to her right eyebrow, her left hand clutching the small oak tree that each of the gold medallists was given. Stella Walsh stood with her arms to her side. The truth about all these women's gender would be established only after the Games.

Stephens's manliness certainly did not stop her being admired by men, and by one man in particular – Adolf Hitler. After the victory ceremony, Stephens and Dee Boeckmann, the women's coach, were approached by a short German official who sported a Hitlerian small toothbrush moustache. In a mixture of English and German, he asked the two women to 'Kommen Sie', as the Fuehrer wished to meet the fastest woman in the world. Much to the official's chagrin, Boeckmann insisted that Stephens did her press interviews first, which the official endured nervously. He then ushered them into a small room behind Hitler's box, where they waited for a few minutes. Eventually, a dozen SS men entered the room through a pair of thick red curtains, and positioned themselves around the room, unbuttoning their holsters as they did so.

Two more SS men stepped into the room, and were immediately followed by Hitler, who was dressed in his brown military uniform complete with cap and black boots. He came towards Stephens and saluted. 'It was sloppy,' she recalled, 'like he didn't really want to give me one.' Stephens didn't return the salute, but instead held out her hand. Hitler took it, and Stephens gave Hitler what she described as a 'good old Missouri handshake'. 'I put extra pressure on it,' said Stephens, 'and that gave him the wrong message because he immediately began to hug me and pinch me and squeeze me and see if I was real.' Hitler's physical familiarity unnerved her, but not enough to dissuade her from asking for an autograph. While Hitler was signing her book, a flashlight illuminated the room, causing a startled Hitler to jump into the air. 'When he landed,' said Stephens, 'fists flaying, he bellowed something like, "*Was fällt Ihnen ein*? Get him! Destroy the evidence!"' Hitler then proceeded to slap the photographer around the face with his leather gloves, and even punched and kicked him. The camera was dropped, and Hitler kicked it hard against a wall. After the hapless photographer was manhandled out of the room by the SS Hitler turned back to Stephens, a smile on his face where there had earlier been a look of utter fury.

'He wriggled his body as if to shake himself back into composure,' she recalled. Hitler then began to speak, his words interpreted by none other than Rudolf Hess, the Fuehrer's deputy and the third-most powerful man in Germany.

'Fräulein should consider running for Germany. Fair hair, blue eyes. Strong, big woman. The Chancellor says you are a pure Aryan. Yes?'

'*Nein danke*,' Stephens replied.

Hitler smiled before speaking through Hess once more.

'You like Berlin better than Fulton homeland?'

'Yes, Mr Hitler, Berlin's very, how do you say, nice, pretty? *Schoen*? Even in the rain.'

This time Hitler beamed, and then he made Stephens an extraordinary offer.

'You would like to spend the next weekend with Chancellor Hitler at his villa in Berchtesgaden?'

It was at this point that Boeckmann interrupted the conversation, pointing out that the women's 4 x 100 metres relay final was due to take place at the weekend. Hitler did not seem to take this revelation seriously, and asked Boeckmann whether she too wanted to come to Berchtesgaden.

'Thank you, but no,' she replied. 'I too cannot accept your kind offer.'

Despite the reply being given in English, a wistful but light-hearted Hitler could tell that it was a refusal. He came up to Stephens and wished her well. 'Then he reached behind me,' Stephens said, 'pinched me, then saluted us both, and marched out.'

The next day, Stephens found that the photographer's camera had survived its kicking from the Fuehrer, for there were photographs of their extraordinary meeting being sold around the stadium.

One female athlete to whom Hitler would have been far less hospitable was the half-Jewish Helene Mayer, who was the subject of much attention from the spectators. Mayer looked the typical Aryan female pin-up, with her long blonde hair plaited and tied over her head. She had made it through the elimination matches with ease, and at 5 p.m. on 5 August, she was standing along with her seven other finalists in the Cupola Hall in the House of German Sport. Her two main rivals for the gold were Ellen Preis from Austria, who the reigning Olympic champion, and the Hungarian Ilona Schacherer-Elek. Coincidentally, like Mayer, both women were half Jewish, but had been brought up as Catholics and did not consider themselves to be Jews.

The finals were a league and not a knockout, so the contest would be decided by points, and not by any one match. In her first encounter with Elek, Mayer fought aggressively, intimidating her opponent with her lunge. A less stylish fencer than Mayer, Elek was nevertheless a superb strategist and was supremely quick. Although the crowd willed Mayer to win, Elek's speed counted, and the Hungarian won all three bouts. Mayer was not as devastated as the spectators. She had been in this situation before and had come back. Elek might well have a bad match with another finalist, which would even the scores. Mayer won her next six matches, which gave her a huge boost of confidence when she came to face Ellen Preis in her final match.

What happened next is regarded as one of the classic fencing matches in Olympic history. With the points being incredibly close between Elek, Mayer and Preis, the winner of the Mayer–Preis match would win gold. Both women were fighting for the ultimate glory – all Elek could do was watch. The hall was in silence as Preis and Mayer lunged and dodged, both women seemingly equal. The result of the first bout was indeed a draw – the score being two all. The next bout was more aggressively fought, but yet again it was a draw – three all. The medal would now be decided by the final three-minute bout. Mayer needed just one more point than Preis and the gold would once again be hers.

To both women's utter disappointment, the result was a draw: four all. The judges added up the points, and found that neither Preis nor Mayer had won. Instead, the gold would be going to the Hungarian, Elek. Mayer won silver and Preis bronze. A friend of Mayer, Doris Runzheimer, recalled that Mayer cried. 'She then said, "It's not so bad that I came in second but I would have loved to get a little oak tree." Instead, she was given a lot of flowers for winning her silver medal. Because of a lack of vases, tubs were filled.' It was on the winner's podium that Mayer did something that she would regret for the rest of her life. After receiving her medal, she then stuck her right arm out and up – she performed a Nazi salute. After the way she and her family had been treated over the past few years – the banning from sports clubs, the denial of full citizenship, the lies uttered by the Sports Ministry – it was an extraordinary act of solidarity with a regime that had treated her like a criminal. For years, Mayer's salute would be regarded as an appalling act of treachery to her fellow Jews. But the truth was that Mayer did not regard herself as Jewish. She had been brought up as a Catholic, and she looked and felt like a non-Jewish German – she really had 'mendelled' to her Aryan side. Her talent, she thought, offered her an opportunity to shake off the stigma of her 'shameful heritage', and would restore her and her family to their rightful place in German society. What better way to prove to the Nazis that she was one of them than to salute? Of course, another explanation was that Mayer feared the consequences of not saluting. Not to have done so would have required an extra-ordinary amount of courage, perhaps even a touch of foolhardiness. More than many other Germans, the Mayer family feared the mid-night knock on the door – an impudent display by Helene would have guaranteed it, not during the Olympics, but a few months later, when the attention of the world had shifted. It is unfair to expect everyone to be a Werner Seelenbinder.

In the meantime Jesse Owens was continuing to wow the Olympic crowds. In the two qualifying heats for the 200 metres on Tuesday, 4th August, Owens ran the distance in 21.1 seconds, which bettered the Olympic record, although he was capable of running it in under 21 seconds. Few were betting against the 'Dark Streak' winning his second gold medal, and fewer still were betting that he would not pick up a third over at the long jump pit. In fact, that Tuesday was Owens' busiest day at the Olympics, as not only did he have to race in the two 200 metres heats, but he also had to work his way through the long jump's elimination trials and semi-finals.

The events of the long jump competition at the XIth Olympiad comprise one of the largest myths associated with the modern Olympics. According to the legend – largely propagated by Owens in countless after-dinner speeches and interviews – Owens won gold in the event only thanks to the heroic sportsmanship displayed by nearest rival, Germany's Carl 'Luz' Long. Like Erich Borchmeyer, Long was the usual archetype of the Aryan athlete – tall, fair, muscular. 'Taller than I was by an inch, maybe two,' Owens wrote in one of his auto-biographies later, 'Long was one of those rare athletic happenings you come to recognise after years in competition – a perfectly propor-tioned body, every lithe but powerful cord a celebration of pulsing natural muscle, stunningly compressed and honed by tens of thou-sands of obvious hours of sweat and determination. He may have been my archenemy, but I had to stand in awe and just stare at Luz Long for several seconds.'

Referring to Long as his 'archenemy' was a classic piece of ghost-written spin to satisfy those with a taste for a tale of good versus evil. (The book even makes preposterous suggestions that Long was personally appointed by Hitler to act as Owens' nemesis.) The truth was that Owens would not have had time to stand and marvel at Long in this uncharacteristically homo-erotic fashion. The elimination trials were running simultaneously with the 200 metres heats, and Owens found himself having to dash from his first race in his tracksuit in order to qualify. Each of the jumpers had three attempts to make the qualifying distance of 7.15 metres, which was just under a metre shorter than Owens' world record of 8.13 metres. There should have been no problem. In the words of John Kieran of the *New York Times*, Owens 'usually removes his jacket, takes one leap, puts on his jacket again and waits for the man to come around with the medal'. According to one version of the legend, Owens took a practice run-up to the pit, only to turn round and see an official had raised a red flag – the run-up had been determined to have been his first attempt, and because he had run past the board, he had fouled. Another version maintains that Owens had simply jumped and fouled, which was not unlikely as he had little time to prepare. Whatever the truth, what was certain was that he had only two jumps left in which he could qualify. 'Forget it, I said to myself,' Owens recalled thinking. 'You've fouled before. There are still two jumps left.'

In later years, Owens would maintain that his concentration was now in shreds, torn apart by a reporter who pestered him as he waited for his second attempt. Apparently the reporter bugged Owens about whether Hitler had indeed snubbed him, and pointed to the Fuehrer's empty box, which was supposed evidence that Hitler had no wish to see '*der Neger*' competing. This story is highly unlikely, as reporters were not allowed to interview athletes in the middle of the stadium. Owens then claimed that before his second jump, he once again looked up at the box to see that it was insultingly devoid of Hitler – 'his way of saying that Jesse Owens was inferior'. Of course, trying to establish Owens' thoughts is conjecture, but the notion that he was more focused on Hitler than on jumping is questionable. Everybody

who met Owens during the Games noted how free he was of political concerns. Owens himself told the famous American sports writer
Grantland Rice after the event that he hadn't 'even thought' about
Hitler. On the boat back home, Richard Helms noted how Owens
'did not feel that he had been insulted [by Hitler], as conventional
reporting had it'. Whatever he was thinking, Owens took his second
jump, and once again the result is disputed. Luz Long claimed
that Owens overstepped the mark, registering another foul, whereas
Owens was later to say that he had fallen short of the target distance
by 3 inches. This again seems unlikely, as Owens, by his own admission, had not jumped less than a foot farther than the qualifying distance for over two years. Most other accounts state that a red flag was
raised for the second time, which indicates that Owens had fouled
once again.

It is at this point that myth takes over from reality. The situation was
certainly dramatic – the world record holder was facing the possibility that he was about to be eliminated in the very first round. As Luz
Long recalled, 'I hardly dared think it: would there be a sensation with
Owens dropping out on the second attempt?' If the American fouled,
Long would almost certainly win gold, as he was capable of jumping
a good 10 centimetres farther than his rivals. Instead of standing back
and hoping that Owens would foul once more, however, Long walked
up to Owens to offer him some advice. According to Owens, the conversation started with a matey 'What has taken your goat, Jazze
Owenz?', to which Owens responded with a brief smile. Long then
proceeded to tell Owens that he knew what was wrong. 'You are 100
per cent when you jump. I the same. You cannot do halfway, but you
are afraid you will foul again.' Long then suggested that Owens jump
off 6 inches before the board, in order to guarantee that he would not
foul. Because he could jump so far, a handicap of half a foot would
not jeopardise his chances of qualification. In fact, Long was so sporting that he even placed his towel at the point at which Owens should
launch himself. 'I could feel the confident energy surging back into
my body,' Owens recalled, 'as I stood still for that brief second before
beginning my run.' He ran as fast as he could and leaped up when he
reached Long's towel, landing well beyond the qualification mark.
Thanks to Luz Long, his 'archenemy', he had made it.

It certainly makes for a lovely story. It is untrue, however. Not one reporter spotted Owens and Long having a conversation before the jump. Nobody saw Long place his towel – or, in some accounts, make a mark – six inches before the board. The eyes of every American journalist were on Owens, and they wrote about his third attempt in such detail that it is inconceivable they would have omitted the fact that Long and Owens were seen to be having a conversation, let alone the sight of Long laying down some form of marker. Grantland Rice was one of those watching – through a pair of powerful binoculars – and he noticed nothing unusual. 'I was searching for some tell-tale sign of emotion,' he wrote. 'Calmly, he [Owens] walked the sprint path to the take-off board, then retraced his steps. Studying the situation a moment, the American athlete anteloped down that runway and took off at least a foot behind the required mark – but qualified!' Crucially, not even Luz Long could recall any such conversation. 'Owens' nerves aren't that bad,' Long wrote. 'He steps up again, jumps far in front of the line so as not to overstep and lands at 7.50 metres.' There is no mention in Long's account that it was his idea for Owens to jump well in front of the line. What makes the story even more incredible is the notion that Owens was not able to work it out for himself. As the American diver Marshall Wayne commented, 'Well, how dumb do you think Jesse was? It didn't take too many brains to figure out that he was going to have to start farther back if they were faulting him.'

By the time the final took place at 5.45 that afternoon, the weather was deteriorating. 'It [the wind] howls in at the north gate,' Long recalled, 'whirls the red ash up into the air taking rugs, caps and hats with it. It's frightening. We're now jumping on the side of the main grandstand. Everyone is tense here too – they're expecting something from us Germans.' Everyone included Hitler himself, who was now in his box, hoping that at least one of the two German finalists – Long and Leichum – would beat Owens. The American had a compatriot in the form of Clark, and Maffei of Italy and Tajima of Japan accounted for the other two places. Although Owens looked invincible – he had broken the old Olympic record three times in the semi-finals – Long was no pushover. He too had beaten the record, although only twice. Maffei and Tajima had done so once. In the semi-finals, Long's best jump had been 7.84 and Owens' had been 7.87 – there was very little between the two men.

In the first round, Long, who was fifth in the running order, managed just 7.73 metres – a relatively poor performance which he blamed on the weather. Nevertheless, it was still a good 13 centimetres ahead of the others. Now it was Owens' first attempt. He sprinted down the track and leaped up, his legs kicking below him. He jumped well, but his distance was not measured, because he had once again overstepped the line. (In his autobiography, Owens claimed he beat Long with his first jump. The official Olympic Report and Luz Long say otherwise.) In the second round, Long excelled himself, leaping a mighty 7.87 which equalled Owens' best that day. 'Luz Long! Luz Long!' rang around the stadium. What Owens did next is undisputed. Instead of starting his run-up, he walked up to Long and congratulated him. 'I rushed over to him,' Owens recalled. 'Hugged him. I was glad. So glad.' Long remembered how Owens 'comes up, congratulates me, sporting and chivalrously'.

The American then returned to the start of the run-up. 'I didn't look at the end of the pit. I decided I wasn't going to come down again. I was going to fly. I was going to stay up in the air forever.' Owens then sprinted down the track at a phenomenal rate. It was his speed which gave him such good results in the long jump, not his technique, which many felt left something to be desired. It mattered little. 'I reached to the sky as I leaped for the farthest part of the ground.' To Long, Owens' jump did not 'look like much', but the tape measure revealed that Owens had jumped 7.94 metres. 'It's hardly possible,' Long recalled.

Once more, the pressure was now on Long. The stadium echoed to the chant of his name. In his box, an excited Hitler rocked back and forth, while Goebbels and Hess had taken to their feet in nervous expectation. Through his binoculars Hitler watched the German run up to the board and leap. As he rose, however, Long lost his balance, and fell forward, clumsily landing on one leg. He had jumped a mere 6.50 – not even enough to register on the scoreboard. Hitler leaned back, disgusted. Goebbels and Hess quickly sat back down. Once more the despised 'Neger' had won. Owens still had a final jump, however, and he decided to make it a good one, one that would emphatically prove his superiority. According to Grantland Rice, Owens 'seemed to be jumping clear out of Germany' with his last jump, and when he landed at 8.06, the first to congratulate him was Luz Long. 'Of all people I can understand what this jump means,' said Long. 'He hugs me and replies, "You forced me to give my best". For me this is the greatest compliment.'

Long and Owens then walked around the stadium arm in arm, acknowledging the plaudits coming from the crowd, whose number did not include Hitler, who had already left. Owens was seemingly not bothered by the departure. 'I suppose Mr Hitler is much too busy a man to stay out there forever,' he told Grantland Rice. 'After all, he'd been there most of the day. Anyway, he did wave in my direction as he left the field and I sort of felt he was waving at me. I didn't bother about it one way or another.' It was in Owens' nature to please others, and not give offence, a characteristic that the apolitical athlete was even willing to extend to Hitler. It is doubtful that Hitler gave Owens a wave – nobody else noticed it, and he was more likely to be waving to the stadium – but if he had, then it would show that Hitler, far from snubbing the athlete, was publicly acknowledging him. Judging by his earlier comments to Tschammer und Osten, Speer and Schirach, Hitler was unwilling to show any friendliness to the black athlete, let alone a matey wave from his box. Nevertheless, it had been a great competition, and Long and Owens formed a deep friendship whose intimacy should have required no embellishment by the American. Sadly, their friendship was not to last long.

Just under twenty-four hours later, Owens won his third gold medal, winning the 200 metres in 20.7 seconds – a new Olympic record, and only four-tenths of a second slower than his as yet unratified world record of May the previous year. One of the American reporters watching the race was the UP correspondent, Richard Helms. Owens would later tell Helms one of the secrets of his technique. 'At the gun, runners tend to clench their fists,' Owens said. 'This causes a tension to run through their body, and this slightly slows the first steps. What I do at the start is to place my thumbs on my first finger – it's just enough to keep me from clenching.' Trailing him by the same margin was Owens' fellow African-American, Mack Robinson, who just pipped Osendarp of Holland, who was delighted to gain his second bronze medal, making him the fastest white man on earth. At the victory ceremony, the entire stadium rose to its feet, celebrating a feat that had not been achieved since the Games of 1900. The author Thomas Wolfe was sitting with the family of the US ambassador to Germany, William E. Dodd, which included his daughter Martha Dodd. He let out such a wild whoop of joy that, according to Martha Dodd, 'Hitler twisted in his seat, and looked down, attempting to locate the miscreant, and frowned angrily.'

'Owens was as black as tar,' said Wolfe, 'but what the hell, it was our team, and I thought he was wonderful.' The writer's racism was of a gentler variety than that of Goebbels, writing in his diary that evening. 'We Germans win a gold medal, the Americans get three, two of which are won by niggers. This is a scandal. White humanity should be ashamed of itself. But what does it matter down there in that country without culture. The Fuehrer is completely carried away with enthusiasm for the German achievements.' Goebbels was right, the Germans were doing well, but for the sport-loathing minister of propaganda the end of the Games could not come too soon. 'If only the Games would finish now!' he wrote. Nevertheless, Goebbels was the first to recognise that the event was doing nothing but good for Germany. After the first day's events, in which Germany had won three gold medals, Goebbels was cockahoop. 'A result of the reawakening of national pride. I am so pleased about it. We can be proud of Germany again.' It was hardly surprising that the minister saw the Games as a 'major breakthrough' that was 'helping us a lot on our cause'. Although many still denied that the Games were being used to promote Nazism, at least one man was privately honest that this was precisely what they were being used for.

In public, Goebbels dissembled. On 30 July he had addressed some twelve hundred foreign correspondents at the Zoo ballroom. Instead of hectoring the correspondents as he did the Berliners, Goebbels spoke softly, reading closely from his notes. He denied that Germany was seeking to use the Games as propaganda. 'I can assure you,' he said, 'this is not the case. If it were I should probably know it. Germany is of course willing to show itself to its guests from its best side. That is a demand of politeness which has nothing to do with political propaganda. We want you to see Germany as it is, but we have no intention of showing you Potemkin villages.' Neither did the Nazis have any intention of showing the journalists the new concentration camps such as Sachsenhausen, which was being built some 20 miles outside Berlin at Oranienburg. As Richard Helms was later to write, 'Most of the foreign press corps, and the embassy staffs attempted to portray German fascism accurately, but there was no such reporting easily available within the Third Reich.' Nevertheless, Goebbels thought the speech was well received. 'World opinion,' Goebbels wrote in his diary. 'Not much talent though. Still they are the ones who decide what people think. I make speech. Short but fearless and clear. Surprised at large amount of applause.' Typically, the journalists were rather more sceptical. 'Few found it [the speech] fulfilled its initial promise that in these Olympic gatherings German propaganda should be wholly eschewed,' wrote Frederick Birchall of the *New York Times*, 'even by Germany's master propagandist.'

At a quarter past four on Thursday, 6 August, what many regard as the greatest race of the Games took place. It was the 1,500 metres final, contested by twelve men, among them Jack Lovelock of New Zealand, Glenn Cunningham and Archie San Romani of the United States, Phil Edwards of Canada, Werner Boettcher of Germany, Luigi Beccali of Italy, Eric Ny of Sweden and John Cornes of Britain. Cunningham – also known as the 'Iron Horse of Kansas' – was without doubt the favourite, considered the greatest American miler of all time. The American section of the crowd was particularly voluble in rooting for their hero, their shouts soon drowned out by the usual hysterical seig-heiling that broke out when Hitler entered the stadium just after four o'clock.

The twelve men started quickly, with Cornes making the running, Beccali tucked in just behind him. Buried deep within the pack, at around seventh, was the diminutive figure of Lovelock, his presence noticeable only by virtue of the fact that he wore a pair of black shorts and his distinctive black vest was emblazoned with a silver fern. After 300 metres, Boettcher launched a bid for the lead, and overtook Cornes and Beccali. The Englishman was having none of it, however, and regained the lead as they drew up to the 400-metre mark. It was at this point that the imposing bulk of Cunningham surged forward to the front, with the 9½-stone frame of Lovelock shadowing him. Compared to his competitors, the New Zealander cut a slight figure, almost feminine. Nevertheless, he looked relaxed and in good shape, his arms gently pumping up and down.

With two laps to go, Ny decided to stake his claim for the leadership, although he was unable to pass Cunningham. Instead, he settled for second position, with the unshowy Lovelock in third place, although the medical student had the advantage of being on the inside, right on Cunningham's heels. Once more, Ny put on the pressure, and for 100 metres Ny and the American ran abreast, the aggressive Swede at one point forcing Cunningham's left foot off the track. Meanwhile, Lovelock stalked them, watching the two men battle it out. By the time the bell sounded for the final lap, Ny was convincingly ahead of both Cunningham and Lovelock, and was pulling away all the time. It was time for Lovelock to pounce.

He did so some 20 metres later. As with Owens, Lovelock's change of pace appeared to be the product of some magical force. He accelerated past Cunningham, and by the 1,200-metre mark he had eased past Ny. It looked easy, childishly so. It also looked cruel, as if Lovelock had simply been toying with the pack. 'It was as usual a case of getting the first break on the field,' Lovelock wrote later, 'catching them napping.' The crowd loved it, though, and cheered him on. A deflated Ny soon dropped out of sight, although Cunningham did his best to keep up, with Beccali in third place. The huge figure of the Iron Horse of Kansas bore down on the fragile New Zealand fern, but just as it looked as if the American was going to close the six-foot gap, some intuition told Lovelock to add just a little more pace. As they rounded the last bend into the home straight, Lovelock finally looked as if he was trying, his arms pumping furiously, although not as manically as those of Cunningham and Beccali. 'I put in another little effort as a second response to dishearten and choke off a further attack,' Lovelock recalled. A few metres before the end, he turned his head to the right and almost had to turn it right back to see what had happened to the competition. Lovelock crossed the tape in 3:47.8, which broke the world record by a second. 'I finished in perfect form, relaxed and comfortable, and jogged on another half lap.' In fact, the race was so quick that Cunningham also broke the record, and Beccali in third, San Romani in fourth and Edwards in fifth had all beaten the Olympic record. Cornes came sixth, just a fraction of a second outside it. The two early challengers, Ny and Boettcher, finished second last and last.

Lovelock's race was followed with much interest in Britain, as the athlete was regarded as being as good as British. Although Harold Whitlock, a thirty-two-year-old garage mechanic from London, had won the 50-kilometre walk the day before, Lovelock's triumph captured the imagination. No one was more excited than Harold Abrahams, who was commentating on the race for the BBC. Discarding any pretence that he was neutral about the result, Abrahams made what is regarded as the most partial commentary in the history of broadcasting. By the end, the former Olympian was screaming into the microphone.

> Lovelock leads by about four yards, Cunningham fighting hard, Beccali coming up to his shoulder, Lovelock leads . . . Lovelock . . . Lovelock . . . Cunningham second, Beccali third . . . Come on, Jack! One hundred yards to go . . . Come on, Jack! By God he's done it! Jack, come on! Lovelock wins! Five yards, six yards, he wins . . . he's won! Hooray!

Abrahams was not the only Briton to get carried away. The *Manchester Guardian* was similarly rapturous, calling it 'a race magnificent beyond all description', and its correspondent, E. A. Montague, sheepishly admitted that 'one's memories of that delirious last lap are a little incoherent'. In his diary that evening, Lovelock was his usual immodest self, but then perhaps he deserved to be. 'It was undoubtedly the most beautifully executed race of my career,' he wrote, 'a true climax to 8 years steady work, an artistic creation.' He then added, 'Later felt a little weary but v. fit.'

Also running hard that day was Charles Leonard, who was competing in the final event of the modern pentathlon – the punishing 4,000-metre cross-country run. The previous day, Leonard had done well in the 300-metre swimming, finishing in sixth place with a time of 4:40.9. In total, he now had 32 points. The athletes' points were the sum of their places in each event – the best overall score possible therefore being 5 points if an athlete came first in all five events. The competition was won by the competitor with the fewest points. Gotthardt Handrick, the German favourite, managed to come ninth in the swimming, completing the distance in 4:51.9. He now had 17½ points. Leonard knew that Handrick was way out in front, and that he would have to beat him by at least fifteen places in order to win the gold. There was other competition too, however, in the form of Thofelt of Sweden, who had 23 points, Orbán of Hungary with 39½ points and Abba of Italy, who had 40½. Before the run started, Leonard was on course for a bronze medal. But he desperately wanted to beat both Handrick and the Swede, who had won the gold in 1928.

The runners assembled at the grounds of the Wannsee Gold Club at nine o'clock that morning. The weather was pleasantly cool, perfect for cross-country running. Leonard was dressed rather more athletically for this event, wearing white shorts and a white vest with red and blue stripes running diagonally across it. Instead of running as a pack, the competitors started individually, with a one-minute delay between them. Leonard knew that he would have to run faster than he had ever imagined possible if he was going to win gold or silver. The first 400 metres were relatively easy, running through pleasant woodland before the course descended down a steep ravine to a glade. Leonard followed the chalk line that designated the course, noting how officials had been placed in the stretches where short cuts could have been taken by unscrupulous athletes. The second kilometre was tougher, half of it uphill. By now some of the competitors were beginning to flag, but Leonard kept pushing himself. He had to do better than bronze, he told himself. For the third kilometre, Leonard found that the line continued to snake its way uphill, this time across a meadow, before plunging down into some woodland. He soon began to pass some of his fellow competitors, who had either dropped out or who were running no faster than walking pace. Halfway through the final kilometre, the course ascended a nastily steep hill and ran through some trees. Leonard was so exhausted that he doubted whether he would be able to get up the hill. He was soon rewarded, however, by a sight that gave him a much-needed boost. It was Thofelt, who was near to collapse. Leonard sprinted past him, realising that the silver medal at least was in his reach. For the last 300 metres he forced himself to go as fast as possible, and to ignore the pain. As soon as he crossed the line, he collapsed into the arms of a German army officer and his coach, who put a blanket over his shoulders. 'The hilly, sandy, rough trail [. . .] was as difficult a trek as I've ever seen,' he wrote in his diary. 'I was worn out when I was done, I'll tell you that,' he later recalled.

Now came the waiting. Leonard changed into his tracksuit and anxiously watched the scoreboard, along with the top brass of the German military. Among the spectators were the Reich war minister, General von Blomberg, the chief of staff of the army, General von Fritsch, and General Milch of the air force. Leonard looked at his time: it was 14:15.8. It was good, but would it be good enough to convincingly beat Handrick? He knew that Thofelt had done badly, but had he done badly enough to drop at least ten places – and therefore 10 points – behind Leonard? Nobody would know the final result until the very last runner came in. The results were finally prepared, and then placed on the board. Leonard came seventh, equal with his fellow American, Lieutenant Starbird, which gave him 7½ points, bring his final score to 39½. Thofelt's time went up: 15:16.2 – a dreadful result for the Swede which gave him a crippling 24 points, bringing his total to 47. Leonard calmed himself down – it looked as if he had won silver, as his nearest rival, Abba, had scored 40½ before the cross-country. Even if Orbán of Hungary came first, he too would end up on 40½.

But what of Handrick? Where had he come? Leonard prayed that the German had come at least twenty-third, which would give him a score of 40½ points. Handrick's time was 14:41.7, just under twenty-six seconds slower than Leonard. Would that put him in twenty-third place? Unfortunately, it did not. It put him in fourteenth, bringing his total to 31½. 'I couldn't overcome Handrick's excellent start in riding and fencing,' wrote Leonard. 'He is known all over Europe as a poor rider; this time he wasn't . . . Anyway, I had the satisfaction of beating him personally in four of the five events.' Leonard knew that if only he had ridden his horse harder down the back straight on that first morning of the competition, then the gold would probably have been his. Such is the nature of sport. Leonard was magnanimous, however. 'He deserves his first,' he wrote.

★

The following morning saw the start of an even more punishing multi-disciplined event – the decathlon. Even though he was the favourite, Glenn Morris found that he was not at all confident. 'The day before I began the decathlon,' he recalled, 'I was all alone in the village and consequently I was not relaxed when the final call was sounded.' Morris's biggest rivals were his fellow Americans Bob Clark and Jack Parker, and for the next two days the three men would battle it out in one of the most nail-biting decathlon contests for many years.

The first event was the 100 metres, and Morris's time of 11.1 seconds earned him a respectable 814 points, which placed him second behind Clark. At the long jump pit, Morris fared less well, managing a jump of 6.97 metres, which was trounced by both Clark and Parker, who both leaped well over 7 metres. After that morning's events, Morris lay in third place, just a few points ahead of Guhl of Switzerland and Huber of Germany. Now the athletes faced a problem none of them could solve satisfactorily – what to do about lunch. After the long jump had finished, there was only two hours to go until the shot put started at 3 p.m., which did not leave enough time for two 45-minute bus rides and a decent lunch. Instead, the athletes had to make do. Morris wolfed down a steak sandwich, washed down by four cups of coffee.

Morris's first attempt at the shot put was a reasonable 13.59 metres, which would have placed him in the top three, but it was his second attempt which proved just how strong he was. The shot sailed a good 10 centimetres beyond the 14-metre mark, earning him a healthy 826 points. Clark could manage no farther than 12.68 and Parker 13.52, and Morris once more found himself in second place behind Clark. In the high jump, Morris easily beat off his compatriots, jumping 1.85 metres, second only to Reindert Brasser of Holland, who cleared 1.90 metres. By now, Morris was attracting the attention of the crowd, not just because of his prowess, but also because he would constantly be practising between events. 'Throughout the long grind, Morris scarcely ever rested,' wrote the correspondent of the *Denver Post*. Perhaps it was just the coffee. The final event of the day was the 400 metres, in which Morris clocked the best time of 49.4 seconds. At the end of the day, he was still second to Bob Clark, but there were only two points in it. With some of his strongest events to look forward to on the next day, Saturday, he looked to be in a strong position.

Morris did, however, have a small problem. It was that coffee. Unused to it, he found it almost impossible to get to sleep, managing only two hours. The lack of rest did not seem to trouble him, as he won the morning's first event, the 110-metre hurdles, in 14.9 seconds. Clark's time was 15.7, and for the first time in the competition Morris took the lead, with a useful 126 points separating the two men. The rivalry was friendly, however. After each event that day, Morris and Clark would spread a blanket on the ground and lie on it together. They would then place towels on their heads, presumably as a means of shutting out the immensity and the noise of the stadium. Morris's meditation was noticed by Peter Gay sitting among the Hungarians. 'Only an American, I thought [. . .] could be so composed and so energetic at the same time.'

It was during one of these companionable rests that Morris was to meet none other than Leni Riefenstahl. The film-maker had noticed him through one of her many lenses, and she asked Erwin Huber, the German decathlete, for an introduction. The encounter would prove to be fateful for both of them. 'With a towel over his head, Glenn Morris lay relaxing on the grass, gathering strength for the next event,' Riefenstahl recalled. 'When Huber presented Morris to me, and we looked at one another, we both seemed transfixed. It was an incredible moment and I had never experienced anything like it.' For Riefenstahl, Morris was the epitome of manhood – a statue from antiquity that had come to life. If Morris was similarly smitten, it did not put him off the competition. He hurled the discus 43.02 metres, which increased his lead over Clark to 236 points. This bought him enough of a margin not to allow Clark to overtake him in the pole vault, which was Morris's weakest event – Clark beat him by 20 centimetres. In the javelin, Morris threw 54.52 metres to come ninth, but this did nothing to alter the positions the three American athletes found themselves in before the 1,500 metres at 5.30 that afternoon. Morris was first, 217 points ahead of Clark in second, with Parker 184 points behind in third. In fourth place lay Brasser, but he was 239 points behind Parker. It was certainly going to be an American triple, but in what order?

The 1,500 metres was delayed by a Hitler Youth demonstration, so the race started just after eight o'clock in fading light. Morris had been told that in order to break the world record he would need to run the race in 4:32, a time that he had never made. He normally ran the distance in 4:49. Nevertheless, the single-minded boy from Simla was determined to try. The 1,500 metres was divided into three heats (there would be no final) and Morris's was the last. In the first heat, Parker ran a rotten 5:07.8, which saw his grip on the bronze severely weakened. Bob Clark crossed the line in his heat with 4:44.4, a time that confirmed his silver medal. By the time Morris started, he knew that gold would be his, but he wanted that world record.

His progress was tortuous to watch; because Morris was pushing himself so hard, he was clearly in agony. During the second lap, Boulanger of Belgium cut in front of him, which caused the crowd to boo. The spectators wanted Morris to beat the record, and even Hitler cheered the American on. The dictator rocked backwards and forwards in his seat, pounding his fist into a cupped hand, willing Morris on. Morris redoubled his efforts, and surged past the Belgian. The last 35 metres were the most painful to watch. 'The American had none of the grace of a Lovelock,' wrote Arthur Daley in the *New York Times*. 'His features were strained and drawn. Every step was painful, but still he came on, running only with his heart. His feet were leaden.' Morris crossed the line in 4:33.2, an astonishing sixteen seconds ahead of his personal best. He collapsed on to the ground, suffering not only from exhaustion but from the disappointment of realising that he had missed beating the world record by a mere second. The crowd sympathised, and cheered him loudly nevertheless. A few minutes later, however, came a sensational announcement. The 4.32 announcement had been an error. Morris had in fact trounced the world record by 76 points. American domination of the event was secured by Clark and Parker taking silver and bronze.

According to Leni Riefenstahl, Morris's behaviour at the subsequent awards ceremony was bizarre. Because the light was now so dim, the director was unable to film the ceremony, which was a shame, as the out-takes might have captured an extraordinary moment. After the ceremony, Morris stepped off the podium and headed straight towards Riefenstahl. 'I held out my hand and congratulated him,' she wrote, 'but he grabbed me in his arms, tore off my blouse, and kissed my breasts, right in the middle of the stadium, in front of a hundred thousand spectators. A lunatic, I thought. I wrenched myself out of his grasp and dashed away. But I could not forget the wild look in his eyes, and I never wanted to speak to him again, never go anywhere near him again.' Riefenstahl's approach to the truth seems once more to have been highly suspect. Notwithstanding the utter implausibility of Morris kissing her naked breasts in what was the largest gathering of people anywhere on the planet, the photographs of the medal cere-mony show that it took place during daylight, which suggests it was postponed because of the lateness of the hour. The photographs also show the three victors in their jackets and ties, which they would not have had at the stadium that evening. This can only mean that the ceremony took place on another day. Despite Riefenstahl's rank fab-rication, however, and protestations that she wanted nothing to do with Morris, the two would in fact meet again.

If Morris had made a Herculanean effort to win his world record, then so too would the marathon runner Son Ki-Jung. Although a Korean, Son was in fact a Japanese subject, as Korea had been conquered and annexed by the Japanese in 1910. Whenever Son raced, he was forced to wear a vest that featured the rising sun, the emblem of a country that had massacred thousands of his fellow countrymen, as well as destroying all but ten of the magnificent 330 buildings that comprised the Korean Royal Palace. For Son, running represented a way of escaping the tyranny. 'The Japanese could stop our musicians from playing our songs,' said Son. 'They could stop our singers and silence our speakers. But they could not stop me from running.' Son spent much of his boyhood running, even running two miles to the bakery every day. He was brought up in Ishu, a small and poor farming and logging community near the Yalu river, on the border with the part of Korea that was not under Japanese occupation. He raced against friends on their bicycles, often beating them. He would also run up and down logging trails, the steepness of their inclines giving him much endurance. His talent was prodigious, and it was soon spotted. He was sent to Yangjung High School in Seoul, a private school that had produced many fine runners.

In April 1935 word filtered to Europe and America from Tokyo that someone had beaten the two-and-a-half-hour barrier for the distance. Then, in November, the world was even more shocked to hear that the same athlete had run the marathon in 2:26:42 – an almost incomprehensible achievement. According to the wires, the athlete's name was 'Kitei Son'. It was the name the Japanese had forced on Son, and it was the name that Son had to use when he represented his conqueror at the Games. During his stay in Berlin, the twenty-three-year-old Son refused to sign his autograph as 'Kitei Son' and insisted on using his Korean name, which was often accompanied by a small outline of Korea in order to emphasise the fact that he felt subjugated to the Land of the Rising Sun.

The marathon was held on Sunday, 9 August. The field was a large one, consisting of some fifty-six competitors who would be running past an estimated million spectators lining the 26-mile (42-kilometre) course around the Grunewald. Son's rivals included Carlos Zabala, an Argentinian who had established the Olympic record of 2:31:36 in Los Angeles in 1932 – some five minutes slower than Son's unofficial world record. Three other threats came in the form of three Finns – Tamila, Muinonen and Tarkianen – who were regarded as being dangerously crafty. The one dark horse came in the form of Englishman Ernest Harper, a miner from Sheffield who at thirty-four was the oldest in the field.

From the start in the stadium, Zabala sprinted away from the pack, eager to prove his supremacy. At the 12-kilometre mark he was one and a half minutes ahead, and it looked as though he was going to smash the world record. Behind him were Son and the rangy Harper, who made an odd couple. At the halfway mark, Harper fell in behind Son, and the two men murmured encouragement and advice to each other. 'Harper kept telling me not to worry about Zabala,' Son said after the race, 'but to let him run himself out. So we paid no attention to him or any other runners and set our own pace.' Nevertheless, it was a painful experience, Son later recalled: 'The human body can do so much. Then the heart and spirit must take over.' Harper kept up with him, his face pulled into a strenuous grimace.

Son's efforts paid off. He and Harper caught up with Zabala at the twenty-eighth kilometre. The Argentinian could not believe it, so sure was he of his imminent victory. After just 100 metres he fell back, and 3 kilometres later he collapsed. The Finns were surprised too, especially at one point in the track when they could see the Korean and the Englishman running towards them on the return loop. Their tactics of bunching together had not worked, and now they had far too much work to do. Nevertheless, they tried, but they could not erode the sockless Son's masterful lead.

The Korean emerged into the Olympic Stadium just under two and a half hours after he had left. He was on his own, his already slight figure rendered minuscule when set against the vastness of the stadium. His face was expressionless, showing no sign of the tremendous effort he had made. In fact, Son seemingly had energy to spare, as he ran the last 100 yards in twelve seconds. He crossed the line at 2:29:19 – an official new world record. Two officials chased after him with a blanket, which seemed to cause Son to collapse. Harper followed two minutes later, his face racked with pain caused by a blister, his shoe filled with blood. He fell on to the grass, and officials piled the mandatory blankets on top of him. Just ten seconds behind him was the unexpected figure of Nam Sung Yong, a fellow Korean, who had managed to outwit the Finnish threesome. The crowd cheered Son, but he was in no mood for celebrating. His mood was not helped by the fact that he was mobbed by weeping Japanese journalists in the dressing room. Bizarrely, while Son lay down to relax, every so often a Japanese would come and press his head against Son's chest and then burst into tears. 'We've been preparing for this victory for twenty-four years,' said one of the weeping genuflectors. 'Now we can hardly believe we've won. It's a big moment for Japan.' Those words must have been bitter for Son to swallow.

Son graciously thanked Harper for his success. 'Much credit for my victory must go to Mr Harper of England,' he said. 'Please say Mr Harper is very fine man for telling me about Zabala.' While Son was being lionised, the 'very fine man' was to be found limping around the depths of the stadium looking for the British dressing room. He had asked twelve policemen where it was, but none could understand him. Nobody from the British team was available to escort him, despite the fact that Harper was exhausted. Eventually, a journalist from the Associated Press helped him, bemused to watch the solitary Harper limp away, holding in his mouth, of all things, a cigarette.

Son knew that he had won a great victory, but the worst moment was about to come – the presentation of his gold medal. 'It was an unbearable disgrace for me that I listened to "Kimigayo" [Japan's national anthem] on the honour platform, seeing the flag of the Rising-Sun on the flag-pole,' Son recalled fifty years later. 'Unconsciously, I hung my head and wondered whether I was really a Japanese. If I were, what did the Japanese maltreatment against my fellow countrymen mean? Anyway, what on earth do the sun flag and "Kimigayo" mean, what do they symbolise?' Son was probably the unhappiest gold medal winner in the history of the Games. The wreath almost covered his eyes, which were moist with tears. Worse was to come. In the press interviews afterwards, Son tried telling the world that he was a Korean, but as his interpreter was Japanese his comments were never translated in full. At his own request, Son was to meet Hitler that day, determined to tell the Fuehrer about his situation. He could not, however, bring himself to raise the matter during the meeting. 'What I was going to say was, "Mr Hitler, I am a man without a country". But I held back. I don't think he would have understood anyway.' It is unlikely Hitler would have cared.

One man who was similarly desperate to tell the world about his country was Werner Seelenbinder. Although he now realised, because of the arrests, that he would never be able to make a broadcast in the event of his winning a medal, he knew that he could still protest plainly enough by not saluting at the medal ceremony. His path to the podium started at the Deutschland Hall just after eleven o'clock on the morning of Thursday, 6 August. Between then and 9 August, Seelenbinder would hopefully face six rounds. At Berlin, the bouts were scored by awarding 'bad points'. Anyone who obtained five bad points was eliminated from the competition. The most points a losing wrestler could gain in a bout was three, which were incurred if he was defeated by a fall. Three points were also awarded if the three judges voted unanimously against the loser. Two points were given to the loser if the judges voted two to one for the victor. One point was awarded to the winning wrestler if he had only won on points, and no points were awarded only if the winning wrestler had triumphed by throwing his opponent.

Seelenbinder did not feel as confident as he should have done, his nerves increased by the arrests made a few days earlier. In his first round he faced the square-jawed Edvins Bietags of Latvia, whom he knew he could beat. Nevertheless, exactly halfway through the twenty-minute bout the Latvian threw a shocked Seelenbinder. For the German, it was a disaster – he now only had to lose two more points and he would be out. The second round took place at seven o'clock the following morning, and Seelenbinder was determined to regain his form. He faced Argast of Switzerland, who felt the full desperate force of Seelenbinder. After just three minutes, Argast was thrown. Seelenbinder now advanced to the fourth round, having been allowed a let in round three. At 7 p.m. on 8 August, Seelenbinder literally wiped the floor with Foidl of Austria, throwing him in a mere thirty-five seconds. The first round was surely unrepresentative of Seelenbinder's mastery.

At eleven o'clock on the morning of Sunday, 9 August, the last four wrestlers faced each other. Bietags still had no points. Axel Cadier of Sweden, his jaw even more lantern-like than that of Bietags, had one point. Like Seelenbinder, August Neo of Estonia, his jaw reasonably lantern-like, was on three points. All four men were well matched, but a betting man would have placed his money on Seelenbinder, despite the disaster of the first round. The first bout took place between Bietags and Neo. It lasted the full twenty minutes, and at the end the judges awarded the victory to Bietags by a margin of two to one. Bietags now had two points; Neo had five, and was therefore ruled out.

It looked as if Seelenbinder's place on the podium was guaranteed. All he had to do was to defeat Axel Cadier to guarantee winning gold or silver. Matters would be made more complicated if Seelenbinder incurred any points by winning on a judge's decision, but given the way the German was wrestling, a victory with no points looked likely. Even if Seelenbinder lost with a judge's decision, then he would be on five points, like Neo. With the two men tied for bronze, they would face a play-off which Seelenbinder would undoubtedly win, as Neo was the weakest of the four. The worst thing that could happen to Seelenbinder was to gain three points by being thrown or suffering a defeat at the hands of unanimous judges.

A podium place, that was all he required. Seelenbinder grappled hard with Cadier, but found the blond Swede tougher than he could have imagined. The two men wrestled hard on the 8-by-8-metre mat, lit up by bright spotlights, their every move analysed by the judges. Seelenbinder felt he did well, but the twenty-nine-year-old Cadier was a tough and experienced opponent. Little did the Swede know that for Seelenbinder there was more at stake than a medal. Neither of the men was able to throw the other, however, and after twenty minutes the bout ended. It would now be up to the judges. At their desks, the judges had three different coloured lights. A white light meant that the judge was neutral. A red light meant that the judge favoured the wrestler wearing red socks, a green light was a vote for the opponent with green socks. That day, appropriately enough, the communist Seelenbinder was wearing red socks. As he stood there, his huge torso glistening in the bright lights, he knew that the illumination of three small light bulbs held his fate. The lights came only on when all the judges had made their decision, in order not to let the judges who had made their minds up quickly affect the decisions of those who were more pensive. Seelenbinder held his breath. The lights came on. They were all of the same colour. It was green.

10

In the Sight of the Heathen

~

ONLY IN DICTATORSHIPS can a 'Week of Laughter' be declared. For Nazi Germany, the eight days from Friday, 17 July were designated thus by the Labour Front. 'The days will be days of jollity and cheerfulness,' the organisation ordered. 'Prior to the strain of the Olympic weeks, Berliners should take stock of themselves, then with merry heart and friendly expressions on their faces receive their Olympic guests. None should miss this chance.' In order to jolly the Germans along, the British and Canadians had decided to show what was termed some 'Olympic spirit' by returning a couple of war relics to the Reich. One was a piece of the Fokker triplane in which Manfred von Richtofen – the famous Red Baron – was shot down near the Somme on 21 April 1918. The other was the bell from the battlecruiser *Hindenburg*, which had been scuttled at Scapa Flow on 21 June 1919. Perhaps there was something a little cheeky in giving back pieces of wreckage that would only serve to remind the recipients of their defeat just eighteen years previously.

Those who visited Berlin during the Olympic fortnight found that the German capital was indeed a place of jollity and cheerfulness. It was a city *en fête*, one that retained much of the glamour of its Weimar days, described by one breathless travel writer as a 'mecca for pleasure-seekers', with 'its midnight path of dalliance [which] offers everything from the finest opera to the jazziest dance-bars'. Berlin's hot spots included the Eden Roof Garden with its distinguished, upmarket clientele, and the rather more racy Rio Rita, where telephones on the tables enabled visitors to indulge in flirtatious chatter with strangers. One of those who enjoyed such clubs was Eduard Falz-Fein, a twenty-three-year-old journalist for *L'Equipe*. 'I enjoyed myself,' he recalled. 'Every minute, there was something going on. I was a good-looking boy, and the girls had a good time with me. I was bewildered by how many good-looking girls there were in Berlin. Every man in the world wanted to have a good-looking girl, but I didn't have to do anything, they just came to me. I took them to restaurants and nightclubs, and after that to bed. They were very good.'

Suffering from hangovers the following day, those who didn't want to attend the Games could consult the recently updated Baedeker guidebook, which had just been reissued and thoroughly Nazified. One of the highlights of the city was nothing less than the grave of the Nazi hero Horst Wessel himself. The Baedeker also told visitors to Germany that the Versailles Treaty was not a real peace treaty, but a 'diktat which the defeated had to accept like a verdict'. As a counter to the Nazification of guides like the Baedeker, secret resistance groups had prepared subversive leaflets mocked up to look like tourist brochures. One, which found its way into the hands of a columnist on the *New Statesman* magazine, featured a map that marked all of Germany's concentration camps, as well as the locations where polit-ical murders had taken place. The columnist grimly wondered 'how many heroic individuals will reach these places of torment for dis-tributing this leaflet during the celebrations'.

What struck most of those visiting Berlin was not just the abun-dance of swastikas and Olympic rings, but also the overpowering sense of militarism. 'I'll not forget the sight of those German storm troop-ers,' wrote Grantland Rice, 'in their severely cut black uniforms, looking every inch the super race. You could see them in the streets, out at the jam-packed Reich Sportsfeld, at the Hofhaus. They didn't stroll, they marched, and gutturalised with the quiet, confident bear-ing that betokened their Cheshire cat scorn of "less endowed" mortals.' For Rice, Germany was, as it was for so many others, 'painted in the garish hues of a nation well primed for war'. The novelist Thomas Wolfe also saw a portent of conflict in the uniforms. '[There were] long lines of Hitler's bodyguards, black-uniformed and leather-booted, the Schutz-Staffel men [the SS], stretching in unbroken lines from the Leader's residence in the Wilhelmstrasse up to the arches of the Brandenburger Tor; then suddenly the sharp command, and instantly, unforgettably, the liquid smack of ten thousand leather boots as they came together, with the sound of war.'

As much as the hosts enjoyed the novelty of having so many guests from all over the world, they soon began to tire of the visitors' obsession with one man. 'There was one question on everyone's mind,' recalled Esther Wenzel, a twenty-year-old schoolteacher from Douglass, Kansas. ' "What do you think about Hitler?" That was the question we asked our German friends at the balls, dinners and entertainments. "Please don't talk about him," we were told. "Are you a member of the Nazi Party?" we often asked someone. If the answer was negative, the reply was always a hushed "no" and "I don't want to talk about it".'

Such abortive conversations were not uncommon. Alfred Gerdes, the German hockey player, had to constantly fend off questions about politics. 'We always said, "Leave it out, that stuff, we don't want to hear anything about all that." ' Gerdes believed, however, that the visitors could detect what he thought. 'They could feel it out of what I said,' he recalled. 'I told them not exactly with words, but they could tell.' Not all the visitors, however, were so politically minded. Halet Çambel, the Turkish fencer, found her fellow female athletes at the Friesian House singularly uninterested. 'The queer thing was that in the Friesian House there was no talk about politics,' she remembered. 'I don't remember that anyone was aware of what was happening. The other girls were just interested in their training and how they were going to do.' Çambel said that the only reason she knew what was going on was that her mother had made friends with many German refugees in Turkey. In fact, many of the female athletes spent their time in Berlin shopping. 'Several of the girls are having to buy trunks and suitcases to get their souvenirs home,' wrote Velma Dunn to her mother. It was during such shopping trips that Dorothy Odam recalled how 'we were quite often stopped because Hitler was coming'. Whenever the Fuehrer drove past, the streets came to a standstill, which Odam at first though strange, until it occurred to her that the British would have done the same thing for King Edward.

One element of the regime that was not in evidence – at least not on the surface – was anti-Semitism. The American swimmer Adolph Kiefer had visited Germany in 1935, when he found the signs of measures being taken against Jews to be 'very obvious'. 'In 1936,' he said, 'they played it down. We didn't see any armbands with Stars of David on them during the Olympics.' Nevertheless, it was clear to some that the Jews, even though they were enjoying the benefits of an all too brief 'Olympic pause', were still frightened. Halet Çambel recalled one conversation she had on a bus. 'A very short dark man came up to me,' she said. 'He asked me in Yiddish whether I was Jewish. I told him that I was on the Turkish Olympic team and that I was indeed Jewish, although I am not. I said it to give him courage. He was obviously happy to hear it, glad to hear that Jews were being allowed to visit. And then he went away.' Not all signs of anti-Semitism had been removed, however, 'I was interested to note, incidentally, that *Der Stuermer* – contrary to rumour – had not ceased publication,' wrote an Alec Dickson to *The Spectator*. '[. . .] I observed copies for sale outside the Gedächtniskirche.' The SS newspaper, *Das Schwarze Korps*, was also noticeable, replacing the pornographically vile, anti-Semitic *Der Stuermer* in the public reading boxes. According to Dickson, the opinion of the former regarding the Games was that they were 'essentially a German festival at which other nations are honoured guests, but still only guests'.

Like Adolph Kiefer, Thomas Wolfe had visited Germany in 1935. Although he too had noticed that there were fewer public displays of anti-Semitism, the worldly thirty-five-year-old novelist was able to see far more than the eighteen-year-old swimmer.

> The pestilence of the year before had spread and deepened so that there was not a person I had known before who had not perceptibly grown, within the space of one short year, sick and stricken as he had not been before. The evidence of pressure and of fear was everywhere sharply more apparent as soon as one reestablished contact with the lives he had known.

One of those lives was that of a 'little man' who had worked in a publishing house, whom Wolfe had met the year before. The novelist had wanted to see him again, and asked the host of a party whether this little man could be also be invited. His host told him that because the man was a Jew, he no longer had a job, and that it would be unwise to meet him in public. Nevertheless, Wolfe insisted on seeing him in private. The two men met in secret, and the first thing Wolfe noticed was the shabbiness of the little man's suit, which was the same suit he was wearing a year ago,

[. . .] except that now his shabby little suit was frayed and patched, and his collar was clean, but he had turned it, and it had the mottled look that collars have when people launder them themselves. He wore a shoe-string of a tie, and his neck and Adam's apple were as thin and stringy as a piece of gristle, and his eyes were like sunk comets in his face. His little claw-like hands were cold as fish and trembled when he talked; and all that I can remember was that he said to me, shaking his head upon that gristle of a neck, 'Sir – sir – the world is very sad, sir; the world is very sad.'

Here, then, was an embodiment of the state of Germany's Jews – unable to work, unable to buy new clothes, unable to get their clothes laundered, unable to feed themselves properly, but still wearing ties, even if they were just shoe-strings of ties. Had Wolfe attended the service for the American Olympic team at the American Church in Berlin, he would have admired Reverend Stewart W. Herman Jr's choice of Psalm 98:

> The Lord hath made known his salvation: his righteousness hath he openly shewed in the sight of the heathen.
> He hath remembered his mercy and his truth toward the house of Israel: all the ends of the earth have seen the salvation of our God.

One Jew similar to Wolfe's 'little man' was Victor Klemperer, who had been a professor of Romance languages until he had been forced to stop teaching because of his faith. Klemperer despised the Olympic Games, regarding them as detestable not only because they married athletic ability to a nation's honour, but also because they were 'not a matter of sports – here in our country, I mean – but rather a political enterprise through and through'. On 13 August he wrote in his diary: 'Natives and foreigners are constantly having it drummed into them that what they are seeing is the upswing, blossoming, new spirit, unity, solidity and splendour, naturally also the peaceful and lovingly world-embracing spirit of the Third Reich.' Klemperer was wise to keep such cynicism within the pages of his diary, for those who openly crit-icised the regime would find themselves in trouble. The daily report of the State Police Office for 15/16 August tells of a man who would constantly approach foreigners in restaurants and ask them what they thought of Berlin. When they told him how much they liked it, he would respond by saying that 'he could show them another side, espe-cially since he had been in a concentration camp'. The Criminal Investigation Office tracked him down and arrested him, and discov-ered that he had in fact not been in a camp, a situation that was soon 'rectified' by Himmler himself, who ordered that he should be sent to one for five years.

Jews were not the only persons of faith who suffered under the regime, and continued to suffer during the so-called pause. Protestants also found themselves under attack, their churches being forced to merge into the Nazi-controlled Protestant Reich Church. Many pastors were opposed to this, and in May 1934, at the Synod of Barmen, the Confessing Church was formally established by, among others, Dietrich Bonhoeffer and Martin Niemoeller. Much to the fury of the Nazis, the new church proclaimed itself the true voice of Protestantism in Germany. The pastors were not afraid to directly oppose the regime. At a 20,000-strong rally at Dahlem in November 1934, Niemoeller declared that 'it is a question of which master the German Protestants are going to serve – Christ, or another'. For a while, the Confessing Church was tolerated by the Nazis, but only just. Over seven hundred pastors were arrested, and members of the church were constantly spied upon and subject to eavesdropping. Higher-profile members, such as Niemoeller and Bonhoeffer, were safe – albeit temporarily – only because they had influential friends and they were well known overseas. Between 1933 and 1935, Bonhoeffer had served as a pastor in two German-speaking Protestant churches in London.

The Confessing Church saw the Olympic Games as an opportu-nity to make itself heard throughout the world. In late July, Niemoeller and others produced a manifesto that was smuggled out of Germany and printed in the foreign press just before the Games.

Our people are trying to break the bond set by God. That is human conceit rising against God. In this connection we must warn the Fuehrer, that the adoration frequently bestowed on him is only due to God. Some years ago the Fuehrer objected to having his picture placed on Protestant altars. Today his thoughts are used as a basis not only for political decisions but also for morality and law. He himself is surrounded with the dignity of a priest and even of an intermediary between God and man [. . .] We ask that liberty be given to our people to go their way in the future under the sign of the Cross of Christ, in order that our grandsons may not curse their elders on the ground that their elders left them a state on earth that closed to them the Kingdom of God.

The pastors did not stop there. On 5 August they wrote a long memorandum to the Nazi government. 'The attempt to dechristianise the German people', it stated, 'is to become the official policy of the Government through the further participation of responsible statesmen or even by the fact that they merely look on and allow it to happen [. . .] We must express our concern that honour is often done to him [Hitler] in a way that is due to God only.'

There was nothing the Nazis could do during the Olympics to silence the Confessing Church. Instead, the regime attempted to prove its supposed devotion to Christianity by getting the Reich Church to erect an enormous tent near the stadium, in which religious services were held. The Nazis vainly hoped that pastors such as Niemoeller and Bonhoeffer might even preach in the tent, but the two men refused. Instead, Bonhoeffer accepted an invitation to speak in a series of anti-Nazi talks in Pauluskirche on 5 August, although he disapproved of the way the talks were being promoted. 'I would rather call the whole thing off,' he wrote. 'I was particularly annoyed when we were asked to send a photograph because they [the organisers] wanted to bring out a propaganda booklet with our pictures in it. This I find both ludicrous and degrading, and in any case, I shall send nothing.'

The booklet did appear – without Bonhoeffer's picture – but it was immediately confiscated by the Nazis. The talks, however, went ahead, attracting what even the pro-Nazi *Christliche Welt* described as 'a huge reverently attentive congregation'. Bonhoeffer was pleased with the way his talk had gone. In it he had demonstrated how the spirit of the Reformation was present only in the Confessing Church, and not in the Reich Church. 'Not a bad evening yesterday,' he wrote. 'The church packed, people were sitting on the altar steps and standing everywhere [. . .] A group of Berlin friends, pastors, etc., met at Rabenau's where I had to continue my talk. I didn't get home until

2 am.' The *Christliche Welt* was less impressed, describing it as 'deeply sad when confronted by such a "view of history" '. For Bonhoeffer, the Games provided the last chance for him to speak to such a large gathering. After associating with the resistance movement against Hitler, the pastor was arrested in 1943 for helping Jews escape to Switzerland. He was hanged in Flossenburg concentration camp on 9 April 1945, just three weeks before its liberation. Niemoeller survived the war, although he suffered greatly in Sachsenhausen and Dachau camps. He became president of the World Council of Churches in 1961 and died in 1984.

Another religious group that was attacked by the Nazis was the Oxford Group. Founded in the 1920s by Frank Buchman, an American evangelist, and a group of Oxford University students, the Oxford Group soon developed into a worldwide network of those who preached a peace-loving message of 'moral rearmament' rather than military rearmament. (The group would later be renamed Moral Rearmament, and is now called Initiatives of Change.) The presence of members of the Oxford Group in Germany was viewed with suspicion by the Nazis, which saw the organisation as one of the 'sinister international forces which wage constant underground war against Germany'. The group was likened to another of those Nazi *bêtes noires*, the Freemasons, and on 21 July 1936 the Bavarian Political Police ordered all their police authorities to report on the activities of members of the group within a fortnight.

Urged by his followers to stand up to the Nazis, Buchman visited Berlin during the Olympic Games. Staying at the Hotel Esplanade, the evangelist managed to arrange a meeting with the head of the SS, Heinrich Himmler. 'The conversation became a complete fiasco,' one observer recalled. Although Buchman somewhat naively wanted to lecture the Nazi on the evils of the 'terrible demoniac force' that were gripping Germany, he instead found himself unable to get a word in. Himmler marched into the Esplanade with a group of SS men, lectured Buchman on the benefits of Nazism, and marched out before the American could respond. 'Here are devilish forces at work,' said Buchman after Himmler had left. 'We can't do anything here.'

Nevertheless, despite his best intentions, Buchman was to attract controversy when he returned to the United States later that month.

Upon his arrival, he gave an interview to a journalist from the *New York World-Telegram,* in which he was reported to have said, 'I thank heaven for a man like Adolf Hitler, who built a front line of defence against the anti-Christ of communism [. . .] My barber in London told me Hitler saved Europe from communism. That's how he felt. Of course, I don't condone everything the Nazis do. Anti-Semitism? Bad, naturally. I suppose Hitler sees a Karl Marx in every Jew. But think what it would mean to the world if Hitler surrendered to the control of God.' Buchman and his aides were later to claim that his words had been heavily edited, giving the impression that he was a supporter of Hitler. Buchman's stance, they maintained, was that Hitler could at least be thanked for being a bulwark against communism, but he had by no means endorsed the Fuehrer or his policies. Nevertheless, the message the public heard was 'Thank God for Hitler', a misrepresentation that still did nothing to help the plight of the group in Germany after the Games.

In November 1936 the Gestapo warned its network that the Oxford Group was a 'new and dangerous opponent of National Socialism', and ordered its operatives to spy on members. Himmler believed that the group was nothing more than a nest of spies, and demanded that its members have nothing more to do with Buchman, an order that they only publicly obeyed. The attacks continued, and in 1939 the Germany army forbade any officers from having anything to do with the group. During the war, the group largely acquiesced with the Nazis, although a minority of its members became active in the resistance.

Such goings-on did not concern the members of the IOC, who were being bounteously entertained by the Nazis. The Olympic fortnight was an endurance test not only for the athletes, but also for those who were invited to the numerous functions hosted by the bigwigs in the Nazi regime. The first of the significant banquets, however, was hosted by the IOC itself on 31 July in the resplendent White Hall of Berlin Castle. Guests were treated to a sensational dinner created by the Kaiserhof Hotel in Berlin, which started with a simple *consommé Julienne* accompanied by an amontillado from A. R. Valdespino. The second course consisted of Black Forest trout and *salade Américaine,* which was washed down by a 1933 Auslese. Then followed *Vol au Vent Toulouse* – puff pastry filled with chicken, mushrooms and truffles – which was served with a 1920 Auslese. The guests now needed to find room for saddle of venison, served with petits pois and a *salade romaine*. The choice of wine was immaculate – a 1918 Mouton Rothschild, a fine vintage which ironically came from the estate of Philippe de Rothschild, who had boycotted the Winter Games. A 1929 Henkell sparkling wine, produced by von Ribbentrop's in-laws, went with the pudding, which was *bombe Florentine*. In case any guests were still peckish, the menu also featured *batons au fromage*.

The food was no less magnificent the following lunchtime, when Hitler hosted a banquet in the Chancellery before the opening ceremony of the Games. Seated around a vast horseshoe-shaped table were 150 guests, who included Hess, Goering, Himmler, Heydrich and Goebbels, who was annoyed by the seating plan. It is easy to see why – the minister of propaganda found himself stuck on one of the 'corners' of the horseshoe, sitting next to Greek IOC member Angelo Bolanachi and French member Albert Glandaz, both of whom the quick-witted Goebbels would have found stultifying. The two men would also have found the German less than ideal company, as his mind was probably more focused on his bust-up with his wife Magda that morning. Goebbels suspected that his wife had been having an affair, although she denied it. Such accusations had the whiff of hypocrisy, as Goebbels himself was notoriously unfaithful. Also present were Lords Burghley and Aberdare from Britain, and from the United States William May Garland and Avery Brundage, no doubt preening himself in such august company. Brundage found himself sitting next to the crass and corpulent Otto Meissner, who was the absurdly titled State Minister of the Rank of a Reich Minister and Chief of the Presidential Chancellery of the Fuehrer and Reich Chancellor. To Brundage's left sat General Leonhard Kaupisch, who had been made Commander of Air District II in Berlin the previous March. Diagonally opposite the American, to his left, was the chief of staff of the SA, Obergruppenfuehrer Viktor Lutze, who was an active participant in the Night of the Long Knives in which Ernst Roehm, the head of the SA, had been murdered. It was Lutze who had supplied Hitler with evidence of Roehm's anti-regime activities.

Seated next to Hitler were Lewald and Baillet-Latour, who before lunch had addressed the Chancellor with the usual ceremonial flannel reserved for such occasions.

I feel certain that the stupendous preparations which Germany has made for the Olympic Games and which are particularly obvious in the excellent organisation of the Festival will constitute a permanent monument to the contribution which she has made to human culture in general. All those who appreciate the symbolism of the sacred flame which has been borne from Olympia to Berlin are profoundly grateful to your Excellency for having not only provided the means of binding the past and the present, but also for having contributed to the progress of the Olympic ideals in future years.

Hitler's reply was no less ironic.

I am deeply grateful to the International Olympic Committee for having allotted the Festival of the Eleventh Olympiad of modern times to the Capital City of the German Reich, thereby affording Germany the opportunity of furthering the eternal Olympic ideals. Germany gladly assumed the task of preparing for the present competitions in a manner which aspires to be in keeping with the ideals and traditions of the Olympic Games, and hopes that she has thereby contributed to the strengthening of the principles of international understanding upon which this Festival is based.

It is unclear how Germany had furthered some of the Olympic ideals. She had not allowed many of her own citizens to compete, and she had made the Games into a Germanic, rather than a cosmopolitan, festival. Her athletes were not primed merely to take part, as Coubertin would have wished, but were programmed to win for the glory of a cruel regime. In many ways, however, the Nazis were putting on an event that sat well with Olympism. It was a festival that celebrated the body, a hybrid pagan festival that married the rituals of the Olympics with those of Nazism.

As well as the banquets, the Nazis also held somewhat smaller, more intimate occasions. On Monday, 3 August, Sigfrid Edstrøm and his wife attended a lunch at the Goerings' which was more epicurean than anything the Kaiserhof Hotel could muster. After starting with a simple *salat rivoli* – chicken, shrimps, celery hearts and melon – the

Edstrøms' eyes would have bulged when a bowl of kangaroo-tail soup was placed in front of them. A more conventional lobster thermidor followed, then poussin (this accompanied by a forty-three-year-old Château Cos d'Estournel), then Parmesan crêpes, and finally a raspberry parfait. Mrs Edstrøm was rather struck by the very fine porcelain, and she enquired as to its provenance. A handwritten wrote was delivered, which informed her that they were eating from a one-off set called 'Stadtschloss Breslau' made especially for Frederick the Great in 1764. The conversation during lunch may also have touched upon the fact that Goering had that morning banned hunting with horse and hounds. In his capacity as Reich Master of the Hunt – a post that reeked of *Gleichschaltung* – Goering had deemed that such hunting was 'unfair to animals'.

The Reichsmarschall also presided over the state banquet that was held at the Opera House on the evening of Thursday, 6 August. The event was truly magnificent, with some two thousand guests in attendance, sitting at round tables on the specially refitted floor of the building, while the Nazis ate in the boxes, surveying those who they hoped to charm with their extravagance. During the dinner, ballet dancers flitted from table to table, their costumes outshone by the vast quantities of jewellery worn by the women, and the medals and orders worn by the men. Typically, Goering looked the most splendid of all, dressed in white, his vast bulk festooned with decorations. Among the guests were Henry 'Chips' Channon and his wife Honor, who was dressed in 'full regalia, with her rubies, but minus tiara'. So far, the Channons had had an indifferent day. After getting up at 12.30 in the afternoon – dinner with the Bismarcks had gone on until 4 a.m. – the couple were taken to the stadium where they watched 'hurdling and running, which bored us'. As the running would have included Jack Lovelock's stunning 1,500 metres, there was presumably no chance of Channon finding any of the events interesting. What he found more engaging was the banquet, at which the food was good and the wine copious. 'Berlin has not known anything like this since the war,' he wrote in his diary, 'and one was conscious of the effort the Germans were making to show the world the grandeur, the permanency and respectability of the new regime.' Channon was right – the Germans were trying to show the world all those things. Goebbels described the party as 'great propaganda' in his diary, full of 'happy people'. With typical boastfulness, Goebbels described himself as being on 'top form', his every word 'apposite'.

After the dinner, Goering addressed the guests, telling them that he hoped they would leave Berlin with the impression that Germany under the Nazis wanted nothing more than to be a friend to every other nation on earth. Goering then stepped down and circulated among the tables, presenting the ladies with a small porcelain model of the Olympic bell. 'He was flirtatious, gay and insinuating,' Channon wrote. The MP felt, however, that perhaps the Nazis were trying too hard to woo.

> At last we left, tired and impressed. The new regime, particularly Goering, are masters of the art of party giving. Tonight, in a way, must have been like the fetes given by the Directoire of the French Revolution, with the upstarts, tipsy with power and flattered by the proximity and ovations of the ex-grand, whom once they wished to destroy.

One person whom Channon met at the banquet was Sir Robert Vansittart. According to the MP, the permanent secretary at the Foreign Office admitted to 'being impressed by the Nazi regime, and the way it had transformed Berlin and rejuvenated the country'. 'Van' was no doubt humouring 'Chips', not wishing to start an argument in the middle of the Opera House with one of the House of Commons' most ardent appeasers. Besides, Vansittart was too wily to display his opinions openly – he was after all a civil servant, not a politician. Such a distinction was not respected by the Nazis, who wooed Vansittart and wife Sarita the moment they arrived in the British embassy in Berlin. Lady Vansittart received a huge display of orchids from Goebbels, and her husband was invited to countless lunches, meetings and dinners.

The purpose of Vansittart's visit was manifold. As well as coming to give support to his brother-in-law, Sir Eric Phipps, Vansittart was also keen to show the Nazis that he was not the zealous Germanophobe of their imagination. In addition, he wished to explore tentatively the possibility of getting Hitler around a conference table in which a 'new

Locarno' could be negotiated. Vansittart knew there was little chance now of getting a response to the questionnaire that Eden had drawn up earlier in the year. Indeed, Hitler's recalcitrance over the issue was the subject of some public jocularity back in Britain. A cartoon in the 5 August issue of *Punch* magazine showed Hitler dressed in athletic garb, clutching a discus on which were the words 'Reply to British Questionnaire'. The caption read, 'I wonder how much longer I can keep this attitude up without letting the thing go?' From the stadium came shouts of 'Let her go, Adolf!' and 'Get a move on!' Vansittart's job, then, was not to bully Hitler into throwing the discus, but to try to wheedle out of him which way he might consider throwing it, and indeed, how far.

When Vansittart met Hitler, he found the dictator to be 'an amiably simple, rather shy, rotundly ascetic, *bourgeois*, with the fine hair and thin skin that accompany extreme sensitiveness'. Ribbentrop had asked Vansittart to avoid 'rough passages and disputable corners', and to concentrate on generalities, partly because 'an Olympic truce lay thick over the city, and had its effect on Herr Hitler's mood'. Vansittart was struck by the presence of Hitler's entourage, although he found him surrounded by fewer yes-men than Mussolini. What he did not find was the demagogue of the newsreels, although he knew that still to be there.

> This, then, was the August aspect. It underlined rather than effaced the other, which is known to history, the harder, more violent, mystically ambitious, hotly and coldly explosive traits, which flare capriciously and keep everyone not only in Europe but in Germany in such a state of nervous tension that I more than once heard the stadium compared with a crater.

It is not known precisely what Hitler thought of Vansittart, but to the bourgeois corporal, the tall Old Etonian must have represented something of the *ancien régime* whose favours he resented having to curry. Perhaps Hitler shared Himmler's view that Etonians were members of a secret society, with their bizarre language that had to be some sort of code. 'In Nazi teaching,' wrote Airey Neave, 'Old Etonians were soft but cunning and should therefore be carefully watched and reports compiled about their activities.'

Vansittart was pleased to discover that he was able to have a conversation with Hitler rather than endure a rant, and that the German
was even able to 'take interruption kindly'. Hitler began the conversation by explaining and justifying to Vansittart what he had done,
both domestically and internationally. The Briton saw no point in
arguing with Hitler, and told him that the British were a practical
people, and wanted only to look to the future. As soon as Vansittart
raised the possibility of a five-power summit – a new Locarno –
however, he found that Hitler was more willing to talk about the civil
war in Spain, which Vansittart was finding to be 'the constant theme
of every man and woman in Berlin'. In Hitler's opinion, if the left
won in Spain, then France might turn communist as well. If that happened, argued Hitler, then the 'contagion' of communism might well
spread to Czechoslovakia, in which case Germany would be 'caught
between two, if not three, fires, and must be prepared'. Vansittart
countered this by saying that the war in Spain might in fact deter
France from going communist, a point that Hitler accepted. Privately,
however, Vansittart was not so sure. 'I made the most reassuring
picture I could,' he wrote. 'For I am by no means convinced of the
accuracy of this picture. France will probably go further left, and
further still in the event of a Communist victory in Spain, with all its
violent consequences. Meanwhile, the Communists in France are
already honeycombing the country with cells.' In essence, Vansittart
and Hitler were in agreement, but the former knew that he could not
possibly say so, as that would look as though he were giving Hitler
a free hand in Spain, and carte blanche to rearm.

The conversation then moved on to Hitler's domestic position,
and the Fuehrer gave an account of 'his own hold on his own people'.
During the course of his stay, Vansittart found that all the leading
figures were entirely confident of this hold, which confirmed
Vansittart's view as to the 'unreality of any German fear as to internal
communism'. What had the Nazis to fear from the Werner
Seelenbinders among them? The Nazi grip on power was so strong
that, in Vansittart's words, 'the underdog stays under'. There was no
need to repress ruthlessly, the diplomat thought, as a 'nod is as good
as a kick, though there are plenty of kicks going on – under the table'.
When Vansittart met Goering, the Reichsmarschall bet the Briton

that he could drive him to the roughest part of Germany he could find, and that they could get out of the car and nothing untoward would happen to them. 'I replied that I had practically given up betting against certainties,' Vansittart wrote.

On 8 August, the British held a party of their own at the embassy. It was not a great success, with Henry Channon describing it as 'boring, crowded and inelegant'. Goebbels, who by now was fed up with the Olympics, was even more damning. '[It was] originally just a small meal,' he wrote, 'but then it turned into a massive reception. A thousand people and a thousand idiotic conversations.' 'Phipps', he wrote, 'is stupid.' Unlike the Nazis, Phipps was not a natural party-giver. Martha Dodd observed that Phipps, 'when he entertained formally, seemed as nervous as a cat, bounced around with his crooked walk – one shoulder hunched up, making one leg seem shorter than the other – his head carried to the side, jerking from one group of his guests to another, emitting almost inaudible, "Yes, yes, how interesting" sounds'. Goebbels was, however, struck by Lady Vansittart, whom he described as 'extremely kind and generous with us'. He also respected her husband, who Goebbels felt had 'opened up a lot' since he had been in Berlin. Goebbels had met Vansittart a few days before, and the meeting, according to Goebbels, had gone well.

> He is a gentleman who is too highly-strung, and whilst clever, he is not energetic. He is still the prisoner of many egg-shells, but he can doubtless be won over for us. I work on him for an hour. I expose the Bolshevik problem to him and explain our domestic political operations to him. He gains a new understanding of the issues, and wants a conference to address the questions, but also understands the German position. He leaves highly impressed. I have turned a light on inside him.

Vansittart also had some respect for Goebbels. 'He seemed to me the deepest of them all,' he wrote. 'I found much charm in him – a limping, eloquent, slip of a Jacobin, "quick as a whip," and often, I doubt not, as cutting [. . .] He is a calculator and therefore a man with whom one might do business.' Vansittart added that he and his wife had got on very well with Goebbels and his wife, noting that 'it is an obviously happy marriage, with attractive devotion on both sides'. The Goebbels were clearly good actors, as Goebbels had just had his suspicions confirmed that Magda had indeed been having some sort of dalliance with a man called Luedecke.

Among the visitors to the British embassy that night was the Indian hockey team, who arrived half an hour late. 'Of course, it was not a novel experience for us,' wrote their captain, 'for we seldom reached any place at the given time [. . .] We had never been punctual at a reception, game or anything, and this fact was known in the Village and outside.' Like the other guests, the Indians found the party over-crowded, although they were happy that Phipps was able to receive them personally. They left after just an hour. With an hour's bus ride there and back, the trip can hardly have seemed worth it.

On the night of Tuesday, 11 August, Ribbentrop held a huge party at his villa in the Dahlem district of Berlin. That morning, what was an open secret in diplomatic circles had finally been announced – Ribbentrop was going to London as the German ambassador. 'No one quite knows why he has been selected,' wrote Henry Channon. 'Is it because his power is waning? Have the machinations of his jealous colleagues led to this dignified banishment? Is it because London is considered so important a post that their best man had to be sent, or is it because there is no-one else?' The truth was a mixture of all these. In the eyes of Neurath, the post was a banishment, whereas Hitler thought that Ribbentrop was the best man for the job.

Ribbentrop and his wife Annelies worked hard at staging a party that they hoped would eclipse all others during the Olympic fort-night. 'Our house in Dahlem was none too big,' Ribbentrop wrote, 'certainly too small for all the guests, and so Annelies very ably turned our garden into a veritable little fairground.' The lawn and the tennis court were covered by a vast marquee, in which the 600 guests would mingle among the rhododendrons and next to the lily-covered swim-ming pool.

When the guests arrived, they were presented with a thick booklet that showed them where to sit. The most prestigious table was no doubt table twelve, around which sat Vansittart, Goering, Mrs Dodd – the wife of the American ambassador – Lady Aberdare, Baillet-Latour, François-Poncet – the French ambassador to Berlin – Annelies

Ribbentrop, the Prinz von Liechtenstein, Countess Szembek – the wife of the Polish secretary of state – General Ernst Udet – the flying ace from the war – Baroness Reischach, and finally, of all people, Avery Brundage. Here then was a motley collection of distinguished guests from different countries, and in some senses worlds – those of diplomacy, aristocracy, politics, the military and sport. Of those five, sport was without doubt the most junior, and it is hard to imagine how the politically naive Brundage would have managed when so out of his depth. There is no doubt that both he and Baillet-Latour, when they looked around the table, would have felt themselves to be every bit as important as an ambassador or a secretary of state. In their minds, the IOC was a sovereign state in itself, and no Mickey Mouse state either. In short, Avery Brundage had arrived.

Also among the guests was Unity Mitford, although her sister and fellow guest of the Goebbels family, Diana, had not been invited. The two Englishwomen and their host got on well, and had chatted into the small hours of the night of 2/3 August. 'The two English girls are actually very nice,' Goebbels noted in his diary. Diana and Unity taught Goebbels and his wife Magda how to play a parlour game called 'Analogies', in which the players had to elucidate what person one of them was thinking of by asking a series of questions that would reveal analogous characteristics of that person. Goebbels was asked what colour his subject reminded him of. 'Fiery red!' he replied, at which everyone guessed he was talking about Hitler. All this badinage must have given Diana some optimism when, on going to see Goebbels in his office on Wednesday, 5 August, she asked whether her lover could have more money for his British Union of Fascists. Unfortunately for Diana, Goebbels put her off, saying that he would need to ask Hitler. 'These are times to help themselves,' he wrote in his diary. The following day, Goebbels spoke to the Fuehrer, who refused to give Oswald Mosley any more money.

The Nazis were more helpful, however, when it came to arranging another private matter for Diana. She and Mosley wanted to marry in secret, but it was impossible to do so in Britain. They had considered Paris, but that would have attracted just as much publicity, as a notice would have to be pinned on the wall outside the embassy. In Munich, Diana discovered that there was a reciprocal arrangement between Germany and Britain which allowed for British subjects to be married by a registrar in Germany, and vice versa. 'Hitler said he would ask the Berlin registrar to keep the marriage quiet,' Diana recalled, 'and while we were staying with her, Magda helped me with all the form-filling.' The wedding day was set for 6 October.

Diana was unfortunate not to go to Ribbentrop's party. 'After dinner, as the marquee was being noiselessly cleaned,' wrote Channon, 'we listened to some very good singing [. . .] perfection, and not too long. About midnight, the older people began to drift away, whilst the others returned to the marquee [. . .] Goering, his merry eyes twinkling, shook us both by the hand: he really is a most disarming man. Frau von Ribbentrop was simply dressed, unlike the other Nazi ladies.' While his guests drank his champagne, Frau von Ribbentrop's husband was concerned about one guest in particular. 'The Vansittarts were among those who stayed longest,' Ribbentrop noted with optimism. 'They danced a lot and seemed happy – was this a good omen? Could it be that Sir Robert did not find Berlin so repulsive after all?' During the evening, Vansittart congratulated Ribbentrop on his appointment as ambassador to London, which prompted Ribbentrop to ask him to a private lunch. Vansittart accepted, which delighted his host. The party went on until the small hours, with Channon describing it as a 'lovely evening' with its 'fantastic collection of notabilities, the strangeness of the situation, the excellence of the Ambassador's (or rather more correctly Frau von Ribbentrop's) champagne, all went somewhat to my head'. Not all were quite so dizzy with the headiness of it all. Martha Dodd and her family 'were greatly bored by the gorgeousness of the celebration', she wrote, 'and figured out that Ribbentrop's wife, a dark, thin snub-nosed woman who looked hard and bitter, had paid the bill'. Dodd also noted how Himmler 'wove his mincing, quiet, and sinister way through the crowds'. The following morning, Ribbentrop recalled how Bohnhaus, his old gardener, shook his head at the damage the guests had wrought on his beloved lawn. 'He made it a point of honour to remove all traces of the night as quickly as possible,' wrote Ribbentrop.

For Ribbentrop, a pockmarked lawn was a small price to pay for the ear of Sir Robert Vasnsittart. The two men met for lunch at the Hotel Kaiserhof, a meeting that Ribbentrop soon realised was going to prove to be completely fruitless. His luncheon partner was totally unforthcoming and evaded all of Ribbentrop's openings for 'a frank exchange of views'. 'I felt from the start as if I were addressing a wall,' wrote Ribbentrop. 'One thing was clear, an Anglo-German under- standing with Vansittart in office was out of the question [. . .] Vansittart, I felt, had completely made up his mind. I gained a firm impression that this man would never even attempt a *rapprochement*, and that any discussion with him would be in vain.'

Vansittart was similarly unimpressed with Ribbentrop. 'With this gentleman we shall have more trouble,' Vansittart was to write. 'He was most markedly unenthusiastic about his appointment to London.' Far from not responding to Ribbentrop's openings, Vansittart found that he was on the receiving end of 'set-pieces'. 'To him one has to listen without much chance of interruption.' The Briton was also perturbed by the threatening nature of Ribbentrop's ramblings. 'Indeed he, and he alone, showed his hand, or perhaps I should say his teeth. He remarked on one occasion that "if England didn't give Germany the possibility to live," there would eventually be war between them, and one of them would be annihilated.' Vansittart was somewhat understating matters when he warned the cabinet after the Games that 'we shall not find the new Ambassador easy, because he will be uneasy himself'.

There were still plenty more parties to go to, however, not least a dinner thrown by Hitler for Vansittart at the Chancellery that evening. It was Vansittart's last night in Berlin, and the Fuehrer was eager to prove that Nazi Germany had not thrown off the grandness of a European court. The 160 guests found themselves being announced as they entered the room by a major-domo in black livery and sporting a court sword. The dining room, which measured some 100 feet long by 50 across, had been designed by Hitler himself. Rows of huge red marble pillars flanked each side of the room, drawing the eye up to the ceiling, which featured an elaborate mosaic in light blue and gold. Tall gold candlesticks were placed around the floor, and on one wall hung a huge Gobelin tapestry. The room soon filled with men and women whose dress matched its sumptuousness, although the only people who looked out of place were the Germans, who lacked the decorations worn by those such as Vansittart. George Ward Price, the correspondent for the *Daily Mail*, noticed this when he saw Rudolf Hess and Vansittart in conversation. 'There was a noticeable contrast between the glittering splendour of the star of the cordon of the Grand Cross of St Michael and St George worn by the one and the field-service-like simplicity of the khaki uniform of the other.'

Lady Vansittart was greeted by Hitler with a formal kiss on her hand, before the dictator took her by the arm and escorted her to the table. She noticed how Hitler's evening dress did not fit him well, the tailcoat slipping off his shoulders. His dietary requests also did not match the party, as he ordered spinach and a poached egg, an ascetic choice that Lady Vansittart copied in order to keep her host company. Over dinner, she caused the Fuehrer to laugh out loud when she enquired as to whether being a vegetarian teetotaller did not make for a rather dull life. Hitler's laugh caused Sir Robert to look up from his conversation with Emmy Goering, and he wondered what his wife had been saying to cause such a reaction. He was rather more perturbed when, after dinner, Hitler took his wife off to his study for half an hour, accompanied only by an interpreter.

'You should come to Berlin more often,' the dictator told Lady Vansittart. 'I can't talk to the British ambassador, but I can talk to your husband.' He then told her, sitting knee to knee, how he had watched *Lives of a Bengal Lancer* no less than five times in his bid to discover how Britain had gained her empire. As the film had only just been released, the Fuehrer must have been quite a fan of this Gary Cooper picture, which boasted the stirring tagline '1750 to 1! Always outnumbered! Never out-fought! These are the Bengal Lancers . . . heroes all . . . guarding each other's lives, sharing each other's tortures, fighting each other's battles . . .' No doubt Hitler particularly enjoyed the torture sequences, which featured bamboo being inserted under fingernails, and the great cliché of such scenes: "We have ways of making men talk'. The conversation then turned to the Games, and Hitler remarked of the athletes, 'You saw all the young men in the stadium today – do you think I'd let them die in battle?' Lady Vansittart told him that it was always the youngest who died in wars, an observation that caused Hitler's mood to change, after which the two of them returned to the dining room.

The Vansittarts left Berlin the following morning, their visit judged to be a success by Sir Eric Phipps, the British ambassador to Berlin. That day, he wrote to Anthony Eden, telling him that Vansittart had many 'long and most friendly meetings and conversations with the principal members of the German government'.

> I have felt for a long time past that Sir Robert should take advantage both of his relationship with myself and of the Olympic Games to come to Berlin in order to dispel the absurd but widely held idea in Germany that he is possessed by a blind and unreasoning hatred of that country. A fortnight's personal contact with prominent Germans has more than sufficed to prick this dangerous bubble, and to convince them that Sir Robert Vansittart is a perfectly reasonable though patriotic Englishman whose great wish is to work for general peace and understanding.

Nevertheless, not everything was rosy. Phipps warned Eden that the goal of peace was probably unattainable. Phipps had heard that Vansittart's request for a new conference had gone down badly, and that Hitler was not minded to sign a treaty, stating that neighbouring Poland was 'more than satisfied' with her relationship with Germany, and that Czechoslovakia was welcome to negotiate an agreement with Germany at any time. Hitler was convinced, Phipps reported, that Britain and Germany 'together constitute a stupendous force [. . .] acting together they could safeguard civilisation and world peace more effectively than any League or any number of pacts'. Hitler was probably right, although the Chancellor's price for such an agreement would have been far too high. Besides, once he had got such an agreement, what would he want next?

There were still two big parties to go. The first, on the evening of Thursday, 13 August, was hosted by Goering, whose appetite for bacchanalia was seemingly endless. The second, two nights later, was held by Goebbels, and the two men did their best to outdo each other – and Ribbentrop – with the extravagance of their parties. Goering's party was held in the Ministerium in the centre of Berlin, and once again Henry Channon found himself entranced. By now he had given up going to the Games – 'we pretend to, and don't, as they are very boring, except when Hitler arrives' – and was in Berlin only for the parties. Goering had excelled himself, and entertained the 800 guests to an evening of fine wine, food and ballet. Many of the guests agreed that 'Goering had indeed eclipsed Ribbentrop', as Channon wrote, 'which indeed we had been told had been his ambition'.

Not everyone, however, was so impressed. William Dodd, the US ambassador to Germany, found the evening cold and damp, with the electric heaters doing little to improve matters. 'I saw that I would take cold,' Dodd wrote, 'but my wife argued against my wearing my hat and overcoat which I had left in the palace as we entered. But as the air grew colder and colder, I got my hat and coat. I felt less conspic-uous when I saw Lewald [. . .] had his hat also, and Sir Eric Phipps was leaving because of the cold.' Dodd left the party at 10.15, a little less than two hours after he and his wife has sat down to eat. Goebbels was also not taken by the party. 'So many people,' he wrote. 'A little formal and cold.'

Dodd's reason for such an early departure may also have had some-thing to do with his detestation of the Nazis. As André François-Poncet, the French ambassador to Berlin, described him, Dodd was a 'rugged and uncompromising liberal, [who] entertained an aversion for National Socialism, which he made no effort to conceal'. A professor of American history, Dodd exuded a donnish, Ivy League air, which made him something of an outsider in the State Department. His opin-ions, however, were respected in the White House. That morning, Dodd had made a report to Roosevelt about the Nazi press, in which he had written about the SS newspaper, *Das Schwarze Korps*, which

[. . .] requests foreign Olympia guests in Germany to open wide their eyes and to see not only official personages but the man on the street and polemicises against an article in the *Basler Nationalzeitung* which stated that in Germany not joy stood in the center of life but fear – fear of spies, agents provocateurs, fear of loss of job, fear of imprisonment etc. (How does the average German, who may be suffering from at least one of these anxieties, feel when he reads his *Schwarze Korps* – or does he?)

Dodd had also been wary of the effect the Games would have on the regime. He had written to the State Department, warning it that 'as the party bases its appeal very largely to the youth of the country, it was recognised at the outset what an instrument the Olympic Games could become in consolidating the position of the party'. In another report, he highlighted the plight of the Jews. 'It is no exaggeration to say that the Jewish population awaits with fear and trembling the termination of the Olympic period which has vouchsafed them a certain respite against molestation.'

As well as damning the regime, Dodd was also highly critical of Lewald, who he had once held in high esteem. Dodd recounted to the State Department how he had once reproached Lewald for misleading the Americans about the extent of the discrimination against Jewish sportsmen. 'He told me, with tears in his eyes, that he had replied that there was no discrimination,' Dodd wrote. '[He said] that I must know what the consequences would be to him if he had made any other reply. To this, I merely remarked that there were times, when, in order to maintain one's self-respect and the confidence of one's friends, one must accept the consequences which come from doing right.'

There was deceit everywhere in Berlin that fortnight, even among Dodd's family, for his twenty-eight-year-old daughter Martha was a Soviet spy. Martha, whom Richard Helms described as a 'lively, intelligent and aggressive woman', had fallen in love with Boris Vinogradov, who was notionally the press secretary at the Soviet embassy in Berlin, but was in fact an officer of the NKVD – the forerunner to the KGB. Acting out of a love for both the Russians and communism, Dodd passed copies of her father's files to Vinogradov, even after he was transferred from Berlin to Bucharest in 1934 and subsequently to Warsaw. Martha described Vinogradov as the love of her life, a love that was undiminished even when he disappeared in Moscow in 1938. What Dodd was not to know was that her Russian lover and handler had been executed in one of Stalin's many purges of intelligence officers. Martha's father was never to discover his daughter's treachery, which was confirmed only in 1995, some five years after her death in Prague at the age of eighty-two.

Dodd's early departure from Goering's party meant that he missed the party's pièce de résistance, which was the sudden appearance at the end of the lawn of an entire fairground. 'It was fantastic,' wrote

Channon, 'roundabouts, cafés with beer and champagne, peasants dancing and "schuhplattling", vast women carrying pretzels and beer, a ship, a beerhouse, crowds of gay, laughing people, animals, a mixture of Luna Park and White Horse Inn.' The guests walked around, mouths gaping, astonished by the sheer extravagance of the event. Goebbels and Ribbentrop were filled with jealousy. A fellow guest approached Channon and told him, 'There has never been anything like this since the days of Louis Quatorze.' '"Not since Nero," I retorted, but actually it was more like the Fetes of Claudius, but with the cruelty left out [. . .]'

If Goebbels could not match the style of Goering, then his party could at least trump him in terms of size. Some 2,700 guests were invited to his *Sommerfest* on the Peacock Island, a nature reserve in the middle of the Wannsee. 'Everyone who has legs is there,' wrote Goebbels, who had been worrying about the rain for days. When the weather finally broke, he compared it to 'a stone removed from inside my heart'. 'Garden parties are so nerve-racking,' he observed, like the good bourgeois. For once, the athletes were invited, although only the female ones. Dorothy Odam recalled going across to the island on a pontoon bridge lined with armed soldiers standing to attention. 'It really was fantastic,' she said, 'all lit up and with huge butterfly lanterns glowing in the trees.' Paths snaked through the trees, each lined with more lanterns and young page girls in tights. Iris Cummings remembered how there were 'tables out on the grass, and each one was laid with these scrumptious gorgeous meals'. In the middle of each table there was 'every wine of Germany', as well as champagne. As it was the last day of the Games, Cummings started to drink, but the diver Marjorie Gestring was clearly some sort of spoilsport. 'She didn't want to see any of these girls getting high on the champagne,' said Cummings, 'and she took this gorgeous Rhine wine and stuff, and poured it straight on to the grass.'

The dignitaries, such as Henry Channon, ate separately from the athletes. Channon found Goebbels 'slightly sinister', although William Dodd was far more repelled by having to greet the minister of propaganda.

We shook hands with the host, the man who had helped on June 30, 1934, to murder Germans who have never been shown to have been guilty of anything but opposition to the Nazi regime. I disliked the hand-shake as I did that with Goering at a similar show two days before. We sat down at a small table near the Goebbels' main table, although I am second ranking diplomat here, the French Ambassador being first, I preferred this and Goebbels had not asked us to his table.

Despite its size and setting, the party did not seem to gel as well as those of Goering and Ribbentrop. Dodd noticed that there was little cordial conversation, 'which is a rare thing at diplomatic functions'. It was hardly surprising that Eduard Falz-Fein described the Nazis' parties as 'just champagne and talking nonsense'.

After dinner, the guests were once more entertained with dancing, a touch of delicacy before a fireworks display that held the guests in a mixture of awe and shock. At first, Dodd thought the noise was 'shooting of a kind that suggested war'. The display went on for half an hour, which caused a great many to complain as the noise was akin to an artillery barrage. 'People at our table trembled when the bombing made such a terrible noise,' wrote Dodd. 'There were of course no real shots or shells, but there were explosions which almost made the ground shake.' Iris Cummings recalled her mother's reaction. ' "I don't like what this says," she said. "This is saying a whole lot more than it needs to say." It was very militaristic.' Even the teenaged Cummings could tell that the whole party had been 'a power show'. 'This was a "look how superior how we are". It was too much and sufficiently evident to most us that it was another one of these "don't tell us that we're reaching too far" occasions.'

For Helen Stephens, the party went too far for other reasons. At some point after midnight, a messenger came up to Stephens and asked whether she would accompany him to see Reichsmarschall Goering. Stephens agreed, and soon found herself stepping into a room upstairs in Goebbels' house, whereupon a goblet of red wine was thrust into her hand. Sitting on a throne-like chair, with a table in front of him, was the enormous bulk of Goering, dressed solely in a black bathrobe, which was partially open, exposing his thighs. 'His sausage-fat arms draped limply over ornately carved armrests,' Stephens recalled, 'and as I was introduced to him, several scantily clad women crawled out from under the head of the long table where he sat.' As Stephens put it, 'things weren't according to Hoyle'. Goering got up, took Stephens's hand and kissed it. She suddenly felt trapped, with one hand on the goblet, and the other still held by Goering, who now asked her whether she wanted to join him in another room for 'a little talk'. Stephens felt herself being pushed towards a huge double door. The athlete protested, saying that she had be back at her dorm, an excuse that would have carried little weight with the lecherous Nazi, who insisted that she join him.

Stephens was saved by an attendant, who told Goering that he had a telephone call. Goering, with faux politesse, asked to be excused, a request that Stephens was very happy to grant. 'It's time to go,' the attendant told her, and led her, away. 'Goering blew me a kiss,' said Stephens, 'and that's the last I ever saw of him. I later thought, gee, I wonder what I missed out on.' Whatever it was, Avery Brundage would certainly have disapproved.

11

The Second Week

~

O N SATURDAY 8 AUGUST, the biggest race of Marty Glickman's
life was just one day away. If the heats that afternoon went
according to plan, then at 3.15 the following day Glickman, along
with his teammates Sam Stoller, Foy Draper and Frank Wykoff, would
be running in the 4 x 100 relay final, a race Glickman knew they had
every chance of winning. So far, the team's training had gone well –
the baton changes were smooth, and Glickman felt in good shape.
The running order was to be Stoller, Glickman, Draper and Wykoff.
It was a good set-up, as Stoller had the best start, Glickman had the
most power down a straight, Draper was the most adept at running
round the turn, and Wykoff had the most experience, a veteran of the
Amsterdam and Los Angeles Olympics.

At nine o'clock, the four sprinters, along with Jesse Owens, Ralph
Metcalfe and Mack Robinson, were summoned to a small bedroom
in the Olympic village by the two American track coaches – Lawson
Robertson, who coached at the University of Pennsylvania, and Dean
Cromwell, who coached at the University of Southern California.
Glickman sat down on one of the beds, opposite Jesse Owens. Lawson
Robertson stood near the door, resting on his cane. Grey-haired and
ageing, Robertson was not in the best of health. Dean Cromwell,
whom Glickman described as the more 'dominant' of the two
coaches – 'brisk, ruddy and vigorous' – sat in the armchair. The
remaining athletes sprawled on the bed, or stood.

Robertson cleared his throat and began to speak. He told the room
that the Germans had been keeping their best sprinters under wraps,
and they were going to unleash them – like a secret weapon – for the
relays. As a result, Robertson felt he had no choice but to replace
Stoller and Glickman with Owens and Metcalfe. Draper and Wykoff,

Cromwell's two runners from USC, would stay on the team. 'There was stunned silence in the room,' wrote Glickman. 'This came out of the blue to me. I was shocked and angry. Being young and brash, I said, "Coach, there's no reason to believe the Germans are any kind of threat to the relay. To be a world-class sprinter, you have to compete in world-class competition."'

Glickman may have been young and brash, but he had a point. The best German sprinter was Borchmeyer, who had finished fifth in the 100 metres final. Both Stoller and Glickman could beat him. What Glickman wanted to know was who these other German sprinters were. If they were so good, then why had they not already competed? Glickman maintained that no matter who the Americans were up against, they would win by at least 15 yards. 'The only way we were going to lose, I argued, was if we dropped the baton.' With just a few hours to go to the heats, Glickman was concerned that neither Owens nor Metcalfe had had any practice baton-changing. It was far better to go with a team that was already coordinated than one that had not practised as a unit. But Robertson was adamant. Besides, he had already told Alan Gould of the Associated Press of his decision the evening before, and in a little under four hours American households would be reading of the personnel change in their morning papers. 'I'd like to let everyone run,' Robertson had told Gould, 'but we're here to win all the events possible. They are likely to criticise any decision I may make, but my job is to put the best possible team into the race.'

While the room contemplated the decision, Jesse Owens spoke up. 'Coach,' he said, 'let Marty and Sam run, they deserve it. I've already won three gold medals, I'm tired. They haven't had the chance to run. Let them run, they deserve it.' Owens' pleading earned him a sharp rebuke from Cromwell in his armchair. He pointed a finger at the three-time gold medal winner and snapped, 'You'll do as you're told.' Owens then fell silent. If Owens did indeed selflessly request not to be placed on the team, then he was being disingenuous, as he had been informed of the decision the evening before, and had even said to Robertson, according to Alan Gould, 'That's swell news [. . .] I haven't known what to do with myself since Wednesday. I'll sure hustle around that corner.' Of course, Robertson could have fabricated the line, in order to win over the hearts and minds of any dissenting armchair sportsmen back home. It seems inconceivable, however, that Owens did not know, as his coach Larry Snyder knew, and he had already speculated to Gould that the line-up would consist of Owens, Metcalfe, Stoller and Wykoff. It seems likely that Snyder would immediately have told Owens that he now had a chance to win a fourth gold medal. If Owens really did plead in that room that morning, then he was going through the motions in order not to make enemies of Glickman and Stoller. This eagerness to please was certainly in Owens' nature, and if Glickman's memory is to be trusted, then Owens was indeed being deceitful in his apparent selflessness. What added a further stink to the proceedings was the rumour that when Cromwell had heard that his USC protégé Draper was going to be dropped – which made sense, as he was the slowest of the American sprinters – he privately lobbied Robertson to reinstate him.

Whatever the truth of the situation, Glickman and Stoller were out. What escaped nobody was that both young men were Jewish, a point that Glickman raised in the meeting. 'Coach, you know that Sam and I are the only two Jews on the track team. If we don't run, there's bound to be a lot of criticism back home.'

'We'll take our chances,' Cromwell replied.

The seven athletes walked out of the room in silence. 'I was an eighteen-year-old kid,' Glickman recalled, 'angry and confused, not able to digest it all. Stoller seemed shattered. We didn't come together on this, partly because we were not particularly close, mostly because athletes in those days were docile, good little boys who didn't protest. Coaches' words were law.' As far as Glickman was concerned, the decision reeked of anti-Semitism. 'I believe that Avery Brundage told Robertson and Cromwell to drop us from the relay team,' said Glickman later, 'to save Hitler embarrassment by having two Jews stand on the winning podium before 120,000 Germans and the world's news media.' What Glickman lacked was proof, although he felt the circumstantial evidence was strong. The counter-argument to Glickman's suspicions was succinctly expressed by John Kieran of the *New York Times*, who wrote that swapping two Jews for two blacks was 'a transfer that would not have sent Herr Hitler off into raptures of delight even if he had paid any attention to it'.

A dejected Glickman went to watch the heats at three o'clock that afternoon. The new team equalled the world record of 40 seconds. The Italians were over a second behind them – some 11 yards – and in another heat the supposedly deadly German team was 1.4 seconds slower, some 12½ yards behind. Even if Stoller and Glickman had been running, the Americans would have still had a comfortable margin. 'The heats failed to show the necessity for shaking up the lineup after Stoller and myself long practised the stick work,' Glickman told a reporter from the Associated Press, before adding, 'It looks like politics to us.'

Nevertheless, Glickman was sporting enough to attend the final the next day. Watching his teammates warm up, he couldn't help but think that it should have been him down on the track, readying himself for what was almost certainly going to be a gold medal. He studied Metcalfe, who was running the second leg – the leg that Glickman was supposed to run. 'He looked strong, powerful, and confident,' Glickman recalled. And then anger coursed through him once more. 'The dirty bastards have me sitting here,' he thought, 'and I want to run. I could show them.' The Americans were drawn in lane four, between Holland in lane three and Italy in lane five. The Germans were in lane two, next to Argentina on the inside. On the outside were the Canadians. The other teams had little chance of winning gold, and they knew it. The only way any of them could win gold would be for the Americans to lose it, and to do that, they would have to drop the baton, or exchange it outside one of the three boxes.

Unsurprisingly, Owens got off to a blisteringly quick start. He streaked past the Italian Mariani in lane five, and a few seconds later he was ready to pass the baton from his left hand to Metcalfe's right. Owens had not had much practice with the baton change, and some maintained that the only reason why he ran the first leg rather than the fourth was so he wouldn't have to perform the far trickier task of actually receiving the baton. Even so, the changeover was not smooth, with Glickman describing it as 'only fair'. Metcalfe roared down the back straight, his style as thunderingly powerful as Owens' was delicate. Metcalfe handed the baton over to Draper, but to one judge it looked as though the change might have taken place outside the box. Unaware of the potential problem, Draper maintained the Americans' ten-yard lead on the field, a lead that Wykoff increased on the last leg to some 12 yards, finishing in a new world record time of 39.8 seconds. Italy was 1.3 seconds behind, narrowly beating Holland, which was anchored by the double bronze medal winner Martinus Osendarp. Osendarp, however, was missing one vital thing – the baton. He had dropped it 30 yards before crossing the line. Once the race was over, he buried his face in the crook of his left arm, knowing that the Dutch would be disqualified and that the fourth-placed Germans would take the bronze.

The judge who had witnessed the handover from Metcalfe to Draper still had his doubts, however. He was simply not sure whether Draper had received the baton outside the box. 'Twice the judge started toward the official jury,' wrote Lewis Burton in the *New York Journal American*, 'seemingly to lodge his complaint, and twice he changed his mind.' The judge then walked on to the track and studied the athletes' spike marks. It was unclear what had happened, so the judge gave the Americans the benefit of the doubt. He wiped out the spike marks and then stayed put. The American gold – and Jesse Owens' fourth – was safe. A study of Leni Riefenstahl's *Olympia* shows that the judge did indeed make the correct decision, although his doubts were understandable. The exchange took place only just inside the box, with Draper's right foot just about to step out when he finally secured the baton. Had the pass been ruled illegal, then there would have been an uproar. 'The coaches would have had to explain to an unsympathetic public their questionable switch,' wrote Glickman, 'and their dubious reasons for making it.'

Despite the win – or maybe because of it – Glickman was furious. 'Those liars,' he thought. 'Those fucking liars, Cromwell and Robertson.' The strength of his feelings was not tempered when he encountered Robertson in the Olympic village later that day. The coach hobbled towards Glickman, and said, 'Marty, I've made a terrible mistake. Please forgive me.' Glickman mumbled some platitude about how good it was the team had won, and the two men turned and walked away from each other.

The women's 4 x 100 relay, which immediately followed the men's race, also had its moment of high drama. Once again, the Americans, including the powerful Helen Stephens, had a good chance of winning, although the Germans looked even stronger. In the heats the previous day, they had actually beaten the world record with a time of 46.4 seconds, some half a second quicker than the Americans. It was going to be an extremely close race. The British wanted a place on the podium as well, however, a prize that looked likely as their time in the heats was the third quickest. On their team was Audrey Brown, whose brother Godfrey would be running with Bill Roberts in the final of the 4 x 400 relay a little later.

Helen Stephens took her place at the beginning of the third leg, which is where the German coach, after watching the Americans in practice, assumed she would run, and he had arranged his team accordingly. As soon as the Germans had taken their positions, however, Stephens, acting on a nod from her coach, Dee Boeckmann, swapped places with her teammate Elizabeth Robinson, who was at anchor. Stephens would now be running the last leg, a last-minute change that visibly upset the Germans, whose running order was now ill suited. Nevertheless, it was too late for them to discuss and then make a change.

The crowd in the stadium went extremely quiet just before the race started at 3.30. The Germans were drawn in lane four, with the British and Americans in lanes one and two. As the runners took their positions, the stadium became almost silent. Hitler watched nervously from his box. To his left sat Goebbels, watching the start through his binoculars. It was the day after that abhorrent party at the British embassy, and Goebbels had spent much of that Sunday morning lying in bed before seeing Hitler at midday, when the two men had discussed 'English policies'. The starter told the runners to take their places. '*Fertig*.' The women got set. There was now a seemingly interminable wait for the pistol, a wait that Emmy Albus found so frustrating that she made a false start. An anguished cry went round the stadium, with Hitler gesticulating at the nervous Albus.

When the race did start, the crowd took to its feet, as did Hitler, who leaned against the handrail at the front of his box, yelling encouragement like any other sports fan. Goebbels, following his beloved Fuehrer's lead, sprung up as well. (Goebbels really did love Hitler. On 7 August, he wrote in his diary, 'When I am alone with him [Hitler], he speaks to me like a father. I love him so much.') Despite her nerves, Albus gave Germany a fine lead, which the mighty Kathe Krauss extended, roaring past Fanny Blankers-Koen from Holland. Annette Rogers ran well for the Americans, although it was proving to be a hectic afternoon for her, as she had to squeeze in the relay while she was competing in the high jump final. Nevertheless, by the time Krauss passed the baton to Marie Dollinger, the German lead was seemingly insurmountable, a lead that grew to some 5 metres by the time Dollinger passed the baton to Ilse Doerffeldt, who hared off towards the finishing line. Not even Helen Stephens, the Fulton Flash, could possibly overtake her.

Stephens was in a unique position to see what happened next. While she accelerated forward, waiting for Elizabeth Robinson to thrust the baton into her right hand, she saw Doerffeldt pull the baton across her chest to place it into her left hand. Such a move was completely unnecessary, as Doerffeldt – who was used to running in one of the middle legs – had no one to pass the baton to. The move was disastrous for the German team, as Doerffeldt did the unthinkable – she dropped the baton. Her mouth wide open in shock, Doerffeldt held up her arms in the position of someone who was surrendering. Her strides grew shorter, and her hands clutched the top of her head. As she turned round to look, the other runners, led by Helen Stephens, stormed past her. For a moment, Doerffeldt looked like a little girl stuck in the middle of a busy street, cars and lorries mercilessly shooting past her. The groan from the crowd must have been heard 10 miles away in the centre of Berlin. Stephens crossed the line with the stopwatch registering 46.9, which cruelly beat the world record set by the Germans twenty-fours before. The British came second on 47.6, just beating the Canadians, who finished on 47.8. Hitler sat back down, banging his right thigh with his fist. Goebbels sat too, and reached for his binoculars to study Doerffeldt, who was in tears, being consoled by her teammates. 'The girls are gutted,' Goebbels wrote in his diary. 'The Fuehrer consoles them.' Indeed he did. Hitler saw the women later, and sent a car stuffed with flowers round to the Friesian House. 'I don't think it helped much,' said Stephens.

Even if Doerffeldt had not dropped the baton, however, it is possible that Stephens might have beaten her. 'Even if we were twelve years behind,' said Annette Rogers, 'Helen would have closed that gap.' She was probably right. Stephens was capable of running the distance in 11½ seconds. The best German runner, Krauss, was at least half a second slower, as was Dollinger. Emmy Albus was seven-tenths of a second slower than Stephens. It has to be assumed that Ilse Doerffeldt was slower than the others, as she had not even been entered for the 100 metres. It is likely that she was a full second slower than Stephens, the equivalent of just under 10 metres, which was twice the gap that Stephens had to close up when she received the baton. Even allowing for Doerffeldt's head start, Stephens would have passed her a few metres before the finishing line. Had the Germans been in the same position with Krauss as the anchor, then they would have won, but only just. If either Albus or Dollinger had anchored, then the result would have been too close to anticipate. But Doerffeldt was the slowest of the German girls, and she lacked the experience to take on Stephens, which was probably why she was nervous enough to unnecessarily change her baton-carrying hand. It looked as if the American tactic of changing positions had paid off.

While Annette Rogers stood on the podium receiving her gold medal, the stadium announced her third and final call for the high jump. 'I jumped off the podium and ran off to compete,' she recalled. 'The crowd was cheering me on because they knew what was happening. It was my third try at one metre fifty-five, but my legs gave out because I was tired.' At least Rogers had more chance that Gretel Bergmann, who was sitting at home, waiting for a letter from her father's rich friend in the United States, who had promised to sponsor her. It came a few weeks later, although the news was not good. The friend moaned at how bad the economic situation was in the United States, and said that Bergmann would have trouble finding a job. He advised her to change her plans. 'Maybe the situation in Germany will soon change for the better,' he wrote. When Bergmann's father read this, he lost his temper and swore copiously. 'We could only surmise that I now seemed a much less valued commodity,' Bergmann wrote. 'No longer could this sterling character brag of having helped an Olympic track star get to the United States.' Bergmann's father dispatched a letter to his friend, reminding him that a 'promise was a promise'. All Bergmann could do, once more, was to sit and wait.

The high jump was a gruelling event. 'We jumped for three hours,' Dorothy Odam recalled. 'They brought the German girls water and things like that, but they wouldn't let anybody bring something through for the rest of us. We thought, 'Can we have some,' but we weren't allowed. It was very unfair.' What made matters even more unfair was that one of the German girls was in fact a man. He was none other than the seventeen-year-old Dora, who had shared a room with Bergmann at Ettlingen the previous autumn, the Dora who never shared the shower room with the other girls, the Dora who always took a bath behind a locked door. Dora – whose full name was Dora Ratjen – was displaying some of the same eccentricities at the Friesian House, where she shared a bedroom with her fellow German high jumper, Elfriede Kaun. 'I thought something was a bit funny,' Kaun recalled, 'because she had a deep voice and she snored in her sleep.' But that was not all. 'She also had to shave,' said Kaun, 'not just her legs and under her arms, but also her face. In the shower, you could hear the voice of Dora, and everybody said, "What's a man doing in here?"'

It was not an unreasonable question. According to Ratjen – whose real Christian name was Hermann, thus giving rise to the inevitable nickname of 'Hermann the German' – he had been forced into competing as a woman by Hitler Youth leaders. Perhaps the Nazis were using Ratjen as a means of defeating Gretel Bergmann, if they were unable to deselect her. The rationale was, presumably, that it was far better to have a transvestite winning for Germany than a Jew. Ratjen may not have been completely male, however, and may have had ambiguous genitalia. Nevertheless, by all counts Ratjen was a lot more male than female, and as such should have been competing against David Albritton and Cornelius Johnson a week earlier.

Hermann would not have done terribly well against his fellow men. In the finals of the women's high jump, he failed to jump over 1.60 metres, which was 10 centimetres shorter than the worst-performing men in the elimination trials. Nevertheless, Ratjen's performance earned him fourth place. The contest for the top three places was decided by a jump-off between Odam, Kaun and Ibolya Csák of Hungary, all of whom had cleared 1.60, but had failed at 1.62. They were then given a fourth attempt at the height. Whoever cleared it would be judged the winner. Both Kaun and Odam failed, but Csák made it – just – and took the gold. The bar was then lowered to 1.60 for Kaun and Odam. The British girl cleared it, but Kaun, her legs worn out after three hours of jumping, was now unable to manage it. Odam won silver, and Kaun took bronze, although under the present high jump rules, Odam would have won gold, as she had been the first to clear 1.60. When she got back to the Friesian House, she found her chaperones' reaction somewhat underwhelming. 'We were having a meal,' she recalled, 'and when it came up that I had won a medal, one of the chaperones said, "Don't forget that the girls won a silver medal in the relay." I was made to feel as if I was nobody. I was just a little sixteen-year-old.' The one woman who felt even more of a nobody was Gretel Bergmann. She could jump 1.60 with ease.

That Sunday was a good day for the British. As well as the high jump and the women's relay, there was one other event in which they hoped to do well – the 4 x 400 men's relay. As the British Olympic Association's official report said, 'it was generally considered that Great Britain's chances of winning the 1600 metres relay event were extremely high'. The BOA was right, but then, as was so often the way, America's chances were also good. The final of the individual 400 metres could not have had a closer finish, with only three-tenths of a second between Archie Williams of the United States in first and Bill Roberts in fourth. Godfrey Brown was just two-tenths of a second behind Williams, with James Lu Valle, who took bronze, a mere one tenth of a second behind Brown. 'A finer final it is impossible to imagine,' wrote Harold Abrahams. Despite the lack of a medal, Roberts could at least congratulate himself that he had beaten his personal best by two seconds.

Although the race was close, Roberts and Brown earned some censure from the newspapers for not starting more quickly. W. Capel Kirby, in the *Sporting Chronicle*, observed that 'our men generally have taken too much for granted and overlooked the fact that in present-day Olympic competition it is courting trouble not to go out hard all the way from "go"'. Kirby indicated that the Americans were great believers in getting to the front as soon as they could, and then staying there. This was certainly correct. Archie Williams recalled the aggressive advice his coach had given him.

> My coach told me, 'Don't get cute out there. You don't have to win every heat, but why not do it? If you don't, you'll fool around out there and think you'll just get a cheap second or third. But that is a good way to wind up in the bleachers [a roofless grandstand].' So each race was a kind of final. There was no sense in saving it for something against some guy you never saw before.

The final took place at 3.45 that afternoon. With the women having just won silver in the 4 x 100, the pressure was on to equal or better their performance. Britain was drawn on the outside lane, with Canada in lane five. In lane four was the United States, with Hungary in lane three, Germany in lane two and Sweden in lane one. Although all six teams were strong, the stadium knew that the race would be between the United States and Great Britain, who had both won their heats. The Americans had recorded a time of 3:13 and the British 3:14.4. In the third heat, Germany and Canada had both finished on 3:15.0, although the Germans were judged to have come first. The running order for the British team was Freddy Woolf, Godfrey Rampling and Bill Roberts, with Godfrey Brown as the anchor. Woolf would have a difficult job at the start. Not only was he the slowest runner, but being drawn in lane six meant that he would have no idea where his opponents were. What made matters worse for Woolf was that he was recovering from some dental treatment, yet he was deemed fit enough to race.

Woolf made a good start, but Limon of Canada was soon right behind him. After 200 yards, the prospects for the British team were already starting to look bleak, as Woolf was labouring. On the final bend, Limon passed him, and all Woolf could do in response was to turn his head to watch him overtake. Woolf slowed down even more as he approached the baton change, and by the time he handed it over to Rampling, the British were in fourth, some 1½ seconds – or 10 metres – behind the Canadians, with the United States and Germany in second and third. Edwards of Canada powered away, but Young of the United States was soon chipping away at his lead. At this stage, it looked as if the North Americans were going to take both gold and silver.

Just as Young was going to pass Edwards, a tall and lanky figure suddenly appeared from behind them, running at a rate that was demonstrably quicker than that of the American or the Canadian. It was Godfrey Rampling, and in the final 50 metres of that leg he passed the North Americans so confidently it made their own efforts look insignificant. 'I just seemed to float around the track,' Rampling recalled, 'passing people without effort.' It was an incredible run, and it had given the British the lead, a lead that Bill Roberts would do his best to increase. As he waited for the baton, Roberts repeated to himself, 'Don't twist round, don't turn, just put your arm out.' It was all he had been taught about baton technique, and it was enough. He took it cleanly from Rampling and began his leg of what was now a two-horse race between Britain and the United States, the opposition taking the form of O'Brien, who was at least half-a-foot taller than the small, wiry Salford lad. As they rounded the bend after the back straight, the thrusting O'Brien drew up and even got slightly ahead of Roberts, but the Englishman was having none of it. 'The iron entered my soul,' Roberts recalled, 'and I dashed off as if I was a sprinter.' He maintained the racing line, and O'Brien found it impossible to get past. It was now Roberts' turn to put on the pressure, and he humiliated the American by drawing away on the final bend, handing over to Godfrey Brown a lead of some 5 metres.

Brown rocketed off, but Fitch of the United States was determined not to let the British run away with the gold quite so easily. As early as the first bend, the American launched his first assault on the bespectacled figure of Brown. Brown was simply too quick, however, and on the back straight the Englishman maintained a comfortable lead of some 5 metres. On the last bend, Fitch mounted another attack, but his energy was beginning to dwindle, while Brown was beginning to look stronger with each stride. This was confirmed on the final straight, as Brown dramatically increased his pace, and belted to the tape to win by two seconds and some fifteen yards. Brown lifted his arms up in a brief display of joy, jumped a little in the air, but then evidently decided that such goings-on were most un-British and looked down at the ground, somewhat embarrassed with himself. The British time was 3:09, eight-tenths of a second slower than the world record set by the Americans four years earlier. Once again, the Germans and the Canadians finished in exactly the same time – 3:11.8 – and again the Germans were judged to have beaten the Canadians. Although Rampling's leg was clearly decisive, Roberts' successful tussle with O'Brien was also seen as essential. 'It really ought to be studied,' said Brown later. 'So relaxed. So powerful. It just broke the American up.'

The men got into their white tracksuits and mounted the podium, their expressions as inscrutable as their ambassador's. Indeed, it was impossible to tell that they had just won the most important race of their lives. 'Of course it was a moving movement,' said Roberts, 'but whether it was the peak of our careers was another matter. We had never run together as a team before, and we never did again.' After the ceremony, there were no victory laps or playing to the crowd. Instead, the foursome posed awkwardly for some photographs and then called it a day. 'After all,' said Roberts, 'it was our view that winning wasn't everything. It was the way that you did it that mattered.' Of this at least, Coubertin would have approved.

If Jesse Owens was the king of the track, then the seventeen-year-old Hendrika 'Rie' Mastenbroek of Holland was the queen of the swimming pool. Her achievements at Berlin were barely less impressive than those of the American, embracing three gold medals and one silver. Although Mastenbroek was blessed with a phenomenal raw talent, it was abetted by a severely strict training regime implemented by the famous Dutch trainer 'Ma' Braun, who had spotted Mastenbroek at the age of eleven. Braun's technique was holistic, and involved not just swimming training but also insisted that her pupils followed an ascetic way of life, which appeared to involve eating a lot of kidney beans and bacon. Braun's approach had been proved to work – her daughter Maria had won a gold and a silver medal at the 1928 Games. By 1934 it had been shown to work again, as Mastenbroek won three golds and one silver at the European Championships at Magdenburg. She was just fifteen.

Mastenbroek's first final in Berlin was the 100 metres freestyle, which was held at three o'clock on Monday, 10 August. She was drawn in lane five, and to her right in lane six was the Argentinian Jeanette Campbell. Also in the race was the German champion, Gisela Arendt, who had finished third behind Mastenbroek at Magdenburg.

Arendt felt she could win, however, In the heats, she had swum next to Mastenbroek, and 'in doing so I had confirmed that I was at my absolute best and that in this condition I could even beat her'. The one thing Arendt didn't want was to be drawn in lane seven – the far-right lane – as she always looked up to her right when she breathed, and when she did so she was able to keep an eye on the competition. In lane seven all she would see would be the side of the pool.

At lunchtime that day, Arendt's trainer, Hans Pausin, told her in which lane she had been drawn. It was lane seven. Arendt's optimism plunged. 'When an unknown old man came over to our table and said how much he admired my composure,' she recalled, 'I thought what a good thing it was that we cannot see inside the heads of other people. Because I would rather not have gone back to the Olympic Stadium at all.' Nevertheless, Arendt did her best, and she led for the first 70 metres in the race, at which point Mastenbroek overtook her, as did Jeanette Campbell. The finish was tight, with Mastenbroek coming in first in 1:05.9, Campbell in second with 1:06.4 and Arendt in third with 1:06.6. All three women had beaten the Olympic record. Despite her bronze medal, Arendt was disappointed. 'The winning of my bronze medal was generally celebrated as a great success,' she recalled. '[. . .] But I will now say quite openly that I did not in any way share this perception of my third place.' Lane seven or not, it is unlikely, however, that Arendt would have beaten Mastenbroek, whose medal haul had only just started.

Thursday, 13 August was a busy day for the seventeen–year-old. At around eleven o'clock, she swam in the heats of the 400 metres freestyle, which she won in the comfortable time of 5:38.6, nearly ten seconds ahead of Schramková of Czechoslovakia in second. At 5.10, she then had to compete in the final of the 100 metres backstroke, in which she faced her fellow countrywoman Dina Senff, Alice Bridges from the United States and Lorna Frampton from Britain. Frampton knew she had little chance of winning, but just to have got to the final was a good result for her. Mastenbroek looked like an awesome oppo-nent. 'My mother, when she saw her,' said Frampton, 'thought she had shoulders like a mantelpiece.' The mantelpiece was tired after her earlier exertions, however, and she found the race tough. Although Mastenbroek had broken the world record for the distance earlier in the year, she managed only to finish second, some three-tenths of a second behind Senff, and 3.4 seconds behind her record. Senff had swum an extraordinary race. At the 50-metre turning point, she had failed to make contact with the end of the pool. Realising that her mistake would get her disqualified, she had turned round, touched the end and then charged back up the pool to win in a time of 1:18.9. Lorna Frampton came sixth in a creditable 1:20.6.

The one woman who could have beaten them was of course Eleanor Holm, who now found herself one of the best-paid journalists in Berlin. Holm watched the race from the stands, sportingly shouting 'C'mon Alice!' to Alice Bridges, who came third. Could Holm – the beauty who trained on nothing but champagne and cigarettes – have won the race? She could have done, but it would have been tough. Mastenbroek's world record was some 3½ seconds quicker than Holm's Olympic record, set in 1932, a time that Senff had also thoroughly bettered by 1½ seconds in the first heat. Nevertheless, because of Mastenbroek's tiredness and Senff's error, the final was a slow race, and had Holm swum in it and equalled her 1932 record, then she would have won by over half a second. Holm claimed that she had swum the distance in 1:14.7 in training in the spring – if she had repeated that time in the final her victory would have been awesomely commanding.

Even though she wasn't swimming, the vivacious Holm was enjoying Berlin. 'I had such fun,' she recalled. 'I enjoyed the parties, the *Heil Hitlers*, the uniforms, the flags. Goering was fun. He had a good personality. So did the one with the club foot.' Goering was clearly captivated by Holm, as he gave her a silver swastika from his uniform. Rumours abounded that Holm had even given a nude swimming exhibition at one of Goering's parties, which she later denied. One person who was not delighted to see her was Avery Brundage. 'I was invited to everything in Berlin,' said Holm, 'and he would be there too. He would be so miserable because I was at all these important functions. I would ignore him – like he wasn't even alive. I really think he hated the poor athletes. How dare I be there and take away his thunder? You see, they all wanted to talk to me.'

Friday, 14 August was another busy day for Mastenbroek. In the morning, she had to qualify for the final of the 400 metres freestyle, and at 4.45 that afternoon she competed in the 4 x 100 metres relay. Mastenbroek anchored the team, and found herself once more racing against Gisela Arendt. Mastenbroek pulled away from the German, but just 2 metres before the finish, disaster nearly struck. An exhausted Mastenbroek inhaled water and started choking. Under normal circumstances, she would have stopped, but there was no way she was going to do that. With her lungs full of water, she swam on and reached the finish to take gold for the team in a new Olympic record of 4:36. Mastenbroek's immediate concern was to cough the water out of her lungs, and her teammates, sensing she was in trouble, hauled her out the water. It was only after she had got her breath back that she was able to celebrate her third medal of the Games.

Just under twenty-four hours later, Mastenbroek was back in the pool, competing in the final of the 400 metres freestyle. Her biggest rival was the Dane Ragnhild Hvegner, whose qualifying time was over ten seconds faster than Mastenbroek's, although Mastenbroek had not pushed herself in the heats. Before the final, the Dutch girl recalled how Hvegner had received a large box of chocolates from her supporters. 'I hoped that Hvegner would offer me a piece of chocolate,' said Mastenbroek. 'Hvegner passed me by, deliberately. I was sorely disappointed with this, and thought of revenge.' What mighty contests rise from trivial things. A miffed Mastenbroek swam the first seven laps – 350 metres – alongside the chocolate-hoarding Dane, and then punished her meanness by sprinting away in the final lap, reaching the finish a good 1.1 seconds ahead of Hvegner. 'This is much better than a piece of chocolate,' thought Mastenbroek. Both girls beat the previous Olympic record, although maybe Hvegner might have done better had she not been weighed down by chocolates. Lenore Wingard of the United States came third, although she was never to know her time, as the two judges allocated to her lane forgot to start their stopwatches, a fate that had also befallen Angyel of Hungary in the heats of the men's 1,500 metres freestyle. Mastenbroek received her fourth medal under the floodlights of the main stadium. Her achievements had been superb, but she failed to reap the same whirlwind of publicity as Jesse Owens, partly because of the 'minor' nature of her sport and because she was a woman, and also because she did not court the attention. When she returned to Rotterdam, she was greeted by a crowd of well-wishers, but her homecoming was not the beginning of a great period of happiness for the most successful swimmer of her generation. 'Ma' Braun, it seemed, wanted more than just a pupil.

Mastenbroek was by no means the youngest girl to win a medal in the pool. That honour fell to Inge Sorensen of Denmark, who had turned twelve just three weeks before she competed in the final of the 200 metres breaststroke. Remarkably, 'Little Inge', as she was affectionately called by the Danish press, claimed that she did not train while she was in Berlin. 'I took a swim once in a while,' she said. 'Even at home, I only swum once a week for one hour – perhaps more in the summer. Other athletes trained more than me. I was never programmed to think that I could go places. I went to the Olympics simply because I enjoyed swimming.' Sorensen was not the only one who didn't train, although others were not able to rely simply on talent alone. Iris Cummings admitted that she was 'not as focused' as she should have been, which did not go unnoticed by her friend and room-mate Velma Dunn. 'She isn't working very hard,' Dunn wrote to her mother. 'I hope she snaps out of it.' Along with the lack of a proper coach, what really militated against American success in the pool was the water temperature. 'The practice pool was an outdoor pool and it was *cold*,' the Californian Cummings recalled, 'a lot colder than we were used to.' Cummings was eliminated in the third heat with a time of 3:21.9.

Despite her youth, Sorensen was calm before the final, which was held on the afternoon of Tuesday, 11 August, watched by, among others, Goering. With Martha Genenger of Germany and Hideko Maehata of Japan in the race, 'Little Inge' was unlikely to win gold, but bronze was within her grasp. Her rival for third place was Waalberg of Holland, who was ahead of Sorensen for most of the race. The two girls turned simultaneously for the last 50-metre lap. 'We were side by side up to halfway,' Sorensen recalled, 'and then I could feel I could do it. Then I started my pull and then I passed her. I was swimming for bronze. I knew I couldn't touch the other two, but I was happy. As soon as I finished I smacked my hands in the water.'

At the medal ceremony in the stadium, Sorensen wore a white dress and a red-and-white scarf that a dressmaker had made specially for her.

'My friends said, 'Wear that, it's perfect. And keep your back straight!'
I cried when I saw the Danish flag going up. I just cried.' The tears
reappeared when she returned to Denmark. 'We were mobbed when
we came off the train on the outskirts of Copenhagen,' she said. 'The
barricades were broken down and the crowd rushed to the train and
we couldn't get out. I couldn't find my parents, and it was too much
and I was crying. Eventually my father found me and pulled me out.'
The image of the crying twelve-year-old and her father made the
front pages the following day, earning Sorensen a place in the affections of the Danish people that she still enjoyed into her eighties. The
New York Times commented wryly on her success. 'The Olympics are
more than a festival of youth,' wrote Albion Ross. 'Pretty soon they
will be getting them out of their cradles to compete for medals and
laurel wreaths.'

The American women fared better in the springboard diving and the
high diving. The former was won by Marjorie Gestring of the United
States at the age of 13 years and 268 days – she remains the youngest
ever individual Olympic champion. The United States won silver and
bronze as well, the former going to to Katherine Rawls, and the latter
to Dorothy Poynton Hill. Along with Eleanor Holm, Poynton Hill
was the most glamorous of the American 'mermaids'. At the age of
thirteen, she had won bronze in the event at Amsterdam in 1928, and
had won gold in the high diving in Los Angeles in 1932. With a huge
smile, bottle-blonde hair, a knowing look and a figure that she was
more than happy to show off, Poynton Hill soon attracted a lot of
attention. She even had bit parts in a couple of movies in 1931 – *Palmy
Days*, starring Eddie Cantor, and *Movie Town* with Marjorie Beebe. By
1936, the pressure for her to win was great, a pressure applied not just
by herself, but by others who had a stake in her. 'I had already made
a commitment to endorse Camel cigarettes,' she recalled, 'Hollywood
bathing suits, and some other things, and if I had lost, all that would
have been gone [. . .] I hadn't signed anything, but you couldn't even
mention that you were thinking about it. If Brundage had even suspected, he would have kicked me off the team.'

Although she had not won at the springboard, Poynton Hill had a
second chance at gold in the high diving, which was held the following

day, on Thursday, 13 August. As in the springboard event, the United States looked as if it might take home all the medals, with Velma Dunn and Cornelia Gilissen both likely to take places on the podium. The trio was not a happy one, however, as Dunn reported to her mother before the event.

> I only hope I beat Dorothy and Cornelia. They have certainly been poor sports and done everything possible to hurt Fred [Cady, the coach], Marge [Gestring] and me. I know now why Georgia hated Dorothy so much. Dorothy is swell to anybody who she can beat or who isn't in her competition. As soon as you are as good as she, she turns on you.
> We are having a swell time in Germany anyway.

Dunn's mother must have read her daughter's pay-off with a raised eyebrow. It looked as if the pressure exerted by the tobacco and clothing companies on Poynton Hill made her behaviour most un-Olympic in spirit.

In the end, the event was a contest between three women – Poynton Hill, Dunn and Käte Koehler of Germany. The girls had to perform four groups of dives, which were scored by seven judges. After the first group, Poynton Hill had scored 7.81 to Dunn's 7.59 and Koehler's 7.26. Between the dives, Poynton Hill would walk coquettishly round the pool, wearing high-heeled sandals with straps around the ankles. Instead of wearing the team-issued black swimsuit, she wore a gingham number with a lower and more revealing décolletage. The effect was enhanced with immaculately plucked eyebrows and waterproof make-up. No wonder girls like Velma Dunn hissed.

But Poynton Hill's diving matched her glamour. In group two, she scored 8.36 to Dunn's 7.92 and Koehler's 8.40. Her third group was even better, earning her 9.36 points. As the women went into the final group, Poynton Hill stood on 25.53, Dunn on 24.39, Koehler on 23.91. Much to Dunn's secret delight, no doubt, Cornelia Gilissen was languishing on 22.07. Poynton's last round was a disappointing 8.40, which brought her final total to 33.93. Koehler scored 9.52 – the highest in any group scored by a woman that day, putting her on 33.43. Velma Dunn now had to score 9.05 to beat the German, and 9.55 to beat the despised Dorothy. The last group called for backward somersaults from the standing position on the 5-metre board. Dunn knew she was good at it, but she would have to surpass her best. She tried as hard as she could, and the judges rewarded her for it, giving her a score of 9.24 – just .30 shy of Poynton Hill. The bombshell had won her gold, and the contract with Camel was now safely tucked down her front. She would retain her somewhat aggressive glamour until her dying day. 'It's great having been the world's best in something,' she said, 'instead of being Suzy Klutz trying to learn how to bake a cake.' She had clearly not listened to Coubertin's words concerning the taking part.

The United States' men's swimming team also appeared to suffer from some bitchy behaviour. Adolph Kiefer, the prodigious eighteen-year-old world record holder in the 100 metres backstroke, found himself on the receiving end of some psychological warfare from his teammate Taylor Drysdale. 'The night before the final,' Kiefer recalled, 'he told me he was going to beat me. He was trying to unnerve me. Well, he was just a pretty boy.' Drysdale must have had some nerve. His fastest time in the heats and semi-finals was 1:08.6. Kiefer's was 1:06.8 in the semi-final, beating the Olympic record of 1:06.9 that he himself had set the day before in the heats. There was no way that Drysdale could possibly beat Kiefer. Indeed, a bookie would have refused to take bets on the young man from Chicago.

Nevertheless, Kiefer was nervous before the race, which was held in the rain on the afternoon of Friday, 14 August. 'I kept thinking about what I would do,' said Kiefer. 'I went to the swimming stadium from the village in an open-top car on my own. The drive was about thirty minutes. After I arrived, I got a massage, and I was just thinking about my event and nothing else. I was interested in getting into my rhythm, getting my muscles coordinated. I would sing to myself as I swam – it gave me a rhythm. I would swim just with my arms, and then with my legs, and then I would be ready.' When the gun went off, Kiefer reached back as far as he could. Like the rest of the swimmers, he had very little idea of what was going on. All he had to do was to swim as fast he could, and he would soon be taking his place at the top of the podium. By the halfway mark, he already had a commanding lead, and it came as no surprise when he finished first, in a time of 1:05.9 – yet another Olympic record, although just over a second slower than his world record. He had barely pushed himself. Taylor Drysdale came fourth. He was 3½ seconds behind the man he said he would beat, finishing in his worst time at the Games.

Kiefer was not the United States' only gold medal winner in the pool. Jack Medica predictably won the 400 metres freestyle, and took silver in the 1,500. The team came second in the 800 metres relay to Japan, who broke the world record in that event. The springboard diving saw the United States take the first three places, with Dick Degener – presumably out of the clutches of Eleanor Holm – taking gold, with Marshall Wayne in second and Al Greene in third. Wayne won gold in the high diving, and Elbert Root took silver, but Germany, in the form of Hermann Stork, won the bronze.

If Britain had very little success in the water, then it did a lot better on it. In the yachting, Peter Scott – the son of Scott of the Antarctic and later to find fame as a naturalist – won bronze in the Olympic Monotype class. Britain's crew won gold in the International Six Metre class, an event normally dominated by the Scandinavians. In the 2,000 metres double sculls, Jack Beresford and Leslie Southwood rowed a thrilling race against the German pair, Willi Kaidel and Joachim Pirsch. The British led at the start, but the Germans caught them, and at the halfway point they took the lead. Beresford and Southwood rallied back, but with just 100 metres to go, it looked as if the Germans would take gold. There were just centimetres in it. They could not stand the pace, however, and the British crossed the line six seconds ahead of the Germans. 'Beresford was much distressed at the end,' commented the *Manchester Guardian*. It was hardly surprising – Beresford was thirty-seven, and that victory represented his fifth Olympic medal. He had won silver in the single sculls in 1920, gold in the same event in 1924, a silver medal as part of the eight in 1928, and a gold in the coxless fours in 1932.

The final of the 2,000 metres coxless fours was no less thrilling. Like Sweden with the modern pentathlon, Britain felt she owned the event as she had won it at the previous three games. The British team – which included Martin Bristow – was determined to do its forerunners proud, and not just throw bread at portraits of Hitler in the refectory. The British were keen to train as hard as possible, as they were missing their stroke, Howitt, who was stuck in his office at Cable & Wireless. The replacement stroke was an Oxford man who was used to rowing a boat with fixed rowlocks, whereas the rest of the crew were accustomed to swivelled rowlocks. 'We had two outings a day,' Bristow recalled. 'Our training was all very regimented.' The British soon found, however, that the bus timetable did not suit them. 'We asked for it to be changed, but we were told that it was all decided in Berlin.'

The race started extremely quickly, with the British leading for a short time. By 600 metres, however, the Germans had nudged slightly ahead. The British put on a spurt to try to overtake, but the Germans were just too strong. 'There was a lack of cohesion because we didn't have Howitt,' said Bristow. 'We lacked that edge.' At the halfway point, the order was Germany, Great Britain, Italy and Switzerland. Once more, the British mounted an attack, but they were unable to get the better of the Germans. When they neared the tribune, the two boats were level, but the Germans had something in reserve, and they managed to pull away decisively, beating the British by a length. 'We felt a bit aggrieved,' said Bristow. 'Nevertheless, we were pleased to win anything. There is no question that we would have wiped the floor had we had Howitt.'

The most exciting rowing race was the final of the eights. This time it was the Americans who had the monopoly on an event, having won it six times since Paris in 1900. The British had marred their clean sweep by taking gold in 1908 and 1912, but there was no doubting that this was the United States' private property. The American eight was that of the University of Washington, an immensely powerful crew which was considered invincible. Although others could row at a faster rate, their pull was so long and strong that they could never be passed. Facing what Arthur Daley of the *New York Times* called 'the lads from the tall timber of the great North-west' were the Italians, the Germans, the British, the Hungarians and the Swiss, none of whom publicly regarded the Americans as anything but beatable.

The race was held at six o'clock on Friday, 14 August. The sky was gloomy, and during the race it started to rain heavily. A crosswind lashed the outside lane, which was where the Americans were drawn, giving them an immediate handicap. Nevertheless, the 'Huskies' got off to a strong start, but it was not strong enough. By 400 metres, the order was Switzerland, Britain, Germany and the United States. The British crew had had to row an extra heat the day before, and at this early stage the exhaustion could be seen on their faces. After another 100 metres, the first three drew level, but at 800 metres Italy was out ahead and the Americans had dropped back to last. The Huskies' cox, Bob Moch, ordered an increase in the tempo, and soon the Americans were rowing at a rate of 35 strokes per minute, churning up the cold grey waters. This saw them draw up to third at the 1,200-metre mark. Italy was now a length ahead of them, with Germany in between. Moch was keen to capitalise on the surge forward, and ordered another increase, which his crew was just about able to provide, stepping up the rate to 36. The gap between them and the Italians soon closed.

At 1,800 metres, the Washington crew enjoyed a slight lead. The Italians started to go at a rate of 40, however, and drew up on the American boat. The Germans, no doubt aware of their Fuehrer's eyes on them, did the same, and soon all three boats were level. Moch now knew that his crew had to push themselves harder than ever. 'Higher! Higher!' he yelled into the megaphone strapped to his face. 'Give her all you've got!' The American stroke, Don Hume, did as he was ordered, and upped the rate from 40 to a punishing 44. The extra effort was worth it, because the prow of the American boat crossed the line first, beating the Italians by a mere six-tenths of a second. The Germans were just four-tenths of a second behind the Italians, and the British in fourth and the Hungarians in fifth were a good length behind. The American coach, Alvin Ulbrickson, was speechless, and when the Huskies came in to dock, all he could do was to make a weak quip. Spotting the victory wreath around the head of Herbert Morris, the bow, Ulbrickson asked, 'Where did you pick up the hay?'

'I picked it up downstream,' Morris replied with a casual wave of the hand.

Robie Leibbrandt would have hated the gentlemanly casualness of the rowers. For the South African boxer, the Olympics were important in the same way as they were for the Nazis – they were about nationalism, not matey internationalism. Winning a gold in his light-heavyweight class would not just be a personal triumph, but also a triumph for his oppressed Afrikaners. It would also be an important leg in Leibbrandt's political journey, a journey that would see him going from Nazi sympathiser to an actual Nazi. But before he could concern himself with such weighty matters, he actually needed to do some boxing.

Leibbrandt's first bout was against Johansen of Norway on the evening of Monday, 10 August. Leibbrandt had been told by his trainer, Jim Fennessey, to stay calm and secure an easy win. There was no point in going for the knockout – he should save his energy for later rounds. The South African, though, was determined to show the crowd in the Deutschland Hall what he was capable of. Despite suffering from a bleeding nose, Leibbrandt harried Johansen around the ring with a series of left swings to his body and rights to the jaw. At the end of the bout, Johansen was barely able to stand, and the largely German crowd cheered Leibbrandt as one of their own when he was rightly awarded the victory by the judges.

The following evening saw Leibbrandt face Amin Mohammed of Egypt. Amin was a far tougher opponent that the Norwegian, and Leibbrandt had to be nimble to avoid the Egyptian's heavy right punches. Nevertheless, Leibbrandt scored well with his left, and in the second and third rounds he landed some vital punches. He won the bout, but towards the end of the match it was clear that he had started to tire. Fennessey questioned the wisdom of Leibbrandt's vegetarianism, but the boxer refused to discuss it. Leibbrandt was now through to the quarter-finals, where he encountered Havelka of Czechoslovakia on the evening of Thursday, 13 August – the same night as Goering's magnificent party. As was to be expected, the fight was tough, and Leibbrandt only just scraped through to the semi-finals. There were now four boxers left – Leibbrandt, Roger Michelot of France, Richard Vogt of Germany and Francisco Risiglione of Argentina.

Back in the dressing room, however, Fennessey noticed that Leibbrandt was in pain. 'What's wrong?' he asked. 'Aren't you glad? There's nothing to stop you now.' Leibbrandt motioned towards his right hand, which was still in its glove.

'You remember that hard right in the second round?' Leibbrandt asked. 'I put all my weight behind it but he brought up his left and

I caught him on shoulder. From that moment I could feel that there was something wrong with my right.'

Fennessey removed the glove, which came off with some difficulty. Leibbrandt's right hand had turned blue, and with the removal of the glove it soon started to swell up. There was no doubt about it – the hand was broken. Fennessey told the boxer that his bid for Olympic glory had finished. There was no way he could carry on. Leibbrandt, however, did not agree, telling Fennessey that he would fight on. The next day, the doctor in the Olympic village confirmed that the hand had been fractured, and told the South African that it was out of the question that he could fight that evening, even if he just wanted to use his left. A useless right hand would not only make it harder for him to launch an attack, but it would also make it harder to defend himself, and would therefore expose him to a greater risk of injury.

Leibbrandt was nothing if not bloody minded, and insisted that he would fight. Eventually, he managed to convince a reluctant Fennessey to support him in the ring, with the proviso that as soon as it looked as if Leibbrandt was going to suffer a permanent injury, then the towel would be thrown. Incredibly, the officials from the International Boxing Federation allowed Leibbrandt to fight, and even sanctioned the use of a painkilling cocaine injection into the right hand. Just a few minutes before the bout, however, the permission was withdrawn, and Leibbrandt entered the ring against Michelot with a glove that had been slit open in order to fit over his swollen hand.

Despite his handicap, Leibbrandt acquitted himself well, using his left with power and precision to stun the Frenchman. Leibbrandt risked the occasional right punch, and when he connected, the pain on his face was obvious to everyone – especially Michelot. By the end of the second round, Leibbrandt was defying his detractors, and it looked as if he was actually winning the bout. In the final round, with the crowd cheering him on, Leibbrandt landed more and more punches with his left. He tried his right one more time, but it lacked any power. Michelot was no walkover, and he got in some hefty body blows, and also managed to get Leibbrandt's nose bleeding. When the bell sounded, the South Africans were sure their man had won. And then the Tannoy sounded. 'The winner on points – Michelot of France!' Boos erupted from the crowd. Leibbrandt shook his head in

disgust. In his eyes, he had been robbed of his victory by a bad decision, his opinion supported not only by the newspapers back home –
which was unsurprising – but also by the British judges who happened
to be watching. The next day, Leibbrandt should have fought for third
place, but the doctors forbade it. Michelot beat Vogt of Germany to
win gold, and Risiglione was given a walkover to take bronze.

Even though Leibbrandt had lost his fight, he would not leave
Berlin without some sort of reward, a reward that would come immediately after the Games. Berlin would change him, and in doing so it
would see him embark on a foolhardy, almost fantastical, journey to
attempt to change the course of his country's history.

Robie Leibbrandt was not the only visitor to Berlin that summer who
was convinced of the rottenness of the judging. In the three-day
event, the Poles were adamant that the Germans were cheating. The
Polish team manager was Colonel Tadeusz Komorowski, who had
not only competed in the 1924 Olympics but had bravely fought
against the Red Army in the last full cavalry battle in Europe just four
years earlier. In the Battle of Komarów, Komorowski had commanded the 12th and 8th Uhlans under Juliusz Rómmel's 1st Cavalry
Division, and during the battle had suffered a head wound.
Komorowski refused to leave the battle, and continued to lead his
regiment until Rómmel ordered him to go to hospital in the evening.
All this was no doubt good training for dealing with the Germans
in 1936.

'The Germans cheated diabolically,' his wife Irena recalled. 'My
husband had a fearful row at one stage during the cross-country. They
had German judges dotted all round the course. Of course there were
also international judges from all the other countries taking part, but
the majority were Germans.' According to Irena, the German judges
awarded some completely fictitious penalty points against the Polish
team. 'It was blatantly untrue,' she said, 'and my husband had one hell
of an argument with them.' Apparently, Komorowski's outbursts had
the desired effect, and the judges withdrew the penalty points.
Nevertheless, there was still bad feeling between the Poles and the
Germans. At the end of the competition, the Germans took gold and
the Poles silver, but the Poles were still certain that the Germans had

cheated. 'If there hadn't been all that business with the cheating,' said Irena, 'then we would probably have won the gold.'

It is impossible now to verify Komorowski's allegations. Even if they are true, then the Germans must have done an awful amount of cheating, as their margin of victory was comprehensive. They had a superior set of riders, including Lieutenant Freiherr von Wangenheim, who completed the cross-country with a broken collar-bone, an injury that did not stop the German competing in the jumping competition in the stadium, his arm bound tightly in a sling. The Poles were no less hardy. One of their horsemen, Captain Kawecki, broke several ribs on the cross-country, but he too competed in the stadium, his entire upper body bandaged.

Despite the ill feeling, the Poles and Colonel Komorowski still attended the grand reception for the riders and pentathletes held on Friday, 7 August. 'There was more braid and highly polished boots than you could imagine,' said Charles Leonard of the occasion. Both Hitler and Goebbels were at the reception; Komorowski had the dubious honour of being presented to the former, and the two men exchanged a few words. 'My husband said there was something about him,' Irena recalled. 'He had terribly penetrating eyes and when he looked you in the eye it felt as though they were boring right into your soul [. . .] It was obvious that this was not your average human being.' While the two men were talking, a photographer took their picture, a picture that the Germans would find of immense value just eight years later.

As well as the Poles, the Peruvians also suspected the impartiality of the judges, and their complaints caused a diplomatic incident that would have been more serious if it had not seemed like something out of a comic opera. The trouble began on the afternoon of Saturday, 8 August in the football match between Austria and Peru. At half-time, the score was 2–0 to Austria, but the Peruvians scored two goals in the second half and the game went into extra time. The first half was goalless, but towards the end of the second half the overly excited Peruvian fans stormed the pitch and started helping their players. One Austrian player later reported that he had even been kicked by a demented fan. In the ensuing chaos, the Peruvians scored two goals in the last five minutes. Unsurprisingly, the Austrians complained, and a jury of FIFA members declared that the match should be replayed two days later.

The Peruvians did not react well to the decision, to put it mildly. In the Peruvian capital Lima, and Port Callao, protesters took to the streets. The Olympic flag was ripped down from an office building used by the Austrian consul, and it was thanks only to the intervention of the police that the building was not ransacked. Undeterred, the mob then marched on the German consulate, whose windows were stoned before the police once more arrived. Stevedores in Callao refused to unload a German ship, the *Ammon*, as well as, bizarrely, a Norwegian ship, the *Remulus*. Presumably those assigned to the Scandinavian vessel wanted the afternoon off as well. President Oscar Benavides – who, needless to say, had come to power through a military coup – summoned members of the Peruvian Olympic Committee to the palace, and ordered them to withdraw the Olympic team from Berlin. Cables were sent out to every other participating country, including the United States. This cable found its way to Avery Brundage staying at the Adlon Hotel.

VIEW UNJUSTIFIED DECISION AGAINST PERUVIAN FOOTBALL TEAM PRESIDENT REPUBLIC AND UNANIMOUS VOTE OF OUR COMMITTEE ORDERING WITHDRAW OF ALL PERUVIAN OLYMPIC DELEGATION WE INVOKE AMERICAN SOLIDARITY = COMITE OLIMPICO PERUANO.

The United States did not withdraw, but President Benavides declared that he had received messages of support from Argentina, Chile, Mexico and Uruguay.

At 5.30 on Monday, 10 August, the only spectators to appear at the football stadium were Berlin policemen. The jury had ruled that no fans could watch the rematch, for fear of another pitch invasion. It promised to be a violent scrap, and the Italian referee, Barlassina, knew that he would have to exert every pound of his authority to keep the game under control. When the whistle blew, however, nothing happened. The Austrians stood and looked around, waiting for their opposition to appear. For the regulation fifteen minutes, they waited patiently in the quiet empty stadium, while the policemen wondered whether it was time to go. At 5.45, Barlassina blew his whistle, and gave the game to the Austrians.

On the morning of Wednesday 12th, the Peruvians left town for

Paris, taking with them the Colombian team (total strength – seven), which had withdrawn in sympathy. The Germans repeatedly stressed to the Peruvians that the decision was not theirs, but FIFA's, but the teams insisted that they were off. Back in Lima, President Benavides, in an attempt to cool the diplomatic temperature over what Goebbels described as an 'embarrassing sports incident', blamed the demonstrations in his cities on 'communists'. Naturally. The only comfort the Peruvians received was the fact that Austria lost 2–1 to Italy in the final.

One of the more unassuming gold medallists of the Games was Endre Kabos, a twenty-nine-year-old Jewish Hungarian fencer. Kabos's sporting career had started when he was given a fencing outfit as a birthday present. Initially, the shy Kabos hid it in a wardrobe, but when a friend discovered it and teased him about it, Kabos went and joined the local fencing club the following day just to spite his tormentor. The Hungarians had a lot to thank Kabos's bully for. At Los Angeles, Kabos won bronze in the individual men's sabre, and also played a vital role in helping the Hungarians to win gold in that year's team event. Tall, dark, good looking and witty, Kabos became quite a hero in his homeland, but he was too modest to bathe in the limelight. Neither would he have been allowed to. Anti-Semitism was widespread in Hungary, and nowhere more so than in the fencing world, which was dominated by army officers with bigoted and antique views. Kabos felt stymied by them, and unable to secure himself flexible employment to allow him to continue fencing, he gave his sabre away and opened a grocery shop. A benefactor noticed his plight, however, and offered him a more suitable position, which enabled Kabos to go on to dominate the European Championships in the years before 1936.

At Berlin, his form was similarly impressive, despite his concerns about German anti-Semitism. Once again, Kabos was the key member of the sabre team. The finals, which were held on the evening of Thursday, 13 August, saw Hungary, Germany, Italy and Poland all face each other. In their match against the host nation, the Hungarians won by a commanding 13–3, which was close compared to their annihilation of the Poles by 10–1. In their final match they faced the Italians, who were also unbeaten – whoever won this match would win gold. In the first bout, Kabos faced Vincenzo Pinton, and he suffered five hits to the Italian's two. It was a bad blow for Kabos, but he was not invincible. Kabos's next bout was the fifth, by which time the teams were level at 2–2. In his duel against Giulio Gaudini, Kabos again lost by the same margin. It looked as though the Hungarian had lost his form. After three more bouts, the Italians enjoyed a lead of 4–3. Kabos now fenced against Aldo Masciotta, and he trounced him 5–1, bringing the two teams level. At last, it looked as if Kabos was back to his winning ways. His victory spurred the team on, and after eleven rounds the Hungarians were beating the Italians by seven bouts to four. There were three round left, and if the Italians managed to draw level, then they might be awarded gold, as they would have received fewer hits.

Kabos's fourth and final bout was against Gustave Marzi, who was Italy's strongest competitor. In fact he was almost flawless, and soon he was beating Kabos 4–1. The situation looked hopeless. Kabos was never one to admit defeat, however, and he counter-attacked with an astonishing display of lunges that thrilled the crowd. By the time the two men were level on 4–4, there was no doubt which man was now the favourite, and when Kabos scored his final touché to bring the score to 5–4, the crowd erupted. Hungary went on to win the match 9–6, and took a well-earned gold. Italy took silver, and the Germans took bronze.

There was more glory for Kabos at Berlin. In the men's individual sabre, the Hungarian fenced his way with ease into the finals, where he faced Gustave Marzi. The Italian was determined take to his revenge on Kabos for his humiliating defeat, and he beat him 5–2. Marzi then went on to face Kabos's fellow Hungarian, Aladár Gerey, but he lost by 5–4. The Italian then fought Sobik of Poland, a match which he should have won with ease, but instead he lost 1–5. This opened a way to gold for Kabos. If he could win all seven of his remaining matches, then he would beat Marzi, who had now lost two matches. Kabos kept his cool, and he saw off all his opponents, including Gerey. By the end of the competition, he had won seven bouts and had received twenty hits. Marzi and Gerey tied with six wins apiece, but the Italian won silver because he received twenty-two hits to the Hungarian's twenty-six. After the match, Kabos found himself mobbed by his fans – many of whom were female – and he happily signed their autograph books. His time in Germany had been good to him, and he suffered little or no anti-Semitism. Although he was never to return to Germany, the Germans would come for him, and many like him.

One of the most exciting sports to watch at Berlin was the hockey, partly because the game was dominated by the Indians, whose skill was vastly superior to that of the other teams. Their speed, power and awesome control of the ball were outstanding. 'They were something else,' recalled Lorna Frampton. 'I remember watching them play, and thinking, this isn't the hockey we played at school – it was so fast and so strong.' The team, which was led by Dhyan Chand, was expected to win gold with no problems whatsoever. On 17 July, however, just two weeks before the Games, the Indians played a friendly against the Germans, and the result did not go the way the Indians had anticipated.

'The match was an eye-opener to most of us,' wrote M. N. Masood, 'for the Germans showed us that they had improved appreciably on their last Olympic form.' What the Indians had not prepared for was a difference in style. The Germans hit hard, made fast runs and thwacked first-time clearances, whereas the Indians were more accustomed to a game that involved short passes, a lot of dribbling and well-planned play. The visitors, who were also unfit after their long journey from the subcontinent, lost 1–4. The Germans were understandably delighted to have beaten the 'wonder boys from the Ganges'. 'After this,' said the German right back, Alfred Gerdes, 'we thought we might have a good result in the Games. It was clear that the Indians were very nervous after the match.'

Gerdes was right. 'As long as I live, I shall never forget this match or get over the shock of defeat which still rankles in me,' wrote Dhyan Chand, who was widely considered the world's best forward. 'Hitler's Germany had made great strides in their game [. . .] The result of the play shocked us so much that we could not sleep that night. Some of us even did not have our dinner.' Instead, a crisis conference was held, and it was decided to call on reinforcements from India. A cable was sent from Berlin to Kunwar Sir Jagdish Prasad, president of the International Hockey Federation, requesting him to send out more players, although they were not to arrive until late into the competition.

If the Indians had been complacent, then they were not now. The game against Germany had woken them up, and in the tournament their progress was spectacular. They beat Hungary 4–0, the United States 7–0, Japan 9–0 – 'Be it said to the credit of Japan that it took twenty minutes for the world's champions to score a goal,' wrote Masood magnanimously – and France 10–0, after which they reached the final. Their opponents were the Germans, who still worried the Indians. 'The impact of the defeat that Germany inflicted on us in the practice match still lingered in us,' wrote Chand.

Another problem was the weather. The final had been scheduled for Friday, 14 August, but the rain was torrential, and the pitch water-logged. The game was postponed until the following morning, a delay that only exacerbated the Indians' nerves. 'All of us were wondering as to what would be the result of the day,' Chand wrote. 'Never before had we ever doubted the issue of a game.' Just before the final, one of the players produced a Congress tricolour, which apparently helped to give the players some mental strength. 'Reverently we saluted and prayed and marched on to the field,' wrote Chand.

A crowd of 20,000 Germans and just fifty Indians had assembled in the newly built hockey stadium. The day was humid and sticky, cond-itions that suited the Indians better than the Germans. Nevertheless, to Chand the home team appeared very confident, which created more anxiety in the Indians. Chand was wrong – the German team was anything but confident. 'As the Indians finished off their oppo-nents effortlessly we suffered a noticeable lack of faith in our own ability,' Alfred Gerdes recalled. 'This atmosphere carried over to the team itself. This was deeply regrettable, for only a self-confident team is in a position to surpass itself.' When the whistle blew, both teams were somewhat shaky, and the play was scrappy and uneven.

'India shook off her nervousness first,' Masood recalled. The team started making short and effective passes, which rattled the Germans, who decided to adopt the same tactic. Throughout the tournament, they had played with their usual 'hit hard and far' tactic, which had served them well, their results being almost as good as India's during the Games. It was a mystery to the Indians why the Germans should suddenly start playing in a style to which they were unaccustomed. The switch seemed to work, however, and the Germans seemed equally matched with their opponents, wowing the crowd with their undercuts and lifts, while the Indians drew much applause with their brilliant half-volleys and sensational long shots. By the interval the game was anybody's, as the Indians were leading only 1–0.

In the second half, the Germans collapsed. They were simply unable to keep up with the Indians' astonishing energy and skill. 'With unbelievable variety this wonder team carried out attack upon attack with unprecedented energy,' wrote Gerdes. 'The forwards were to be found at the front and at the back and fought for every ball with full commitment. It could not possibly go well for our team in its current state if the Indians were able to maintain this tempo.' Unfortunately for the Germans, they were able to maintain it. Soon, the Indians had scored three more goals, and a savage defeat looked likely. Some little German face was saved when the team scored a goal, but it was to be the only goal scored against India in the Olympics that year. Before the final whistle, the visitors managed another four goals, bringing the score to a humiliating 8–1. The Germans felt devastated, as Alfred Gerdes recalled. 'For five weeks nothing but sport – and on top of this the vast pressure of the Olympic Games – had left our team, without our really being aware of it, tired, worn down and having had enough of sport.'

The hockey players were not the only Germans who had had enough. Even on 8 August, Goebbels was moaning in his diary, 'Today the Olympics have been going on for a week. Hopefully they will end soon.' The Games finally did end on the evening of Sunday 16th with a closing ceremony held in the early evening. The event was described by the propaganda minister as being 'rather dry'. 'Very protocol driven,' he wrote. 'This must be tightened up, made more effective.' This last comment showed just how proprietorial the Nazis felt about the Games. Still, after the flags had come down and the flame had gone out, Goebbels admitted to being 'deeply moved and rather melancholy'. Henry Channon was also in the stadium. After the crowd had listened to the umpteenth rendition of 'Deutschland über Alles', 'there was a shout, a speech or two, night fell, and the Olympic Games, the great German display of power, and bid for recognition, were over'.

12

The Legacy

~

THE EXODUS FROM Berlin started quickly. On the Monday morning after the closing ceremony, every train, bus, plane and taxi was full, and heavy traffic lined the roads out of the city. The one person who was not stuck in a jam was Hitler himself, who immediately decamped to his mountain retreat at Berchtesgaden. His minister of propaganda allowed himself his first few days off in weeks, and was able to enjoy the fine weather that occurred as soon as the Games were over. By the middle of the week, the city was deserted. 'Berlin is practically empty,' Goebbels wrote. 'Where have all the people gone? Sad lonely feeling.' Describing himself as 'very chuffed to be at rest', Goebbels spent much of his time gleefully perusing the overseas newspapers, which were unanimous in their praise for the XIth Olympiad. He would particularly have enjoyed the article in the *New York Times* by Frederick Birchall that was headlined 'Olympics Leave Glow of Pride in Reich'. Birchall noted how the Germans, anxious to impress their visitors, had been 'happy and amiable beyond reckoning'. As a result, 'they are back in the fold of nations who have "arrived"'.

> Foreigners who know Germany only from what they have seen during this pleasant fortnight can carry home only one impression. It is that this is a nation happy and prosperous beyond belief; that Hitler is one of the greatest political leaders in the world today, and that Germans themselves are a much maligned, hospitable, wholly peaceful people who deserve the best the world can give them.

Birchall was not completely convinced. He did note that the 'black spots have been covered', but he ended by expressing the hope that the effects of the so-called Olympic Pause would remain. The pause, such as it was, ended swiftly. On the evening of Friday, 21 August, Captain Wolfgang Fuerstner, the partly Jewish officer who had masterminded the Olympic village, excused himself from an Olympic farewell dinner, citing ill health. He returned home, put a gun to his head and shot himself. He was unable to live with his impending dismissal from the army. According to the authorities, Fuerstner was killed when his car hit a tree.

During that first week after the Games, the Berliners, who had spent the past fortnight doing their best to be friendly to their visitors, suddenly showed their true faces. One who witnessed it was Domnitsa Lanitis, who had stayed on in Berlin for a few days after the Games. 'One day, I was on a tram,' she recalled, 'with a Greek lady – Mrs Spanidou – and her daughter. However, Mrs Spanidou was rather fat, and she was pushing against people as she tried to get past them. The Germans began to moan at her when she tried to get past. "Now that the Games are over," she said to them, "I can see your politeness has finished." It was clear that the Germans had been told to be nice to us.' Clearly, a tussle on a tram can happen in any city at any time, but the departing athletes noticed some far more sinister undertones. Adolph Kiefer saw one when he was on a coach on the way to the airport to fly to Holland. 'One of our party took some pictures of the airport,' Kiefer said, 'and this big guy came along, took his camera, removed the film, and handed the camera back to him, saying, "We don't take pictures of airports". When we took off, we weren't allowed to look out of the windows and we had to shut our blinds.'

Despite their bragging to Charles Lindbergh, the Germans were clearly attempting to conceal their ever growing Luftwaffe. It had been impossible to do so over the entire Olympic fortnight, however, especially when some of the four thousand athletes were rather more nosy than was good for them. Archie Williams and his fellow American athlete, the miler Gene Venzke, were both interested in planes, and one day at the Olympic village they decided to take a look at the nearby airport. 'We crawled under this fence,' Williams recalled, 'and someone yells, "Halt!" Well, it was *Hogan's Heroes* time. We got the hell out of there. Then we saw this plane go by – whoosh! I'd never seen a plane that fast before.' Williams asked one of the Germans what sort of plane it was, and he was told it was a mail plane. The 400 metres runner was unconvinced. 'Well, shit, that was an ME-109 [. . .] And they were supposed to be flying gliders. That was the fastest "glider" in the world.' It was not just the air force which was being built up. On 24 August, just one week after the Games, Hitler extended the length of conscripted military service from one year to two, which had the effect of increasing the size of the army from 600,000 to 800,000 – the same size as it had been at the outset of the First World War.

In the immediate aftermath of the Games, however, public attention in Britain and the United States was more focused on the performance of their athletes. Despite the impact of Jesse Owens, Germany was undeniably the victor of the Games, winning a total of 89 medals, of which 33 were gold. The United States came second, with 56 medals, of which 24 were gold. The British came tenth with just 14 medals, of which a mere four were gold. The British performance was considered dire. A letter to the *Daily Telegraph* from a Reverend F. Brompton Harvey of Leicestershire summed up the national mood: 'The failure of Englishmen in the Olympic Games should give a jolt to our national complacency. England is admittedly the Mother Country of sport; yet the pick of her athletes [. . .] have been outclassed.' Harold Abrahams thought that such complaints were unfair. The gold medal winner argued that the difference between winning gold and bronze or silver was so slight that 'any argument as to a nation's prowess based on mere victories is apt to be somewhat fallacious'. In fact, Abrahams questioned the very desirability of the German approach, which insisted on victories. 'There are those who would urge us to make a similar effort,' he wrote, 'but not only do I doubt whether we could manufacture the psychological background necessary for such a drive, but even if we could, I have even more serious doubts as to whether it would be desirable.' Part of the reason for Britain's failure was that her athletes were still truly amateurs, many of whom, like Bill Roberts, had full-time jobs. Germany had coddled their athletes, given them time off work, and had all but paid some of them. As Sir Robert Vansittart acidly commented, 'One does not feel much amateur spirit in the air, but rather a jealously-guarded political demonstration.'

Avery Brundage's reaction to the American showing was to call for a similar programme of nationwide physical training to that seen in

Germany. Although he was broadly pleased with the athletes' performance, Brundage suggested that the United States had a lot to learn from the Germans, with their 'perfect national organisation, the intensive training and the almost supernatural determination to win'. 'If we want to hold our own,' he said, 'we will have to begin to train in the same intensive way and on a national scale. We must cease to be a group of athletic clubs and must become a national organisation.' It was not just the Germans' sporting prowess which Brundage admired, however. 'We can learn much from Germany,' he said in a speech a few weeks later. 'We too, if we wish to preserve our institutions, must stamp out communism. We too must take steps to arrest the decline of patriotism [. . .] Germany had progressed as a nation out of her discouragement of five years ago into a new spirit of confidence in herself.'

The Nazis were of course delighted with the German showing. *Der Angriff* was exultant: 'If one may be permitted to speak of intoxication from joy, then every German may be said to have reeled from happiness. It is an odd but familiar experience and once again we have discovered after sturdy struggles what reserves are contained within us.' The German performance naturally pleased Hitler, who saw the Games as proof that Germany was once more a strong nation. What was more, the results could be improved on; a few years later, he called for the formation of 'Reich Schools' that would be 'inspired with the principles of National Socialism'.

> The results we obtained at the Olympic Games have shown me that these Reich Schools will be able to raise the standard of German youth to an exceptionally high level. The British, notwithstanding the advantages of their college system of education, were only able to win eight gold medals [*sic* – four]. The young sportsmen of the Reich took thirty-three! Think, then, what will happen when the youth of the whole Reich will receive its upbringing, including intensive sports training, in the new Reich schools!

Furthermore, Hitler's opinion of the Olympics had now completed its inversion. A festival he once regarded as a 'an invention of Jews and Freemasons', and which 'could not possibly be put on in a Reich ruled by National Socialists', was now something he wanted to Germanise. In the spring of 1937, Hitler visited Albert Speer in his

Berlin offices to look at a model of a new stadium that would seat 400,000 spectators. While Hitler inspected it, Speer told him he was concerned that the athletic field in the projected stadium did not have the correct Olympic proportions. Hitler dismissed Speer's worry. 'No matter,' he said. 'In 1940 the Olympic Games will take place in Tokyo. But thereafter they will take place in Germany for all time to come, in this stadium. And then we will determine the measurements of the athletic field.'

One issue arising from the Games that the Nazis found hard to explain was the success of the American black athletes. The solution was found in a pseudo-scientific claim that with an abnormally large 'animal' heel-bone, the blacks were bound to be faster. Therefore, as the blacks were in fact animals and not humans, the Americans had cheated – they might as well have entered racehorses. Such thinking was not confined to Germany. On 22 August, *The Economist* noted that 'persons of Aryan sympathies in England have written to the Press suggesting that negroes should be excluded from the Olympic Games on the ground of their "physical abnormality"'. *The Spectator* regarded the 'wonderful negroes' as the heroes of the Games, observing that 'the real trouble is that the success of the Japanese and negroes throws doubt, even in German minds, on the supremacy of the white races'.

Nevertheless, to Nazi minds, the Olympics proved the efficacy of their system of government. If the Games were a political litmus test, then the result was a triumph for fascism. fascist Germany had beaten the liberal United States. Fascist Italy had beaten the liberal France. Totalitarian Japan had beaten the liberal Britain. As the *Deutsche Volkwirkschaft* pointed out: 'The preparations rested on the totality of the nationalist art of government and its fundamental idea of the community of the whole people. The world stands in honest admiration before this work because it has totalitarian character. Without unitary will, that which today has astonished the world would have been impossible. It is the supreme achievement of the totalitarian state.' For the time being, this 'unitary will' was being harnessed to produce gold medals. What diplomats such as Sir Robert Vansittart feared was how it was going to be used in the future. 'These tense, intense people are going to make us look a C3 nation if we elect to continue haphazard,' he wrote, 'and they will want to do something with this stored energy [. . .] These people are the most formidable proposition that has ever been formulated; they are in strict training now, not for the Olympic Games, but for breaking some other and emphatically unsporting world records, and perhaps the world as well.'

Thomas Wolfe would have agreed with Vansittart's presentiments. For the novelist, Germany did not send a team to the Olympics; rather the entire country acted as the team. 'The whole united power of Germany's enormous organising and disciplining genius went into their effort,' he wrote in his notebook in the autumn of 1936. 'No one really knows how strong America is: we are a loose-jointed, shambling, and disengaged people. But from the effort of these games some idea may be gained of Germany's strength. It was an enormous strength, and it was collected in a single stroke as compact as the blow of a fist.'

Such sentiments were shared by only a very few athletes. The victorious Godfrey Brown, for example, showed very little 'honest admiration' for the XIth Olympiad. 'The fact is that some of us went to Berlin with a mistaken idea – that we were going to watch or take part in a sports meeting,' he wrote. 'Instead, we were treated to a piece of political propaganda [. . .] On the last day we were inflicted with the sight of thousands of gross, flabby Germans, so-called Hitler Youth, clad in nothing but shorts and performing ridiculous evolutions on the grass. We cried, "Sweep on, you fat and greasy citizens," and made a dash for the first train home.'

Charles Leonard's opinion was less splenetic. 'I wouldn't say the Games were hijacked by the Nazis,' he said, 'but they were used for propaganda purposes. They were determined that the German nation should capitalise on this good feeling that they were out to generate. I talked to a German woman at the embassy in Berlin, and she said, "Frankly we're trying to make a good impression in Berlin". She didn't say, "We are trying to redeem our bad reputation from the last war", but that's what she meant. They did very well.' Leonard also noticed numerous manifestations of the 'unitary will' during his visit.

I have seen a number of mass demonstrations – 5000 or more boys and girls performing their calisthenics and field exercises without error. They are well trained and disciplined; they strive for perfection. It may be because this is a sort of festive time, but it strikes me that everyone is doing his very best – for Germany. Incidentally, there is much movement in formation – columns of twos and fours – all in step and all singing. The army sings going anywhere; kids march around town singing stirring marching tunes, happily. National flags fly out from at least half the windows. In summary, NATIONALISM sticks out – even to the ends of their noses. Competitors do not win medals as individuals – Germany wins each and every one of them. The people have realised one thing – they must all pull together to survive; so far they are sticking together peacefully and we hope they do not try to force Nationalist Germany down someone else's throat.

The majority of athletes, however, were not as sensitive to such matters. As Alfred Gerdes said, 'The Games gave Germany a big push – the visitors almost forgot that Hitler stuff.' Adolph Kiefer thought that the Nazis had done nothing but good for the Games. 'It made the Olympics more popular,' he said. 'It brought it to the attention of the public.' What was more, the hosts had succeeding in making a good impression: 'Germany was encouraging health, sports, exercise for all ages, and it was obvious that it was having an effect on the morale of the people.' Iris Cummings denied that she had taken part in a 'piece of political propaganda'. 'We didn't feel that way,' she said. 'And we didn't come across anyone else who felt that way. We were not the pawns of anybody. The idea of being used like that is counter to the Olympic ideal. The Olympic spirit and the competitors are not there to support a particular regime. If there is a violation of the rules of the Olympics, then it is up to the IOC to deal with it. They're not always very strong, but that's what they're operating under.'

The problem with Cummings' argument is that just by being in Berlin – even in good faith – the athletes participated in a show that helped the hosts to promote Nazism. There were no gas chambers as yet, but there were certainly pogroms, political murders and concentration camps, all of which were widely known and reported in every newspaper in the democracies. This is why Adolph Kiefer is wrong when he claims that it was 'a few years after the Games that things went wrong'. Things were already going very badly wrong, and yet the athletes chose to ignore it, or thought it too sanctimonious if they cared. João Havelange put it bluntly when he said, 'At that age we didn't think about people. As Olympic athletes we were never disturbed [by such matters] and we had a very good life.'

Most of the athletes were of course very young. Not only were many of them apolitical, but they also had a hunger to achieve some personal sporting glory. If older and supposedly wiser heads had deemed that going to Berlin was acceptable, then who were they to contradict that? And once they had returned, the last thing they would admit to was that they had been used as pawns by the Nazis. They had been there only for the sport, and that was all. For them, the Olympics were above politics, and therefore by being an Olympian they were running over hallowed moral high ground above the mire of grubby talk of boycotts and propaganda. The only problem was that Olympism had been dirtied and sullied as well, which resulted in a drastic lowering of that high ground. The Nazis had defaced Olympism by corrupting its leaders, who had been bribed, had lied and had actively taken part in the discrimination against Jews.

When Coubertin was interviewed after the Games about the question of propaganda, he replied by asking, 'What's the difference between propaganda for tourism – like in the Los Angeles Olympics of 1932 – or for a political regime? The most important thing is that the Olympic movement made a successful step forward.' Leaving aside the issue of the massive difference between promoting tourism and promoting Nazism, Coubertin's response was extraordinary. All that mattered to him by now was that his beloved Olympics were safe. What good they stood for no longer mattered – they were now little more than a circus, or rather a flea circus. Besides, Coubertin was in no position to say anything critical of the Games, for fear that the Nazis would reveal his dirty little secret. If the athletes had known it, how many would have felt comfortable about going to the Games? With the athletes being presented with only a sanitised version of the truth, they were not in a good position to judge. As Thomas Wolfe wrote, 'There have been too many false stories – too many distortions of fact, twisting of evidence, and just plain lies.' Despite Jesse Owens, the Games did propagandise the regime, and they did it well. 'I'm afraid the Nazis have succeeded with their propaganda,' wrote William Shirer on 16 August. 'First, the Nazis have run the Games on a lavish scale never before experienced, and this has appealed to the athletes. Second, the Nazis have put up a very good front for the general visitors, especially the big businessmen.' Owens may have shown the world that Hitler was wrong – and the world had a good laugh at the dictator's expense – but Hitler laughed last. Germany had not just won the athletic games, it had also won the political games.

It would take many years for some of the participants to realise what their attendance represented. In 1974, thirty-eight years after the Games, Harold Abrahams was interviewed about going to Berlin. 'I wasn't happy – being Jewish – about going at all,' he replied, 'but it was an enormous temptation being asked by the BBC – the first time they'd broadcast the Olympics. I went, I'm not sure I was right . . . it's rather . . . you know . . . I was advised by Lord Vansittart that it was a good thing to go, to let the Germans see that over here Jewish people were treated just like anyone else. But I'm not terribly happy about having been there.'

Jesse Owens may have been the hero of the Olympic fortnight, but he was rarely treated as one. The first sign that all would not be well came immediately after the Games, when along with the rest of the team he was invited to compete in Sweden. Owens, who had no regular income, had decided, however, that he needed to capitalise on his success by going back to the United States to take up some of the numerous and lucrative offers he was receiving. Avery Brundage was furious and threw him out of the AAU, thereby ending Owens' career. The normally mild-mannered athlete was livid: 'All we athletes get out of this Olympic business is a view out of a train or airplane window,' he told reporters. 'It gets tiresome, it really does. This track business is becoming one of the biggest rackets in the world. It doesn't mean a darned thing to us athletes. The AAU gets the money. It gets all the money collected in the United States and then comes over to Europe and takes half the proceeds. A fellow desires something for himself.'

Despite numerous appeals against his expulsion, Owens was never to regain his amateur status. The lucrative offers that had flooded in never quite materialised, and Owens was reduced to running against race-horses up and down the country. If that was not *infra dig* enough for the world's fastest man, he soon found himself fronting a dry-cleaning business and then working as a petrol pump attendant. Owens eventually filed for bankruptcy, and matters improved as he set about reinventing himself as a United States 'goodwill ambassador', travelling round the world preaching the American way and demonstrating his still-considerable athletic prowess. His espousal of what his fellow blacks regarded as 'white values' led to accusations that he was an Uncle Tom, a charge that Owens frequently refuted.

In 1966, Owens was successfully prosecuted for tax evasion. His problems with the IRS were similar to those experienced by his great friend Joe Louis, although Owens merely had to pay a small fine rather than suffer anything like Louis's ignominious return to the ring in order to finance the interest on his tax debt. By the 1970s, Owens was partly rehabilitated. A grand old man, he made countless appearances at awards dinners and various functions, telling and retelling tales of his time in Berlin, tales that grew slightly taller on each occasion. His health was rapidly failing, however, chiefly because he was a heavy smoker – a habit he had acquired at the age of thirty-two. Switching to a pipe made little difference, and in 1980 Jesse Owens died of lung cancer. At least he lived to a good age. His fellow gold-winning African-American, Cornelius Johnson, contracted bronchial pneumonia while working as a ship's baker in 1946. He died while being taken from the ship to a California hospital. He was only thirty-two.

Owens returned to the scene of his glories just once, in 1951. At his hotel in Berlin, he was met by a woman and a young boy. They explained that they were the family of Luz Long – the young boy being Long's son, Karl, who had seen his father only three times before he had been killed fighting in Italy during the war. Owens and Karl wrote to each other until Owens' death, the former considering Karl to be one of his best friends.

Glenn Morris did have an affair with Leni Riefenstahl that August. 'We couldn't control our feelings,' the director recalled. 'They were so powerful that Morris did not rejoin his team, and I imagined that he was the man I could marry. I had lost my head completely. I forgot almost everything, even my work.' Morris returned to the United States, leading the ticker-tape parade through New York. The black athletes – including Owens – were crammed into two cars, but Morris had a car to himself. Although he married Charlotte, he continued to write to Riefenstahl. She sent him dramatic photographs that she had taken, photographs that helped Morris win the part of Tarzan starring opposite the beautiful Eleanor Holm.

The film, *Tarzan's Revenge*, was made in 1938, and it was a spectacular turkey. There was no chemistry between him and his co-star, who regarded him as 'a dull country boy'. *Variety* magazine was damning: 'Even the youngsters, at which this type of production is aimed, will not be much impressed.' With his Hollywood career stillborn, Morris found himself confronting failure for the first time. He was not good at it, and he and Charlotte got divorced just three years after they married.

With the outbreak of war, Morris joined the navy. As a lieutenant, he was assigned to the USS *Banner*, an attack transport ship. Morris's job was to act as the beachmaster, which involved getting the men from the ship on to solid ground during an attack. Being a beachmaster was not an easy task, but Morris appeared to perform his duties well. On 9 January 1945, however, Morris snapped during a landing on the Philippines. 'Lieutenant Morris ran up behind me and a couple of others on the beach brandishing a submachine gun,' recalled Jim Larson, one of Morris's comrades, 'swinging it around and shouting, "Where's my gas mask? I'm going to shoot whoever took my gas mask!" He was yelling wildly, pointing the submachine gun at all of us.' Larson found the gas mask back in the landing craft, and gave it to the wild-eyed Morris. 'I don't know what would have happened if the gas mask had not been there,' said Larson.

Morris was never to recover from the war. Suffering from post-traumatic stress disorder, although it was never diagnosed as such, he spent his remaining three decades drifting, like Owens, from menial job to menial job. He was a steel rigger, a construction worker, a security guard and even a parking attendant before he was committed to a veteran's hospital suffering from severe psychological problems. A heavy smoker, he died in 1974 from heart disease. The descent from Olympus had been especially harsh.

Rie Mastenbroek was another star of Berlin for whom post-Olympic happiness was to prove elusive. After the welcoming Rotterdam crowds had dissipated, Mastenbroek found that her trainer, 'Ma'

Braun, wanted to take control of more than just her life in the pool. 'She tried to get my mother out of official parenthood over me,' said Mastenbroek. 'This was meant to bring me completely under Ma's influence.' Braun even took the case to court, claiming that Mrs Mastenbroek was an unfit mother, evidenced by the fact that Rie had been born out of wedlock. (Mastenbroek's parents in fact remained together for forty-six years.) The judge ruled against Braun, with the result that Mastenbroek's links with her trainer were severed.

The experience deterred the Queen of Berlin from competitive swimming, and Mastenbroek became a swimming instructor, a decision that she was soon to regret. On 16 August 1937, just a year and a day after she had won her last gold medal, the Dutch Swimming Association ruled that she now had to be considered a professional, and would no longer be allowed to compete. Mastenbroek protested, as she did not have a teaching diploma, but the Association was adamant. A succession of jobs as a nanny followed, until she married in 1939 and had two children, a boy and a girl. The marriage ended in 1945, however, and in order to raise the children she worked as an interpreter, a bookkeeper in a doctor's clinic and even as a building inspector. She married again, this time happily, and bore another son.

Mastenbroek never enjoyed good health, however. Even as early as 1935 she had suffered from breathlessness in races, which the doctors diagnosed as being due to a problem with her thyroid gland. Some thought she had a mysterious blood disease, although she was later to discover that the most likely explanation was that she suffered from extremely low blood pressure. One doctor said to her, 'We certainly would like to know what your achievements in sport would have been if you had performed in a healthy and normal body!' Mastenbroek died in November 2003, a forgotten and undervalued figure.

Eleanor Holm retained her bumptiousness until she died in January 2004. After the Games, as well as appearing in the abysmal *Tarzan's Revenge*, Holm also starred in many of Billy Rose's aquacades alongside Buster Crabbe and Johnny Weissmuller, which earned her some $4,000 ($50,000 in 2005) a week. Holm married Rose after divorcing Art Jarrett, and she gave up swimming just before the war. Her marriage to Rose ended in a spectacular divorce case in the early 1950s, which was famously referred to as the 'War of the Roses'. Holm later married her true love, oil executive Tom Whalen. She spent her days playing tennis and perusing the *Wall Street Journal*, but still retained her flirtatiousness even into old age. In 1999, at a reception at the White House, she said to Bill Clinton, 'Mr President, you're really a good-looking dude.'

Jack Lovelock gave up running shortly after the Olympics and concentrated on his medical training. During the war, he served as a major in Northern Ireland, and then moved to New York with his American wife, Cynthia James. However, he regularly suffered from dizzy spells after being thrown from a horse in 1940, an accident in which he had broken a leg and an arm, as well as damaging an eye. On the afternoon of 28 December 1949, Lovelock called his wife and two daughters to say that he would be returning home from work at the Manhattan Hospital early, as he was feeling dizzy. Instead of taking a taxi, he went on the subway. Standing at the platform at Church Avenue station, the dizziness grew worse, and Lovelock collapsed, falling into the path of an oncoming train. He was killed instantly, just a few days before his fortieth birthday. Although he had spent much of his adult life away from New Zealand, the country rightly regards him as one of its heroes. Bars, streets and playing fields are named after him, and he has been the subject of a novel and a play. 'New Zealand doesn't have any myths yet, other than the Maori ones,' said Roger Robinson, an English professor at Victoria University. 'I believe Lovelock has the makings of a mythic figure.'

Son Ki-Jung was another who attained mythical status in his homeland. After the Games, he returned to Japanese-controlled Korea as a national hero. The newspaper *Dong-a-Ilbo* published a picture of Son Ki-Jung in which the rising sun on his vest had been painted out. The Japanese were furious and jailed eight people connected with the paper and ceased its publication for nine months. Japanese rule in Korea ended in 1945, and three years later Son Ki-Jung carried the South Korean flag into the stadium for the opening ceremony of the London Olympics. A prouder moment was to come forty years later, however. During the opening of the 1988 Seoul Olympics, a sprightly old man bounded into the stadium carrying the Olympic torch. Leaping with joy, Son Ki-Jung reduced his entire nation to tears.

Although Son Ki-Jung had been good to the Olympic movement, it proved to be less good to him. In October 1983 the Korean Olympic Committee wrote to the IOC, asking for Son's medal to be ascribed to Korea rather than to Japan. 'In view of the Olympic ideals and humanity to be achieved,' wrote Man-Lip Choy, the KOC's secretary-general, 'we hope that you should kindly refer to our proposal to correct the nationalities of the Olympic winners who participated in the Olympic Games not under their original nationalities.' The IOC refused the request, claiming that it would be in contravention of Rule 8 of the Olympic charter, which stated that 'only citizens or nationals of a country may represent that country and compete in the Olympic Games'. 'Thus, in accordance with the "Olympic Charter" and the principles of international law,' said the response, 'modification of the nationality of an athlete who has competed in Games already held is unfeasible and legally unjustified.' This was nonsense. Not only was the Korean request not a contravention of Rule 8, but neither was it asking for something that was illegal under international law. The IOC is not a public body, but a private one, and it is up to it and its national committees if it wishes to alter its records. Presumably the IOC did not wish to antagonise the Japanese. The Koreans did not give up, and four years later the KOC again requested that Son's nationality should be changed, and even asked that the inscription on the stadium be altered. Once again, the IOC refused, saying that it would be an 'alteration to the Olympic history'. Despite his treatment, Son remained a devoted Olympian, insisting that without the Olympics there would be more war. When it was put to him that the Berlin Games did not stop the Second World War, he replied, 'That was the fault of politicians.' Son died at the age of ninety in November 2002. The inscription at the stadium in Berlin still bears the word '*Japon*' after his name.

It would be tempting to say that those who won gold medals at Berlin suffered some sort of curse, but it was not so. Bill Roberts stayed in the timber trade, although in a more rarefied form, as he became a successful antiques dealer. In 1984, Roberts' house in Cheshire was broken into. The thieves took many valuables, but the biggest blow to Roberts was the loss of his gold medal. Devastated, he thought he would never see the medal again. Help came in the form of Sir Arthur Gold, a former high jumper and a senior

administrator in the world of British athletics. Gold had heard that
the moulds for the original medals had been taken to the United
States after the war, and he was able to use his influence to get
another gold medal struck from the original mould. In 1990 Roberts
was presented with the new medal by Princess Anne, the president
of the British Olympic Committee. 'The replacement medal was of
much greater meaning to me than the original,' he explained. 'You
see, I knew where the Nazis had got their gold from to make those
medals in 1936, and the action of Sir Arthur, himself Jewish, and of
the German Olympic Committee more than fifty years later meant
so much more to me.' Roberts died in December 2001 at the age of
eighty-nine.

Helen Stephens retired from athletics shortly after the Games, and
played professional baseball and softball. Until 1952, she ran her own
semi-professional basketball team. She died in St Louis in 1994 at the
age of seventy-five. The fate of Stella Walsh was somewhat bizarre.
On 4 December 1980, the sixty-nine-year-old Walsh was shopping
in a discount store in Cleveland, Ohio, buying ribbons for the Polish
women's basketball team, who were shortly to play at Kent State
University. As she entered the car park, Walsh suddenly found herself
caught in the crossfire of a bank robbery that had gone wrong, and
was killed. Because she had died from unnatural causes, she was subjected to an autopsy, which revealed that she had both male and
female genitalia. Like everyone else, Stephens had always suspected
that something was not 'kosher' with her competitor at Berlin. Her
suspicions had been confirmed in 1975, when a friend told her that
she had seen Walsh actually having sex with a woman and that 'Stella
had male sex organs'. The friend was so shocked that she said she
would go to the police, whereupon Walsh punched her, and 'told
her if she did that, then Stella would "get her" when they returned
to Cleveland'.

At the time of writing – early 2006 – Dora Ratjen is still alive,
married and living quietly in Germany as Hermann after undergoing
corrective surgery. Before he retired, he ran a pub, and played a lot of
football. According to Elfriede Kaun, Ratjen was the subject of an
inquiry by the Reich Sports Ministry in 1938, after she was appre-
hended by some soldiers on a train, who suspected that she was a

foreign spy masquerading as a woman. 'The soldiers took her off the train,' Kaun recalled, 'and they took nude pictures of her and sent them to Berlin. A fellow athlete and I received letters from Berlin asking if we had known anything.' Kaun and Dorothy Odam are both alive, and live in Kiel and Croydon respectively. Odam has earned an MBE for her services to sport.

If Ratjen was coerced by some element of the Nazi regime to work for them, then there were some athletes who willingly helped the Nazis. One was Martinus Osendarp, who had gone on to win the 100 and 200 metres in the 1938 European Championships. When Germany occupied Holland in 1940, Osendarp joined not only the Dutch Nazi Party but also the SS, serving as a member of the Security Police. As a collaborator, Osendarp was successfully tried after the war and served four years in prison. After his release, he became a miner, and he died on 20 June 2002.

Robey Leibbrandt met his hero Adolf Hitler just after the Games. The boxer told the dictator that he was a huge admirer, and that he hoped that the Afrikaners would soon throw off the English yoke. 'Yes,' Hitler is reported to have said, 'the English, they are everywhere.' Leibbrandt spent the next few years on the boxing circuit, and returned to Germany in 1938 to study at the Reich Gymnastics Academy. When war broke out, Leibbrandt stayed in Germany, attending the leadership school in Neustralitz, where he became a glider pilot. He then joined the army, and trained as a parachutist. Itching to fight for both the Afrikaners and Nazism, Leibbrandt was the natural choice for Operation Weissdorn, which was an Abwehr plot to assassinate Jan Smuts and replace his government with one sympathetic to the Germans. The headstrong Leibbrandt was viewed with scepticism by some in the Nazi regime, but he was the best candidate available.

After a sea voyage of 9,000 miles, Leibbrandt was landed in a rubber dinghy at Mitchell's Bay in South Africa on 10 June 1941, equipped with nothing more than a radio, a suitcase and three bottles of soda water. The dinghy capsized, however, and Leibbrandt had to swim ashore empty handed. With some difficulty, the boxer managed to make contact with the Ossewa Brandwag, a militant anti-war, pro-Nazi Afrikaner organisation. Leibbrandt and the OB spent the next six months causing as much havoc as they could, but cursed with factionalism, poor planning and suspected infiltrators, they made little progress towards their goal of establishing an Afrikaner Reich. Leibbrandt never came close to assassinating Smuts, although the general had been warned that the renegade was out to kill him.

Leibbrandt was arrested on Christmas Eve of that year. He was not tried until the following November, in a case that lasted until March 1943, making it the longest criminal trial in South African history. Leibbrandt was unrepentant, even giving the Nazi salute in the court-room. When he was sentenced to death, he again saluted, and announced, 'I greet death! *Die Vierkleur Hoog!* [The Afrikaners high!]' Smuts commuted Leibbrandt's sentence to life imprisonment, however, and when the National Party won the election in 1948, he was pardoned and released. He married, and had five children, one of whom was called Izan – 'Nazi' backwards. Another was called Rayna, an anagram of 'Aryan'. Unlike many other Nazis, Leibbrandt was unashamedly unapologetic.

Diana Mosley also remained unapologetic in her admiration for Hitler. On 6 October 1936, she and Sir Oswald Mosley married in Goebbels' drawing room, in a short ceremony that was attended by the dictator, who gave them – somewhat unimaginatively – a silver photograph frame, although this cliché of a wedding present was at least emblazoned with the initials A.H. and the German eagle. Shortly after the outbreak of war, the Mosleys were interned under Defence Regulation 18B until 1943, after which they were placed under house arrest until the war's end. The couple eventually settled in France, and became friends of the Duke and Duchess of Windsor. They had two children, one of whom, Max, is the president of the FIA, the governing body of world motor sport. Mosley died in 1980, and Diana in August 2003 in Paris. The fate of her sister Unity Mitford was far more tragic. When war broke out, Unity was so distraught that she went to the English Garden in Munich, and shot herself in the head. The suicide attempt failed, and she was returned to Britain by the Nazis, although she was severely mentally disabled. It was too dangerous to remove the bullet, and she contracted meningitis caused by the swelling around it, which killed her in May 1948.

Helene Mayer also died young. Cancer claimed her in 1952 when she was just forty-one. Although she was no Nazi like Osendarp, her decision to salute on the podium earned her a notoriety that followed her to America. Her fellow German Jew, Gretel Bergmann, also made it to the United States, where in 1937 she won the US women's high jump championships with a jump of just over 1.57 metres – a height that she cleared easily. Bergmann refused to go back to Germany until 1999, when she opened a Berlin arena named in her honour. She is still alive.

Joachim von Ribbentrop was not a great success as the German ambassador to London. Although he felt sure that he would be able to integrate successfully into British society – he even sent his son Rudolf to Westminster School – he was loathed. His behaviour, such as giving King George VI a fascist salute, was regarded as bizarre, and he was unable to pull off an Anglo-German agreement. It is doubtful whether anybody could have done so, but Ribbentrop was hopelessly ill equipped. Ribbentrop fulfilled his dream of becoming the German foreign minister, however, when von Neurath resigned in February 1938. The war saw a diminution in his influence, although he was still found guilty of war crimes at the Nuremberg trial. He was hanged on 16 October 1946. Ribbentrop always maintained that the British were responsible for the war, and in particular one man. 'There are those who contend that Vansittartism and the hatred of Germany which this word implies were a result of Hitler's policy,' he wrote. 'To this I reply – and I believe with a better right: Hitler's policy was a consequence of Vansittart's policy in 1936.'

Ribbentrop's views are not widely shared today, much as Sir Robert Vansittart's views were not shared by many members of the British government. Ignored, sidelined, he was eventually kicked upstairs to the House of Lords. He regarded his diplomatic career as a failure. He died in 1957. Sir Eric Phipps became the ambassador to France in 1937, a post he held until his retirement two years later. He died in 1945.

The years after the Olympics were certainly kind to one man – Avery Brundage. Between 1936 and the start of the Second World War, Brundage courted the Nazis in order to win building contracts. On 8 August 1938 he received a letter from Tschammer und Osten that would have delighted him.

Mr von Halt forwarded your letter to me at the beginning of July, in which you asked whether your firm could participate in the building of the German Embassy in Washington. Having brought your proven record of your friendly attitude toward German sports before the responsible authorities, I can happily tell you that both the German foreign minister as well as General Building Inspector Speer have declared to me that you take part.

Brundage wrote back later that month, thanking Tschammer und Osten effusively. By November, however, the deal had fallen through, and the project was indefinitely postponed.

This did not stop Brundage maintaining immensely cordial links with those who were taking the world to war. On 20 October 1939, some seven weeks after the outbreak of hostilities in Europe, Brundage wrote to the Reich Sports Minister, expressing his desire that the war would end early so that the next Olympic Games could take place. Typically, he repeated his view that sport would be able to cure the world's ills. 'It is unfortunate that the sportsmen of the world are not numerous enough to demand boldly an armistice so that the Games can proceed normally,' he wrote. Brundage was more concerned about his beloved Games than those who were dying. For him, sport was seemingly more important than life itself.

The pro-German Brundage would have had no issue with the German subsuming of the Olympic movement into Nazism, a process made possible by Coubertin's death in 1937. With Lewald now removed from the German Olympic Committee, it fell to Diem to start permanently Nazifying the Olympics. Little by little, the Germans staked their territory. The International Olympic Institute was founded in Berlin, and placed under the authority of the Reich Sports Minister. The IOC bulletin was incorporated into Diem's own Olympic magazine. The Olympic Cup was awarded to the Strength through Joy movement. The Olympic Diploma was presented to Leni Riefenstahl for *Olympia*. Karl Ritter von Halt joined the IOC executive committee in place of Lewald. The list was exhaustive.

When Belgium was invaded in 1940, Baillet-Latour found that it was not just his country which was being taken over, but also the Olympics. Carl Diem was dispatched to see the president, to tell him that he would be able to continue in his role, but that the Germans meant to 'rejuvenate' the Games, with a new IOC stuffed with German members. Baillet-Latour had little choice. If he hadn't been able to stop the Nazis stealing all his racehorses, then there was no way he could stop them stealing the Olympics. He died in January 1942, a broken man after the death of his son the previous month. Although he requested a simple family funeral, the Nazis put on a large service at the St Jacques Cathedral in Brussels. Typically, they turned the event into a propaganda opportunity, with an Olympic flag draping the coffin, over which was placed a swastika-festooned wreath. A German honour guard stood next to it, and Hitler and Goebbels sent flowers. With Baillet-Latour out of the way, Diem was now able to travel to Lausanne to take the IOC's and Coubertin's papers to Berlin. His efforts were stymied, however, by a Madame Lydia Zanchi, who hid the most important documents in a cellar. She then alerted Sigfrid Edstrøm in Sweden, who travelled to Switzerland later in 1942, and hid the papers in a bank vault. It is thanks to the efforts of Madame Zanchi and Edstrøm that books such as this can be written.

For Diem, the war provided an excellent testing ground for the value of sport and of Olympism. In June 1940 he had declared that the military victory over France was due, in part, to the German soldiers', officers' and leaders' love of sports. 'Thus it came to the storming of Poland, Holland, Belgium and France,' Diem crowed, 'to the triumphant race to a better Europe!' Five years later, in March 1945, the troilism between Nazism, Olympism and war was celebrated at the Olympic Stadium itself. Gathered there were thousands of Hitler Youth, who were about to do battle with the Russians as they assaulted Berlin. Speaking to them was none other than Diem, who called upon them to show 'the Olympic spirit' by refusing to capitulate. In case this was not enough to strengthen the boys' backbones, execution stakes were set up around the stadium, ready to be used if there were any displays of cowardice. Two thousand of the children Diem addressed that day were killed. There is no doubt that some of their blood spilled on to Diem's hands. Nevertheless, he was one of the few Nazis who managed to be completely rehabilitated after the war. He was even seen as an anti-Nazi, an impression brought about by his reputation as an intellectual. He died in 1962. Theodor Lewald also survived the war, and died in 1947.

Karl Ritter von Halt had a good war as well. He assumed the position of acting Reich Sports Minister when Tschammer und Osten died in March 1943, and like Diem took part in the defence of Berlin. As a leading Nazi, however, he was incarcerated after the war, locked up in Buchenwald of all places, and finally released in 1950. For both him and Diem, life was tough in post-war Germany, but matters were significantly helped by Avery Brundage, who sent them food parcels from the United States. Brundage, who was now vice-president of the IOC under Sigfrid Edström, did not seem to mind that both Germans had not only been convinced Nazis but had also attempted to steal the Games from the IOC. No matter. Brundage would do anything to support his old friends, even lie for them. In October 1950, the American testified that von Halt was a 'gentleman of the highest calibre'. 'He has never been in politics, he was never a Nazi, and he is worthy of the highest confidence.' These were lies, and Brundage must have known them to be so. Not only was acting as the Reich Sports Minister a political role, but von Halt had also been a brigade leader in the SA, having joined the Nazi Party in 1932. He was a complete Nazi. By 1957, von Halt had regained his seat on the executive committee of the IOC, which he held until 1963, the year before his death.

Brundage became head of the IOC in 1952. He continued bitterly to oppose any form of professionalism within the Olympic movement, and disqualified the legendary Austrian skier Karl Schranz during the 1972 Winter Olympics in Sapporo on the grounds that he was a professional. Despite Schranz collecting a petition with several thousand signatures that testified that he was in fact an amateur, Brundage was not to be moved. Brundage is best remembered, however, for being the head of the IOC during the 1972 Munich Olympics, when Palestinian terrorists took eleven Israeli athletes hostage. Controversially, Brundage insisted that the Games 'must go on', a decision that earned him worldwide opprobrium. Many of the hostages were later killed during an appallingly botched rescue attempt at the airport. In 1973, Brundage married a German princess many years his junior in Garmisch-Partenkirchen, the German town that had hosted the 1936 Winter Olympics. He died there two years later. Although Brundage had made the Olympic movement immensely strong, he had severely stained it with fascism. It is a stain that today's IOC is still trying to bleach out.

Finally, there were many who competed in 1936 who became the victims of the regime that they had unwittingly helped to promote. At least twenty-one members of the Polish Olympic team lost their lives in the war, either in battle, in the resistance or, like fifth-placed 5,000 metres runner Jozef Noji, in a camp such as Auschwitz. Twenty-five German medal winners were killed or went missing in action. Silvano Abba, the bronze medal winner in the pentathlon, was killed leading his battalion at Stalingrad. (Gotthardt Handrick survived the war, as did Leonard, who spent the war at Fort Benning. Leonard went on to command the 27th Infantry in Korea in 1953, as well as the 1st Cavalry Division, before retiring with the rank of major-general.) Colonel Komorowski went on to lead the Polish Home Army, and as General Bor-Komorowski directed the Warsaw Rising of 1944 that was so brutally put down by the Germans. The photograph taken of him with Hitler at the Games was used by the Nazis to help track him down. He surrendered on 2 October, and was sent to Colditz. After the war, he settled in London, as the Russians would not allow him back to his homeland. From 1947 to 1949 he was the prime minister of the Polish government-in-exile, and he died in 1966 at the age of seventy-one. The British Labour government refused to send a representative to the funeral for fear of upsetting the Russians. In 1984, Komorowski's son, Adam, was invited to the White House, where he received the Legion of Merit on behalf of his late father. Ten years later, Adam exhumed his parents from Gunnersbury cemetery in North London, and took their remains back to Poland, where they were given a state funeral.

There were many more victims. Endre Kabos, the Hungarian fencer, was imprisoned in a labour camp in Vác in Hungary. One of the Hungarian officers recognised him, however, and discharged him. Kabos joined the resistance, and on 4 November 1944, as he was driving a lorry loaded with explosives across the Margit Bridge, one of the last links between Buda and Pest, an oil pipe under the bridge exploded – most likely caused by a bomb – and Kabos and his lorry were thrown into the freezing Danube, where he was killed.

Despite his failure to win a medal, Werner Seelenbinder still struggled hard against Nazism. In 1938 he formally joined the Uhrig Group, and ran messages between Germany and Denmark until the Nazis stopped him travelling. During the war, Seelenbinder continued both his wrestling and his resistance work. He won the German championship in 1940 and 1941, although this did not stop him being arrested on 4 February 1942. He was tortured for eight days, but he gave nothing away. For two and a half years he endured nine camps and prisons, often being locked up in their punishment blocks for helping Soviet prisoners. And then, in September 1944, he was tried by the People's Court in the last of four trials of the Uhrig Group. He was sentenced to death. On 24 October 1944, in Brandenburg prison, Werner Seelenbinder was beheaded with an axe. Just before his death, he wrote a farewell letter.

> The time has now come for me to say goodbye. In the time of my imprisonment I must have gone through every type of torture a man can possibly endure. Ill health and physical and mental agony, I have been spared nothing. I would have liked to have experienced the delights and comforts of life, which I now appreciate twice as much, with you all, with my friends and fellow sportsmen, after the war. The times I had with you were great, and I lived off of them during my incarceration, and wished back that wonderful time. Sadly fate has now decided differently, after a long time of suffering. But I know that I have found a place in all your hearts and in the hearts of many sports followers, a place where I will always hold my ground. This knowledge makes me proud and strong and will not let me be weak in my last moments. My dear Father! I am sorry I can't spare you this pain, having given you so much pleasure with my sporting success. So, good health! I know you won't forget me. Give my best wishes to all my acquaintances and fellow sportsmen.

Seelenbinder's ashes are buried at the site of his old club, the Berolina 03 Sports Club stadium in Berlin. Unlike so many at the XIth Olympiad of the Modern Era, Seelenbinder was a rare thing. He was a good sport.

Postscript

The Sprinters

Owens the nigger is sprinting,
The Aryans tasting defeat.
The blond arena is musing,
Der Fuehrer frowns in his seat.
But more cheerfully they may consider
All the Jewish women and men
Who ran for their lives in the streets –
With them they caught up in the end.

Nordahl Grieg,
translated by Lars Finsen

Acknowledgements

I OWE AN enormous debt to the many sportsmen and sportswomen I have interviewed. As the Berlin Olympics are now seventy years distant, many of the competitors are extremely elderly, and I am very grateful to them for taking the trouble to speak to me. They also showed me much hospitality, and in many cases fed and watered me, which went beyond the call of any interviewee's duty. Although their names are listed in the Bibliography, I would also like to thank their family members, without whom many of the interviews would not have taken place. They include Pippa Ayres, Doug Ayres, Eva Baier, Heidi Leseur, Barbara Bishop Popovsky, Kathleen Kelly and Land Washburn.

I have received much linguistic assistance from Tory Wilks, who translated countless fiendish German documents, and carried out some telephone interviews with me. She has been a boon, as has Edgar Bettridge, who translated the relevant sections of Goebbels' diaries. My Bulgarian is non-existent, and here I relied on Nadka Gouneva's services. She can be reached at gouneva@aol.com. Belinda Venning and Pippa Campbell used their knowledge of Italian and Spanish to contact Olympic associations around the world. In Korea, Andrew Salmon fished out many newspaper articles relating to Son Ki-Jung, for which I am very grateful. In Kiel, Berit Odebrecht helped me interview Elfriede Kaun, a job she undertook with much skill at the last minute.

Tracking down the surviving athletes has been no easy task. Some Olympic organisations are extremely helpful while others are downright useless. The useful ones include the United States Olympic Committee, where the mighty fine Cindy Stinger even went to the trouble of sticking stamps on to my letters. Chris Baillieu, who represents British Olympians, was no less helpful in putting me in touch with veterans of Berlin. At the British Olympic Association itself, Ellen Shoesmith was very accommodating in allowing me free access to their archives. There are good and bad archives as well, but among the best was that at the University of Illinois, where Deborah Pfeiffer tolerated the beeping and fake shutter sound of my digital camera for days. Archives that allow digital photography make the task of writing books like this so much easier. It enables researchers to view documents in the comfort of their own homes, rather than spending weeks in dim basements. Archives that do not allow digital photography – please take note. At the IOC headquarters in Lausanne, the ebullient Ruth Beck-Perrenoud made research a joy, a task helped along by a liquid lunch overlooking the lake. I would also like to thank the staffs at the London Library, the Churchill College Archives Centre and the London School of Economics. I would *not* like to thank the British Library's Newspaper Archive at Colindale in London, where I found the truculence of the staff an immense hindrance, and the policy of closing at 4.45 utterly absurd. That institution needs to be pulled by its hair into the twenty-first century.

In the course of my travels, I have received much hospitality. I must particularly mention George Pendle and Charlotte Taylor, who allowed me to stay for several nights in their Manhattan apartment. I still maintain that I had nothing to do with jamming their front door lock. In Los Angeles, I was treated to a superb dinner by Simon and Lisa Andreae, and stood several drinks by Susie Tobin. In Illinois, I would like to thank the police officer who caught me speeding at 113 mph on the freeway, and was good enough to call it 95 mph, thereby sparing me a jail sentence. In Berlin, I would certainly not wish to thank the plainclothes policeman who arrested me on the Underground without a ticket, despite my reasonable protestations that the ticket machine at Kurfürstenstrasse Station was invisible.

I have also received much expert advice. In no order, this has come from Dr Christopher Young at Pembroke College, Cambridge, whom I chanced upon in Lausanne. He has been a real help and given me much confidence in my efforts to tackle the subject matter. Dr Michael Emmerich in Japan spent many hours on my behalf attempting to establish whether the writer and critic Masamune Hakucho wrote anything of note after his visit to the Games. Sadly, his quest proved to be fruitless. Dick Booth was kind enough to take time off from writing his history of sports broadcasting to discuss Harold Abrahams. Charles Palmer-Tomkinson supplied with me some useful information about his father James at the Winter Olympics. James Holland, James Owen, Tobyn Andreae and Adrian Weale have talked much good sense into me, and Olly Figg was shrewd in putting me on to Niemoller and Bonhoeffer. At John Murray, Roland Philipps and Rowan Yapp have been enormously supportive and professional. Claire Wachtel and Sean Griffin at HarperCollins have been equally good to me. Once again, Tif Loehnis and Luke Janklow have represented me with their usual charm and panache, and Claire Dippel, Molly Stirling, Rebecca Folland and Christelle Chamouton at the offices of Janklow & Nesbit have all proved to be great props.

It is traditional to reserve one's greatest thanks for one's family, and I shall prove to be no exception. My parents, Martin and Angela Walters, and my parents-in-law, Richard and Venetia Venning, have all been of inestimable help. My young children William and Alice, and my wife Annabel, have endured their father's and husband's absences with good grace. To invert Cyril Connolly's aphorism, there is no more sombre enemy of good family life than the man in his study, and I am so grateful that the three of them have given me the encouragement and the love that I so often required. They are more precious than any book, but at times it must have been hard for them to believe it. They all deserve gold medals.

Notes

NB: Abbreviations for archives and publications are listed in the Bibliography. I have not annotated quotes from any of those I interviewed privately during the research for this book. Interviews with João Havelange, Charles Leonard, Iris Cummings Critchell, Velma Dunn Ploessel, Albert Washburn, Annette Rogers Kelly, Alfred Gerdes and Elfrieda Kaun are all on mp3 and I am happy to burn any or all of them on to a CD if my costs are covered. Regrettably, the files are too large to be e-mailed. I can be contacted via my website, www.guywalters.com.

PROLOGUE

p. 1   **'I looked down that field'**: Jesse Owens, *Saturday Evening Post*, January/February 1936, quoted in Cohen, *The Games of '36*.

p. 1   **'The temperature was mild'**: XIth Olympic Games, Berlin, 1936, Official Report.

p. 1   **'Imagine you're sprinting'**: McRae, *Heroes without Country*.

p. 2   **'There never was a runner'**: TMG, 4 August 1936.

p. 2   **'Ralph and I ran neck and neck'**: Cohen, *The Games of '36*, p. 89.

p. 3   **'The greatest moment of all'**: ibid., p. 89.

CHAPTER ONE

p. 4   **'Gathered there on the morning of Sunday, 26 April 1931'**: There is some confusion as to when Berlin was awarded the Olympics. According to the *Official Bulletin of the IOC*, the meeting and vote took place on this date and the second vote took place in

Lausanne on Wednesday, 13 May 1931. Mandell, however, suggests that the decision was not announced until nearly a year later, which seems unlikely.

p. 9   **'It will be my most ardent desire to arrange the Olympic Games of 1936'**: CIO JO 1936S Notice 0083817.

p. 9   **'A French educationist and historian, Coubertin believed'**: For Coubertin's philosophies and revival of the Olympic Games, see Hill, *Olympic Politics*, and Guttmann, *The Olympics*.

p. 11   **'He seemed in excellent health, though he still pronounced that he wished soon to die'**: CIO JO 1936S CORR (Notice 0083816).

p. 15   **'During the last few weeks the foreign press reported in many instances'**: CIO JO 1936S CORR (ID Chemise 203362).

p. 16   **'On 5 May, Baillet-Latour wrote to Lewald, von Halt and the Duke of Mecklenburg-Schwerin'**: CIO JO 1936S Notice 0083817.

p. 16   **'An incensed von Halt replied on 16 May'**: CIO JO 1936S Notice 0083817.

p. 17   **'Baillet-Latour was clearly affronted by von Halt's attitude'**: CIO JO 1936S Notice 0083817.

p. 18   **'One Jew who was affected by these measures was the eighteen-year-old Margaret "Gretel" Bergmann'**: See Bergmann Lambert, *By Leaps and Bounds*.

p. 19   **'The President of the International Olympic Committee asked the German delegates if they would guarantee'**: *Official Bulletin of the IOC*, CIO.

p. 20   **'There is no room in the German land for Jewish leadership'**: Quoted in Mandell, *The Nazi Olympics*, p. 60.

CHAPTER TWO

p. 23   **'I am not personally fond of Jews and of the Jewish influence'**: ABC Box 42.

p. 24   **'Perhaps we are about to witness the development of a new race'**: Quoted in Maynard Brichford, 'Avery Brundage and Racism', 4th ISOR, p. 130.

p. 25   **'What I believe should be a useful move'**: ABC Box 42.

p. 25   **'On Saturday, 18 November 1933, the grand William Penn Hotel in downtown Pittsburgh'**: See NYT issues for 19 November 1933 onwards.

p. 26   **'One of them was a German–American called Dietrich Wortmann'**: For a discussion of Dietrich Wortmann see JSH, vol. 17, no. 2 (summer 1990), p. 214: 'Devotion to Whom? German–American Loyalty on the Issue of Participation in the 1936 Olympic Games', by Wendy Gray and Robert Knight Barney.

p. 27   **'1) Neither Reich government nor I have issued any order excluding Jewish members from athletic clubs'**: CIO JO 1936S CORR (ID Chemise 203362).

p. 27   **'At the American Olympic Association meeting in Washington on Wednesday 22nd'**: See NYT for coverage of meeting and reaction.

p. 28   **'. . . knew that the Jewish athletes in Germany were being discriminated against'**: JSH, vol. 11, no. 3 (winter 1984), p. 62: 'The Voices of Sanity: American Diplomatic Reports from the 1936 Berlin Olympiad', by George Eisen.

p. 29   **'On New Year's Day, 1934, Lord Aberdare wrote to Lewald'**: CIO JO 1936S CORR (ID Chemise 203362).

p. 30   **'He went on the attack, saying that the fate of the sportsmen Aberdare wrote about were of no consequence'**: CIO JO 1936S CORR (ID Chemise 203362).

p. 30   **'On 5 February, Aberdare adopted a far more conciliatory tone'**: CIO JO 1936S CORR (ID Chemise 203362).

p. 33   **'On 26 May Baillet-Latour cabled Brundage . . .'**: ABC Box 42.

p. 33   **'His opinion was shared by the IOC's vice-president, Sigfrid Edstrom . . .'**: ibid.

p. 34   **'Before Brundage arrived in Germany, he attended the International Association of Athletics Federations' meeting'**: See Guttmann, *The Games Must Go On*.

p. 35   **'The notes for the same speech also reveal'**: ABC Box 248.

p. 36   **'It came as no shock that Brundage returned to the United States'**: See NYT, 27/28 September 1934.

p. 39   **'On 16 December, Lord Aberdare wrote to Lewald'**: CIO JO 1936S CORR (ID Chemise 203362).

p. 40   **'Aberdare offered Lewald a pathetically simple solution'**: ibid.

p. 40   **'On 14 May 1935 he wrote to the British Olympic Association, asking'** BOA.

p. 41   **'In April, Arnold Lunn had written to Temple, telling him that he would be officiating'**: AL Box 2, Folder 31.

p. 41   **'One BOA member who supported Temple's letter was Harold Abrahams '** BOA.

p. 42   'Evan Hunter informed Temple that writing to Hitler': ibid.

p. 42   'In August, a brief interview in the *New York Times* with the Reich's sports leader': NYT, 12 August 1935.

p. 42   'We felt that we had suddenly been lifted from our everyday spheres of life': CIO JO 1936S ECRIT (Notice 0093288).

p. 44   'In September, Gustavus Kirby wrote to Avery Brundage, stating that he had heard that Mayer': ABC Box 29.

p. 45   'Sherrill recalled the meeting in oozing detail': FDR – see (c)(iii) in Bibliography.

p. 46   'But did so later in a letter to Marguerite Lehand': ibid.

p. 46   'At a lunch in Berlin with Tschammer und Osten': ibid.

p. 49   'The Jewish proposal to boycott the Games of the Eleventh Olympiad which I thought was safely buried last year': ABC Box 42.

p. 51   'On 27 September, he wrote to the key members on the AOC': ABC Box 29.

p. 51   'In October he wrote to Garland, Sherrill and Jahncke': CIO JO 1936S CORR (Notice 0083816).

p. 52   'On 16 October, William Garland declared to Baillet-Latour': CIO JO 1936S CORR (ID Chemise 203362).

p. 52   'In a letter written on 20 October, Mahoney reminded Lewald': CIO JO 1936S ECRIT (Notice 0093288).

p. 53   'Lewald's response was considerably shorter than Mahoney's accusatory letter': CIO JO 1936S COJO (Notice 0083818).

p. 54   'He dismissed Mahoney in a letter to Coubertin': ibid.

p. 55   'Many would have agreed with the words expressed by sports writer John Kieran': NYT, 27 July 1935.

p. 56   'Baillet-Latour regarded this climb-down as a significant triumph': ABC Box 42.

p. 57   'Now it was the turn of Ernest Lee Jahncke to strike': ibid.

p. 58   'This enabled Brundage to immediately dispatch a telegram': ibid.

p. 58   'Baillet-Latour was not to reply, however, until after the crucial AAU vote': ibid.

p. 59   'At the British Olympic Association committee meeting on 3 December': BOA.

p. 59   'Philip Noel-Baker, who captained the British Olympic team at Antwerp in 1920': TMG, 7 December 1935.

p. 59   'Neville Laski, president of the Board of Deputies of British

Jews, wrote to Harold Abrahams': LMA ACC/3121/B/05/003/010.

p. 60 'As Evan Hunter, the secretary of the BOA, told Brundage': ABC Box 130.

p. 60 'In a subsequent letter, he enclosed a copy of the Association's latest minutes': ibid.

p. 61 'Jeremiah Mahoney convened the executive committee of fifteen delegates that Friday afternoon': See NYT, 6 December 1935 onwards.

p. 62 'A few days later, he received a letter from the Olympic president': ABC Box 42.

p. 63 'A satisfied Brundage wrote back to Baillet-Latour in the new year': ibid.

CHAPTER THREE

p. 64 'The Olympic year was greeted by the *Reich Sports Journal*': NYT, 1 January 1936.

p. 65 'the German Organising Committee hand-wringingly attempted to mollify the Americans': ABC Box 35.

p. 65 'When Robert Livermore, one of Washburn's fellow skiers, received his uniform': *Atlantic Monthly*, n.d. (presumably 1936). In the collection of Albert Washburn, Seattle.

p. 66 'On 6 January, Gustavus Kirby, the AOC's treasurer, wrote to Carl Diem': ABC Box 29.

p. 66 'The secretary of the BOA, Evan Hunter, held a pretty low opinion of the event': ABC Box 130.

p. 66 ' "The hotels are absolutely packed," he wrote to Brundage on 16 January': ibid.

p. 66 'Many were struck by the picture-postcard prettiness of the place': NYT, February 1936.

p. 68 'Funk laid into the foreign journalists for not presenting the "true" side of Nazi Germany': ibid., 5 February 1936.

p. 68 'Visitors were even welcome at Dachau concentration camp': ibid., 3 February 1936.

p. 68 'A few days before, Shirer had been telephoned by Wilfred Bade': Shirer, *Berlin Diary*.

p. 71 'The faces turned upward toward him seemed to say it was no formal courtesy': NYT, 7 February 1936.

p. 83   **'I am informing you of a flagrant violation of Germany regarding her promise'**: ABC Box 152.

CHAPTER FOUR

p. 87   **'especially when housewives found butter costing 1.6 Reichsmarks per pound . . .'** CAC Phipps Collection 1/17.

p. 87   **'At the end of January, Phipps wrote to Sir Robert Vansittart'**: CAC Phipps Collection 2/18.

p. 88   **'a lightweight (I place him near the bottom of the handicap)'**: CAC Phipps Collection 10/2.

p. 88   **'Vansittart found him "shallow, self-seeking and not really friendly"'** CAC Vansittart Collection 1/17.

p. 89   **'I realise that in our free country the Government cannot always prevent Mayfair'**: CAC Phipps Collection 10/2.

p. 92   **'The press reaction in Britain was just as Hitler would have hoped it to be'**: See Reid Gannon, *The British Press and Germany 1936–1939.*

p. 92   **'[He] sat down in a corner of the room where he had never sat before'**: See Churchill, *The Second World War.*

p. 93   **'"With dictators nothing succeeds like success," Phipps wrote to Eden'**: CAC Phipps Collection 1/16.

p. 93   **'Later in the month, Vansittart wrote to his brother-in-law'**: CAC Phipps Collection 2/18.

p. 93   **'"WE DON'T want nigger money!" the fat man shouted'**: See McRae, *Heroes without Country.*

p. 94   **'a pogrom held in July 1934 in Hirschberg'**: See Dunelm, *The Yellow Spot.*

CHAPTER FIVE

p. 114   **'Let me say that I shall not resign from the International Olympic Committee'**: ABC Box 58.

p. 114   **'The boycotters were badly whipped'**: ABC Box 29.

p. 114   **'the words Gustavus Kirby uttered when he returned from Germany'**: NYT, 18 February 1936.

p. 115   **'Brundage returned at the end of February, and was even more effusive than Kirby'**: NYT.

p. 116 '**where its boys trained under banners that shouted: "Our duty is to die for Germany"**': See Ward Price, *I Know These Dictators*.

p. 117 '**"In 1930, German youth was undersized, anaemic and undernourished"**': See speech notes contained in ABC Box 244.

p. 118 '**the organisation was "in a hell of a hole financially"**' ABC Box 29.

p. 118 '**Shall we allow Communists, in whatever disguise and for whatever specious reasons**': ABC Box 233.

p. 119 '**In April, Ornstein told the *New York Times* that the AOC was "representative not of the sporting spirit of American tradition"**': See JSH, vol. 17, no. 2 (summer 1990) for an account of Wortmann's activities.

p. 121 '**Kirby, however, was convinced that the actions of the AOC**': NYT, 18 February 1936.

p. 121 '**He let his full anti-Semitism slip in a letter to Brundage on 27 May**': ABC Box 29.

p. 122 '**Brundage replied calmly to Kirby's spirited letter**': ibid.

p. 122 '**the Grafton Athletic Club in London was considering not allowing its athletes**': Elvin papers, LSE. Much of the material concerning the English boycott movement, the BWSA and the Barcelona Olympiad is contained in this collection.

p. 126 '**. . . the BOA held on 19 May at the Dorchester Hotel**': TT, 20 May 1936.

p. 128 '**In the magazine *World Sports*, Lord Aberdare informed readers**': CIO JO 1936S CNO.

p. 129 '**. . .Indeed, their invitation to the AAU in the United States was sent out only on 22 June**': ABC Box 238.

p. 129 '**For British organisations such as the British Workers' Sports Association**': See Elvin Papers, LSE.

p. 130 '**On 17 June, Sir Eric Phipps wrote to the British Foreign Secretary, Anthony Eden**': CAC Phipps Collection 1/17.

p. 132 '**Hitler has never meant business in our sense of the word**': CAC Vansittart Collection 2/26.

p. 135 '**Sir Robert Vansittart, who had decided to come to the Games**': CAC Phipps Collection 2/18.

p. 143 '**During the Winter Games, Lewald told Coubertin**': CIO JO 1936S COJO (Notice 0083818).

p. 144 '**On 25 May, Lewald wrote to Coubertin at his house in Geneva**': ibid.

p. 145 'At the end of June, Lewald curtly informed Coubertin that his idea of giving a short address': ibid.

CHAPTER SIX

p. 147 'Iberian Interlude': See Elvin Papers, LSE.

CHAPTER SEVEN

p. 160 'Before the team disembarked the following morning, Avery Brundage made a speech': ABC Box 248.

p. 161 'The London correspondent of the *Manchester Guardian* was withering': TMG, 27 July 1936.

p. 161 'Outside the station, a chocolate seller had been monitoring their arrival': ibid., 30 July 1936.

p. 163 'One of them succinctly summed up the state of Germany': LHA CP/ORG/MISC/6/5.

p. 164 'On the Bismarckstrasse in Berlin, one Jewish woman refused to hang up any flags': LMA ACC/3121/C/11/012/024.

p. 166 'Lewald, who welcomed the British as "the finest team that Great Britain has ever had"': TMG, 31 July 1936.

p. 177 'On 22 March, at the Albert Hall in London, Mosley had advocated': ibid., 23 March 1936.

p. 177 'in the gangsterish form of used notes in different curren-cies': For details of the BUF finances see Dalley, *Diana Mosley*, Lovell, *The Mitford Girls*, Skidelsky, *Oswald Mosley*.

p. 178 'Diana baldly told the Nazi leader that Mosley required £100,000': See Dalley, *Diana Mosley*.

CHAPTER EIGHT

p. 185 'The British journalist George Ward Price had ridden in the back of Hitler's car': Ward Price, *I Know These Dictators*.

p. 186 'That month, Helmuth von Moltke, a young lawyer who had a passionate hatred of Nazism': Quoted in MacDonogh, *A Good German*.

p. 189 'although the seven-strong Bermudan team doffed their

white solar topees and made the fascist salute': Photograph in collection of John Young, Bermuda.

p. 191 **'Strauss was not proud of his collaboration with the Nazis'**: Konno; see (c) (ii) in Bibliography.

p. 193 **'The torch arrived in Vienna in the early evening of 29 July'**: TMG, 30 July 1936.

CHAPTER NINE

NB: Many of the athletes' reminiscences in Chapters Nine, Ten, Eleven and Twelve are gleaned from five principal sources – interviews with the author, the *New York Times*, 'A Proper Spectacle', *Tales of Gold* and Maegerlein, *Die Wille siegt*. For reasons of space, I have refrained from listing the provenance of each quote as most are readily found in these sources. If researchers require assistance, then I would be more than happy to help. I can be contacted via my website, www.guywalters.com.

p. 203 **'J M Loraine in Britain decided to write to the new hero of the Games'**: See Rürup, *Die Olympischen Spiele*.

p. 209 **'Doping had been present in sports since the Ancient Olympics'**: *Lancet*, 16 September 2000, p. 1008.

p. 211 **'Stephens's manliness certainly did not stop her being admired by men'**: Stephens's encounters with Hitler and Goering are recounted in Kinney Hanson, *The Fulton Flash*.

p. 215 **'Owens wrote in one of his autobiographies later'**: Owens, *Jesse: A Spiritual Autobiography*.

p. 218 **' "It [the wind] howls in at the north gate," Long recalled'**: *Die Wille siegt*.

p. 223 **' "It was as usual a case of getting the first break on the field," Lovelock wrote later'**: From Lovelock's diary, reproduced in the front papers of McNeish, *Lovelock*.

p. 232 **'His mood was not helped by the fact that he was mobbed by weeping Japanese journalists'**: Much of this and the account of the lost Harper are from an undated newspaper cutting in the collection of Velma Dunn Ploessel. A copy can be e-mailed by the author if required.

CHAPTER TEN

p. 236 'Only in dictatorships can a "Week of Laughter" be declared': NYT, 18 July 1936.

p. 236 'In order to jolly the Germans along, the British and Canadians had decided to show': ibid., 5 August 1936.

p. 236 'described by one breathless travel writer as a "mecca for pleasure-seekers"': *North American Review*, vol. 235, no. 1, January 1933.

p. 237 'could consult the recently updated Baedeker guidebook': NYT, 26 July 1936.

p. 237 'One, which found its way into the hands of a columnist on the *New Statesman* magazine': *New Statesman*, 1 August 1936.

p. 240 'Reverend Stewart W. Herman Jr's choice of Psalm 98': ABC Box 152.

p. 240 'The daily report of the State Police Office for 15/16 August': See Rürup, *Die Olympischen Spiele*.

p. 241 'Our people are trying to break the bond set by God': *Time*, 27 July 1936.

p. 244 'the numerous functions hosted by the bigwigs in the Nazi regime': The menus and the seating plans contained within this chapter can be found in CIO JO 1936S INVIT.

p. 247 'a forty-three-year-old Château Cos d'Estournel': This was incorrectly printed on the menu as 'Cos d'Es Tournel' – a small indicator of Goering's *arriviste* tendencies.

p. 247 'Goering had deemed that such hunting was "unfair to animals"': TMG, 4 August 1936.

p. 249 'When Vansittart met Hitler, he found the dictator to be': Vansittart's post-Olympic Report, 'A Busman's Holiday', can be found at CAC Vansittart Papers 1/17.

p. 252 'some sort of dalliance with a man called Luedecke': Possibly Kurt Luedecke, a fund-raiser for the Nazis in the United States.

p. 256 '"You should come to Berlin more often," the dictator told Lady Vansittart': See Hart-Davis, *Hitler's Olympics*.

p. 257 'That day, he wrote to Anthony Eden, telling him that Vansittart': CAC Phipps Papers 1/17.

p. 258 'That morning, Dodd had made a report to Roosevelt about the Nazi press': FDR Digital Archive; see Bibliography, (c) (iii).

p. 259 'He told me, with tears in his eyes, that he had replied that there was no discrimination' JSH, vol. 11, no. 3 (winter, 1984); Eisen, *The Voices of Sanity*.

p. 259   **'had fallen in love with Boris Vinogradov'**: See Helms, *A Look over My Shoulder*.

p. 260   **'Some 2,700 guests were invited to his *Sommerfest'***: There are various estimates of the number of guests. We can be sure that it was a big party; 2,700 is Goebbels' figure.

p. 261   **'For Helen Stephens, the party went too far for other reasons'**: See Kinney Hanson, *The Fulton Flash*.

CHAPTER ELEVEN

p. 265   **'Whatever the truth of the situation, Glickman and Stoller were out'**: As well as Glickman, see, NYT 8 August 1936.

p. 275   **'Hendrika "Rie" Mastenbroek of Holland was the queen of the swimming pool'**: See JOH, summer 1937, p. 30.

p. 290   **'The Peruvians did not react well to the decision, to put it mildly'**: See NYT, 11–14 August 1936.

p. 290   **'This cable found its way to Avery Brundage'**: ABC Box 152.

p. 293   **'A cable was sent from Berlin to Kunwar Sir Jagdish Prasad'**: A kunwar is the younger son of a small feudal chief – a thakur. The term may sometimes be used for the first younger son of a raja.

CHAPTER TWELVE

p. 296   **'Olympics Leave Glow of Pride in Reich'**: NYT, 16 August 1936.

p. 298   **'Harold Abrahams thought that such complaints were unfair'**: *The Field*, 21 November 1936.

p. 298   **'Avery Brundage's reaction to the American showing'**: NYT, 5 October 1936.

p. 299   **'We can learn much from Germany'**: ABC Box 244.

p. 299   **'The results we obtained at the Olympic Games'**: Hitler, *Hitler's Table Talk*.

p. 303   **'When Coubertin was interviewed after the Games'**: Quoted in Bale and Christensen, *Post-Olympism?*

p. 306   **'Rie Mastenbroek was another star of Berlin'**: See JOH, summer 1937, p. 30.

p. 309   '**Although Son had been good to the Olympic movement**':
CIO JO 1936S CORR.

p. 313   '**On 8 August 1938 he received a letter from Tschammer und
Osten**': NYT, 21 February 1999.

p. 314   '**Brundage wrote back later that month**': ABC Box 127.

p. 314   '**On 20 October 1939, some seven weeks after the outbreak
of hostilities in Europe**': CIO PT BRUND CORR Notice
0061522.

p. 315   '**It is thanks to the efforts of Madame Zanchi and Edstrøm
that books such as this can be written**': See 6th ISOR,
pp. 93–104; Paton and Barney, *Adolf Hitler, Carl Diem* . . .

p. 315   '**"Thus it came to the storming of Poland"**' See Rürup, *Die
Olympischen Spiele.*

p. 316   '**In October 1950, the American testified that von Halt**': ibid.

Bibliography

UNPUBLISHED SOURCES

(a) Interviewees

Abrahams, Harold M., interviewed by John Dunn, 12 July 1974 (from Dick Booth)

Bristow, Martin, interviewed telephonically by author, 23 February 1936

Çambel, Halet, interviewed telephonically by author, 26 March 2005

Cummings Critchell, Iris, interviewed by author, Downey, CA, USA, 25 July 2005

Dunn Ploessel, Velma, interviewed by author, Downey, CA, USA, 25 July 2005

Falz-Fein, Eduard von, interviewed telephonically by author, 22 February 2005

Frampton, Lorna, interviewed telephonically by author, 23 February 2005

Gerdes, Alfred, interviewed by author, Lake Constance, Germany, 2 September 2005

Havelange, João, interviewed by author, Zurich, Switzerland, 3 May 2005

Herber Baier, Maxie, interviewed by author, Garmisch-Partenkirchen, Germany, 23 September 2005

Hill, Harry, interviewed by author, Manchester, UK, 4 March 2005

Kaun, Elfriede, interviewed by author, Kiel, Germany, 20 September 2005

Kiefer, Adolph, interviewed telephonically by author, 7 July 2005

Komorowski, Adam, interviewed by author, London, UK, 12 July 2005

Komorowski, Irena, interviewed by Eugeniusz Romiszewski, 1967/8 (from Adam Komorowski)

Kurland, Simon, interviewed telephonically by author, 4 April 2005

Lanitis, Domnitsa, interviewed telephonically by author, 23 February 2005

Leonard, Charles, interviewed by author, Fort Belvoir, VA, USA, 22 July 2005

Obretenov, Lyuben, interviewed telephonically on author's behalf by Nadka Gouneva, early May 2005

335

Odam Tyler, Dorothy, interviewed by author, Croydon, UK, 21 February 2005
Oliver, Percy, interviewed telephonically by author, 9 August, 2005
Proksch, Alfred, interviewed telephonically by author, 7 March 2005
Rogers Kelly, Annette, interviewed by author, Niles, IL, USA, 27 July 2005
Sorensen, Inge, interviewed telephonically by author, 13 April 2005
Washburn, Albert, interviewed by author, Seattle, WA, USA, 26 July 2005
Webster, Dick, interviewed by author, Winchester, UK, 3 March 2005
Zamperini, Louis S., interviewed by George A. Hodak for the Amateur Athletic Foundation of Los Angeles, Hollywood, CA, USA, June 1988 (from Louis Zamperini)

(b) Archives

Avery Brundage Collection (ABC), University of Illinois, IL, USA
Arnold Lunn Papers (AL), Georgetown University Library, Washington, DC, USA
British Olympic Association (BOA), London, UK
Cambridge University Library, Department of Manuscripts and University Archives (CUL), Cambridge, UK
Churchill College Archives Centre (CAC), Cambridge, UK
British Library Newspaper Archive, Colindale, London, UK
International Olympic Committee Archives (CIO), Lausanne, Switzerland
Labour History Archive and Study Centre (LHA), People's History Museum, Manchester, UK
London Library, UK
London Metropolitan Archives (LMA), London, UK
London School of Economics Archives (LSE), London, UK
New York City Public Library, USA

(c) Academic papers and lectures

Young, Christopher, *When Adolf Met Pierre? The Olympic Games in the Age of Technical Reproduction* (University of Cambridge, UK, March 2005)
Whiteing, Charles, *Robey Leibbrandt and Operation Weissdorn* (South African Military History Society, Kwazulu Natal Branch, 2002)

(d) Diaries and letters

Charles Leonard's diaries and letters (from Charles Leonard)
Velma Dunn Ploessel's letters (from Velma Dunn Ploessel)
Albert Washburn's letters (from Albert Washburn)

PUBLISHED SOURCES

(a) Printed

(i) Biographies and memoirs

Avon, The Earl of, *The Eden Memoirs: Facing the Dictators* (Cassell, 1962)
Baker, William J., *Jesse Owens: An American Life* (Macmillan, 1986)
Bergmann Lambert, Margaret, *By Leaps and Bounds* (United States Holocaust Memorial Museum, 2005)
Bethge, Eberhard, *Dietrich Bonhoeffer* (Collins, 1977)
Bloch, Michael, *Ribbentrop* (Abacus, 2003)
Bruccoli, Matthew J. and Park, Bucker, *To Loot My Life Clean: The Thomas Wolfe–Maxwell Perkins Correspondence* (University of South Carolina Press, 2000)
Channon, Henry, *'Chips': The Diaries of Sir Henry Channon* (Phoenix, 1999)
Chapman, Mike, *The Gold and the Glory: The Amazing True Story of Glenn Morris, Olympic Champion and Movie Tarzan* (Culture House Books, 2003)
Churchill, Winston S., *The Second World War: The Gathering Storm* (Folio Society, 2000)
Dalley, Jan, *Diana Mosley: A Life* (Faber & Faber, 2000)
Dodd, Martha, *My Years in Germany* (Gollancz, 1940)
Dodd, William E. and Martha, Dodd, *Ambassador Dodd's Diary 1933–1938* (Gollancz, 1941)
Donald, David Herbert, *Look Homeward: A Life of Thomas Wolfe* (Bloomsbury, 1987)
Fromm, Bella, *Blood and Banquets: A Berlin Social Diary* (Birch Lane Press, 1990)
Gay, Peter, *My German Question* (Yale University Press, 1998)
Glickman, Marty, *The Fastest Kid on the Block* (Syracuse University Press, 1996)
Goebbels, Joseph, *Der Tagebücher von Joseph Goebbels* (K. G. Saur, Munich, 2005)
Guttmann, Allen, *The Games Must Go On: Avery Brundage and the Olympic Movement* (Columbia University Press, 1984)

Helms, Richard, *A Look over My Shoulder: A Life in the Central Intelligence Agency* (Ballantine, 2004)

Holman, C. Hugh and Sue Fields Ross, *The Letters of Thomas Wolfe to His Mother* (University of North Carolina Press, 1968)

Jones, Thomas, *A Diary with Letters 1931–1950* (Oxford University Press, 1954)

Kinney Hanson, Sharon, *The Fulton Flash: The Life of Helen Stephens* (Southern Illinois University Press, 2004)

Kennan, George F., *Memoirs 1925–1950* (Little, Brown, Boston, 1967)

Kennedy, Richard S. (ed.), *The Notebooks of Thomas Wolfe* (University of North Carolina Press, 1970)

Kershaw, Ian, *Hitler 1889–1936: Hubris* (Penguin, 2001)

—— *Hitler 1936–1945: Nemesis* (Allen Lane, 2000)

Kirkpatrick, Ivone, *The Inner Circle* (Macmillan, 1959)

Klemperer, Victor, *I Shall Bear Witness 1933–1941*, vol. 1 (Phoenix, 1999)

Lean, Garth, *Frank Buchman: A Life* (Collins, 1988)

Lindbergh, Charles, *Autobiography of Values* (Harcourt Brace Jovanovich, 1992)

Lovell, Mary S., *The Mitford Girls* (Little, Brown, 2001)

MacDonogh, Giles, *A Good German: Adam von Trott zu Solz* (Quartet, 1994)

McRae, Donald, *Heroes without Country: America's Betrayal of Joe Louis and Jesse Owens* (HarperCollins, 2002)

Mahoney, Barbara S., *Dispatches and Dictators: Ralph Barnes for the Herald Tribune* (Oregon State University Press, 2002)

Mogulof, Milly, *Foiled: Hitler's Jewish Olympian, the Helene Mayer Story* (RDR Books, 2002)

Mosley, Diana, *A Life of Contrasts* (Gibson Square Books, 2002)

Mosley, Leonard, *Lindbergh: A Biography* (Dover, 2000)

Neave, Airey, *They Have Their Exits* (Pen and Sword, 2002)

Nowell, Elizabeth (ed.), *The Selected Letters of Thomas Wolfe* (Heinemann, 1958)

Owens, Jesse, *I Have Changed* (William Morrow, 1972)

—— *Jesse: A Spiritual Autobiography* (Logos International, 1978)

Phillips, Bob, *The Iron in His Soul: Bill Roberts and Manchester's Sporting Heritage* (Parrs Wood Press, 2002)

Radetz, Walter, *Werner Seelenbinder* (Sportverlag Berlin, 1969)

Ribbentrop, Joachim von, *The Ribbentrop Memoirs* (Weidenfeld & Nicolson, 1954)

Rice, Grantland, *The Tumult and the Shouting* (A. S. Barnes and Co., 1954)

Riefenstahl, Leni, *A Memoir* (Picador, 1992)

Schmeling, Max, *An Autobiography* (Bonus Books, 1998)

Shirer, William L., *Berlin Diary 1934–1941* (Promotional Reprint Company, 1997)

Skidelsky, Robert, *Oswald Mosley* (Macmillan, 1990)

Speer, Albert, *Inside the Third Reich* (Phoenix, 1995)

Strydom, Hans, *For Volk and Führer: Robey Leibbrandt and Operation Weissdorn* (Jonathan Ball, 1983)

Ward Price, George, *I Know These Dictators* (Harrap, 1937)

Weitz, John, *Hitler's Diplomat: Joachim von Ribbentrop* (Phoenix, 1997)

(ii) Histories

Bachrach, Susan D., *The Nazi Olympics* (Little, Brown, 2000)

Bale, John and Krogh Christensen, Mette, *Post-Olympism? Questioning Sport in the Twenty-first Century* (Berg, 2004)

Barry, James P., *The Berlin Olympics, 1936: Black American Athletes Counter Nazi Propaganda* (Franklin Watts, 1975)

Burleigh, Michael, *The Third Reich: A New History* (Pan, 2000)

Buruma, Ian, *The Missionary and the Libertine: Love and War in East and West* (Faber & Faber, 1996)

Carlson, Lewis H. and John J., Fogarty, *Tales of Gold: An Oral History of the Summer Olympic Games Told by America's Gold Medal Winners* (Contemporary Books, 1987)

Cohen, Stan, *The Games of '36: A Pictorial History of the 1936 Olympics in Germany* (Pictorial Histories Publishing Co., 1996)

Cross, Colin, *The Fascists in Britain* (Barrie and Rockliff, 1961)

Daniels, Stephanie and Tedder, Anita, *'A Proper Spectacle': Women Olympians 1900–1936* (ZeNaNA Press, 2000)

Dawson, Buck, *Mermaids on Parade: America's Love Affair with Its Olympic Women Swimmers* (Kroshka Books, 2000)

Die XI. Olympiade de Berlin 1936 (Heinrich Franck Söhne, Berlin, 1936)

Dunelm, Herbert (foreword), *The Yellow Spot* (Gollancz, 1936)

Graham, Cooper C., *Leni Riefenstahl and Olympia* (Scarecrow Press, 1986)

Graves, Robert and Hodge, Alan, *The Long Week-end* (Penguin, 1971)

Guttmann, Allen, *The Erotic in Sports* (Columbia University Press, 1996)

—— *The Olympics* (University of Illinois Press, 2002)

Handler, Andrew, *From the Ghetto to the Games: Jewish Athletes in Hungary* (East European Monographs, Boulder, distributed by Columbia University Press, 1985)

Hart-Davis, Duff, *Hitler's Olympics: The 1936 Games* (Coronet, 1988)

Hill, Christopher R., *Olympic Politics: Athens to Atlanta 1896–1996* (Manchester University Press, 1996)

Hitler, Adolf, *Hitler's Table Talk*, trans. Norman Cameron and R. H. Stevens (Weidenfeld and Nicolson, 1973)

Hoberman, John, *The Olympic Crisis: Sport, Politics and the Moral Order* (Caratzas, 1986)

Holmes, Judith, *Olympiad 1936: Blaze of Glory for Hitler's Reich* (Ballantine, 1971)

Kieran, John and Arthur, Daley, *The Story of the Olympic Games* (Lippincott, 1952)

Krüger, Arnd and Murray, William, *The Nazi Olympics: Sport, Politics and Appeasement in the 1930s* (University of Illinois Press, 2003)

Lipstadt, Deborah E., *Beyond Belief: The American Press and the Coming of the Holocaust 1933–1945* (Macmillan, 1993)

Lovett, Charles C., *Olympic Marathon: A Centennial History of the Games' Most Storied Race* (Greenwood Press, 1997)

Maegerlein, Heinz, *Der Wille siegt* (Verlag Dürrsche Buchhandlung, Bonn, 1950)

Mandell, Richard D., *The Nazi Olympics* (University of Illinois Press, 1987)

Mayer, Paul Yogi, *Jews and the Olympic Games* (Vallentine Mitchell, 2004)

Olympia 1936, Band I (Cigaretten-Bilderdienst Hamburg-Bahrenfeld, 1936)

Olympia 1936, Band II (Cigaretten-Bilderdienst Hamburg-Bahrenfeld, 1936)

Preez, Max du, *Of Warriors, Lovers and Prophets: Unusual Stories from South Africa's Past* (Zebra Press, 2004)

Reid Gannon, Franklin, *The British Press and Germany 1936–1939* (Oxford University Press, 1971)

Rürup, Reinhard (ed.), *Topography of Terror* (Willmuth Arenhövel, Berlin, 2001)

—— *Die Olympischen Spiele und der Nationalsozialismus* (Argon, Berlin, 1996)

Senn, Alfred E., *Power, Politics and the Olympic Games* (Human Kinetics, 1999)

Taylor, Paul, *Jews and the Olympic Games* (Sussex Academic Press, 2004)

Tschammer und Osten, Hans von and Baeumler, Alfred, *Sport und Staat* (Deutsche Sport, 1934) (BOA)

Wallace, Max, *The American Axis: Henry Ford, Charles Lindbergh and the Rise of the Third Reich* (St Martin's Press, 2003)

Webster, F. A. M., *Olympic Cavalcade* (Hutchinson, 1948)

(iii) Bulletins, journals, newspapers and magazines

NB: Titles marked with an asterisk are available digitally from AAFLA (see (c) (iii) below)

ASSH Bulletin★
Atlantic Monthly
Bulletin du Comité International Olympique (BDCE)★
Daily Telegraph (DT)
Daily Herald
Daily Mirror
Daily Worker
The Economist
The Field
Glasgow Evening News
Jewish Chronicle
Journal of Olympic History (JOH)★
Journal of Sport History (JSH)★
Harper's Magazine
International Symposium for Olympic Research (ISOR)★
Manchester Guardian (TMG)
New Statesman
Newsweek
New York Times (NYT)
North American Review
Official Bulletin of the International Olympic Committee★
Olympic Review★
Olympika★
Saint Louis Post-Dispatch
Saturday Review
South Wales Evening Post
Spectator
Time
The Times (London) (TT)
World Sports

(iv) Pamphlets

American Olympic Committee, *Fair Play for American Athletes* (1935) (AB)
Citrine, Walter, *Under the Heel of Hitler: The Dictatorship of Sport in Nazi Germany* (1936) (BOA)

Committee on Fair Play in Sports, *Preserve the Olympic Ideal* (1936) (CIO)

Organisationkomitee für die XI. Olympiade Berlin 1936, *Guide Book to the Celebration of the XIth Olympiad* (1936) (CIO)

(v) Novels

McNeish, James, *Lovelock* (Hodder & Stoughton, 1986)

Mitford, Nancy, *Wigs on the Green* (Butterworth, 1935)

Wolfe, Thomas, *You Can't Go Home Again* (HarperPerennial, 1998)

(vi) Official reports

IV Olympische Winterspiele 1936, Amtlicher Bericht, Organisationkomitee für die IV. Olympischen Winterspiele

The XIth Olympic Games, Berlin 1936, Official Report, Organisationkomitee für die XI. Olympiade Berlin

The Official Report of the XIth Olympiad, ed. Harold M. Abrahams, British Olympic Association

British Ski Year Book, 1952

(vii) Reference

Taylor, James and Shaw, Warren, *Dictionary of the Third Reich* (Penguin, 1997)

(b) Film

Charlie Chan at the Olympics (1937)

Olympia, Parts 1 & 2 (1940), Homevision, 2000 (VHS available from www.amazon.com)

Tarzan's Revenge (1938), Roan Group, 2004 (DVD available from www.troma.com)

(c) Electronic

NB: The following Web addresses were accessed on 23 January 2006. Links to all these URLs may be found on my website, www.guywalters.com

(i) Biographies and memoirs

Chand, Dhyan, *Goal!*, www.bharatiyahockey.org/granthalaya/goal/1936/page1.htm

Gentle, Peter, *Stella the Fella*, www.radio.com.pl/polonia/article.asp?tId=13495

Jesse Owens Foundation, *Who Is Jesse Owens?*, www.jesse-owens.org/about1.html

Jewish Virtual Library, *Marty Glickman*, www.jewishvirtuallibrary.org/jsource/Holocaust/glickman.html

Masood, M. N., *The World's Hockey Champions 1936*, www.bharatiyahockey.org/granthalaya/champions/

Nordmark, Birger and Houda, Patrick, *Rudi Ball*, http://web.comhem.se/~u87152366/RudiBallbiography.htm

Robinson, Roger, *Lovelock, John Edward*, www.dnzb.govt.nz/dnzb/default.asp?Find_Quick.asp?PersonEssay=4L14

Traces, *Martha Dodd*, www.traces.org/marthadodd.html

Ward, Paul, *Jack Lovelock: Come on Jack!*, www.nzedge.com/heroes/lovelock.html

Webber, Ken, *Glenn Morris: Colorado's Tarzan Recalled*, www.erblist.com/erbmania/kw/kwglennmorris.html

Wenzel, Esther, *Memories of the 1936 Olympic Games in Berlin*, www.iwitnesstohistory.org/ResidentPages/Wenzel/Wenzel%2036%20olympics.htm

(ii) Histories and articles

1936 Olympics – Berlin, http://frankwykoff.com/1936.htm

Dean, Fred and Joan, *Account of 1936 Winter Olympics*, www.iceskate-magazine.com/page53.html

Jewish Virtual Library, *The Nazi Olympics*, www.jewishvirtuallibrary.org/jsource/Holocaust/olympics.html

Konno, Satoshi, *Olympische Hymne*, www.geocities.com/Vienna/Studio/2891/olympia.htm

Richards, Annie, *Transsexual Women and Female Sports*, http://transwoman.tripod.com/sports.htm

United States Holocaust Memorial Museum, *The Nazi Olympics Berlin 1936*, www.ushmm.org/museum/exhibit/online/olympics/

Vercamer, Arvo and Pipes, Jason, *The 1936 Olympic Games in Germany*, www.feldgrau.com/1936olymp.html

(iii) Reference and archives

The Amateur Athletic Foundation of Los Angeles' digital archive features searchable pdf versions of, among others, the following titles: *ASSH Bulletin, Journal of Olympic History, Journal of Sport History, Olympika, Olympic Review, Revue Olympique*, http://www.aafla.org/search/search.htm

Centre for Olympic Studies and Research, Loughborough University, UK, www.lboro.ac.uk/departments/sses/institutes/cos/index.html

Inventory of the Avery Brundage Collection at the University of Illinois, http://web.library.uiuc.edu/ahx/ead/ua/2620037/2620037f.html

Lynching statistics, www.law.umkc.edu/faculty/projects/ftrials/shipp/lyn chingyear.html

Currency conversions and comparisons are provided by the Economic History Services website, www.eh.net/

The Franklin D. Roosevelt Presidential Library and Museum (FDR) contains online versions of the letters from Charles Sherrill and William Dodd, www.fdrlibrary.marist.edu/online14.html

I have also consulted the excellent www.questia.com/ to locate journals, books, magazines, newspapers and books. This requires a subscription. For looking up and confirming general information, I have used Wikipedia, the free encyclopedia, at http://en.wikipedia.org/wiki/Main_Page

Index

100 metres: men's event in Berlin Games, 1–3, 195–7; weather conditions for Berlin Games, 1, 195, 196, 199; AAU championships in 1935, 100; New York Metropolitan Championships, 107; women's event in Berlin Games, 210

200 metres, 215, 216, 220–1

220-yard low hurdles, 99

400 metres, 272

1500 metres, 222; in decathlon, 228

AAA *see* Amateur Athletics Association (UK)

AAU *see* Amateur Athletic Union (US)

Abba, First Lt Silvano (Italian pentathlete), 206, 225, 226, 317

Aberdare, Clarence, Lord, 29; correspondence with Lewald over Jewish athletes, 29–30, 39–40; and proposed boycott of 1936 Games, 29; at 1936 BOA dinner, 126; on treatment of Jews in Germany, 128; at Chancellery banquet before Berlin Games, 245; at Ribbentrop's party, 252

Abrahams, Harold, 41, 60; on Olympism, 41–2; on boycott, 59, 124–5; commentary on Lovelock's triumph, 224; on 400 metres final, 272; on British successes in Berlin, 298; on his attendance at Berlin Games, 304

admiration of the body *see* physical culture

African-Americans: at Berlin Games, 1, 197, 200, 202; comparison with Jews and prejudice against, 26, 52; racist abuse, 93–4; lynching, 94; treatment compared to German Jews, 94–5; on SS *Manhattan*, 156; welcome for athletes at Berlin Games, 167–8; success at Berlin Games, and Nazis, 300; and supposed Aryan superiority, 300; *see also* black

competitors in Games; Metcalfe, Ralph; Negroes; Owens, Jesse

Afrikaners/Boers: and Hitler, 190; Leibbrandt as representative, 286

Albritton, David (African-American athlete), 93–4, 97, 197, 198

Albus, Emmy (German athlete), 211, 268, 269, 270

Allais, Emile (French skier), 75

Amateur Athletic Union (US): annual convention in 1933, 25–6; and proposed boycott of 1936 Games, 26, 36, 39; Mahoney appointed president, 39; Miami convention in 1934, 39; relinquishing of presidency by Brundage, 39; New York convention in 1935, 50, 61; boycott vote, 61–3; championships in 1935, 100; and Owens' amateur status, 100, 304; Owens on, 304

Amateur Athletics Association (UK): Roberts in Championships, 112–13; 1936 AGM, 123–4; and proposed boycott, 123–5, 127; boycott vote, 127; and People's Olympics, 129–30

amateur status of athletes: at Berlin Games, 82, 298; after Berlin Games, 304, 307; Brundage and, 316

American Amateur Athletic Union *see* Amateur Athletic Union (US)

American Hebrew: and Mayer, 44, 48

American Jewish Congress: support from Sherrill, 16

American Olympic Association: meeting in 1933, 27–8; proposed boycott of 1936 Games, 27–8, 36; Brundage's visit to Germany on behalf of, 34–6; examination of conditions of Jewish sportsmen and women, 34–6; right to certify athletes' participation in 1936 Games, 51

345

Woolf, Freddy (British athlete), 113, 140, 273
working class athletes, Britain, 112
world records: swimming, 54, 105, 277, 283; individual track events, 98, 99, 138–9, 161, 197, 211, 223; field events, 99, 197; decathlon, 229; marathon, 231, 232; relays, 266, 267, 268, 269
World Sports, 128
Wortmann, Dietrich, 26, 119; on proposed boycott of 1936 Games, 26, 27–8; Nazi sympathies, 119–20; fund-raising letter to German-Americans, 120; as Olympic sportsman, 120; support for Olympics, 120
wrestling, 233–5
Wykoff, Frank (American athlete): in 100 metres final, 1; in US try-out finals, 137; in 100 metres semi-final, 199, 200; and relay final, 263–4, 265; in relay final, 267

yachting competitions, 283
Yack, Norman (Canadian Jewish boxer), 139
Yata (Japanese high jumper), 198
Yoshioka (Japanese athlete), 196
Young (American athlete): in relay final, 273
Youth Service *see* Honorary Youth Service (German)

Zabala, Carlos (Argentinian marathon runner), 231–2
Zamperini, Lou (American athlete): on voyage to Germany, 154, 158; and Brundage's sacking of Holm, 159; on Olympic village, 170; on German military presence in Olympic village, 171; on military presence at Olympic village, 173; on opening ceremony, 191; on Owens, 199
Zanchi, Madame Lydia: salvage of Olympic papers, 315
Ziegfeld, Florenz: on Holm, 104